The Historicism of

Charles Brockden Brown

The Historicism of

Charles Brockden Brown

Radical History and the Early Republic

❊ ❊ ❊

Mark L. Kamrath

The Kent State University Press
Kent, Ohio

Frontis: Portrait of Charles Brockden Brown by James Sharples (circa 1798). As was fashionable for young men in his day, Brown wore his hair short, in a style consistent with interest in Greek and Roman classical revival. Courtesy of the Worcester Art Museum, Worcester, Massachusetts.

© 2010 by The Kent State University Press, Kent, Ohio 44242
ALL RIGHTS RESERVED
Library of Congress Catalog Card Number 2009047068
ISBN 978-1-60635-032-4
Manufactured in the United States of America

"Charles Brockden Brown and the 'Art of the Historian': An Essay Concerning (Post) Modern Historical Understanding," by Mark L. Kamrath. *Journal of the Early Republic* 21 (Summer 2001). Copyright 2001 Society for Historians of the Early Republic. Reprinted by permission of the University of Pennsylvania Press.
"American Exceptionalism and Radicalism in the 'Annals of Europe and America,'" by Mark L. Kamrath. *Revising Charles Brockden Brown: Culture, Politics, and Sexuality in the Early Republic.* Edited by Philip Barnard, Mark L. Kamrath, and Stephen Shapiro, 2004. Copyright 2004 by The University of Tennessee Press/Knoxville. Reprinted by permission of the University of Tennessee Press.

LIBRARY OF CONGRESS CATALOGING-IN-PUBLICATION DATA
Kamrath, Mark.
The historicism of Charles Brockden Brown : radical history and the early republic / Mark L. Kamrath.
p.   cm.
Includes bibliographical references and index.
ISBN 978-1-60635-032-4 (hardback : alk. paper) ∞
1. Brown, Charles Brockden, 1771–1810—Criticism and interpretation.   2. Brown, Charles Brockden, 1771–1810—Knowledge—History.   3. Brown, Charles Brockden, 1771–1810—Knowledge—United States.   4. History in literature.   5. Historicism in literature.   6. United States—In literature.   7. United States—History—Philosophy.   8. Literature and history—United States—History—19th century.   I. Title.
PS1137.K36 2010
813'.2—dc22   2009047068

British Library Cataloging-in-Publication data are available.

14 13 12 11 10   5 4 3 2 1

For Erik, Christian, and Marie—

and the lifelong pursuit of honesty,

understanding, and truth

In Memoriam

Charles W. Mignon 1933–2009

"Ad astra per alia porci"

Contents

Acknowledgments

I wish to thank Professor Sydney J. Krause, general editor of *The Novels and Related Works of Charles Brockden Brown*, for introducing me in the early 1990s to Brown's historical writing, and being a source of scholarly support for so many years.

I also want to express my gratitude to Institute for Bibliography and Editing at Kent State University, Special Collections at Bowdoin College Library, the Clifton Waller-Barrett Collection at the University of Virginia, the American Antiquarian Society, the Harry Ransom Center at the University of Texas–Austin, the Historical Society of Pennsylvania, the Library Company of Philadelphia, the Interlibrary Loan and the Graduate School at the University of Nebraska–Lincoln, and the Interlibrary Loan office at the University of Central Florida. I am particularly thankful for the help of James Green, who always had ready knowledge of eighteenth-century print culture—along with the much valued library, reference, reproduction, and other assistance of Linda August, Vincent Golden, Cornelia King, Richard Harrison, Nicole Joniec, Phil Lapsanski, Cheryl Mahan, Karen Mansfield, Charlene Peacock, Nola Pettit, Erika Piola, Sara Weatherwax, Kate Wilson, and other librarians over the years.

Charles Mignon provided generous dissertation direction and support while I was at the University of Nebraska, and Sharon Harris, Robert Stock, Robert Narveson, and Ken Winkle, along with Patrice Berger and George Wolf, also contributed significantly to my ideas and critical sensibility during those formative years. Since coming to the University of Central Florida, many colleagues have supported my work. In addition to Rose Beilor, Lisa Logan, Kevin Meehan, and Rick Schell, I am grateful to Dawn Trouard, David Wallace, Kathy Seidel, and José Fernandez for their academic support and for release time at the University of Central Florida. Such support and resources over the years have been invaluable.

I am grateful to Larry Buell, Bruce Burgett, Mary Chapman, Michael Cody, Ray Craig, Jared Gardner, Thomas Gillan, Sean Goudie, Philip Gould, Norman Grabo, Janie Hinds, John Holmes, David Levin, Robert Levine, Chris Looby, Carla Mulford, Jeffrey Richards, Wolfgang Schäfer, David Shields, Frank Shuffelton, Fredrika Teute, Wil Verhoeven, Michael Warner, Bryan Waterman, Alfred Weber, and Ed White for their answers to questions, reading of materials, generous suggestions, sharing of resources, and overall support for scholarship on

Brown. Each helped shape my understanding of Brown, his contemporaries, and the period. I am also thankful to members of the Charles Brockden Brown Society, and the Society for Early Americanists for their interest in my work and that of Brown's. I also want to thank Joanne Hogan of Proquest's American Periodical Series Online, and Remmel Nunn and Georgia Frederick of the Readex Corporation for help with access to Archive of Americana databases, namely the American State Papers; Early American Imprints, series 1: Evans; Early American Imprints series 2: Shaw-Shoemaker 1801–1819; and Early American Newspapers. Over the years, these research tools have made all the difference. Likewise, I am grateful to Joyce Harrison, Mary Young, and especially Erin Holman for their expert advice and editing at Kent State University Press.

Last, I want to give special thanks to Philip Barnard, Seth Cotlar, Fritz Fleischmann, John Larson, Stephen Shapiro, Karen Weyler, and the anonymous press readers. They read the entire manuscript, or significant parts of it; offered rich commentary and provocative questions I hope that I have addressed with some success; and variously inspired me to complete the book. Philip Barnard, expert on electronic databases and British periodicals, provided invaluable information about Brown's authorship and has significantly updated Brown bibliographical scholarship. Without their insights, the manuscript would not be what it is. I also wish to thank Joanna Hildebrand Craig of the Kent State University Press, and Karol George Kamrath, my wife, for their support; both have patiently waited for, and gently encouraged, completion of this book over many years.

Introduction

"Philadelphia, Mr. Charles B. Brown, editor of the American Register; as an
annalist he acquired much reputation."
        —Obituary, from the *Boston Gazette*, March 5, 1810

After publishing his fourth volume of the *American Register* on May 20, 1809,
Charles Brockden Brown struggled amid exhaustion and growing illness to produce his last volume, which concentrated on the impact of the Embargo, congressional debates, the Constitution, and what he called the "motives of human conduct."[1] It was published in December 1809. On November 10 of that year, Brown,
says his biographer and friend William Dunlap, experienced a "violent pain in his
side, for which he was bled."[2] From this day until February 22, 1810, when he died
at age thirty-nine, Brown suffered greatly, dying of an advanced case of pulmo-
nary consumption, or tuberculosis.

Such were the last days of America's first professional novelist turned editor,
pamphleteer, and historian. While news in 1810 of a writer's death might have
circulated fairly quickly in a city the size of Philadelphia, Brown's passing away
attracted less attention from local newspapers and magazines than one might
expect. Publications like the *Philadelphia Repository and Weekly Register*, the
Pennsylvania Evening Herald, and the *Pennsylvania Gazette* did not even mention
Brown's death. Yet, for the time, substantial obituaries were written by Brown's
friends and published in places such as *Poulson's American Daily Advertiser*, the
New York Evening Post, and Brown's own magazine, the *American Register*. And
newspapers like the *American Watchman* in Wilmington, Delaware, and the *Tren-
ton Federalist*, in New Jersey, also mentioned his passing.

In *Poulson's American Daily Advertiser*, for example, Brown is remembered by his
childhood friend as having a "brilliant imagination—the unwearied inquisitiveness
of a rich and active mind."[3] He had a "liberal education, which he greatly improved
by study and research," and was naturally disposed to "scrutiny and investigation,"
admitting "nothing on trust, when in search of the truth." His "criticisms," he says,
"were generally admitted to be acute, liberal and profound." By comparison, Anthony Bleecker writes in the *New York Evening Post* that after Brown relinquished

his pursuit of "speculative knowledge," he turned to the more "substantial and profitable branches of science" in his publication of the *American Register*.[4] The publication demonstrated Brown's "vigour and comprehensiveness as an annalist."

However, it is in a third, significantly longer obituary that appeared in Brown's magazine and was, says Daniel Edwards Kennedy, also possibly written by Bleecker, that offers an assessment of Brown the annalist and a vantage point for understanding how Brown's historicism compares with his contemporaries and, equally as important, engages historical and historiographical issues in his day and ours.[5] The author notes, for instance, Brown's "ardent curiosity" and his habit of using the smallest detail or incident to generalize about larger matters: "Ever on the alert in quest of information, he patiently enquired, he read, reflected, examined and compared, opposing facts and arguments—the result was a judgment luminous, consistent, and just." Brown, he continues, was noted for his peculiar "habits of analysis," and

> added to this, there was another trait in his character, that peculiarly fitted him for the office of an annalist, the philosophic candour he maintained in his record of political events. As an annalist inaccessible to the biases of party, he seemed more to write in the style of an historian of past ages, than the recorder of those passing occurrences that tincture our public councils, and embitter the charities of domestic life. We but echo the opinion of the public, when we pronounce this *Register* under his superintendence to have put all competition at defiance.[6]

Although such remarks might be read as mere sentiment on behalf of a friend and as offering no further clarification on Brown's worth as an annalist or historian, the obituary actually encodes a rich archive of references to significant historical and historiographical issues.[7] It references forgotten late Enlightenment debates about history and objectivity and may be read as archiving ideas and issues that are central to how a democratic republic—both then and now—might represent its immediate past. It calls attention to contested and even changing conceptions of historical impartiality, enlightened thought, and liberal political journalism.

And that is the essential problem with the "later Brown" and his thinking and writing about history. Historians and literary critics alike have relied on accounts of historiography that have become calcified by time and generations of misreadings about historical representation and the debates about narrative and truth that took place at the end of the eighteenth century. For if Brown's historical and historiographical reflections were culturally significant in his time, his claim on our attention begins with asking why his generation characterized him as someone who wrote in "the style of an historian of past ages," why subsequent generations have variously referred to his later periodical and historical writing as either "hackwork" or the work of a "pioneer American historian in the modern manner," and why today his historical thinking and writing strike us as having a self-conscious, meta-critical quality in the mode of Hayden White or Robert Berkhofer. Although such a range of contradictory historical and critical responses suggests that the controversy surrounding Brown's writings may say more about the cultural and historiographical values of his readers than anything else, we need to ask what historical and historiographical forces have led to the erasure of his contribution to history and enable us to gauge his work so variously.[8]

Some tentative answers to these questions might focus on the critical reception of Brown since his death, and in reassessing the still lingering perception that he was a flawed writer who prefigured but could not fully embody the aesthetic greatness of later generations.[9] Critical assessments of this type seem linked to the critical and cultural values that were in place during earlier periods. Likewise, inquiry into the underlying assumptions about American exceptionalism and continualism that inform reception of his historical writing are appropriate.[10] Only now, decades after Alfred Weber, Sydney Krause, Norman Grabo, and others turned our attention to Brown, and recent poststructural and cultural theories have been applied to his work, are we beginning to fully appreciate his contribution to early American history and culture.[11]

In fact, since the early 1980s the consensus interpretation of Brown's overall achievement and significance has undergone radical change, with scholars devoting increased attention to the breadth of his achievement as a prolific novelist, essayist, historian, and editor. As Mary Chapman has astutely observed, for instance, contemporary scholarship on the American and Gothic novel, in response to the New Criticism's emphasis on aesthetic unity, "has begun to explore how, in challenging aesthetics, the two hybrid forms also challenge the organizing hierarchies of class, gender, sexuality, race, ethnicity, and nation that culture has naturalized."[12] This wholesale reassessment of Brown's work is largely due to developments in literary and cultural theory and the availability of a critical discourse responsive the ideologies and discursive structures in marginalized texts.

As has been underscored in *Revising Charles Brockden Brown*, "the complexity of his response to and exploration of key concerns and issues in early national culture—republicanism and revolution debates, expansionism, nationalism and counter-subversive paranoia, sensibility and gender dynamics, or the emergence of bourgeois liberalism, to cite only a few—makes him a crucial figure for contemporary scholars of the period, a writer whose idiosyncratic artistic strategies can be understood on their own terms, apart from anachronistic or normative criteria."[13] As scholars are more fully understanding, Brown's writing across a range of genres and cultural debates offers a unique lens through which to understand early republican interests, concerns, and contradictions. It is fair to say that Brown is now viewed as an interdisciplinary "touchstone for understanding the cultural transformations and conflicts of the early republic" and that his "histori-cal" interests and often self-reflexive writing constitute a field of inquiry that is of interest to literary scholars and historians alike.[14]

Brown's lifelong interest in "history" and issues of representation argue, I be-lieve, for seeing him as a significant writer of history in the early Republic. Brown's philosophical reflections on history and historical meaning and his analysis of political, military, and economic events argue for regarding him not only as a neglected historian of the Jeffersonian era—what Henry Adams believed was one of the most influential periods in American history—but also as a writer of "radi-cal history" whose historical observations and historiographical meditations offer important insights into cultural and critical issues in his day and our own.[15]

Using New Historicist, narrative discourse, post-colonial, and other reading strat-egies, the central argument, then, of *The Historicism of Charles Brockden Brown: Radical History and the Early Republic* is that Brown lived during an era of in-tensely democratic change and disruption and that scholarship has carelessly por-trayed post-Revolutionary Americans as living in a flat, rational universe without historical self-consciousness or dialogue.[16] Brown's evolution as a historian chal-lenges enduring misconceptions such as this about late Enlightenment historical consciousness and modern objectivity. In addressing why Brown's historical rep-resentation was so different from those of earlier eighteenth-century historians, why it is familiar to contemporary ones, and why he wrote "novelistically" or ironically, I argue that Brown, a dissident Quaker and member of the New York Friendly Club, was among the first of his generation to wrestle with the limits of late Enlightenment historiography and to challenge emerging metanarratives about historical objectivity and American exceptionalism, including the manipu-lation of democratic processes for political purposes and power.

Brown's evolving historiographical reflections on narrative meaning and truth, in other words, ask us to reconsider stereotypes about the Enlightenment as wholly "rational" or "objective" and related myths about American destiny and progress. His inquiry rubs up against the postmodern idea of history as a "textual construction" in three important ways: first, Brown's self-conscious historiogra-phy and inquiry into the differences between "history" and "romance" points to an ignored tradition of linguistic self-consciousness that applies epistemological doubt to grand narratives. Analysis of Brown's historicism, as it matured in his pe-riodical writings and novels, suggests an intellect that raised philosophical ques-tions about memory, historical accuracy, and truth relative to late Enlightenment ideas about narrative objectivity and impartiality. Brown's self-reflexive inquiry into modes of historical representation tested assumed boundaries between "fact" and "fiction" in eighteenth-century writing.

Second, his efforts at historical representation call attention to our own interest in reassessing the neglected pasts of particular individuals and peoples. Brown's Quaker idealism in regard to gender equity, his sympathy for the lives of marginalized others, and his Godwinian sensibilities translate into a historicism that rises above the "great man" history and interrogates teleological metanarratives of enlightened progress. In this way, he spearheads a forgotten ironic tradition of American historical writing that questions or disrupts essentialist constructions of race and empire and participates in the process of decolonization.

And third, his contrapuntal use of primary documents, in lieu of a monological historical narrative, offers readers a history that imaginatively participates in what Robert F. Berkhofer Jr. calls a "dialogic and reflexive contextualization" of the past—a moment where democratic reading practices intersect with the processes of historical fact and interpretation.[17] Brown's inclusion of voices other than his own in his historical narrative and his focus on engaging his readers' critical sensibilities carnivalize historical representation and meaning in ways that run counter to a fileopietistic tradition of historical writing.

Taken together, Brown's historicism and "novelistic" use of documents qualify traditional monolithic conceptions of historical narrative and meaning and prompt the reader to participate in the dialectical construction of meaning—a method that permeates his novels and other writings. Indeed, as his writings indicate, the notion of relative "truth" or the idea that historical sources are but "imaginative representations of reality" are *not* twentieth-century ideas, nor is the concept that some form of truth is attainable with access to historical evidence. Rather, the evolution of Brown's understanding of historical inquiry and representation in both his novels and in his historical essays, reviews, sketches, and annals may be seen as providing a rich vein of historical, cultural, and ideological information, a radical alternative, for the time, to consensus history and historiography.

Thus, this study, which seeks to be historically self-conscious and attend to the intertextual deep structure of narrative and meaning, juxtaposes the beginning and end of Brown's career in ways that illuminate relationships between his novel and history writing and the relationship between his earlier career and his later, supposedly more "conservative," days. Further, it assumes that Brown's interest in and evolving theory of history are properly situated in his reading and understanding of classical, European, and colonial traditions of history writing and the changing market conditions of the early Republic after the revolution. From his earliest writings and private correspondence through his reviews and philosophical essays to his reflections about the construction and meaning of history in his prefaces to the *American Register*, his radical historicism took shape. To be sure, his novels, fictitious history, and political pamphlets fertilized his ideas about the meaning of history and contributed to his understanding of how to write it. But at the heart of Brown's lifelong engagement with history was his innate sense of "curiosity" or, as one obituary writer said of him, his "brilliant imagination—the unwearied inquisitiveness of a rich and active mind." As Brown patiently "enquired . . . read, reflected, examined and compared, opposing facts and arguments," this part of his being, more than any others, enabled him to develop a "novel" historicism.

This study is divided into three parts. The first, "Remembering the Past," focuses on European and colonial models of historiography and the context they provide for understanding historical representation in Brown's day. It also concentrates on Brown's emerging interests in history and the manner in which his early writings and novels chart his efforts to understand the past, especially as it related to the present. Chapter 1, "European and Colonial Traditions," examines the historiographical traditions in place as Brown developed his ideas about the meaning and function of "history," particularly as the "idea and ideal of 'objectivity'" manifested itself during the late enlightenment and the colonial and early national periods. When measured against the "providential" historicism of Mather and the rationalist, teleological histories of contemporaries such as Jeremy Belknap or Abiel Holmes, Brown may be seen as employing Quaker beliefs yet also departing from, like other contemporaries, the historiographical status quo and traditional notions of historical meaning. Moreover, I suggest, in contrast to filiopietistic histories of the day, Brown's secular historiography signals a radical departure from that of his eighteenth-century contemporaries.

Chapter 2, "'Domestic History' and the Republican Novel," examines the earliest conception of Brown's historicism, from his youthful journal entries and poems to his novels, and attempts to trace the ways his settings and plots resonate with contemporary historical circumstances such as yellow fever. Brown's explicit interest in and focus on, I argue, "domestic history" and the "motives" behind the actions of individuals, especially women, in familial situations further clarifies his engaging historicism and use of historical reality in his novels. In addition to recording how Brown's representation of women's experiences in historically accurate and sympathetic ways continues to inform his developing ideas of the meaning and function of history, I contend that his evolving understanding of "history" as a category for understanding shifts in late Enlightenment philosophy is also significant. He not only used historical circumstances in his novels to explain the motivations behind people's actions, but he used the novel as an initial platform for reflecting more fully on the meaning and function of history—and historical truth—itself. The metahistorical reflections in Brown's novels register his continued interest in and interrogation of domestic issues and the status and subjectivity of women within patriarchal power structures. At the same time, they also provide a basis for understanding the "novelistic" or political qualities in his later historical writing.

Part 2, "Historiography and the 'Art of the Historian,'" charts more explicitly Brown's evolving understanding of the complicated relationships between "history" and "fiction" when representing the past, especially as it occurred in his two periodical publications, his historical sketches, and his "Annals of Europe." Similar to the ways his early periodical reviews and essays informed his understanding of history in his novels, and vice versa, so his later periodical writings and historical sketches prepared him to delve further into issues of historical impartiality and representation, especially in regard to his growing interest in "domestic history" and European events concerning imperialism and Napoleonic rule. Chapter 3, "Historical Representation in the *Monthly Magazine and American Review* and the *Literary Magazine and American Register*" lays out the way "history" emerges as a subject in Brown's early periodical publications and other writings. His review of contemporary histories by Benjamin Trumbull, Abiel Holmes, Hannah Adams, and others in the late 1790s enables him to simultaneously be critical of and conceptualize historiographical principles and practices. In tracing Brown's historical reviews and self-conscious engagement with contemporary historians, one sees a mind immersed in the historiographical and cultural issues of his time, including the generic boundaries between history and romance, the role of bias and judgment in historical method, and the value of history as moral instruction.

By 1806, Brown's continued attempts to reconcile rationalist and romantic historiographical principles are illustrated by his selection and editing, for instance, of essays on history from Isaac D'Israeli and British periodicals. His publication, for example, of "Historical Characters are False Representations of Nature" and "Modes of Historical Writing" show his most intense engagement with contemporary writers and debates about the epistemological limits of history and the constructed nature of historical writing. These essays illustrate not only Brown's interest in history and aesthetics but also his own readiness, methodologically, to write historical narrative. More important, as a result of reassessing his periodical essays and scholarship, one can no longer ignore Brown or his era or claim that late Enlightenment intellectuals lived in a flat, rational universe, devoid of questions about the certainty or subjectivity of history. The meta-assumption that nineteenth-century "romance" birthed the "grand narrative of history" and that it, along with the "linguistic turn," is responsible for today's historiographical debates about historical representation, narrative, and truth completely elide the philosophical self-consciousness and originality of Brown and the late Enlightenment.

In chapter 4, "The Historical Sketches—and a 'Government, Ecclesiastical and Civil,'" I argue that like his early political pamphlets on the Louisiana Purchase, Brown's fictitious histories—the "Sketches of a History of Carsol" and "Sketches of a History of the Carrils and Ormes"—provide a bridge to his later "Annals of Europe and America" (1807–09). They serve as a practice field for his engagement with "domestic history" and a lens or vantage point from which to gauge his historicism. Brown engages medieval religious and familial history as a means of responding to ecclesiastical and political debates in his day concerning the separation of church

and state in governance, enabling his historical sketches to become a practical extension of his meditations on history in his novels and early reviews and essays in periodicals like the *Monthly Magazine and American Review.* His imaginative rendering
of the history of the Carril and Orme families illustrates his willingness to stage—
and then, theoretically, interrogate—the dynamics of political power and cultural
hegemony in an era of colonial expansion, ideological instability, and empire.

In chapter 5, "Empire and the 'Annals of Europe,'" which appeared in his *American Register; or, General Repository of History, Politics, and Science* (1807–09), I suggest that Brown's annals pick up where his historical fiction left off, with his engagement of emerging European events, or contemporary history, and the implications
of Napoleonic imperialism. Using postcolonial, feminist, and other reading strategies, I argue that Brown's interrogation of the premises and practices of European
imperialism, particularly British rule in India, places him within a democratic,
progressive tradition of anti-imperial thought and unveils how assumptions about
race, gender, social class, and religious belief combine with "political self-interest"
to oppress the "rights of others." The Godwinian and sympathetic tone that accompanies Brown's rendering of European events and motives places his historical
writing within a postcolonial tradition of historical and political thought, enabling
him to eventually examine American pretensions of power.

Part 3, "The Politics of History," focuses on lessons Brown learned from recent
European history and acts of political and economic self-interest as they apply to
American events during and immediately after the Jefferson administration and
Brown's increasing critical response to political pretense and manipulation. Building
on earlier arguments about Brown's continuing willingness to interrogate the political status quo—and the evolution of his historical thinking—chapter 6, "American
Exceptionalism and the 'Annals of America,'" calls attention to what Amy Kaplan
and Donald Pease early on called the "absence of the United States in the postcolonial study of culture and imperialism."[18] In it, I show how Brown's earlier Quaker
"instinct of social reform and cultural radicalism" remained intact during the time
of the Louisiana Purchase and enabled him, as he began to understand the full implications of European events and political history, to turn his attention to this side
of the Atlantic and assess American adventurism and foreign policy toward Santo
Domingo and the Spanish in South America, along with the Aaron Burr incident,
as representative of American pretensions toward expansion and imperialism.[19] As
his historicism evolved or matured, Brown began to interrogate, in other words,
American imperial ambitions in the name of "democracy" and did so in a manner
established within an ironic tradition of American historians.

In chapter 7, "Constitutional Limits—and 'Liberalism,'" I trace Brown's final
and, arguably, most imaginative and politically significant foray into history, especially as it concerns his efforts to alert readers to a crisis in presidential nomination procedures. Responding to congressional proposals to amend the Constitu-

tion and Stephen Bradley's controversial 1808 republican caucus memo, Brown's historiographical and political experience emboldened him, I argue, to represent the past to people in provocative ways. His focus on debates to move the capitol and the crisis caused by the Bradley memo highlights serious questions about the Constitution and how it is interpreted. Brown's concern with the absence of debate and the presence of power in the hands of a few recalls the liberalism of the American Revolution and its "radical" response to authoritarian government. Moreover, his imaginative reconstruction and juxtaposition of primary historical documents in lieu, essentially, of a formal historical narrative hail readers in ideologically and rhetorically sophisticated ways similar to his earlier novel writing. By disavowing a teleological or filiopietistic history and engaging his readers, dialogically, with voices other than his own, Brown's historical writing not only challenges the political status quo but revises our understanding of early American history and historiography.

Last, in the epilogue I read Brown's historicism against historical events and historiographical assumptions and practices in our own time. Both historians and literary historians, I argue, will find that Brown's metahistorical reflections and philosophical "reflexivity" raise useful but thorny questions about the meaning of a "postmodern" sensibility and historical representation. Additionally, Brown's history provides an intriguing perspective on early republican ideology and contemporary debates about constitutional powers and presidential authority. That is, just as Brown's historical writings and self-conscious historicism may be read as "dialogic interventions in an ongoing debate on the constitution of republicanism" in his time, so they offer useful ways to consider debates about the meaning and spread of democracy in our own.[20]

Part 1

❀

Remembering the Past

Chapter 1

European and Colonial Traditions

At the very center of the professional historical venture is the idea and ideal of "objectivity." It was the rock on which the venture was constituted, its continuing raison d'être. It has been the quality which the profession has prized and praised above all others—whether in historians or in their works. It has been the key term in defining progress in historical scholarship: moving ever closer to the objective truth about the past. Anyone interested in what professional historians are up to—what they think they are doing, or ought to be doing, when they write history—might well begin by considering "the objectivity question."

—Peter Novick, *That Noble Dream* (1988)

If Brown, as his contemporaries assert, had a capacity for "fancy" and "imagination" yet "patiently enquired . . . read, reflected, examined and compared, opposing facts and arguments," it is worth investigating what exactly such traits meant in Brown's time and how they relate to the idea that he "seemed more to write in the style of an historian of past ages, than the recorder of those passing occurrences that tincture our public councils, and embitter the charities of domestic life."[1] For, if as his contemporaries suggest, Brown, who was raised as a Quaker, was not merely reporting or describing passing events, then he was, it would seem, instead bringing a degree of philosophic candor and analysis to those events, especially in terms of cause and effect. Such analysis or pursuit of truth amid conflicting circumstances and evidence invites inquiry into what political, cultural, philosophical, and even familial forces shaped Brown's concept of history and enabled him to think and write "in the style of an historian of past ages."

That is, in addition to clarifying what was meant by historical "objectivity" in Brown's time, inquiry into the cultural milieu of his era illuminates the ways Brown's historiography related to, and was eventually at odds with, a providential or filiopietistic tradition of historical writing that privileged assumptions of providential design and, often, national destiny. Brown's affiliation with "an historian of past ages" or a generation of historians whose own methods of historical representation arguably anticipate elements of late Enlightenment historiography raises provocative questions about the evolution of modern "objectivity," and more recent claims at the end of the twentieth century about the final arrival and practice of a "bottom-up" history, historical self-consciousness or constructionism, and "truth"—issues I also examine in later chapters.

If, as Novick suggests, the "idea and ideal of 'objectivity'" is indeed at the center of modern historiography, it is useful then to examine those traditions as Brown inherited them and to try and discern how Brown himself negotiated the "the objectivity question." For if representing the past objectively as possible is the "continuing raison d'être," it is also one of the primary criteria by which not only Brown's contributions but also those of other historians should be measured. While it is beyond the scope of this study to comprehensively reassess whole generations of historians, in the case of Brown, I want to argue, scholars of American historiography have inaccurately recorded and judged the experimental historiographical efforts of Brown's era. Indeed, filiopietistic principles and practices Brown engaged—and ultimately broke away from—are illustrative of the period's ideological deep structure and construction of the past. Brown's freethinking, Quaker engagement with history forces us to rethink assumptions and clichés about early American historiography, and, equally as important, truth claims about historical consciousness associated with the rise of modern history writing. As Eileen Ka-May Cheng argues about antebellum historiography that focused on the American Revolution, "modern historians have not advanced beyond their early nineteenth-century predecessors as much as they would like to think they have." These early historians "anticipated many of the concerns of modern historians and the sophistication and complexity of their ideas about truth."[2]

European History

In considering how classical historians approached history, Harry Elmer Barnes importantly remarks that while the birth of historical writing is often associated with Greece and Homer's poems, the qualities of objectivity and analysis usually associated with historical inquiry and representation can be traced to the emergence of "speculative Ionic philosophy."[3]

The beginnings of "free thought and critical philosophy" emerge in fifth-century Ionia, where Greeks such as Hecataeus identified two elements of modern historicism in *Genealogies:* "setting up truth as the test of his statements and assuming a frankly critical attitude toward the conventional Greek creation myths."[4]

Along with an interest in geographical and genealogical origins, these early philosophers used "reason" and "free speculation" to interrogate conventional mythologies about Greek beginnings and, in effect, the cultural status quo.[5]

Greek historians like Herodotus (ca. 484–425 B.C.), Thucydides (ca. 456–396 B.C.), and Polybius (ca. 203–120 B.C.) also variously aspired toward impartiality and fairness in the reconstruction of historical events and their causes.[6] Of Herodotus, for instance, Maurice Croiset has written that he traveled much and sought to "inform[ ] himself about everything, about customs, laws, forms of government, and religions, without preconceived ideas and prejudices, but with a singular mixture of acuteness and credulity, of insatiable curiosity and religious discretion."[7] In his *History* and account of the Persian wars, Herodotus could have indulged a patriotic bias in favor of the Greeks but instead analyzed the clash of Hellenic and Persian cultures, only occasionally relying on supernatural intervention as a way of explaining causes and effects.[8] According to Donald Lateiner, however, Herodotus tried to provide a "studiously fair account" of historical events and often indicated "the limits of his knowledge" or his "uncertainty." Just as Herodotus anticipates Gibbon and his use of irony, so his *History* also avoids a teleological approach to the past and is absent of "a single 'systematic interpretation of universal history in accordance with a principle by which historical events and successions are unified and directed toward an ultimate meaning.'"[9] Likewise, if Thucydides wrote more "contemporary history" and considered more fully issues of "historical and political causation," Polybius, remarks Barnes, "came closer to the ideal of impartiality in treating Greek and Roman history than any other historical writer of antiquity." His interest in causation and effect and sound historical method is, in general, a legacy of the period.[10]

Importantly, then, if establishing what was meant by saying Brown wrote in a style of "past historians" means understanding that such a remark references early Greek and Roman historians and conceptions of impartiality, Brown, like these early philosophers, wrote history in a mode that was, for its time, a secular and innovative departure from the existing cultural mythos. The remark, in other words, in Brown's obituary that he wrote in the manner of a historian from past ages suggests that Brown's spirit of inquiry and search for knowledge, general analysis, and attempts at impartiality departed, quite radically, from historiographical standards and methods in his day and recalled the historicism of an earlier period. If true, Brown's historical method and attempts to represent the past objectively not only have a unique and, arguably, radical Greek analogue but raise provocative questions about what exactly late Enlightenment historiography accomplished relative to "the objectivity question." Were histories written during the Enlightenment informed, as most scholars assume, by reason and objectivity, or were they somehow lacking in those more modern qualities? Did early American historiography by writers such as Mercy Otis Warren objectively represent the past, or did it understand events as part of a larger providential, teleological design?

Greek analysis favored accuracy and was generally imitated by the Romans until Christianity and religious bias in the Middle Ages affected Western historical
writing. The resulting histories tended to be teleological and to privilege theological and allegorical explanations of the past that justified progress to the present.
However, it was not until Enlightenment science and rationalism took hold that
historiographical practice would return to its roots.[11] As part of a reaction to the
doctrinal or providential historical writing of the Middle Ages, the idea of rational "objectivity" was, in other words, central to Enlightenment historiography.

George H. Callcott concurs, observing how late Enlightenment philosophers
and historians developed scholarly principles and introduced the idea of progress into history writing. Giambattista Vico especially influenced the historical
writings of Montesquieu, Voltaire, Condorcet, Hume, Robertson, and Gibbon—
works that Brown either read or reviewed during his lifetime. Vico, explains Callcott, thought history was meaningful only when the historian went beyond the
mere chronicling of an event and connected it to society itself.

> When the historian grasped the totality of man's achievement—his laws,
> manners, institutions, and culture—then the past becomes understandable
> and historical knowledge useful. Vico called upon historians to cultivate a
> self-conscious method—a "scientific" method—for arriving at truth about
> the past. The method really only amounted to a conscious effort at objectiv-
> ity. The historian must ask whether a fact were reasonable, if it were relevant
> to a larger truth, if witnesses were reliable; he must be aware of his own
> biases and his own standard of judgment.

Regardless of the historian's "effort at objectivity," suggests Callcott, the themes he
included or excluded in his history reveal ideological inclinations, or the presence
of private and public biases. Similarly to how works like Montesquieu's *Spirit of
Laws* (1748) and Voltaire's *Age of Louis XIV* (1751) applied a "scientific" or objective point of view, histories by men like Turgot, Condorcet, Priestly, and Godwin
also espoused various concepts of human "progress." English historians Hume,
Robertson, and Gibbon have, for example, variously incorporated the idea of
secular progress into history. While Hume searched for "causation—or theme—
in the affairs of men," Gibbon wrote of the triumph of religious superstition, and
Robertson's histories tended to acknowledge the providence of God in historical
events—an approach that made his histories popular in America.[12]

During the eighteenth century, however, late Enlightenment ideas in historiography about reason, natural laws and progress, and the moral and literary
appeal of history entered a period, observes Hayden White, when Europeans disagreed about "the proper *attitude* with which to approach the study of history." In
response to the embrace of rationalism in historiography, critics such as Johann

Gottfried Herder moved toward "'empathy' as a method of historical inquiry" and acknowledged those elements of the past that had been ignored by Enlightenment historians. "Enlighteners," writes White, "never rose to full awareness of the creative possibilities contained in their own Ironic apprehension of the 'fictive' nature of historical reflection."[13] Instead, they were skeptical of any historical truths contained in myths, legends, or fables. As I argue elsewhere, Pierre Bayle's, Godwin's, and Brown's philosophical reflections on the nature of history and fiction qualify these observations, but by and large White's characterization of late Enlightenment ambivalence over historiographical method is accurate.

In particular, Herder, along with other German historical thinkers, put forth an organic, teleological model of history—one that questioned the idea of historical events or the past being separate from the present and instead saw history as contributing to, and defining, the present.[14] If rationalist historians looked down upon medievalism and believed in "progress as a law of history," so romanticists, he said, "stressed the organic wholeness" of historical evolution.[15] Toward this end, Herder strove in *Yet Another Philosophy of History* (1776) for a higher degree of historical empathy, emphasizing the need to focus more closely on facts and to place greater emphasis on individuals and on what was "local."[16] While rationalist historians viewed history as the "accidental result of cumulative cultural progress," Herder identified providential purpose as informing or connecting historical events.[17] As with the romantic movement elsewhere, the emphasis on feeling or empathy and providential design was, in part, a reevaluation of medieval values and central to Herder's and others' understanding of historical development. It was a clash of ideas that Brown would immerse himself in intellectually, especially after 1800, when he turned from novels to political and historical writing.

In England the response by historical writers to late Enlightenment rationalism was less pronounced than it was in Germany. English literary writers, of course, such as Wordsworth, developed an aesthetic in reaction to neoclassicist ideals, but historical writers were slower to absorb rationalist conceptions of history. Edmund Burke, for example, while not typically considered a romanticist or a historiographer, refuted tenets of rationalism in his political writings and in putting together his *Annual Register,* which he edited until 1788, defended a "conservation of the accumulated achievements of the past and condemned the rationalists for their disdain of history."[18] Not until historians such as John Whitaker, John Pinkerton, and Sharon Turner published their histories on Britain's Anglo-Saxon past could one identify anti-Enlightenment tendencies in English historical writing.[19] Of course, beyond the achievements of Wordsworth, writers like Sir Walter Scott and Robert Southey wrote historical novels that were part of the English revival of the past. But British historiographical achievements in the first half of the nineteenth century remained sparse, highlighted by the didactic studies of Thomas Macauly and Thomas Carlyle and, later, James Anthony Froude's twelve-volume *History of England.*

Contemporary historiographical scholarship has loosened its "objectivist creed" and recognized the role of ideological preconceptions and bias in writing history, but historians like Novick are accurate in saying that the objectivist point of view has remained "the key term in defining progress in historical scholarship." Even today, the avoidance of partisanship or bias in one's narration reigns supreme, and the historian is, like his classical counterparts, expected to conduct empirical research into the past and render the results with neutrality or impartiality. While Novick concentrates on "historians of some consequence or visibility" during the last hundred years, his examination of the objectivist creed's problematic nature and philosophical assumptions is useful in setting up the parameters for a discussion of colonial and early national historiography.[20] In particular, his assertion that the "idea and ideal of 'objectivity'" is at the heart of contemporary historical practice provides an important lens for assessing how European historiographical traditions came to inform colonial and early national historiography in the United States and set the stage for Brown's own interest in and, later, practice of history writing.

One of the more provocative questions that emerges from a transatlantic intellectual history such as this is how European traditions of history writing, themselves rooted in certain philosophical assumptions, influenced early American historiography both before and after the American Revolution. Were such attitudes simply appropriated, or did they take on unique features and purposes as they were employed in the recording of American "settlement"? Did the American Revolution, for instance, as a political and philosophical phenomenon alter fundamental categories about human agency and historical representation? Would Brown, a Quaker, and others of his generation have approved or contested the mythic and typological historiography of his Puritan predecessors? Or were historians of his generation skeptical of not only a providential theory of interpretation but also, eventually, a rationalist paradigm for understanding historical events? If they did pursue questions of this sort, to what extent were they self-conscious about historical writing, and how should we characterize Brown's departure from historiographical assumptions of his day, the rise of romantic historical writing in subsequent years, and similarities between Brown's understanding of "historical objectivity" and our own metacritical stance toward historical narrative and the representation of historical "truth"?

I believe that answers to these questions are mutually illuminating and that if after the American Revolution men such as Dr. Benjamin Rush urged "above all" that youth be "instructed in the history of the ancient republics, and the progress of liberty" both abroad and at home, Brown would have been, for example, familiar with various clerical and even secular histories of New England.[21] However, the manner in which such chronicles or histories record a narrative self-consciousness and attempt to be "impartial" is complicated by the rhetoric and rationale of filiopietistic history—the idea, as Jack P. Greene has articulated it, that

America was "an '*exemplary* nation,'" destined by providence to lead or redeem the world.[22] For, despite the impact of late Enlightenment rationalism, the fact is that history after history of colonial America and the early Republic anchored its representation of America's past in the assumption that as Winthrop's "city upon the hill" it was responsible for manifesting God's Divine Providence. The purpose of history in the eyes of the vast majority of historians, even after the American Revolution, was to simply and accurately record the workings of God's providence in New England and the rest of America. This is true for historians during the colonial and early national periods, from William Bradford, William Hubbard, and Thomas Prince to David Ramsay, Jeremy Belknap, Mercy Otis Warren, and others at the state and national levels.[23]

As indicated, surveying the "idea and ideal of 'objectivity'" as it appeared in colonial and early national histories is a study unto itself. In the remainder of this chapter, I provide a brief overview of how an increasingly rationalist approach to the past gradually manifested itself in the typological histories of Puritan historiography, Brown's contemporaries, and later nineteenth-century historians. Such developments, especially as they contextualize Brown's own historical self-consciousness, lay a crucial foundation for rethinking some of the assumptions that are associated with the formation of early American history writing and help identify Brown's distinct contribution to early American—and modern—historiography.

Colonial Historiography

Beginning with the chronicles of John Smith, William Bradford, John Winthrop, and others, historical narratives move from travel accounts to records of events that were both autobiographical and testimonials of providential destiny. To be sure, several early historical narratives were written by English explorers, the most significant perhaps being Richard Hakluyt's *The Principall Navigations, Voiages and Discoveries of the English Nation* (1589). Composed mainly of eyewitness reports, Hakluyt's history gathers together numerous manuscripts dealing with early English exploration of America and offers insight into the discoveries and imperial interests of the English, especially on the sea. Like Hakluyt's travels, the Norse sagas and even the travel narratives of individuals such as Bartolomé de las Casas represent some of the earliest historical narratives, especially of early contact, concerning America. Such historical narratives, while they fall outside traditional colonial histories, provide a context for understanding how travel writing, at least during the colonial period, provided a lens through which historical facts, "relations," and narratives could also be generated.[24]

Despite recording the difficulties of settling in the New World, "the need," observes Michael Kraus, of explorers "to render unto God a statement of actions done in His name, and the desire to thank Him for beneficent guidance also found an outlet in our earliest historians."[25] William Bradford's *History of Plymouth Plantation, 1606–1646,* for instance, is the classic example of the "chosen people" myth or typology in colonial histories. Bradford begins his text by stating that after their departure from England to Holland, there was uncertainty: "But these things did not dismay them (although they did some times trouble them) for their desires were sett on the ways of God, and to injoy his ordinances; but they rested on his providence, and knew whom they had believed." Incidents ranging from the "spetiall worke of God's providence" with the "profane young man," relations with Squanto and the Indians during the starving time, to the English victory over the Pequots all testify to the manner of God's favor toward his chosen people. Upon receiving, for example, corn and beans from the natives, Bradford explains, "Here is to be noted a spetiall providence of God, and a great mercie to this poore people." And of fighting with the Indians: "Thus, it pleased God to vanquish their enemies, and give them deliverance; and by his spetiall providence so to dispose that not any one of them were either hurte, or hitt, though the arrows came close by them, and on every side them, and sundry of their coats, which hunge up in the barricade, were shot throw and throw."[26]

Although Bradford's work later expressed harsh criticism of Morton's consorting with the natives and uncertainty about Divine Providence, his history of Plymouth largely parallels the Old Testament and Israel's covenantal relationship with God. His retrospective history or "typology" establishes itself, in other words, as a primary method for rendering the Puritan past in New England. As Harvey Wish observes, "Calvinists felt that that this story, but for a few alterations of names and places, was essentially their own." For Puritans, he remarks, "unsparing self-examination, recorded faithfully in detailed, introspective diaries" and "contemporary history itself" combined to make history, like the Bible, a "revelation of God's will."[27] Biblical history, the history of the Reformation, and the unfolding story of New England were seen for generations of historians as complementary texts about redemption and progress, divine or otherwise.

Similar to the way Bradford's text uses the Puritan "plaine style" and records a "conscious artistry," Cotton Mather's rendition of the Salem witch trials in *The Wonders of the Invisible World* (1692) also attempts to register a measure of historical objectivity. In noting what the reader might expect in terms of "Entertainment" and what he has been requested to provide to William Stoughton, Mather writes that he can "do no other than shortly relate the chief *Matters of Fact,* which occurr'd in the Tryals of some that were Executed" and that the reader should "take the *Truth,* just as it was." He aims to report matters, he says, "not as an *Advocate,* but as an *Historian.*" This last statement—that Mather aims to represent the past as "an historian"—speaks to his desire to avoid "personal prejudice" in his abridgement of the court papers. To be sure, his assumption that the "New

Englanders are a people of God" threatened by the Devil testifies to his typological understanding of God's providential designs for New England. Likewise, his relation of the events surrounding the trial of Martha Carrier and calling her a "Rampant Hag" in his "Memorandum" betray the presence of personal bias.[28]

But to the extent that historians like Bradford and Mather commented self-consciously on their history writing, only a handful of historians at this time can be seen as attempting to infuse rationalist "objectivity" into their narratives. That is, beyond the subtle ways Edward Johnson's *Wonder-Working Providence of Sions Saviour in New England* (1653) contributes to a self-conscious tradition of Puritan history writing, chronicles or histories in seventeenth-century America that contain explicit reflections on narrative "objectivity" are few. The majority of relations or histories—from John Smith's *A True Relation* (1608) and *The Generall Historie of Virginia, New-England, and the Summer Isles* (1624) to William Hubbard's *Narrative of the Troubles with the Indians in New England* (1677) and Cotton Mather's *Magnalia Christi Americana; or, the Ecclesiastical History of New England* (1702)—rely almost exclusively on a providential paradigm to narrate events and comment on their historical significance. It was a set of historiographical assumptions, and a practice, that would, at least in terms of relating American destiny, extend into Brown's era as well.

By the early eighteenth century, however, local and regional histories such as Robert Beverly's *History of Virginia* (1705) and Thomas Prince's *The Chronological History of New England in the form of Annals* (1736) record more overt attempts at historical self-consciousness and how they intended to use or ignore particular historical resources.[29] Kraus notes, "American historians continued to speak of colonial beginnings in awesome wonderment, grateful for divine guidance," but "most of the later colonial historians, with their strong secular approach, tended to locate the causes of events in a mundane and not in a supernatural plane." This is not entirely accurate. While historians became increasingly interested in identifying mistaken English perceptions of America and presenting histories that represented colonial America in a more favorable light, they nevertheless remained conscious of the role of providence in shaping America's past and future.[30] As many of their prefaces, narratives themselves, indicate, God or providence still played an important role in historical events.

Prince, for instance, is a classic instance of a colonial historian who overtly reflects this position as a historian. For the most part, he was regarded as an "American pioneer in scientific historical writing" and was "aridly factual." After "paying his critical respects to writers who protest their impartiality," says Kraus, Prince relates:

> I own I am on the side of pure Christianity; as also of civil and religious liberty, and this for the low as well as the high, for the laity as well as the clergy,

I am for leaving everyone to the freedom of worshipping according to the light of his conscience; and for extending charity to everyone who receives the gospel as the rule of his faith and life; I am on the side of meekness, patience, gentleness and innocence. And I hope my inclination to these great principles will not bias me to a misrecital of facts, but rather to state them as I really find them for the public benefit.

Like many of his contemporaries, Prince embraced rationalist principles but also still interpreted God's providence and interventions in the New England in terms of their relevance to the "chosen people" myth and its attendant millennial or typological images. He even used the medieval convention of beginning his history with the birth of Christ. And while his alignment with "pure Christianity" is clear, he, nevertheless, realizes that his religious beliefs might "bias" him toward a "misrecital of facts." Prince's conscious attempts, says Kraus, to give "unadorned facts" distinguishes him from his Puritan peers.[31] But there was still, paradoxically, a lingering belief in providence as an agent of colonial history.[32]

William Douglass's *Summary, Historical and Political . . . of the British Settlements in North America* (1747–52), however, examines British settlement in North America and provides, as noted at the time by England's *Monthly Review,* a "fuller and more circumstantial account of North America, than is anywhere else to be met with." Despite claims, says Kraus, that he had "no personal disregard or malice," "the partisanship of Douglass was so obvious that it hardly offends today."[33] His shortcomings were many, with his historical narrative resembling a mass of "ill-digested notes" and "misinformation" rather than a complete history. Still, his outlook on history and his views on manuscript sources—he thought they were a "laborious affair"—reflect a willingness to remark more openly on historical method and to position his account of the past relative to other New England historians. His historical writing also records an imperfect albeit self-conscious effort to identify his own historical biases and to gravitate toward a more impartial historiography.

Amid such historiographical developments, Americans began to embrace history, mostly classical or English history at first, as a genre both for pleasure and instruction. As Frank Luther Mott observed long ago about the popularity of history writing, both before and after the Revolution, Americans increasingly read histories: "By the firesides of Colonial America, in the long winter evenings, our serious-minded forebears read many an extended and leisurely historical work. Rollin, Josephus, Voltaire, Plutarch, Robertson's and Buchanan's histories of Scotland, Hume's and Smollet's works on English history, Rapin's and Rider's ditto, Neal's *History of the Puritans* and Fox's *Book of Martyrs* were favorites. Most of these histories were read from imported copies in many-volumed sets of small sextodecimos." William Robertson's *History of Scotland* (1750) was the most popular imported history in America for almost a decade. Hume's *History of Great*

Britain was also immensely popular and "reprinted in Philadelphia in 1795–96, when Samuel Harrison Smith issued a six-volume edition in octavo for Robert Campbell, the bookseller." Mott does not comment on the popularity of American state or colonial histories but observes that toward the end of the eighteenth century Franklin's *Autobiography* and Weems's *Life of Washington* were the two best sellers in American biography. Not until Sir Walter Scott popularized the historical romance were the masses consuming works of a historical nature.[34]

History writing, then, as formulated by early colonials, still largely, if not unequivocally, assumed that American settlement and progress were guided by the hand of God and that providential design, combined with millennial aspirations, had prepared the way for the creation of God's New Israel. The providential history of the early Puritans aimed, on the one hand, at impartiality but failed, on the other, to completely separate itself from a "chosen people" mythology and typological images. Without doubt, some historians articulated a relative degree of historical self-consciousness and attempted to limit the presence of personal bias—a pattern of thought that continues into the revolutionary era. But even as colonial America moved toward political and economic independence from England, it continued to admire British history and biography and to more actively imagine its own developing history. It also started to believe more fervently, especially on the eve of 1776, that it had a special destiny under God and would play a pivotal role in the future events of world history.

Historians of the Early Republic

"Accompanying the American Revolution," writes Lester H. Cohen, "was a historical revolution, a radical transformation of assumptions and ideas about the nature and meaning of history and about man's location in the historical process both as a participant in events and as interpreter and shaper of them." In addressing how Americans, mostly Federalists, moved from a providential model of history toward a revolutionary or, further down the road, romantic model, Cohen reminds us of how "history" became a conduit for "enlightened republicanism" and an emblem of political change. In fact, he writes, even though revolutionary historians like Thomas Hutchinson, David Ramsay, and Jeremy Belknap shared the language of republican virtue, it is not always clear that their belief in historical providence was keyed to the same set of theological assumptions as their predecessors.[35] For them, argues Cohen, man was both independent and responsible for his actions, thereby placing causation for events with human nature and choice. American historical writing after the Revolution may have continued to allude to God or providence, but it did so minus the philosophical certainty and conviction of previous generations. "God," observes Robert Skotheim, did not always "appear in the pages of the chronicles as an immediate, temporal causal force," but Puritan doctrinal biases lingered in New England histories even after religious toleration and ideas of independence became more pervasive in the colonies.[36]

This "growing self-consciousness of Americans," remarks Kraus, "in the era of the Revolution fostered the study and writing of history, and was itself nurtured by historical narratives."[37] While the belief, in other words, that providence somehow played a role in America's destiny and that it, as a result, had a special responsibility was always present, the Revolution also caused a desire to account, as rationally and accurately as possible, for how the human agency of "We the People" and religious liberalism combined to free the colonies from political and economic oppression.

Such is the case with Jeremy Belknap. In contrast to Prince's efforts of historical self-consciousness, Belknap, who wrote his history during the revolutionary period, clearly exhibits a more rationalist—or modern—approach to history writing in his three-volume *History of New-Hampshire* (1784–92). While, like his peers, Belknap acknowledges the role of "Divine Providence" in historical events, it is only rarely and then in the context of his narrative proper.[38] However, unlike his Puritan predecessors and many of his contemporaries, he reflects more self-consciously on his attempts to write an impartial historical narrative per se.[39] For example, in the preface to his first volume he writes: "The author makes no merit of his regard for truth. To have disguised or misrepresented facts would have been abusing the reader. No person can take more pleasure in detecting mistakes than the author in correcting them if he should have opportunity. In tracing the progress of controversy it is impossible not to take a side, though we are ever so remote from any personal interest in it. Censure or applause will naturally follow the opinion we adopt." Belknap's recognition of the role of bias and error in his construction of the past did not stop him from critiquing Puritan excesses in the realm of "capital executions" and remarking that "impartiality will not suffer a veil to be drawn over these disgraceful transactions."[40] From the "height of a rationalist's seat in the late eighteenth century," apparently, Belknap attempted to pass an objective sentence on the past; he even remarked once to his friend Ebenezer Hazard that he wished they could "be together to laugh at Mather's *Wonders of the Invisible World*."[41] Brown, as later chapters in this study demonstrate, embraced similar ideas about historical impartiality and objectivity in his historical writing. However, he also developed a more sophisticated and self-reflexive understanding of the limitations of such a posture, both as a matter of practical application and as a philosophical issue.

The growing interest in historical matters, especially as they pertained to the emergence of the early Republic, suggests that history writing—especially providential history—was not solely relegated to books, imported or otherwise. As Mott's *History of American Magazines 1741–1850* demonstrates, colonial and early national history also made its way into the ever-expanding medium of the periodical press, with periodicals contributing "an invaluable contemporaneous history of their times."[42] In addition to "The History of North America" in Samuel Neville's *New American Magazine* (1758–60), magazines such as the *Royal American* (1774–75) reprinted much of Governor Hutchinson's *History of Massachusetts Bay*, and the *Universal Asylum* (1786–92) published a history of the Revolution.[43]

Periodicals "devoted hundreds of pages to general and national history, and in the 1780s there was a special interest in ancient history which, it was hoped, would furnish moral and political guidance to the young Republic." The American Revolution was a major source of magazine histories, with serial histories such as the "History of the Late War," originally published in the *Annual Register* (London), running in the *Worcester Magazine* (1786–88). The *Boston Magazine* (1783–86), in particular, distinguished itself by frequently providing in-depth historical accounts of recent political and military events. Men such as John Eliot, James Freeman, and George R. Minot, who had helped launch the magazine, later played roles in starting the Massachusetts Historical Society.[44] The periodical became, as it was in Brown's day, a primary medium for gaining perspective on the Republic's young past and for promoting those virtues that were consistent with republican society and providential design. More so than state and local histories, in other words, histories that appeared in periodicals had the potential of being read by a greater number of citizens.

As indicated earlier, despite the continuing presence of Puritan historiographical principles, romantic attitudes toward history began to contend with rationalist ones, and if by the 1780s "American nationalism was the most intense in the world," it was because religious and romantic beliefs had combined with Scottish "common sense" philosophy to fan the fires of patriotism. Although by the early 1800s enthusiasm for English writers like Hume, Robertson, and Gibbon had lessened, post-Revolutionary American historians themselves did not enjoy any kind of windfall from this shift away from England. Anxious for a first-rate American historian, reviewers wrote that almost everything seemed "too biased, too local, too lacking in coherence and style," and that if by "eighteenth-century standards these historians did not deal with universals, . . . by nineteenth-century standards they were dull." "Seldom," writes Callcott, "did historians consider what really constituted a fact, or the likelihood of bias in their selection."[45] The level of historical self-consciousness had increased in terms of imagining a national polity and destiny, but interest in constructing a more immediate historical identity often precluded inquiry into the philosophical limitations of such a narrative.

To illustrate: Benjamin Trumbull, pastor of the North Haven Congregational Church subscribed to the idea that providence had demonstrated divine intervention during the American Revolution. As early as 1801 in *A Century Sermon; or, Sketches of the History of the Eighteenth Century*, he would remark that major revolutions and other events should be understood as "the operations of the divine hand" and that his publication was "a sketch of the works of God in the century past and especially His dispensations toward America, the United States, New England, and this town."[46] Here, Trumbull ascribes God's divine assistance over time to several venues, including where he lived and preached, North Haven, Connecticut. It is, however, in his *General History of the United States of America; from the Discovery in 1492, to 1792; or, Sketches of the Divine Agency, in Their Settlement, Growth, and Protection; and Especially in the Late Revolution* (1810) that Trumbull articulates assumptions about American destiny and the role of providence that were in play during Brown's time. As his history makes clear from the first sentence of the narrative, "Very conspicuous have been the assertions of providence in the discovery of the new world, in the settlement, growth, and protection of the states and churches of North America." Trumbull's sketches were merely an effort to "transmit them to succeeding ages, as a tribute of honour to their great and beneficent AUTHOR"—a direction Brown clearly chooses to avoid when writing his history during the same time.[47]

Like many of his and Brown's peers, then, Trumbull understood the history of the American Revolution and even the recent past to be part of God's larger plan for New England or special destiny for America. On this point, the influence of God and nationalism after 1776, Callcott astutely remarks:

> Americans never fully rejected their Puritan past, never fully embraced Enlightenment skepticism, never entirely broke the line between the Great Awakening that began in 1740 and the Great Revivals, which began in 1757. While Voltaire, Hume, and Gibbon vented their emotions against the Church, similar American feelings found outlet in the development of a pious Unitarianism. Among the American historians who began their careers as clergymen, for the most part Unitarian clergymen, were Jedidiah Morse, Abiel Holmes, Alexander Hewat, Jeremy Belknap, Benjamin Trumbull, Mason Locke Weems, John Gorham Palfrey, Jared Sparks, Frank Lister Hawks, George Bancroft, and Richard Hildreth.[48]

This lineage and the amalgam of Puritan and patriotic beliefs alluded to here—that God's hand guided American progress and destiny in unique ways—reached its literary apex with works like Joel Barlow's *Vision of Columbus* (1787), which was later revised, toned down in terms of its religious sentiments, and published in 1807 as *The Columbiad*. The concurrent publication of *The Columbiad* alongside Brown's secular brand of historical interpretation helps illustrate the era's heightened patriotism and, simultaneous, philosophical upheaval—and how much Brown was going against the historiographical grain and historical status quo.[49]

Of fundamental importance here, then, is the idea that colonial and early republican historiography clearly embraced a providential paradigm for understanding the past, a set of ideas about America's founding and special purpose that would shape historical accounts for generations to come. As Anthony Molho and Gordon S. Wood observe in *Imagined History: American Historians Interpret the Past* (1998), "Until quite recently many Americans thought of their history and their role in the world as not merely different from those of other nations but as 'exceptional'—as a beacon or model for other nations, with a special and unique destiny to lead the rest of the world to freedom and democracy."[50] Daniel T. Rodgers concurs, saying, "From John Winthrop to Oliver North, the 'rituals of God's country' (as Sacvan Bercovitch once called them) have run: a sense of God acting within and through the history of His specially chosen land."[51] In yet another essay, Wood underscores this point as it pertains to early American historiography:

> The Revolutionary leaders took the colonial period seriously indeed. They tended to look back to the seventeenth-century settlements, in John Adams's words, "as the opening of the grand scene and design in providence for the illumination of the ignorant and the emancipation of the slavish part of mankind all over the earth." In such Revolutionary sentiments lay the sources for the emerging notion of America as an exemplary nation. . . . Right from the beginning of the United States historians and fiction writers began using the colonial period to work out problems of national identity.[52]

What becomes clear, in other words, is that a filiopietistic historical tradition was largely in place after the American Revolution and that historians largely sought to understand America's past in light of a providential teleology that was anchored in historical and millennial time.[53]

However, equally as important for understanding the gaps or exceptions in such a historiography, for gauging Brown's own history writing, and even for reassessing—and, I believe, revising—modern claims for historiographical evolution or progress, Callcott observes that "while critics abused most turn of the century historians for being old-fashioned, they were puzzled and angered by other historians who were radically different." For instance, Mason Locke Weem's *Life of Washington*, which imaginatively combined "literary forms in unprecedented manner—history, biography, epic, lyric, sermon—and was an immediate best seller" was later trashed by reviewers as an outrage and "as entertaining and edifying matter as can be found in the annals of fanaticism and absurdity." By contrast, in response to the denigration of Jeremy Belknap's *History of New-Hampshire* and the charge that he was as a mere compiler, a critic reading a reprint of Belknap's history in 1832, some forty years after its initial publication, reconsidered the quality of its analysis and simply remarked, "We misjudged."[54]

But if amid this transitional and in some ways experimental period of historical writing, works by Robert Proud and George Chalmers seemed too loyalist for democratic tastes, some, like Mercy Otis Warren's popular three-volume *History of the Rise, Progress, and Termination of the American Revolution interspersed with Biographical, Political and Moral Reflections* (1805), bathed themselves in providential rhetoric and patriotic exuberance—what Kraus calls the celebrated "Warren bias." Like Ramsay and other historians in their day, she freely appropriated material from various sources, and her text "antagonized both Federalists and Southerners."[55] Warren's history, though, provides a useful lens for examining the history of the Revolution and its cultural beliefs from a female point of view and for beginning to understand what motivated Brown's interest in the past.

As Jeffrey H. Richards observes, despite using a historiographic method that was highly moral or resembled an "extended jeremiad," Warren understood, among other human sufferings, how Indians were victimized by white savagery, and she attempted to show compassion. She also held out hope that "reason and humanity" would contribute toward an equality for all nations and people, including women and, in the case of Shay's Rebellion (1786–87), debt-ridden farmers.[56] Her historical narrative focused, in other words, less on military troop movements and more on issues of politics and moral character, addressing in quite liberal ways the philosophical tensions—political "self-interest" as opposed to "self-sacrifice"— and the intellectual status quo of her day. Indeed, in her closing assessment of John Adams's actions after the war, she candidly writes: "The veracity of an historian requires, that all those who have been distinguished, either by their abilities or their elevated rank, should be exhibited through every period of public life with impartiality and truth. But the heart of the annalist may sometimes be hurt by political deviations which the pen of the historian is obliged to record."[57]

Sharon M. Harris underscores Warren's commitment to truth and justice, saying that her history not only "moved beyond the specifics of the Revolution to contemplate the nature of a republic and the character traits necessary in its citizens to survive," but "from a seat of concern over the corruption and pursuit of wealth that seemed to characterize the newly freed states." In fact, she remarks, "What is unusual about such history writing of this period is that many of the authors were writing about very recent history, about *lived* history." Moreover, she further explains how we might account for Brown's lifelong investment in history and historical writing, insightfully explaining that history writing, while a genre in and of itself, often included or blended with various subgenres from the captivity narrative and travel writing to historical dramas and poetry, making "imaginative" historical accounts part of the fabric from which early republican intellectuals and other classes understood and constructed its past.[58]

Just as Warren aspired toward historical "impartiality and truth," so Brown, according to his contemporaries, methodically and candidly "compared, opposing facts and arguments." That is, if early chroniclers and writers of seventeenth- and eighteenth-century American history "did not analyze at length the ideas which they stressed—nor did they explore the environmental contexts from which these ideas emerged," Skotheim's observation about early historians points up one of the distinguishing features about Brown and his engagement with what was "historical" in his day.[59] Whether it was in the context of his novels, essays or reviews on historical representation and truth, or the prefaces to his "Annals of Europe and America," Brown attempted to analyze not only the underlying political and private motivations behind historical events but also, like Warren, the moral ramifications of such actions and their impact on how one understands the past and lives in the present. Unlike Warren, however, and the vast majority of his peers, Brown's embrace of historical writing was less nationalist and much more inclined toward philosophical or critical self-consciousness in terms of historical method. Both, though, made a critical examination of causes and effects.

Although coverage of early national history in newspapers and magazines often neglects to mention Brown's annals, commentary from Ebenezer Hazard about why he himself "did not write history instead of publishing historical materials" helps account for this omission. Asked this question by Belknap, Hazard responded that a "regular history of the United States would be a more popular and profitable work than such a collection" but that "it would cost . . . years of labor," a deterrent in and of itself during this time period. A number of these histories, such as Samuel Nevill's "Historical Chronicle," merely "compiled" recent political news. Or they extracted and collected previous works. But by and large the aim of such magazines was not only pecuniary but preparation for "participation in politics."[60] While Brown's own annals may be seen as using recent historical events for commercial or capital gain, they also register a response to key historical and political developments. And when compared to what Jeremy Belknap called "regular history," such as Robert Proud's and Abiel Holmes's, both of which rely on a providential sense of destiny or "divine patronage," assumed historiographical and generic distinctions begin to blur.[61] This is especially true when a "regular history," such as Holmes's, lapses literally into annalistic writing in the medieval sense and into a chronological list of dates and events.[62]

If domestic histories became more popular toward the end of the eighteenth century and well into the nineteenth, Callcott is right in observing that beyond how the "historic theme" entered art, fiction, and theater, the most "impressive evidence of the place of history in popular thought is statistical: of the 248 best-selling books in the United States from 1800 to 1860, ninety of them, or 36 percent, dealt with history." Before 1800, however, only about 15 percent of the most popular books were historical. Nevertheless, history was becoming so popular, says Callcott, that publishers for periodicals such as the *American Review of History and Politics* (1811–12) and the *Historical Register of the United States* (1812–14) used the word "history" because it helped sell books and periodicals.[63] Neither of these were historical journals.

Washington Irving, author of Diedrich Knickerbocker's *A History of New York* (1809), seems to have understood this appeal. Composed and published in 1809, two years after Brown had begun his own history writing, and then revised up until 1848. He invoked the spirit of Herodotus in seeking to "rescue from oblivion" Dutch history and the name of Xenophon in striving for the "utmost impartiality and the strictest adherence to truth." Along with delving into the origins of the American Indians and how America was discovered, Irving's persona Knickerbocker also detailed the natural wonders and delights of the Hudson River and the conduct of Peter Stuyvesant and other civic heroes in governoring New Amsterdam and the surrounding area. He commented on New York's political elite and on the multiple "tastes and dispositions of the enlightened *literati* who turn over the pages of history" as well as the extent his book would satisfy their imaginations.[64]

However, while Irving's work is historically self-conscious for its time, its main focus is satirical, and it does not plumb the depths of historical uncertainty to the same degree that Brown does. It does, though, as James B. Hedges remarks, call attention to Brown's efforts to formulate "a theory of 'fictitious history'" and "equate novelist and historian as purveyors of truth through allegory." And, as Hedges suggests, if Brown early on understood the "uncertainty of history," the *History of New York* follows suit and "consistently ridicules the possibility of acquiring certain or reliable knowledge."[65] As Irving admitted in his 1848 "Apology," the "main object" of his work "had a bearing wide from the sober aim of history. . . . It was to embody the traditions of our city in an amusing form." Toward that end, for instance, he humorously depicts the "reign" of Governor William Kieft, a "brisk, waspish, little old gentleman" who became known as "William the Testy," and he mocks the conservatism of "fat, self-important old burghers" in defending the city against military aggression. However, if in his history Irving limited himself to ridiculing ethnocentric and religious claims for colonizing the Americas by "*right of discovery*," so Brown, as I argue later, understood the enduring, and politically disturbing, ties between the past and the present on that particular point.[66]

Last, even as more recent scholarship by early American historians and literary scholars is finally beginning to properly understand the imaginative form and content of early American history writing, misconceptions linger about what the "new history" of the 1960s accomplished relative to the old history. In *History's Memory* (2002), for instance, Ellen Fitzpatrick claims that the alternative or "new history" that emerged in the 1960s and 1970s "lifted from obscurity the lives of those who had been swept to the sidelines in the metahistory of progress," restored history to the people, addressed "conflict," and countered or challenged the "generalizations about American exceptionalism." In an effort to address the role of social and economic forces in history, historians used "novel methodologies" to uncover the past, thereby bringing to the table a "radically different perspective on the American past" and throwing into "sharp relief" the standards of earlier generations of gentleman scholars. Likewise, Joyce Appleby echoes the "bottom-up" approach of change in American historiography, saying, "Many of our contemporary battles over history can be traced to the 1960s" and that younger historians then developed a "template for challenging nationalistic histories everywhere" and more fully engaging the American public.[67] Both Fitzpatrick and Appleby are half correct, for if historical knowledge "comes not from remembering the past, but from taking questions to it," a major misunderstanding, as I demonstrate later, still exists among historians about the historicism of Brown and his era relative to our own.[68]

It is, then, amid the turbulent political and philosophical backdrop of the 1790s and a national historiography that was in constant flux and increasingly tied to ideas about national identity that Brown meditated on, and probed, for several years the cultural meaning and function of history. At once recalling the historical approach and methods of Herodotus and also anticipating more modern, and even postmodern, inquiries into historical self-consciousness, relativism, and representation by more than a century, Brown, I argue, imaginatively and "radically" interrogated the relationship between history and literature not only in his novels but also in his periodical essays, historical fiction, and, ultimately, his "Annals of Europe and America," which he published serially in the *American Register; or, General Repository of History, Politics, and Science* (1807–09). Long before the 1960s, he examined the lives of marginalized others and used novel methods of historical representation to challenge nationalistic history and the political status quo. In this way, his theory and writing of history provide a unique radical vantage point on late Enlightenment historiography and the claims and assumptions of both old and new historians.

Brown's Historical Writing

Brown's understanding of "historical objectivity" and the range of cultural and philosophical assumptions in Europe that have contributed to its development can be traced to Greek historians such as Herodotus and to the rationalist historians of the late eighteenth century and their effort to achieve a measure of impartiality when narrating events of the past. Vico, in particular, as read by Montesquieu, Voltaire, Hume, and Robertson, urged historians to practice a self-conscious or "scientific" method for examining the past. In reaction to the rationalist elements of late eighteenth-century historiography, Herder and other German romanticists turned inward and placed greater emphasis on rendering the past empathetically rather than objectively—a focus in English writing that was highlighted by Sir Walter Scott and Thomas Carlyle. Later in the nineteenth century, romantic concepts were also challenged as a new generation of scientific historians questioned the idea that history could be traced through documentary processes without the help of philosophy.[69]

Brown himself had, of course, classical training, and he was fond of Cicero's works. Joseph Pemberton, for instance, retired in 1769 from teaching in Philadelphia, but he left a list of works belonging to the school that included "Buckham's Universal Penman, 7 Bibles, 3 History of England, 3 Roman History, 2 Barclay's Apology, 6 Collection[s] of Tracts."[70] When Brown entered the Friends Latin School, around 1781, he was eleven years old and was "exposed to the rudiments of Latin and Greek" by Robert Proud.[71] Peter Kafer concurs, writing in his biography on Brown that Proud had a "rare combination of Quaker piety and sound classical training" and was hired as the school's headmaster of classics. In addition to reading Quaker materials, the Bible, and English literature, Brown most likely had exposure then to works by Virgil, Ovid, and Plutarch as well as popular Greek and Roman historians.[72] Jean S. Straub's inquiry into the Friend's Latin School in Philadelphia and its practices at this time also confirms the likelihood of Brown's rich reading in the classics and modern history. She writes that among the memoranda Robert Proud gave to the Latin School board was advice about the school's "Collection of Books" and that a "Renewal" of some books was necessary, as was the "addition" of others "not only among the Classics, in the first Place, but also modern History, Mathematics & the most useful Parts of Philosophy."[73]

What is not only intriguing but essential here is to understand what exactly Brown might have thought regarding Quaker beliefs, the Bible, and the study of Greek and Latin, especially as such subjects pertain to questions of historical knowledge, method, and truth. As Kafer tells the Brown family history, Brown's ancestors were caught up in Quaker reforms and preserving beliefs about "the 'Light of Truth' within," specifically one's duty to "attend to the presence of the Spirit of God, of the 'light,' of the 'voice,' within himself or herself." Of the "*inward objective manifestation in the heart*," Kafer writes: "Here was the gist of the matter in the technical language of the sect. Quakers believed that personal or 'inward' revelation—what others might term 'subjective' revelation—could be 'objective,' that revelation, in the words of historian J. William Frost, "could be infallibly known because God spoke to the spiritual senses, and one could determine the origin of the clear and distinct ideas that resulted."[74] Such beliefs shaped both Brown's sense of philosophical truth his entire life and, importantly, the independent way in which he constructed it in his personal life and his political and historical writings. Although Quakers like William Penn would try to distinguish between one's Inner Light and the use of natural reason, asserts Howard Brinton, they generally believed that "as conscience gives us our judgments about good and evil, so reason gives us our judgments about truth and error."[75] To practice "free rational inquiry" with one's natural reason is at the core of Quaker doctrine. And this is an important point for understanding Brown's method of historical inquiry, early political radicalism, and, ultimately, what later drives his historical ethos—and self-conscious efforts in obtaining historical impartiality, applying rational judgment, and locating truth.

In addition to the Bible, Jonathan Edwards's *Two Dissertations,* Samuel John-son's dictionary, multiple volumes of Abraham Rees's *Cyclopedia,* and some two hundred other books, another important book was part of Brown's personal li-brary.[76] As Kafer notes, Brown called William Godwin's *Enquiry Concerning Political Justice, and Its Influences on Modern Morals and Happiness* his "oracle." Beyond espousing atheism, the book is a "single-minded pursuit of 'truth' and in its criticisms of particular aspects of the modern European political world, is a very Quaker-like performance." Similar to Foucault's work on cultural hegemony and power, Godwin interrogates institutional forms of power and human "coer-cion," especially as they oppress "individual conscience" and one's sense of truth, an ethos Brown would carry with him the rest of his life. For Brown, observes Kafer, Quaker belief about following one's "inner light" in pursuit of truth and knowledge and Godwin's credo about "'truth' and 'justice'" were perfectly com-patible. "It is in the sense that Godwin's radical rationalism, his belief that 'truth is omnipotent,' has a Quaker ring to it."[77] Thus, in Brown's day, inquiry, reason, and truth—qualities Brown's friends associated with his historical writing—are also fundamental tenets of Godwinian *and* Quaker belief and, relative to the political and religious culture of the day, a radical historicism.

In *Charles Brockden Brown: Pioneer Voice of America,* David Lee Clark ob-serves that in Brown's "early days he was strongly pro-French and radical." Brown had read Rousseau, Montesquieu, Helvétius, and Holbach and was familiar with existing ideas about institutional power and corruption, natural morality, and in-dividual freedom.[78]

In his recent study, *Republic of Intellect* (2007), Bryan Waterman deepens our understanding of Brown's radical background and ideas, especially as shared by Elihu Smith, William Dunlap, and others in the late 1790s, when he remarks that "religion, not politics, was the group's chief concern." Contrary to histori-cal perception about the club's ties to Federalist politics and religious orthodoxy, what "most united the club's inner circle—Smith, Brown, Dunlap, and Johnson in particular—was not an antipathy toward Jacobins or Jeffersonians but a shared derision of established Christianity."[79] As Waterman rightly suggests, Brown's late Enlightenment skepticism is present throughout his novels and, one can argue, elements of his later periodical and historical writing as well.

Brown himself says as much early in his career in a letter to Joseph Bringhurst on October 24, 1795. Explaining how his "*system* of Christianity" differs from Bringhurst's and that he believes "the belief of the divinity of Christ and future retribution" has been "pernicious to mankind," Brown writes:

It is not the rational business of men to settle what is the creed of Moses, of Christ, of Mohamet, of Confucius, of Pythagoras or Solon. It is indeed not without use: it is, in certain degree, properly the theme of historical curiosity,

but the chief business is to ascertain the dictates of moral duty, by consult-
ing his understanding, and measuring the opinions of others whatever may
be their pretensions, by the standard of his own judgment.—You say I have
mistaken the Christian tenets. It is of little moment: I deny that religious sanctions are friendly to morality. I deny the superhuman authority of any teacher:
and a future retribution. Were these affirmed by Jesus Christ or merely by
you? It is indifferent: The truth is the same independently of any one's assertion or authority.

Brown clearly sees inquiry into the past of Moses, Christ, and others as a useful
"theme of historical curiosity." At the same time, if, according to Quaker belief,
"conscience" helps decipher good from evil, and natural reason facilitates "judgment" about truth and error, Brown's emphasis on the need for one to consult "his
understanding" and to use the "standard of his own judgment" speaks to both the
kind of independent inquiry and analysis associated with Quakerism and historical inquiry, especially as it concerns "the truth" and is completely antithetical to
a filiopietistic understanding of the past. Brown's subsequent suggestion to Bringhurst later in the letter that he undertake a "profound and impartial reflexion
upon these subjects" underscores the ways in which Brown's personal philosophical ethos informs his approach to historical judgment.[80]

About this time (1790–93) in a letter to "Henrietta," a young woman he fell in
love with, Brown would write that he valued "knowledge of Greek and Roman
literature" and the ways it facilitated the study of English. While study of "British,
French, or Italian literature" might be helpful in learning English, he thought one
could learn the language without classical training. In responding further to the
importance of learning English, he admits that he had received "some knowledge
of the Greek and Latin at a Grammar School" but that his level of learning did not
qualify him to "instruct others."[81] It is clear from remarks such as these that Brown
appreciated a classical education but also had doubts about, at age twenty or so, his
own knowledge base and the efficacy of learning Greek and Latin to improve one's
understanding of the English language. Study of contemporary romance languages
offered a means of mastering the rudiments of English grammar.[82]

Still, Brown, as later letter manuscripts indicate, read ancient historians like
Herodotus and understood their intellectual achievements. In a letter to Samuel
Miller dated March 16, 1803, almost ten years after Brown's letters to Bringhurst
and his meditations on classical learning in the Henrietta letters, he comments
on a recent publication of Miller's (probably *A Brief Retrospect of the Eighteenth
Century*) and asserts that "Geography . . . [is] the only subject" in which he feels
qualified "to correct any mistakes." Proceeding to offer criticism on that particular
topic, he points out that Miller's work on geography is good but that it could benefit from a "survey of the actual boundaries of our former & present knowledge."

The facts, he says, "actually added to the science and the mistakes rectified, might have been brought within small compass. The chief glory of Rennel has been to *verify,* & thus to *revive* the knowledge of Herodotus & Shaba."[83] The reference here to Herodotus reveals Brown's familiarity with such classical authors and suggests that even though Brown may not have been interested in a classical education in his early years he, nevertheless, derived his appreciation of historical inquiry, impartiality, balance, and the use of engaging detail from this "Father of History."[84]

Couched, therefore, between Holmes's *American Annals; or A Chronological History of America* (1805) and Benjamin Trumbull's *General History of the United States of America* (1810), Brown was in a position to offer historical perspective of a more immediate sort. While Holmes, for instance, would write in his preface that "professions of impartiality are of little significance" and that he was "not conscious of having recorded one fact, without such evidence," there is evidence in his narrative, as well as that of Trumbull's, that a providential interpretation of the past was still fashionable—even when one acknowledged his or her biases.[85] In fact, writes Lawrence Buell, the historiography of the early Republic's Puritan ancestors was very much in the center of ideological conflicts between Arminian Unitarians and Calvinist Congregationalists.[86]

To put it another way, as sectarian ideologies and differences began to play themselves out more fully in historiographical arenas and terms, historiographical disputes over "the facts, meaning, and authority of the New England past," says Buell, began to play themselves out more forcefully. Broadly speaking, "the trend in · New England historiography during the colonial period had been from orthodox to latitudinarian, from partisanship to qualified objectivity, resulting in a critical, rationalist appraisal of Puritanism." In addition to Belknap, Samuel Peters's *History of Connecticut* (1781) and Isaac Backus's *History of New-England, with Particular Reference to the Denomination of Christians Called Baptists* (1777–96) were among the first in the "dissenting tradition" of early national historiography. Likewise, Richard Hildreth was also in opposition to filiopietism. His six-volume *History of the United States* (1849–51) was forward-looking in the sense that it avoided "gush" and it contained a "more empirical study of history than the Brahmin Romantics practiced."[87] Yet, even though Hildreth's history often aimed at being a corrective to orthodox narrative, it did not reach a level of "independent synthesis"—a major factor, I want to suggest, that distinguishes Brown's work from that of other late-eighteenth and early nineteenth-century history writers whose work was aligned with filiopietistic assumptions or, say, Federalist party belief.[88]

In terms, then, of locating Brown's history writing in the landscape of colonial and early national historiography, one may reasonably conclude that he was not the first, nor the last, to broach questions about historical objectivity and bias. However, if Buell and historiographers like Kraus and Callcott *all* agree that George Bancroft's multivolume *History of the United States from the Discovery of the American Continent* (1834–74) was a high-water mark in nineteenth-century American history writing and that Bancroft, most generally considered the "Father of American History," raised historical writing to new heights, early Americanists and historians need to reassess canonical and noncanonical histories.[89] We need to ask, for instance, why Bancroft's work, in its breadth and depth, surpassed state histories such as those of Proud and Trumbull, and what happened to the late Enlightenment meta self-consciousness we find in early national historical writing? Was it momentary? If so, why? Why also do we remember Belknap, in other words, and not Brown? How did Bancroft's moral optimism and eloquence raise history writing to a high art form, and why for so many readers was his commingling of historical event with providential design evidence of the supreme historical narrative?[90]

As Kraus rightly observes then, although Bancroft is known for effectively placing the "history of his own country in some sort of definite relation to that of Europe," he omitted economic conflicts or influences in history, lacked objectivity, and indulged in loose editing practices, plagiarizing and editing text beyond recognition.[91] Skotheim concurs, adding that Bancroft "did not depict ideas in detail nor investigate the environments from which they emerged. . . . He [merely] synthesized the traditionally emphasized ideas of Puritanism, toleration, and national independence into a progressive development toward democracy."[92] If this is true, we need to seriously question the assumption, as put forward most explicitly by Dorothy Ross, that "'romance' shaped the 'grand narrative of history,' and today's historiographical debates."[93] As I argue later, such an interpretation, and its assumptions about late Enlightenment historiography, clouds an accurate understanding of early national historiography, and needs to take into greater account the debates Brown and his peers engaged in concerning the meaning and function of such terms as "history," "narrative," "truth," and "objectivity."

To properly reassess history writing of the early Republic up until the twentieth century involves, then, comparative analysis with colonial and early national histories and supposedly more sophisticated or developed histories such as Bancroft's—histories that by the end of the nineteenth century were being revised by more modern or "objective" ones, such as Henry Adams's *History of the United States* (1889–91). It involves an accounting, in some fashion, of the manner in which historians relied on or, in Brown's case, shunned existing providential models of history and sought to eliminate, or ignored, the role of bias in their writing. It involves a serious consideration, in other words, of how Brown examined the philosophical and imaginative ramifications of historical representation, and a willingness to consider the extent to which he linked historiographical and epistemological inquiries with an interrogation of American exceptionalism—that is, challenged, in a radical Quaker fashion, standard or lingering assumptions about providential design and destiny in American history.

In short, if, as Novick suggested, "historical objectivity" was and is the primary means of measuring a historian's worth, its assimilation into American historiography vis-à-vis late Enlightenment influences and the relaxation of Puritan standards has been by no means clear or agreed upon; nor have the reputations of historians like Belknap and Bancroft remained fixed. Not until after the great romantic history writers Bancroft and Prescott in the 1830s were these early historians or compilers "accepted on their own terms."[94] Indeed, as historiographers became more conscious of the fluid boundaries between "objectivity" and personal or political bias, so the history writing of writers such as Belknap has been viewed more positively. By modern standards, "historical objectivity" is still the "raison d'être" of history writing and, as Buell suggests with Hildreth and others with Belknap, even a means of *revising* a historian's standing.

Given this long view of historical "objectivity" and the possibility of a "dissenting tradition" in early American historiography, one naturally wonders where Brown's theorizing about history and actual history writing fit in. To what degree, if any, for instance, do Brown's reflections on history and history writing echo European attitudes toward the past, or a "providential" interpretation? Should we consider him as a historian in the mode of Belknap? An Abiel Holmes? Or, because of his Quaker background and the ways he engages, like Greek historians, the ambiguities of modern historical representation and interrogates the political status quo, as a "radical" writer of early American history—a forerunner of postmodern historiography? That is, if Brown writes history in a secular, Godwinian manner, countering, as do Belknap and Hildreth, a patriotic, filiopietistic view of the past, and he also embraces historically and philosophically self-conscious attitudes toward history writing, might we see his historicism—his early musings about history, his essays, his reviews of contemporary histories, his historical fiction, and his annals—as constituting an independent, self-reflexive, and sustained inquiry into the nature and function of historical writing? If so, his writings seem to offer a unique vantage point for more precisely assessing historicist issues during his time, and for more self-consciously and accurately historicizing current debates about the nature and function of historical meaning.

Indeed, as Brown's career suggests in the mid- to late 1790s, especially with his burst of novelistic productivity in novels like *Wieland, Ormond, Edgar Huntly,* and *Arthur Mervyn,* he focused on history as a subject, his novels using a range of historical circumstances, personal and familial histories, and reflections on the meaning and function of history as part of his ongoing efforts to represent the past. His early fiction not only initiates his inquiry into historical conditions of the past, and specifically the ways women become central subjects and narrators of domestic history, but it establishes a sustained record of theoretical inquiry on the differences and similarities between history and romance—and the important role Brown's novel writing played in his evolving conception of history and what it meant, at least between 1798 and 1802, to be a historian.

Chapter Two

"Domestic History" and the Republican Novel

In the history of man there is this great and evident distinction. He is either a solitary, a domestic, or a political being. It is domestic history that pleases me beyond all others. So far as the characters of men are influenced by political events, political history is interesting, but it is not for me always to so abstract my attention from the personages and fix them as events, always to consider men, no otherwise than collectively to employ my attention only in the consideration of general events flowing from general causes. The formal character of individuals, their visages, their dress, their accent[,] their language[,] their habits, manners and opinions; their *personal behaviors* I am desirous of knowing. *Life and Manners,* I must repeat is my favorite science. These are the materials of conversation. These the objects of universal curiosity.
—Charles Brockden Brown to Joseph Bringhurst, July 29, 1793

Some of Brown's earliest reflections on history and history writing may be found in his journal or notebook entries. Loose, mutilated page manuscripts like "Sample of Liberty of Conscience 1783," which remark on the need to "unfold the page of [h]istory" and the history of the Protestant reformation, refer specifically to "Hume" and his "History of England," suggesting that even as a young boy, Brown was familiar with Hume's *History of England* at least in part.[1] Likewise, in a page from one of his notebooks, Brown comments on the "Dying expressions of General Harrison" as recounted in "Hume's History of England."[2]

However, it is in a verse manuscript like "Aretas," composed in 1787, when Brown was sixteen years old, that one gets a more complete glimpse of his thinking about "sensibility" and history. In this poem, which Brown's father transcribed, Brown's speaker espouses "Truth o'er Satires rank'rous pen" and desires that "Candour" shall be an "impartial guide" as he sings the "virtues" of his friend Aretas.[3] Such sentiments in turn lend themselves to "contemplation" in nature and eventually "pleasures of the mind," pleasures that are by "Education Taste refin'd" and manifest themselves in the form of "Instruction from historic page" and the "search . . . [of] records of a distant age." In this respect, the poem gestures toward a sensibility or concept of history that is romantic yet modern in orientation and sees the reading of history as an aesthetic experience and vehicle for moral and intellectual improvement. It shows that Brown's reflections on the purpose of history are consistent with his Quaker upbringing and lifelong pursuit of truth and integrity and the emerging ideology of leading intellectuals such as Dr. Benjamin Rush, who urged after the Revolution: "Above all . . . let our youth be instructed in the history of the ancient republics, and the progress of liberty and tyranny in the different states of Europe."[4]

However, if, as a youth of sixteen, Brown saw the "historic page" as something he could consume more for pleasure than instruction, such a view becomes qualified throughout the late 1790s, especially when he began to write novels and to understand their potential to operate as agents of political and social change.[5] By the mid-1790s, Brown understood "domestic history" to mean "the formal character of individuals"—"their visages, their dress, their accent[,] their language[,] their habits, manners and opinions"—and "political history" to refer to "general events" and "general causes." His attempt, for instance, in a letter to Joseph Bringhurst in 1793 to distinguish "domestic history" from "political history" signals a distinct shift in his thinking about historical representation and society, a change that offers insight into the construction of his novels and their handling of historical materials.

That is, to the extent, then, that Brown sought to gain readers, he variously depicted scenes of domesticity in his novels, sometimes in sentimental or conventional ways, and sometimes not. Although Brown may have registered in his early writings an awareness of an emerging romantic and even republican ideology, it is not entirely clear if he completely disassociated himself from lingering neoclassical arguments for elevating poetic or fictional discourse over that of historians. His novels, for instance, variously register use of historical settings and modes of representation; his historical sketches blend historical realism with utopian fiction; and when, toward the end of his life, he composed his historical annals, he embraced fictional, and arguably poetic, methods of representation as a way of engaging the reader's imagination. Thus, his earlier inquiry was clearly with "*personal behaviors,*" whereby he equated "domestic history" with the circumstances of the home and family and, to a certain degree, social history. During the last several years of his life, Brown would concern himself almost exclusively with "political history."

In gothic and epistolary novels, therefore—such as *Wieland* (1798), *Ormond* (1799), *Edgar Huntly* (1799), and *Arthur Mervyn* (1799, 1800)—Brown renders "domestic history" and the lives of individuals and families in historical and philosophically self-conscious ways. He does so in a manner that enables him to articulate distinctions between a "historian" and a "romancer" and, at the same time, to reflect, like his characters, on the limits of those such categories as they pertain to human knowledge. Similar to his periodical essays, Brown's novels operate as a philosophical workbench for him to experiment with methods of representation. In addition, however, one can see Brown's engagement with the novel and his sustained interest in "domestic history" as he pays particular attention to women as the subject and agents of history. In this respect, his interest in late Enlightenment European philosophy, reason, and historical objectivity is intertwined with emergent forms of liberal republicanism and a sympathetic understanding of the everyday lives of women.

Here, I make two claims. First, by the late 1790s, Brown's serial fiction and, in particular, his novels—from *Wieland* to *Clara Howard* and *Jane Talbot*—testify to an intense interest in "history" or "the past" as both subject matter and a vehicle of philosophical expression. I argue that both his "major" and "minor" novels illustrate the provocative ways his interest in the republican home and family enabled him to further develop his sense of "the historical," particularly as it concerned emerging cultural issues related to race, gender, class, and religious belief and the act of narrative representation.

Second, as analysis of the full trajectory of his novels illustrates, Brown's growing interest in familial matters, specifically the "formal character of individuals," provides a unique perspective on both his evolving sense of biography as history and his continuing reflections on the boundaries between history and romance. I argue that as his inquiry into personal histories, especially of women, extends into family histories, a subject he takes up more fully in his later historical fiction, his novels are driven by historical and epistemological concerns, especially the manner in which feeling and memory can supplement historical "facts" and inform his narrator's—and his readers'—ability to recall the past and live in the present. The use of "memory," in particular, for Brown becomes a means not only of approaching the past but, when informed by sentiment or emotion, of actively ascertaining knowledge and truth.[6]

That is, if Brown's earlier novels move, generally, from historical incidents and historically accurate representations of religious fanaticism, Indian displacement, and yellow fever in Philadelphia, especially as it concerns the lives of men, to plots more narrowly focused on family relations, the interpretation of characters, and female subjectivity, they continue to probe past lives of individuals and issues of memory and historical representation—to examine people's actions and motives and the process, collectively and individually, of constructing knowledge in historically and philosophically self-conscious ways. In this respect, Brown's novels are less about republican self-sacrifice or "virtue" and maintaining the status quo and more about the cultivation of a late Enlightenment critical sensibility geared toward greater historical self-consciousness, the presence of political and other injustices, and social and individual change.

Wieland

In her provocative study, *Intricate Relations: Sexual and Economic Desire in American Fiction, 1789–1814*, Karen A. Weyler observes that the American novel was not authored in isolation and that the term "novel" had much more fluidity in the eighteenth century than it does today. And while it is difficult, she notes, to nail down the first American novel per se, almost all the novels, from, say, Jeremy Belknap's serialization, beginning in 1787, of *The Foresters, An American Tale* and William Hill Brown's *The Power of Sympathy* (1789) to those published as late as Hannah Webster Foster's, "explicitly appeal to literary nationalism"; but their greater importance "lies in how they, as a body of work, contribute to developing bourgeois subjectivity, particularly as related to economic aspirations and moral virtue in the post-Revolutionary era." However, various texts articulated their themes, "broad-based, pervasive bourgeois concerns, as well as narrative style, unite these works." It would not be until around 1814 that the "beginnings of radical changes in the style and subject matter of American fiction become noticeable, with sustained attention beginning to be paid to the problems of more diverse groups of people." This is true to a great degree, with the sole exception perhaps of Brown's novelistic efforts in the late 1790s.[7]

Novelists in the early Republic continued, in other words, like their European counterparts, to situate narratives in the context of historical "fact" or truth and in quasi self-conscious ways—some more fully than others. For example, William Brown Hill's *The Power of Sympathy: or, the Triumph of Nature. Founded in Truth* (1789), Jeremy Belknap's *The Foresters, an American Tale: Being the Sequel to the History of John Bull the Clothier. In a Series of Letters to a Friend* (1792), and Hannah Webster Foster's *The Coquette; or, the History of Eliza Wharton; A Novel; Founded on Fact* (1797) all engage, at least in their titles, questions of history, narrative, and truth. Foster's title implies that if there were any uncertainty about the veracity of her story or, at least, its origins, the novel was "founded on fact," and the history or story of Eliza Wharton, in reality the seduction and ruin of Elizabeth Whitman of Hartford, Connecticut, offered an important moral lesson.

The prefatory material in Susanna Rowson's novel *Charlotte Temple* (1791) used claims of historical veracity as a means of justifying the novel's didactic intent. Rowson, for instance, asked her readers to consider her novel "as not merely the effusion of Fancy, but as a reality," claiming that out of necessity she had thrown over the facts "a slight veil of fiction, and substituted names and places" according to her own fancy.[8] Although Foster's novel was based in fact and Rowson's only claimed to be, assertions of historical veracity were not just empty rhetorical gestures or attempts to distance oneself from novel writing. They were efforts to engage readers on the basis of biography or true stories and to participate successfully in the public and economic spheres of the early Republic—to use fiction as means of writing history.

As Shirley Samuels argues in her now classic study *Romances of the Republic,* if "a powerful nation constitutes much of its political identity through the language of heterosexual and patriarchal family relations . . . fiction carries this message—that it operates in the dissemination of national presence into the families."[9]

But while novelists during the revolutionary and early national periods may have claimed a basis in historical fact so that they could publish novels with risqué content, almost none, really, contained extended or abstract analysis in the mode of Brown of what constitutes "history" and "fiction."[10] Just as historians like Jeremy Belknap and Abiel Holmes offered limited commentary on the role of bias or objectivity in their historical narratives, so early novelists rarely considered, at any length, what comprised a fact. Likewise, early historians seldom reflected on the possibility of bias in their own sources or narrative. Unlike most of his contemporaries, Brown, however, contemplated such matters and reflected self-consciously on the relationship between "history" and "fiction" in not only his periodical publications but also in his novels. Like his periodical essays, which address the deficiencies of ancient and Enlightenment histories and the ability of realistic fiction to render human motivation and action more fully, his fictitious histories or sketches also later became a vehicle for him to further explore the imaginative—and instructive—aspects of "domestic history."[11]

Brown's interest in the intersection of history and fiction first presents itself in his 1798 publication of *Alcuin: A Dialogue,* which may be said to mark his foray into "domestic history" or the cultural mores for women relative to family, home, and society. While Alcuin and Mrs. Carter are decidedly fictional characters, their discussion about inadequate education and the institution of marriage nevertheless touches upon realities for women in Brown's day. It focuses attention on the rights of women within a republican society and the ways in which codes and institutions favor one sex over another.[12] It also initiates reflection on the meaning and function of "history"—that is, it contains a self-reflexive commentary on the role of the historian during the late Enlightenment. In reference, for instance, to "the past" and the manner in which that knowledge is systematically withheld from women, Alcuin addresses Mrs. Carter's concerns, saying that "Artists may want skill: Historians may be partial" and that he is opposed to the assumption that women have particular defects. Brown stakes out a consciousness of the limits of historical impartiality and also of a progressive position regarding women.[13]

While the extent of Brown's radicalism concerning the rights and status of women continues to be a matter of debate, scholars increasingly agree that his text registers an acute awareness of the historical status and oppression of women.[14] As Fritz Fleischmann accurately and insightfully observed early on, especially in regard to Mrs. Carter's defense of the social utility of marriage, "If Brown is hedging on his radicalism here, as has been alleged, he does so tongue-in-cheek, relying on his readers' wits and sense of irony. His later works show that he never abandoned his feminism and that he continued to hope for social reform." "The cause," he says, "Brown makes for women's rights extends to all his novels" and also appears in his later writings.[15] Bruce Burgett concurs, saying that, for instance, Mrs. Carter's response to Alcuin that she was "tired of explaining this charming system of equality and independence" is Brown being ironic "in his most radical drag."[16] The fictional dialogue within *Alcuin* about the domestic sphere of women illustrates, in other words, Brown's "habit of working rather close to contemporary events" and his interest in probing subjects of domestic interest.[17] It is representative of the manner, early on, in which he married historical "fact" with "fiction" and allowed his interest in historical matters to inform his fiction writing and vice versa. This type of historical self-consciousness and rhetorical play is typical of all of Brown's writing, fiction and nonfiction. However, it is *Wieland,* Brown's first novel, where one finds a fusion of biography, history, memory, and representation—and where characters like Clara begin to meditate on the meaning of family history and the difficulties inherent in reconstructing the past.

Written in epistolary format, *Wieland; or, The Transformation* (1798) uses actual events—a murder in New York of a wife and children in 1781 by religious fanatic James Yates—as the basis of its story. The novel begins by recounting the lives of Clara Wieland and her brother, Theodore, whose own father is a religious enthusiast and dies mysteriously. Raised by their aunt, the sister and brother develop close relationships with Catherine Pleyel and her brother, Henry. Theodore eventually marries Catherine and has four children, while Clara and Henry also develop a close relationship that promises marriage. Theodore, however, eventually begins to hear voices, which test the rationalist assumptions and beliefs of the group. As they try to sort out sensory impressions and their own reasoning processes, another character, Carwin, arrives on the scene. An Irish immigrant who can mimic other voices, he makes Clara uneasy, yet she is also fascinated by him. A series of events occur that, in gothic tradition, ultimately lead to Carwin being found in Clara's bedroom closet. Henry concludes that Clara and Carwin are having an affair, but the group then hears a series of mysterious voices, which lead to further confusion and anxiety. It is Theodore, however, who, like his father, hears "divine" voices urging him to kill his wife and children. As Clara attempts to reason with him and he, in turn, prepares to stab her, Carwin intervenes and saves her by using his abilities as a ventriloquist. The novel ends with Henry killing himself and Clara reflecting, years later, on the processes of human reasoning and morality.[18]

As Donald Ringe notes, "Always in the background lies the history of the elder Wieland, the father of Theodore and Clara."[19] Without doubt, the "Advertisement" to the novel itself addresses the problem of "historical evidence" or veracity and places Clara in the role of historian. "If history furnishes one parallel fact," writes Brown, "it is sufficient vindication of the Writer; but most readers will probably recollect an authentic case, remarkably similar to that of Wieland." In addition to relating her father's "ancestry" and the history of those sources that influenced his spiritual beliefs, she also narrates her brother's history and "the history" of those disasters that generally befall her family.[20] Clara, in other words, is the central narrator in the story, the filter through which events are translated and one of the main characters through which Brown explores rationalist, sensationalist psychology and religious fanaticism of the day as well as illustrates how each belief system fails to fully explain human motivations and actions.[21]

Early on, for example, Brown fuses Wieland's biography with religious history. Clara relates how her father's ancestry was "noble" on the "paternal side." Upon her grandfather's death, her father, she says, was apprenticed to a "London trader, and passed seven years of mercantile servitude." Working hard and in relative poverty, he eventually slid into "gloomy reflection" and depression before he encountered a book written by a sect of French Protestants known as the Camissards, which provided "an historical account" of their origins. Her father, she continues, was receptive to its teachings and sentiments and immersed himself in Biblical study and extreme behaviors associated with that particular "empire of religious duty." Once his apprenticeship expired, we learn, the elder Wieland felt compelled to bring his faith to the North American Indians, so he moved to Philadelphia and purchased a farm on the Schuylkill, where he married. A religious enthusiast, he built a temple and became increasingly "engrossed in his own reflections" and reclusive. Feeling that he failed to follow God's will for his life, he visited his temple at midnight, where, according to his "imperfect account," he saw a light and suffered a mysterious blow.[22] He eventually contracted fever and died.

While his account, says Clara, seemed an "imperfect tale" and her uncle was "inclined to believe that half the truth had been suppressed," it also raises questions for her about the "conclusions" that can be drawn on such "facts." Similar to her uncle, who exhibits a "skeptical" temper and believes in "natural causes," Clara, as she ages, makes the incident the "subject" of her thoughts. And as more recent events recall the "memory" of her father, she reflects on whether or not the stroke of the "invisible hand" upon her father was "fresh proof that the Divine Ruler interferes in human affairs, meditates an end, selects and commissions his agents, and enforces, by unequivocal sanctions, submission to his will" or whether or not what happened was more subjective—"the irregular expansion of the fluid that imparts warmth to our heart and our blood, caused by the fatigue of the preceding day, or flowing, by established laws, from the condition of his thoughts."[23] Clara's meditations on the veracity of her father's story raise fundamental questions about historical knowledge and epistemology in the late eighteenth century,

Facing page: Title page of Brown's first edition of *Wieland,* published in New York for Hocquet Caritat on September 14, 1798, by Thomas and James Swords. Courtesy of the Library Company of Philadelphia.

WIELAND;

OR THE

TRANSFORMATION.

AN

AMERICAN TALE.

From Virtue's blifsful paths away
The double-tongued are fure to ftray;
Good is a forth-right journey ftill,
And mazy paths but lead to ill.

COPY-RIGHT SECURED.

NEW-YORK:

Printed by T. & J. Swords, for H. Caritat,
—1798.—

ADVERTISEMENT.

THE following Work is delivered to the world as the first
of a series of performances, which the favorable reception of
this will induce the Writer to publish. His purpose is neither
selfish nor temporary, but aims at the illustration of some important branches of the moral constitution of man. Whether
this tale will be classed with the ordinary or frivolous sources
of amusement, or be ranked with the few productions whose
usefulness secures to them a lasting reputation, the reader must
be permitted to decide.

The incidents related are extraordinary and rare. Some of
them, perhaps, approach as nearly to the nature of miracles
as can be done by that which is not truly miraculous. It is
hoped that intelligent readers will not disapprove of the manner in which appearances are solved, but that the solution will
be found to correspond with the known principles of human
nature. The power which the principal person is said to possess can scarcely be denied to be real. It must be acknowledged
to be extremely rare; but no fact, equally uncommon, is supported by the same strength of historical evidence.

Some readers may think the conduct of the younger Wieland impossible. In support of its possibility the Writer must
appeal to Physicians and to men conversant with the latent
springs and occasional perversions of the human mind. It will
not be objected that the instances of similar delusion are rare,
because it is the business of moral painters to exhibit their subject in its most instructive and memorable forms. If history
furnishes one parallel fact, it is a sufficient vindication of the
Writer; but most readers will probably recollect an authentic
case, remarkably similar to that of Wieland.

It will be necessary to add, that this narrative is addressed,
in an epistolary form, by the Lady whose story it contains, to
a small number of friends, whose curiosity, with regard to it,
had been greatly awakened. It may likewise be mentioned,
that these events took place between the conclusion of the
French and the beginning of the revolutionary war. The
memoirs of Carwin, alluded to at the conclusion of the work,
will be published or suppressed according to the reception
which is given to the present attempt.

                                                    C. B. B.

September 3, 1798.

questions about historical representation, individual agency, and truth both Clara and Brown reflect on more self-consciously later in the novel.

Like his father, Theodore Wieland is also interested in the "history of religious opinions" and has a knowledge of that history and Calvinism that rivals that of rationalist Henry Pleyel. Although intellectual debate dominates their lives, it is when the Irish immigrant Carwin appears that Clara narrates, again, another personal history. To be sure, Carwin's life history is expostulated fully in Brown's publication *Memoirs of Carwin the Biloquist,* which he published from 1803 to 1805 in the *Literary Magazine and American Register.* In *Wieland* though, Clara provides an initial sketch of his life, remarking that while Carwin was quiet concerning the subject of "religion and of his own history, previous to his *transformation* into a Spaniard*,*" he had met Pleyel in Valencia, Spain, and had "no aversion to intercourse" with him on a variety of topics. In addition then to having an "affection for Pleyel," Carwin is "highly intelligent and communicative," and on different occasions throughout the novel, he uses his power to mimic voices.[24]

However, it is in the process of seeking to understand the value of sense impressions, as well as why certain events have occurred and what caused them, that Clara reflects self-consciously, in the mode of a self-conscious historian, on the veracity of her own narrative and its effect on the reader. For instance, one evening as she approaches her house, she notices the dimming of a light in her bedroom. Entering her home with her penknife open, she contemplates Carwin's possible motives for being there and remarks on her own actions: "Yet I will persist to the end. My narrative may be invaded by inaccuracy and confusion; but if I live no longer, I will, at least, live to complete it. What but ambiguities, abruptness, and dark transitions, can be expected from the historian who is, at the same time, the sufferer of these disasters." While her remarks are made as part of her larger recollection of finding her way to her bedroom, believing she has seen Carwin's face in the dark, and then stumbling, to her horror, upon Catherine's corpse, they also highlight Brown's continued interest in probing the limits of human narrative and memory as well as how "motives" can be assigned to "actions." Whether "the spectacle," he says, Clara experiences at that moment exists in her "fancy or without, might be doubted."[25] As Shirley Samuels writes, Clara's "description of herself as a historian may explain how the issue of authorship and authority in the narrative appears as an issue of familial and national history."[26] Because she is sometimes the subject of her own story, her own narrative, like others in the novel, is sometimes

Facing page: The advertisement for *Wieland,* dated September 3, 1798. Brown's advertisement alerts readers to the veracity of his "tale" and the extent to which a "fact" may lack "historical evidence." His business, he suggests, is to be a moral painter and offer readers memorable instruction. Courtesy of the Library Company of Philadelphia.

ambiguous or unreliable and can only be substantiated with the passing of time and other events—a theme Brown explores repeatedly in his novels.

Finally, after Henry accuses Clara and Carwin of being lovers and Theodore, like his father, descends into madness and kills his family, Carwin defends Clara from the younger Wieland's attack, Theodore commits suicide, and Clara withdraws from society for three years. It is here, in the often maligned last part of the novel, that Clara, "in her last letter," returns to the subject of history—and the present. In "relating," she says, "the history" of past "disasters," she's "changed": rather than being immersed in despair and ready for death she is, instead, "in full possession of life and health." When she reflects on her earlier reasoning process and emotional state, she claims that she now has acquired stability and solace. She has survived a house fire, moved to France with her uncle, and married Pleyel. In the process, she claims her "curiosity was revived" and she again passionately "contemplated . . . the spectacle of living manners and the monuments of past ages."[27]

However, echoing his earlier assertion that "it is the business of moral painters to exhibit their subject in its most instructive and memorable forms," Brown returns to the moral importance of history when Clara briefly recounts the history of Conway, Major Stuart, and Maxwell. Asking the reader to "moralize on this tale," Clara focuses on the "deceitful and sensual" Maxwell, in particular, and apprises us of his success in seducing Mrs. Stuart and of his interest in Clarissa. As we soon learn, the murder of Stuart and the "history of Maxwell" on the eve of combat between the two leads Clara to conclude that Maxwell was the likely suspect and that "the evils of which Carwin and Maxwell were the authors, owed their existence to the errors of the sufferers." If characters like Stuart and Wieland, she says, had "not admitted the spirit of absurd revenge" or "framed juster notions of moral duty," events might have transpired differently.[28] Indeed, if she had been "gifted with ordinary equanimity or foresight," her own history might have been less tragic and evil might have been avoided.

Thus, for Clara, like Brown, "domestic history" can, at once, be a source of truth and an "imperfect tale." Brown's reminder to his readers of the "authentic case" of a father murdering his family develops into an inquiry into the "ancestry" and histories of a range of characters, with Clara as the primary narrator. Like Mrs. Carter's, Clara's reflections on the veracity of her father's story lead to subjective and self-conscious questions about the "ambiguities, abruptness, and dark transitions" of her own story or history. And in the end, Clara changes as a result of her experiences, and she prompts the reader to consider the moral implications of her story both for particular characters and themselves. This theme of history and historical subjectivity becomes a subject of even more concern in Brown's next novel, *Ormond; or, The Secret Witness*.

Ormond

In *Ormond; or, The Secret Witness* (1799), Brown included "many references to recent events in both America and Europe, especially the French Revolution," creating again, says Ringe, "a rich historical background."[29] Chapman concurs, writing that *Ormond* "tells the story of the young chaste Constantia Dudley's attempts to support herself and her family and to preserve her republican virtue, in a community threatened by a yellow fever epidemic, rising tides of immigrant refugees from political crises around the world, and confidence games associated with emergent market capitalism."[30] It is a story about Constantia Dudley's life and her encounters but also about family histories and the personal histories of Martinette and Ormond. The histories of these characters, and especially Sophia Westwyn, as they are intertwined with each other and events in Europe, are central to the form and content of the novel and further inform our understanding of Brown's metacritical ideas about historical narrative, novel writing, and truth— his inquiry, in the context of the novel, into how individuals are constructed, and construct themselves, as historical subjects.

The novel opens in post-Revolutionary New York by sketching how Thomas Craig swindled Dudley out of his stock and property and forced him and his family into bankruptcy. Dudley then moves to Philadelphia, where his wife dies and he develops cataracts and blindness. His daughter, Constantia, takes care of him and lives frugally, sharing "domestic duties" with Lucy, a girl whom Mrs. Dudley had adopted before her death, and pursuing intellectual interests in her spare moments. Amid the spread of yellow fever, fear, and poverty, Constantia bravely helps the diseased of the city, provides for her father, and shuns marriage to Balfour and others in an attempt to hold on to her independence. With the return of Craig, however, she is also introduced to Ormond, whose indulgent manner, rationalist distaste of marriage, and infatuation with her lead to the suicide of Ormond's mistress, Helena Cleves. Constantia's meeting with Martinette de Beauvais, Ormond's radical sister, interests her momentarily in the actions of women during the French Revolution. Sophia Courtland confesses how her life as an orphan with the Dudleys led to a "romantic passion" for Constantia. Ormond learns of Constantia's plans to leave for Europe with Sophia and, after using Craig to murder Constantia's father and then killing Craig himself, confronts Constantia in a jealous rage and attempts to kill her. Using a penknife, Constantia defends herself, killing Ormond, and then relocates, with Sophia's help, to Europe.

As Brown indicates in the novel's prefatory material to "I. E. Rosenberg," Sophia Courtland's desire to communicate the "history of Constantia Dudley" and to be a "faithful biographer" is one that simultaneously casts light on Brown's own interest in the role of individuals in history. Specifically, the promise to compose an "authentic, and not a fictitious tale"—to imitate reality as closely as possible—is in keeping with not only the conflicting views of history and romance of the time but also the purposes of biography.[31] The desire to avoid relating events in an "artificial" manner and with "harmonious congruity and luminous amplification" is, for Brown's narrator, an effort to relate her story not from a "unity of design" but rather from "facts," however plentiful or scarce. In this way, says Sophia, the imperfections of characters such as Constance and Ormond will more closely resemble real life, and what a "faithful biographer" can accomplish, than the contents of a romance novel. Moreover, even if Constantia's personal history is of no interest to readers, Sophia believes that "modes of life" and "public events" associated with her story warrant attention insofar as they pertain to a uniquely American culture that is devoid of European class distinctions based on birth. Similar, in other words, to what Brown had indicated earlier about "society and manners" in a letter to Joseph Bringhurst, the story of Constantia would also be a study that resembled reality in terms of its content and factual "detail." Indeed, if the details she presents prove unsatisfactory, she advises Rosenberg and, by implication, the reader to "go and examine for yourself."

Beyond Craig's embezzlement of Dudley's stock, news that the "history of the Wakefield family" was "entirely fictitious," and the fact that Dudley's "paroxysms of drunkenness" contribute to the "mournful period in Constantia's history," it is Brown's depiction of the yellow fever in Philadelphia that holds historical significance for literary scholars and historians alike. Whiston's death, for instance, from "*yellow fever*" prompts Constantia's "reflections" on the contagion's progress in "one quarter of the city" as well as on the history of "contagious diseases" in "Greek and Egyptian cities." "The predictions of physicians," relates Brown's narrator, "the measures of precaution prescribed by the government, the progress of the malady, and the history of the victims who were hourly destroyed by it, were communicated with tormenting prolixity and terrifying minuteness."[32] The deaths of Whiston and his sister Mary illustrate the manner in which victims' bodies are disposed.

For instance, even as Constantia's arrival at the Whistons' allows her to observe Mary's "exertions to vomit" and a floor "moistened and stained by the effusions from her stomach," we witness the effects of yellow fever on individuals. Mary is described as being restless, having a "flushed and swelled" face with "languid eyes," and, as she dies, a "corroded and gangrenous stomach" that produces vomit of a "dark hue and poisonous malignity." Whiston, after deserting his sister and then being shunned in the countryside, is also found "burning with fever, tormented into madness by thirst." His body, left unburied for fear of contamination, rots and leads to the deaths of the rural family that had "too much regard for their own safety to accommodate him." In Philadelphia, "negroes" and others of similar "colour and rank" are seen carting bodies to burial, accompanied, especially at night when the removal of corpses takes place, by the "sounds of wheels" and the "shrieks and laments of survivors."[33] By all accounts, the images of yellow fever Brown provides and the manner in which temperature and air changes contribute to its "remission" or disappearance are accurate and part of the novel's historical appeal.

Constantia's personal history is, of course, at the core of the novel and in many ways accents feminist issues initiated in *Alcuin*. Aside, for instance, from how she is physically and sexually accosted on the lower-class streets of Philadelphia, her rationale for not marrying Balfour, her rescuer, is both provocative and progressive for its time. Reflecting, for example, on the advantages and disadvantages of "nuptial life," she comments that once married "the choice of a more suitable companion, if such an one should offer, is for ever precluded" and that "now she was least mistress of the product of her own labour." "Marriage," she believes, would cause the loss of her "personal freedom" and make her "the property of another." Moreover, "education . . . had created in her an insurmountable abhorrence of admitting to conjugal privileges, the man who had no claim upon her love."[34]

Similar to the yellow fever of 1793 that gripped Philadelphia and finds its way into the novel, Constantia's meditations, then, on marriage and her own personal agency or "freedom" tap into women's rights debates and discourses of the day. Such reflections place the fictional "history of Constantia Dudley" within an undeniably real historical context concerning marriage, being the "property of another," and education. Constantia's assertion concerning marriage to Balfour that "homely life was better than splendid servitude" underscores for anyone familiar with the writings of Mary Wollstonecraft or Judith Sargent Murray, the presence of a feminist politics in Brown's novels. It provides further context for understanding Constantia's motives, thoughts, and actions in the remainder of the novel and for gauging later reflections about how the "ignorance and cowardice" of women themselves concerning their rights sometimes contrives to subject them. Indeed, as Russel Nye notes of Brown's essay "Remarks on Female Education," published in June 1798, "Far from being inferior to men in intellectual capacity, 'were all circumstances of education equal, the fair sex might claim an equality, perhaps a superiority in mental abilities.'"[35]

Like Constantia, "the history of Ormond" is revealing of Brown's philosophy of history and historical representation in its own right. Ormond, in psychologically and sexually manipulating others for selfish motives, moves the plot forward in the ways he becomes obsessed with Constantia. His attempted rape of her at the end of the novel and his subsequent death encapsulate the thrust of his character. In remarking, though, on how men generally "chuse a wife as they chuse any household moveable" and that Ormond was more calculating in his views of women, Brown's female narrator draws attention to Ormond's "domestic system" and, specifically, the case of Helena Cleves, Ormond's mistress. Brown sympathetically depicts Helena, writing that while endowed with "every feminine and fascinating quality," her "understanding bore no disadvantageous comparison with that of the majority of her sex" and Ormond came to regard her "merely as an object charming to the senses." Helena is passionately in love with Ormond, unable to "separate" from him because her "education" has "disabled her from standing alone," and she commits suicide once Ormond makes Constantia his main love interest. Insofar as Constantia's "meditations" about Helena and her emotional dependence are also Sophia's, so the histories of Brown's characters intersect with one another and combine to explain a character's motives and how historical subjects are constructed in time.[36]

This interest in literally depicting "domestic history" is clearly represented by the character of Martinette de Beauvais, Ormond's sister. Unlike Helena, she has "large experience, vigorous faculties, and masculine attainments," and her "acquaintance with history" is "exact and circumstantial." Her knowledge of events in the "theatre of France and Poland" is related in a manner that suggests intimate knowledge of them. In fact, remarks Sophia, "while this historian described the features, personal deportment, and domestic character of Antonelle, Mirabeau and Robespierre, an impenetrable veil was drawn over her own condition." There was "a warmth and freedom in her details which bespoke her own coagency in these events. Constantia's curiosity about Martinette's Greek and Sclavonic "history" and how it compares "with other incidents" leads to additional narrative about Martinette's upbringing and religious instruction in Italy and Spain. "New manners and a new language" interest her until she becomes engaged to a "political enthusiast" named Wentworth and they decide to travel to America to fight during the Revolutionary War. Assuming "male dress" and acquiring skill with the sword, she reaches Santo Domingo, helps "repulse" the "Americans at German-Town," and then meets Madame de Leyva before arriving in France and participating in the French Revolution as an ardent "adorer of liberty."[37]

According to Paul Lewis, Brown's representation of the "woman warrior" and of female independence is radical—making him "the one U.S. novelist of the 1790s who went beyond 'Wollstonecraft in reevaluating woman's potential empowerment'"—and propels Ormond two centuries ahead to "the kind of gender trouble that Judith Butler described in the 1990s."[38] Kristin M. Comment concurs, writing that Brown's novel "contains the first extended fictional portrayal in America of what the novelist calls 'romantic passion' between women." The end of the 1790s, she argues, witnessed, in response to excesses of the French Revolution, a "conservative turn in American popular culture and politics" and an effort to control women's desires and behavior. Brown's novel not only "reflects both the cultural fascination with lesbian possibility and patriarchal efforts to contain it," but its "ambivalent treatment of female independence leaves that containment tenuous at best and ultimately affirms the power of female homoerotic bonding it seeks to limit."[39]

Moreover, "both Martinette and Ormond are allied with masquerade and the public sphere, with contemporary wars, world politics, and masculine military exploits," and Brown represents "both heterosexual marriage and queer romantic union as possible means by which Constantia might preserve her 'homely liberty.'" The novel's "digressions, embedded narratives, and biographical sketches" as well as its ending suggest that individuals like Constantia can participate in the public sphere to the extent that they imagine or see themselves as part of a larger political fabric or community.[40] Bryan Waterman concurs on this point insofar as he sees Brown's affiliation with the New York Friendly Club and its engagement with Godwin's and Wollstonecraft's "religious and sexual radicalism" as key to Brown's fiction. For him, despite the ways "politeness of speech" in social circles and mixed company may have inhibited the development of "American feminism and intellectual 'radicalism,'" "*Ormond* shares Wollstonecraft's belief that for women to play a full part and to benefit from the march of intellectual progress they would have to overcome the limitations imposed by a false sense of decorum and by essentialist notions of gender, whether they posit women as incapable of violence or of intellectual improvement."[41] This novel, in other words, like *Alcuin*, is a philosophical and political inquiry into the status and agency of women.

Nowhere is this type of historical and aesthetic self-consciousness—the female subject's contemplation of the real or factual and the imagined—more evident than in Sophia Westwyn, the novel's female narrator and last major character. Through Sophia's history and reflections, the reader can chart, in the mode of earlier essays, Brown's historicism—his developing notions of historical narrative, novel writing, and truth—and, specifically, the idea that it is difficult to know any kind of truth, historical or otherwise, because of one's personal biases and interests.

To illustrate: admitting her identity at the end of the novel, Brown's narrator writes: "I must be forgiven if I now introduce myself on the stage. Sophia Westwyn is the friend of Constantia, and the writer of this narrative."[42] The "stage" or performance metaphor is an important key for understanding Brown's works in general and his novels in particular, for it suggests the manner in which Brown's plots aim to engage the reader for the purposes of prompting reflection on the actions and motives of individual characters.[43] Sophia, for instance, recalls how "indebted" she is to Constantia as an adopted member of the Dudley household and how the memory of her mother—a woman who prostituted herself in search of marriage and stability until saved by the "exhortations of a Methodist divine"—pains her. Her mother's subsequent "moral history" and illness take them both to Europe, where Sophia learns the "history of Craig's imposture" at the Dudley household and imagines Constantia's demise. Despite getting married to Courtland, her desire to learn the "history of the Dudleys" and her memory of Constantia drive her to find Constantia, which, after returning to the Dudley's abandoned home and examining a field of yellow fever graves, she does. Their reunion consists of sharing "the story of each other's wanderings" and reflecting on the role of destiny and chance in human events.[44]

Sophia's philosophical reflections here on her own narrative vividly illustrate Brown's conception of historical representation, fiction, and truth. If early in the

novel, Brown's narrator endeavored to be a "faithful biographer," she also acknowledged, in regard to the "character of Ormond," that to "truly pourtray the
motives, and relate the actions of another, appears utterly impossible" because of
the difficulties in ascertaining absolute "truth." "No representation will be wholly
false, and some though not perfectly, may yet be exempt from error." Likewise,
in reflecting on the effects of human choices and action, she remarks that "in no
case, perhaps, is the decision of an human being impartial, or totally uninfluenced
by sinister and selfish motives." However, it is in sharing her past with Constantia
and reflecting on the history and "machinations" of Ormond that Sophia remarks:
"Human approbation or censure, can never be exempt from injustice, because our
limited perceptions debar us from a thorough knowledge of any actions and motives but our own."[45]

As in "Walstein's School of History" (1799) and Brown's reviews about historical representation, *Ormond* underscores the "uncertainty of history," how "actions
and motives cannot be truly described," and how "we can only make approaches
to the truth." The novel's instances of "domestic history," especially of women, use
"memory" as a means of remembering the past and, at the same time, as a way
of thinking about how to accurately represent the lives of individuals in a larger
historical context. Thus, Brown's novel renders the details of "domestic history"
on the one hand, and, like *Alcuin* and *Wieland,* the practical and philosophical
limitations of historical representation on the other—a subject he continues to
investigate in his next novel, *Edgar Huntly; or, Memoirs of a Sleep-walker.*

Edgar Huntly

In their recent edition of Brown's *Edgar Huntly; or, Memoirs of a Sleep-walker*
(1799), Philip Barnard and Stephen Shapiro argue that "unlike" many of his contemporaries, Brown had a theoretically complex method for writing his novels,
one that draws upon the period's "British radical-democratic writers," specifically
"Mary Wollstonecraft, William Godwin, Thomas Holcraft, Robert Bage, Helen
Maria Williams, and Thomas Paine." These "Woldwinite (Anglo-Jacobin)" authors
distrusted institutions and saw "social change as resulting from the amplification
of transformed local and interpersonal or intersubjective relations." This ethos,
combined, they suggest, with a fictional method that was outlined in essays like
"Walstein's School of History," and made for novels that "explore how common,
disempowered subjects respond to damaging social conditions caused by defects
in dominant ideas and practices." For Brown, "history describes and documents
the results of actions, while fiction investigates the possible motives that cause
these actions." A novel like *Edgar Huntly* is unique because it stages the "precon-
ditions for historical events or behaviors" and prompts readers to reflect on their

own cultural conditions or "motives" in an effort to "construct a more 'virtuous,' equal, and fulfilling society."[46]

If *Ormond* focused primarily on the domestic lives of women as they pertain to select historical events and might have more aptly been entitled "Sophia; Constantia's Secret Historian," *Edgar Huntly* focuses on the history and motives of Edgar Huntly relative to other characters and issues of frontier settlement in western Pennsylvania. Published in July 1799, its epistolary structure and male narrator, Edgar, frame the novel's larger historical inquiries, yet the histories of characters like Clithero, Sarsefield, and Waldegrave are also uncovered as they pertain to characters' motives and actions and Brown's general inquiry into late Enlightenment epistemology. That is, just as the novel's focus on "remembrance" and "memory" aims, as Brown hints at in his preface "To the Public," to engage the "sympathy of the reader," so, I contend, characters like Edgar immerse themselves in the role of philosophical historian and comment on the differences, and similarities, between "history" and "romance." It also examines the historical and philosophical implications of forgetting the past, colonial or otherwise, and being under the impulse of "misguided . . . but powerful benevolence."[47]

Edgar Huntly opens with remarks "To the Public" about providing new themes for the "moral painter" and using sources that grow out of "the condition of our country," such as "incidents of Indian hostility, and the perils of the western wilderness." He declares that in this "performance" he will seek the reader's "sympathy" and that the "success of his efforts" must be judged by the "liberal and candid reader." In the novel proper, Edgar writes a letter to Mary Waldegrave and attempts, much like a historian, to "recollect" the past and to "place in order the incidents that are to compose my tale." He focuses on being able to relate events, without "indistinctness and confusion" and with accurate and precise "remembrance." At the same time, however, he is conscious of how his own "perturbations," personal "sentiments," and "time" itself may affect his story. He confesses that as his tale is "deliberate and slow," so also "incidents and motives which it is designed to exhibit will be imperfectly revived and obscurely portrayed."[48] Like Walstein, in other words, and as seen in self-reflective parts of *Wieland* and *Ormond,* Brown expresses ongoing concerns about the moral imperatives and "uncertainty of history" and how we can "only make approaches to the truth."

The plot of the novel revolves around Edgar's perceptions—often misguided, though sometimes not—of other people and the proper role of benevolence. Edgar, writing to his former fiancée, Mary Waldegrave, recalls seeing a distraught man, Clithero Edny, digging one night at the foot of an elm tree, the place where Edgar's friend Waldegrave had been murdered. Edgar confronts Clithero about his actions and learns about Clithero's past in Ireland, his patroness Mrs. Lorimer and his engagement to her daughter Clarice, and his accidental murder of Mrs. Lorimer's brother, Wiatte. Clithero disappears, and Edgar pursues him through the wilderness in an effort to convince him that because of his momentary insanity he is blameless in Wiatte's death and in his benevolent belief that killing Mrs. Lorimar is a reasonable way to rescue her from the torment of her brother Wiatte.

The novel's plot takes a turn when the letters of the late "freethinking" Walde-grave to Edgar disappear. Highly critical of religious belief and espousing atheism, the missing letters are a major source of anxiety for Edgar and eventually cause his own sleepwalking. Weymouth's appearance, and claim that Waldegrave's estate of $8,000 is his, sends Edgar into his own delusional journey into the wilderness, where he wakes up in dark cave, encounters Indians, and is accidentally shot at by whites in pursuit of renegade Indians. In making his way back from the frontier to civilization, Edgar increasingly resembles "the savage" until he meets Sarsefield, his former instructor and mentor. Clithero, wounded and rescued from Indian captivity, encounters Edgar and Sarsefield, but Clithero escapes after Sarsefield denies him medical help. The novel ends with a series of letters indicating Ed-gar's attempts to inform Clithero that he had not killed Mrs. Lorimer, Sarsefield's indictment of Edgar's actions and resistance to paternal authority, and Clithero's suicide while accompanying Sarsefield to an asylum.

Brown's use of "history" as a subject here largely follows two trajectories: the novel's rural setting of 1787—and debates about the federal Constitution, Indian policy on the frontier, female agency in marriage, and hospital reform—and Ed-gar's reflections, relative to Clithero's past, on the meaning of history and its re-lation to Enlightenment epistemologies of truth.[49] Just as Brown, in other words, draws upon a usable past that ranges from historical relations with the Delaware Indians to the contemporary "confinement of lunatics" in New York City, so he also examines in the novel the roles of "memory" and "truth" as they pertain to an accurate understanding and representation of the past.[50] The intersection of these trajectories, through constant "reflection" and "recollection," lends itself toward a conception of "domestic" history that is broader or more complex than that seen in his earlier *Wieland* or *Ormond*. That is, aside from the novel's focus on somnambu-lism and the shortcomings of rationalist and benevolent belief systems, Clithero's "history of ... disasters" and Edgar's reflections on his own actions and motivations make for moments of self-conscious inquiry—moments where the reader may also reflect on his or her knowledge of English colonialism and historical relations with the Delaware Indians.[51]

What are we to make, for example, of how Edgar's and Clithero's self-reflexive "histories" reference British colonialism in America, Ireland, and India? Brown's sympathetic rendering of Old Deb's resistance to the abuses and "perpetual en-croachments of the English colonists"? The expectation of an "exterminating" war? Defying her "oppressors"? Or even Edgar's repeated reluctance to engage in "vio-lence and bloodshed" against the Indians he encounters? What is the significance of having Clithero, a dispossessed Irish immigrant, speak as a subject and recall the history of Sarsefield in India? Of having Clithero relate how Mrs. Lorimer procured Sarsefield a "post in the service of the East-India company," where a "war broke out between the Company and some of the native powers"? Or having Clithero rely on his memory of conversations with Mrs. Lorimer in order to tell of Sarsefield's escape from the prisons of Hyder and the means by which he finally managed to escape west through Hindoostaun, Turkey, and Europe to America?[52] Such discourse, like Brown's later representation of the East India Company in his "Annals of Europe," seems aimed at prompting the reader to remember the past and reassess the historical reality and politics of race, colonization, and ethnocentrism.

Generally, since publication of Jane Tompkins's *Sensational Designs: The Cultural Work of American Fiction 1790–1860* (1985), scholars have increasingly agreed that Brown's representation of Indians in the novel is historical, if not performative, in a political way. Brown stages or reenacts Indian displacement and, with exception of Old Deb, uses captivity narrative character types and drama as part of the plot. In his introduction to the novel, Grabo asserts that the fraudulent Walking Purchase of 1737 is the origin of Queen Mab's displacement and the primary source of resentment. Likewise, he identifies Easton as the place between 1756 and 1758 where the government of Pennsylvania made a peace treaty with the Delaware Indians. "So," suggests Grabo, "when Brown conflates the two episodes, he is right in spirit if not entirely in fact."[53] Sydney Krause agrees, adding that Brown's symbolic use of the "Elm tree" in the novel references the "legendary 'Treaty Elm'" where William Penn seems to have negotiated a treaty of friendship with the Lenni Lenape, the same Delaware Indians who are dispossessed in the novel. For this reason, if "we have a subtext in *Edgar Huntly* that, consistent with its symbolism, awakens dark thoughts about the whites' past treatment of Native Americans, it correspondingly awakens a compassionate attitude toward the Indians themselves."[54] Edgar reenacts the racism and Indian hating of the period but also reflects on the historical circumstances and political injustice associated with Indian resistance to English settlement.[55]

The historical circumstances of the Delaware aside, Brown also specifically meditates on "domestic history" as it pertains to the historical condition of women. In relaying, for instance, the history of Mrs. Lorimer and her choice of a marriage partner, Clithero remarks, "There is no event on which our felicity and usefulness more materially depends, and with regard to which, therefore, the freedom of choice and the exercise of our own understanding ought to be less infringed, but this maxim is commonly disregarded in proportion to the elevation of our rank and extent of our property." Influenced by her brother, Wiatte, who despised "love and friendship" as reasons for marriage, her parents "denied the husband of her choice," and "another was imposed upon her." The impact of such events is not lost on Mrs. Lorimer years later when her daughter seeks marriage to Clithero. Rather than maintaining that Clarice marry at a suitable rank, she supports marriage between Clarice and Clithero, saying, "I see that you love each other, and never, in my opinion, was a passion more rational and just."[56] Clithero's account of Mrs. Lorimer's life is typical of the way Brown embeds cultural commentary in fictional narratives and blends romance with history.

As in his other novels, aside from hammering on the egotism or evils of male characters, Brown's socially progressive intervention on behalf of women is present, notably in the scene at Selby's son's dwelling, where Brown details an incident of domestic abuse.[57] Here, Brown radically undercuts the home as an "icon of classical republican values" and reveals the underside of domestic tranquility on the rural frontier.[58] Edgar's approach to the house, a "model of cleanliness and comfort," immerses him in the presence of a drunken and enraged husband and the trauma of a recent Indian attack. Domestic abuse becomes clear as Edgar hears the husband say "Is't you Peg? Damn ye, stay away, now; I'll tell ye stay away, or, by God I will cut your throat . . . I will" and reflects further about his use of "the oak-stick." Even as Edgar contemplates the "miseries which a debauched husband or father inflicts" and experiences "tears of anguish," he realizes the "true nature of the scene" when he hears the mother's efforts to quiet her crying baby and recollects similar incidents of domestic abuse by men. Brown's emotional rendering of "heart-breaking sobs" in this scene leads, finally, to Edgar's assessment of the "domestic miseries . . . the unhappy lady suffered." Edgar's egotistical reasoning for why it was not a time to "waste" his "sympathy on others" prevails, however.[59]

Although the scene, like "the history of Mrs. Lorimer" and marriage, is brief and demonstrates the limits of Edgar's benevolence, it also points up Brown's interest in using "remembrance" and "sympathy," especially in regard to the response of his readers, to portray the historical and domestic realities of women's lives—a topic covered graphically in his personal correspondence. This same sort of historical consciousness and interest in trying to determine the truth of events, domestic or otherwise, is evident, finally, in Edgar's reflections on Clithero's narrative. That is, in keeping with the novel's predominant theme of attempting to "ascertain the truth" behind events and people's actions, Brown positions characters to also inquire into the subject of "history" itself, enabling them, along with the reader, to act as a kind of metahistorian.[60]

For instance, in his relation of the "history" of Sarsefield's "actions and opinions," especially concerning Wiatte, Clithero remarks, "The tale of that man's misdeeds, amplified and dramatized, by the indignant eloquence of this historian, oppressed me with astonishment." "If a poet," Clithero states further, "had drawn such a portrait I should have been prone to suspect the soundness of his judgment."[61] As in his earlier writings, Brown's juxtaposition of "the historian" with the "poet" reflects his longstanding interest in the distinctions—and similarities—between "history" and "romance." On the one hand, it calls attention to historical attitudes about history as a form of "truth," and poetry as an exercise in imagination; on the other hand, it also invites the reader to reflect on his or her own judgment or construction of historical representation and knowledge and existing assumptions about historians, poets, and their impartiality in constructing the past.

Brown's interest, however, in historical representation becomes most apparent immediately after Clithero has finished his life's story and in the way Edgar reflects on its meaning. Responding to Clithero's "history of my disasters" and his insistence of innocence in regard to Waldegrave's murder, Edgar remarks: "Not a circumstance, from the moment when Clithero's character became the subject of my meditations, till the conclusion of his tale, but served to confirm my suspicion. Was this error to be imputed to credulity? Would not anyone, from similar appearances, have drawn similar conclusions? Or is there a criterion by which truth can always be distinguished. . . . I had communed with romancers and historians, but the impression made upon me by this incident was unexampled in my experience."[62] Similar to Clithero's reflections on Sarsefield's life and on the role of the historian and the "soundness of his judgment," Edgar reflects on the truthfulness of the "tale" he has heard. Unlike Clithero, however, he reflects more self-consciously on his own potential for mistaken assumptions and interpretation—and ponders whether anyone, including "romancers and historians," can completely ascertain the truth in a set of circumstances. Such reflections recall both "Walstein's School of History" and, during this period, Brown's "The Difference between History and Romance" (April 1800), where he discusses how distinctions between historical actions in the past and the "motives" associated with such events provide insight into the fictional aspects of history writing. As in the later essay, where Brown observes that "HISTORY and romance are terms that have never been very clearly distinguished from each other," in *Edgar Huntly* Brown also examines the supposed distinctions between history and romance concerning the truth of what "*might* have happened," "what has *actually* happened," and "what never had existence."

Thus, like *Alcuin* and, in some ways, *Wieland* and *Ormond*, *Edgar Huntly* examines the subject of history in terms of the historical condition of women, especially the ways that patriarchal beliefs constrain women's choices in marriage or condone domestic abuse, and allows that inquiry to influence considerations of plot and thematic development. In particular, the novel's inquiry into "memory" and "truth," as they pertain to one's understanding of the past, lead to a provocative illustration and, in some instances, interrogation of "domestic history" and philosophical issues associated with historical representation of the past. In repeatedly prompting the reader to reflect on characters' motivations, actions, and tales, Brown explores epistemological issues of truth and knowledge—as they pertain to late Enlightenment constructions of history and the novel—and tests the limits of philosophical certainty. This inquiry into "domestic history" continues in his next novel but in a way that expands Brown's construction of "family" and history.

Arthur Mervyn

As Charles Bennett has suggested, Brown used "historical materials" in his novels most conspicuously in *Arthur Mervyn* (1799, 1800), where urban Philadelphia and yellow fever provide background for the misfortunes of its protagonist.[63] Brown writes in his preface that the "evils of pestilence by which this city has lately been afflicted will probably form an aera in its history" and that the disease has been cause for "reflection to the physician and the political economist." Brown hopes that his novel will also afford "moral" instruction on "human passions and motives" and communicate "lessons of justice and humanity." If he is successful in supplying a "faithful sketch" of the city during this period, he believes the novel can foster "benevolence" in those capable of offering "relief" and, at the same time, depict examples of civic "disinterestedness and intrepidity."[64] In short, the novel is designed to both entertain and instruct, to offer, as Grabo observes, a "model of right conduct" that proceeds from principles "similar to those that inspired Engle," and were "embodied in Walstein's 'School.'"[65] Stephen Shapiro concurs, adding that in tales like *Arthur Mervyn*, "Brown defines romance's function as being no longer simply a statement of radical intent and rationale alternative, but now as a mechanism for driving through its own status as a textual object and indicating the presence of actual existing networks of oppositional cultural authority."[66]

Arthur Mervyn; or, Memoirs of the Year 1793 is also Brown's novel that most fully develops the familial or domestic history of its female characters and uses their "past" as a means of further exploring issues of historical representation, agency, and epistemology. That is, although published in parts (serially and as part one) prior to the publication of *Edgar Huntly*, it continues to focus on historical circumstances of the yellow fever in Philadelphia but, unlike his previous novels, expands the scope of "domestic history" in terms of subject matter beyond the lives of women to also include extended family histories—the histories of multiple families and in-laws, not just that of a daughter or a mother and her children.[67] It also focuses on the relationship between history and identity, on how Arthur Mervyn, like Carwin, can be read as a study of the dangers of anonymity when people are allowed to tell their own histories in a way that deceives others and hides their real motives.

First appearing as nine chapters in the Philadelphia *Weekly Magazine* between June 16 and August 25, 1798, *Arthur Mervyn* was then published as part 1 between March 7 and May 21, 1799, about three months before *Edgar Huntly* was published and "Memoirs of Stephen Calvert" began its serial appearance.[68] Part 2, the bulk of the novel, was published most likely in August or early September of 1800, almost a full year after *Edgar Huntly* appeared. In part 1, the novel's plot and subplots indeed focus on Arthur's struggle to make his way in the yellow fever– and crime-infested city of Philadelphia in 1793. Dr. Stevens tells how he found the afflicted Arthur; nursed him back to health; and, in the face of Wortley's concerns, encouraged him to reveal his personal history. Arthur's tale is about how his sad boyhood in rural Pennsylvania prompted him to come to Philadelphia for a better life and how upon his arrival he falls prey to a swindler, losing his clothing and money, before meeting Thomas Welbeck. While Welbeck hires him to copy a stolen manuscript, Arthur eventually learns that Clemenza Lodi, Welbeck's "daughter," is really a woman Welbeck had taken advantage of financially and then kept, against her will, as a mistress. Arthur later observes Welbeck's murder of his competition, Amos Watson, and participates in burying the body and starts to realize that Welbeck is a criminal. But Welbeck disappears in the Delaware River, prompting Arthur to flee the city for fear of his own demise. He returns to the countryside and finds work with the Hadwins, a Quaker family, where he falls in love with Eliza Hadwin and discovers $20,000 of embezzled monies in Lodi's book. Arthur decides to go back to Philadelphia in order to return the money and to locate Wallace, Susan Hadwin's fiancé. Arthur, however, contracts yellow fever, is almost buried alive, and again encounters Welbeck, who is in search of the $20,000 in banknotes. Deathly ill yet desiring to be virtuous, he confronts Welbeck, burns the notes, and travels to Medlicote's house, where he collapses and the novel's narrator, Dr. Stevens, finds him.

To the extent that Dr. Stevens's story about Arthur displays fears and attitudes associated with yellow fever in 1793 and how "cleanliness, reasonable exercise, and wholesome diet" can help counter illness, it is a narrative, like *Ormond,* that has historical bearing and usefulness. The atmosphere in which victims of yellow fever died and were buried is made abundantly clear. However, as "memoir" or fiction rooted in historical circumstances, Dr. Stevens's story also embeds the stories or histories of other characters, such as Arthur, Welbeck, and Clavering. Stevens relates, for instance, how he nursed Arthur back to health from the fever and found it necessary in the process to learn more of Arthur's past, especially as it concerned Arthur's connection to Welbeck, who had defrauded Stevens's friend Wortley. Arthur's subsequent tale in part 1 amounts, in other words, to an attempt to explain his motives and actions relative to the histories of other characters. Beyond learning how the wives of Dr. Stevens and Arthur's father govern their better judgment or about Arthur's knowledge of Betty Lawrence, a "wild" "milk-maid and market woman" with "defective morals" who eventually marries his father but comes to despise Arthur, the reader is repeatedly exposed, then, to inquiries and narratives concerning Arthur's past, first by Dr. Stevens but also by Welbeck, his mistress, and others.[69]

To illustrate: before offering Arthur employment as a "copyist," Welbeck questions him about his "history" or origins, which Arthur relates. Although he is not confident that his tale will be believed, he nevertheless shares his rustic background. A similar interview takes place a few days later, but, says Arthur, when

Welbeck made allusions to Arthur's earlier history and "made more particular inquiries on that head" he was "not equally frank"; rather, he "dealt in generals." Arthur's relation of the "history of Clavering" to Mrs. Wentworth also forces him to weigh the importance of "truth" versus "falsehood" in his story. However, even as potential incest on Welbeck's part becomes the subject of "vague and tumultuous ideas" for Arthur, he tries to ascertain the relationship between Welbeck and his mistress. Additionally, "Welbeck's tale" of how Watson was killed, along with and his own past, dominates the novel in terms of action until Arthur leaves Philadelphia and then returns during the plague.[70]

Besides weaving together different strands of history and narration, Brown continues to use the novel as a self-reflexive means of shaping ideas about history, fictional narrative, and truth. Dr. Stevens, for instance, makes the following remarks after listening to Mervyn's tale: "Mervyn's pause allowed his auditors to reflect on the particulars of his narration, and to compare them with the facts, with a knowledge of which, their own observation had supplied them."[71] With such commentary, Brown returns the reader to questions of historical veracity and, as Frank Shuffelton has argued, moral judgment.[72] Like Arthur's listeners, the reader is prompted to "reflect" on "the crimes and misfortunes of Welbeck" and, by implication, Arthur's own "human passions and motives." Thus, Arthur's claim that in the last five days he has "gathered more instruction than from the whole tissue of my previous existence" requires Dr. Stevens and other "auditors," including the reader, to closely ascertain what is "fact" and "fiction"—what is "truth" and falsehood.[73]

However, Brown probes this subject more fully in part 2 of *Arthur Mervyn* almost a year later, especially in regard the "domestic history" of the Hadwins and Mervyns. Like *Edgar Huntly,* Brown's publication of "Thessolonica" and "The Death of Cicero" in his *Monthly Magazine* in the spring and fall of 1799 testifies, observes Charles E. Bennett, to his continuing interest in fiction and history.[74] Brown's focus on ancient history and fictionalized autobiography in these works suggests that they influenced his theories about history and romance. In part 2 of *Arthur Mervyn* (1800), Brown expands and diversifies his use of "domestic history"—focusing on urban conditions for women in Philadelphia, family histories, and the past of a marginalized Jewish woman named Achsa Fielding—and the ways that individual and family histories intersect. Beyond, then, the explicit or realistic ways his novel provides a "faithful sketch" of the conditions of yellow fever in Philadelphia during the summer of 1793, and beyond Grabo's observation that in "Walstein's School of History" the "fictitious history" called "Olivo Ronsica" anticipates "the story in the *First Part* of *Arthur Mervyn*—including even the appearance of 'a pestilential disease . . . in the city,'" in part 2 Brown's novel continues to focus on individual and family histories in historically accurate and self-conscious ways.[75]

Part 2 begins with Arthur stepping forth "upon the stage," eager to demonstrate "benevolence" and concerned about Wallace and the Hadwins. Stevens relates various "facts" as they pertain to his experiences and the "history of the Mervyns." Hadwin, we learn, died from yellow fever when returning to Philadelphia to help Wallace. Susan also dies shortly after Mervyn visits the farm, and Mervyn feels compelled to help Eliza, whose abusive uncle takes her inheritance. After returning to Philadelphia and finding a safe place, with Achsa Fielding, for Eliza to live, Mervyn searches for Clemenza Lodi, whom Welbeck has put in Mrs. Villars's house of prostitution as his mistress. Mrs. Villars, relates Brown's narrator, "stooped to the vilest means of amassing money" yet, at the same time, had "secure[d] to herself and her daughters the benefits of independence."[76]

Upon later encountering the dying Welbeck in the Prune Street Debtors Prison and recovering a money belt that Welbeck had taken from a corpse, Mervyn later goes to Baltimore to help rescue the Watson family. After traveling back to Philadelphia, Mervyn finds a home for Clemenza Lodi, and he continues to fall in love with Achsa Fielding, who is also wealthy and whom he is eager to marry and to travel with to Europe.

Part 2 does continue to provide a view of Philadelphia during the yellow fever outbreak. But it also yields, unlike other novels of the period and even Brown's own earlier writing, a realistic account of a darker "domestic history"—the urban economic, social, and sexual conditions, particularly as they affect the domestic lives of working-class women. Aside, for instance, from Bob and Cato's "habitual deference for every thing *white*" at the house of Mrs. Maurice, which references the reality of race relations during this period, her property has been exploited financially by Welbeck, putting her and her three daughters in an economic bind. Arthur's search for Clemenzi at Mrs. Villars's home provides a historically accurate picture of brothels in late eighteenth-century Philadelphia.[77] Similar to Brown's representation of yellow fever and prostitution in *Ormond,* Arthur's visit provides the reader with historically accurate and minimally fictitious spatial and sexual details.

Moreover, as Weyler has argued, novelists like Brown wrote "compelling narratives that synthesized the sexual and economic anxieties associated with the rise of bourgeois consciousness and culture," and "while sex and property are not made perfectly analogous in fiction, both are sites of desire, expenditure, and exchange."[78] In the case of *Arthur Mervyn,* such sites are indeed analogous. Arthur's inquiry into the domestic household of the Villarses literally reenacts the tension between commercial and sexual exchange as Arthur arrives at the home in order to determine if Clemenza is present.

Despite being told Mrs. Villars is not home, Arthur instructs Achsa, who answers the door, to communicate that he is on "important business" and begins to wander into various rooms. As he enters the interior of the parlor, for example, it is described as having an "air of negligence and disorder," with "wrinkled and unswept" carpet, "embers scattered on the marble hearth," "tongs lying on the fender with the handle in the ashes," and a "harpsichord, uncovered, one ended loaded with *scores*." "In short," we are told, "no object but indicated the neglect or igno-rance of domestic neatness and economy."[79] Learning that Miss Hetty had gone to town with Mrs. Villars, Arthur doubts the information and remarks, "This was a tale not to be credited," despite Achsa's persistence in "maintaining the truth of it."

Arthur then proceeds to move about the house from one floor to the next, driven by ambivalence about the information he received at the door and, presum-ably, his own prurient interests, until he encounters "two females, arrayed with voluptuous negligence, in a manner adapted to the utmost seclusion, and seated in a careless attitude, on a sofa." Arthur admits to his "distaste" for the woman's erotically suggestive attire, and his antagonistic questions of the older female allow him to speculate about her trade in "licentious pleasures" as he attempts to "know the truth" of Clemenza and the house he is in. He remarks: "Who, where, what are you? Do you reside in this house? Are you a sister or daughter in this family, or merely a visitant? Do you know the character, profession and views of your com-panions? Do you deem them virtuous or know them to be profligate?"[80]

While Achsa's receptiveness to Arthur's questions seems to suggest her desire to be found out and rescued from what appears to be forced prostitution, Mrs. Villars's response is one of the "utmost alarm."[81] Regulating, as Weyler points out, republican vice, Arthur goes on to verbalize further suspicions about how Mrs. Villars and her daughters were "suspected of carrying on the trade of pros-titution."[82] Correspondingly, angry response of Mrs. Villars to Arthur's actions—saying he entered the house by "fraud"—prompts him to reflect on whether or not he acted "illegally" and whether or not his "motives" in rescuing Clemenza were "unquestionably pure." Brown leaves the reader to meditate on the degree to which one's intentions, moral or otherwise, desire to "know the truth," and ac-tions are always justified or ethical.[83]

This "domestic" scene, then, like the one Brown presents of Selby's son's house in *Edgar Huntly*, not only highlights the diversity of women's lives and living con-ditions but immerses the reader in contemplation of scenes and events, and, like the historian, the search for truth among conflicting appearances and sources of evidence. In this regard, Brown's novels repeatedly expose the reader to a moral and epistemological process similar to how historians approach and, importantly, repre-sent the past. In *Arthur Mervyn*, as well as in his other novels, "domestic" scenes and manners provide a ready vehicle for Brown to practice rendering historical circum-stances and, at the same time, deliberate on the actions and motives of individuals as well as how people's lives are, or are not, represented in a fictional medium.

In this way, *Arthur Mervyn*, more than Brown's other early novels, systemati-cally probes the histories of other families—the "history of the Mervyns" and the Hadwins as well as the "history and condition" of Mrs. Maurice's family—and makes these histories a key element of the plot. In the opening chapters of part 2, for example, Stevens recounts "the incidents" of Mervyn's "tale," the various "facts" associated with his story, and how impossible it was "for such a family to keep together." Later, as the novel unfolds and Arthur relates more about his youth and other parts of his past, he remarks: "I did not detain you long, my friends, in pourtraying my parents, and recounting domestic incidents, when I first told you my story. What had no connection with the history of Welbeck and with the part I have acted upon this stage, I thought it proper to omit." Arthur goes on to painfully relate his father's occasional drinking bouts and abuse; his sister's out-of-wedlock-pregnancy and suicide; the temperamental behavior of his brothers; and "the wrongs which . . . [his] mother endured in the person of her only and darling daughter." And, later, after refusing to "justify" himself by further "expatiating on domestic miseries," he asserts that he no longer needs, or wants, to "conceal what passed in domestic retirements" and that he was ready to tell "the truth before any audience." He says he is now living a "changed" life and seeking an honest livelihood in the service of Mr. Hadwin.[84]

Just as Mervyn's past becomes intertwined with the history of Welbeck and Watson, so his ties to the "domestic history of the Hadwins" lead to a deepening of the plot and novel's action. Mervyn's desire, for instance, to see Eliza Hadwin "independent and free" and not under the "authority" of her tyrannous uncle prompts him, after her profession of love, to go to Malverton and inform an uncle, Philip Hadwin, of the true circumstances surrounding his brother's death. Curling, relates Arthur, "had lately commented on the character of Philip Hadwin." He is a "noted brawler and bully, a tyrant to his children, a plague to his neighbors"— a drunkard who curses Mervyn repeatedly upon their meeting. "Not three words," we learn, "were uttered without being garnished with a—God damn it! Damnations! I'll be damn'd to hell if." After several unsuccessful entreaties with Hadwin to forfeit rights to his brother's property, the scene closes with Mervyn telling Hadwin "the truth" in regard to his "own history, so far as it was connected with the Hadwins" and learning that Hadwin was indeed in debt with a mortgage and not in a position to give Eliza "the house and land" that "were his by law."[85] However one wants to interpret Brown's "feminist" agenda or sympathies, he clearly understood the relationship between political and domestic tyranny and represented women as wanting to be "independent and free."

In addition, just as Brown's novel relays the "domestic history of the Hadwins" and, using profanity, portrays the pasts of characters like Mervyn, it also reflects more philosophically on the role of the historian in representing the past and performing or enacting historical inquiry. For instance, similar to how Arthur tells the "little story" of his "family," and particularly "the history" of his "dear country girl," Bess, so Brown also has Stevens "compile" much of his own "history with his own hand" and places him in a position to reflect on Achsa Fielding and, in particular, how "her history" or biography might be told.[86]

Likewise, Achsa plays the role of historian when she confesses to being Jewish and relates, through Arthur, the history of her family and upbringing—how her father became successful in London and how she was "trained up in the most liberal manner." Arthur's representation of her "renunciation" of religion, her marriage, her "sudden loss of fortune," and her arrival in America further illustrate how Brown's protagonist engages in historical pasts beyond his own. The novel ends with an exchange of biographical pasts between Mervyn and Achsa, which leads to Mervyn's confession of undying love for her and his expectation of domestic felicity in marriage.[87]

From the wives of Dr. Stevens and Arthur's father to characters such as Mrs. Villars, Mrs. Wentworth, and Achsa Fielding then, women are represented as having or desiring some measure of domestic agency, particularly in regard to their historical circumstances and representation of themselves. Brown portrays women as domestic subjects and as agents of historical self-consciousness and change.[88] By extension, the narrated pasts of Arthur, Welbeck, Clavering, and other minor characters combined with inquiry into the "history of the Mervyns," the Hadwins, and the "history and character" of Mrs. Maurice's family raise questions about Arthur's innocence and ambitions and generate elements of the novel's plot. Brown's interest in domestic circumstances concerns the lives of both individual women and their extended families. Unlike in his previous novels, Brown takes his interest in domestic history and develops it beyond matters of marriage or the histories of individual women toward a larger inquiry into the meaning and function of families.

Yet, the narrator in *Arthur Mervyn* is also historically self-conscious in ways that are uncommon, especially in the early American novel. As with Brown's earlier novels, issues of historical representation emerge when he says he wants to consider the "facts" on their own terms, and that he wants "time to revolve them slowly, to weigh them accurately, and to estimate their consequences fully." The novel is self-reflexive about historical representation, in other words, when Dr. Stevens tells Wortley his "judgment is unfurnished with the same materials; your sufferings have soured your humanity and biased your candor." The only person capable of being somewhat impartial is his wife: "She is mistress of Mervyn's history; an observer of his conduct during his abode with us; and is hindered, by her education and temper, from deviating into rigor and malevolence." Once again, Brown here highlights a female character when it comes to those qualities of mind capable of rendering one's personal history or the past impartially. Wortley's wife enacts the role of the historian, performing, like Stevens and Arthur, an enduring "office" with his pen.[89]

Thus, as Steven Watts observes, scenes of "familial failure" permeate Brown's novel and suggest the impact of liberal change on traditional family structures.[90] The novel's use of multiple embedded individual and familial histories further enhances its representation of individual ambivalence and domestic change. At the same time, women in novels like *Arthur Mervyn* are represented not only

sympathetically but also as resilient agents of moral truth and political change—
as having an ethos or perception of judgment that in regard to domestic situations is independent of the status quo and consistent with historical impartiality
of the modern historian. In fact, Bennett observes that after the publication of his
early novels, particularly *Arthur Mervyn,* Brown was about to "enter a new and
major phase of his literary career; he was about to leave the romance behind him,
about to become an historical novelist."[91] Indeed, he was, and, as the discussion of
Brown's last two novels shows, his interest in "domestic history" and especially the
lives of women continued to evolve in ways that would point to his later historical
sketches or fiction.

Clara Howard

Clara Howard; In a Series of Letters (1801), like *Jane Talbot* (1801), is typically
dismissed from analysis of Brown's novels because they are seen as failures in
plot. But they both focus, as suggested by their titles, on women. In her essay
"Epistolarity, Anticipation, and Revolution in Clara Howard," Michelle Burnham
remarks that Brown's "expectant narrative economy has more than a little to do
with the historical and political condition of postrevolutionary America, where
citizens rush in frenzied pursuit of political possibilities that somehow appear
to have been left far behind." Instead of writing a failed epistolary romance for
readers that features a heroine, Brown, she says, offers a novel that is a "politically
charged representation of historical time," a text that registers, through its de-
lays and "frequent interruptions of domestic life," his awareness of an unfulfilled
utopian promise of democratic ideals for women. His suggestive use of the word
"revolution" is both political and social, she argues, suggesting that rather than
merely writing fiction in 1801, he was commenting on the "forestalled temporal
progress of American political history."[92]

Brown, as I have been arguing thus far, used personal histories, especially the
lives of women, and, increasingly, family histories as a platform for exploring a
range of domestic circumstances and historiographical concerns. On occasion, as
in the explicit reference to the "Elm tree" or displacement of Delaware Indians in
Edgar Huntly, his plots integrate or imaginatively represent past historical events
or circumstances and their surrounding debates. The scenarios, and even "personal behaviors," he stages, whatever the degree of historical correspondence, are
often geared toward generating feelings and memories that, in turn, inform his
narrator's—and his readers'—ability recall the past and reflect on its moral or political relationship to the present. *Clara Howard,* as Burnham insightfully argues,
aims to historically represent anxieties about revolutionary promise in women's
lives and their domestic situations. Although the novel contains noticeably fewer

overt references to historical representation and the differences or similarities between history and romance, Brown continues to use "history" as an explicit mechanism for plot and character development and, as Burnham suggests, a way to "remember" past promise.

In terms of plot, *Clara Howard* departs from conventional novel formulas to the extent that it eschews traditional seduction themes of the day and sentimental moralizing and reverses gender roles, motivations, and action. As the novel opens, Edward Hartley, a penniless boy from the country, is going to the city to become an apprentice to a watchmaker. He meets Mary Wilmot, a plain woman older than he, who supports herself and her brother by sewing. She falls in love with Hartley, who agrees to marry her despite the absence of similar feelings. When her brother dies, Mary inherits $5,000, which a fellow named Morton claims is his. Meanwhile, Edward is taken in by Mr. E. Howard, an English gentleman who tutors him but then leaves for Europe, and by his attractive and resourceful step-daughter, Clara. Mary then disappears with a man named Sedley, a development Edward doesn't learn about for several months due to a misplaced letter. Thinking his engagement is broken, Edward expresses an interest in Clara, who benevolently reasons that he has to find and marry Mary. Faced with an ethical and emotional dilemma, he attempts to find Mary but becomes sick with a fever when he rescues a girl from drowning. Both Edward and Clara think Mary is alone and unhappy, but she has instead fallen in love with Sedley. Brown imaginatively reverses traditional republican gender expectations by having Clara rely on reason and Edward on sentiment, and Edward eventually becomes distraught because it appears neither woman wants him. The novel concludes with Mary marrying Sedley and with Edward finally free to marry Clara.

Brown's inquiry into the past and into the domestic lives and manners of his characters is first evident in a pair of letters from Edward Hartley to Clara Howard and their discussion of Mary's whereabouts. Edward, in his March 7 letter to Clara in New York, reflects in despair on Mary's departure, saying, "Why do I write? For whose use do I pass my time thus?" Uncertain of what has become of Mary, to whom he is engaged, Edward essentially relates that he cannot fully direct his attention to Clara until he knows what has happened to Mary. His anxiety about his relationships with both women is compounded when in a second letter to Clara at Hatfield, dated March 20, he remarks on the "hospitable mansion" of Mr. Hickman and learns the "truth" about Mary's misplaced letter to him. He reveals that in "comparing circumstances" and "gradually recollect[ing]" the letter's history, Mr. Hickman's sister then "remember[ed]" her actions that day and how she put the letter in a drawer and forgot about it. After hearing the anecdote, Mr. Hickman exclaims, "Such is the history of your pacquet, which, you see, was mislaid through accident and my sister's bad memory." The scene concludes with Edward hurrying over to "Cartwright's hovel" to retrieve the letter, then reading it.[93]

Mary's letter highlights her displeasure with not hearing from him sooner and her passion and love for him, despite their age difference. Saying that "the narrative of Morton is true," she confirms details about money inherited after her brother's death and explains her motives to marry to Edward. She then clarifies her "reluctance" and "misgivings" about marriage to him and using her inherited money to rescue him and his sisters from "indigence and dependence." Clara, she insists, is a better choice for him because she herself is "homely and uncouth" and lacks the education and "the refinements of learned and polished intercourse." Saying that her lack of manners disqualifies her as a suitable wife, she closes the letter by urging Edward to "forget the unhappy Mary" and "make haste to the feet" of Clara.[94]

While some critics have found the love triangle between Edward, Mary, and Clara to be "absurd," Brown anchors the plot of *Clara Howard* in domestic relations between friends and lovers and, in this case, the economics of marriage as it involves specific individuals and families like Edward's.[95] Although sentimental in some instances, Brown's novel attempts to represent the real-world financial, emotional, and social strains and negotiations that attend courtship and marriage in culturally relevant and revealing ways and to speculate on what might truly constitute "mutual" "happiness."[96] Moreover, as in his earlier novels, and in the context of the "sensational, formulaic plots," "stereotyped characters," and perhaps even clichéd language Tompkins locates in Brown's novels, his narrators and other characters continue to reflect on the epistemological limitations of narrative, historical or otherwise, and the role of individual judgment in the construction of historical representation or meaning, suggesting that Brown's later novels were part and parcel of his evolving historicism and, arguably, prepared him to tackle more ambitious historical fiction projects.[97]

To illustrate: in Letter XIX to Edward Hartley, dated May 6, Clara reveals her pleasure in receiving two of Edward's letters at once, saying that once she retired to her chambers she "eagerly, rapturously, kissed and read" his letters. Just as his May 5 letter wishes for a "more lively and congenial intercourse of eyes and lips," claims that he is "undesirous of power," and longs for "some *parity*" between them, so her response is one of both "pleasure" and uneasiness. Remarking on her mother's interest in her situation and the "truth" of matters in general, Clara goes on to comment on the role of the "nurse's tale" in prompting inquiry about Mary's past and how that information affected her and her mother:

> I did not conceal from her the cause. I made her pretty well acquainted with the history of Mary. She was deeply interested in the story I told, and suggested many inquiries respecting her, which I had overlooked. She has made me extremely anxious as to some particulars, on which perhaps you can give me the desired information.

Pray tell me what you know of the history of her family before her father's leaving Europe. Where was he born? Where lived he? What profession did he follow? What know you of the history of Mary's mother?[98]

The series of questions Clara asks about Mary's past and the past of her mother
serves, of course, to move the plot forward. And as with Brown's earlier novels, such
questions about personal and familial history also provide Brown's characters opportunities to further meditate on the relationship between history and romance,
especially as mediated by the biographies of certain characters. But Brown's emphasis on "history" here—"history of Mary," "the history of her family," "history
of Mary's mother"—underscores Brown's interest in "domestic history" and the
ways history and identity are intertwined, and familial histories inform individual
ones and vice versa. In this respect, narrative and memory become a vehicle for approaching the truth and understanding the past as it relates to the present.

Hartley's response to Clara's questions about the past is twofold: first, he says
that her letter has "put me on the task of recollection" and that remembering
earlier circumstances is difficult; second, he says, "The Wilmots were either very
imperfectly acquainted with the history of their parents, or were anxious to bury
their history in oblivion." Part of the reason for this difficulty, is that Mary may
have been guilty of "contradictions and evasions" in her story or "pretended ignorance, for the sake of avoiding the mortification of telling the truth." Brown's
rehearsal or whole and partial conversations related to one's individual or familial
past highlights the role of "remembrance" for understanding Mary's past, offering
now and then only "a glimpse into their family history."[99]

Mary shares biographical information about her German father, English
mother, and French nurse, and Edward's letter closes with questions for Clara,
such as, "Is your mother acquainted with any of the family in Europe? With the
history of Wilmot before he came hither? Pray tell me all you know in your next."
In Letter XXI, Clara responds, saying that she talked with her mother who, in turn,
was able to document the Wilmot family history—"A native of Holstein. . . . Family
abode near Taunton. . . . Victim of some early distress"—and confirm that these
particular "circumstances place the truth beyond controversy." Offering to tell the
story "somewhat with more order," she reenacts her mother's recollection of the
past:"Wilmot . . . Wilmot . . . said she. An English family. . . . Came over twenty-
four years ago. I think I know something of them. Their story was a singular one;
a disastrous one. I should like to know more of their history. I think it is not im-
probable that these are the same Wilmots with those whose history I am perfectly
acquainted." Similar to a historian, Clara goes on to relate "the early history of this
family" in "the words" of her mother, which later ends with her remark that "time
insensibly wore away the memory of these transactions, and 'tis a long time since

my sisters and I have been accustomed, in reviewing past events, to inquire 'What has become of poor Mrs. Wilmot and her children?'"[100]

Brown's repeated reference to "history" and "family" and one's ability to inquire into or recall the past, and his focus in letters such as this on "time," "recollection," and truth speak to his interest throughout the novel in discerning the ambiguities related to one's representation of the past and the ability of language to accurately represent reality. Like any number of personal factors, time may be seen as compromising one's memory and judgment of the past. It is no coincidence, then, that by the end of the novel Brown brings together these elements as a way of suggesting how subjective our interpretations of the past are and how such constructions themselves are subject to the limitations of time and memory.

That is, beyond Edward's self-reflexive comments about the "ambiguous medium" of letters for relating the past or present and Clara's confession as a writer—and narrator—that she "concealed . . . struggles" because they were "past," the last several letters in the novel also reveal a collective desire by all of the major characters to relate the past and judge it, each other, or themselves more accurately or truly. Mary, for instance, addresses Edward one last time, imploring him not to go West and saying: "You used to be circumspect, sedate, cautious; not precipitate in judging or resolving. What has become of all these virtues?" In the letter that follows, addressed to Clara in Wilmington on May 17, Edward acknowledges that his "past conduct" has been self-indulgent and says, "Clara, thou has judged truly. My eyes are open to my folly, and my infatuation." "In truth," he remarks, as he hastens to return to her, "I have been sick." And, finally, Clara confesses her love for Edward, adding, "With the improvements of time, very far wilt thou surpass the humble Clara; but in moral discernment, much art thou still deficient. . . . Our modes of judging and our maxims, shall be the same."[101]

In short, *Clara Howard* represents Brown's heightened efforts to use family or domestic histories like he had earlier and seems to return, in the mode of his narrator in *Edgar Huntly,* to the act of "remembrance." That is, characters relate and rely on each other's personal and familial biographies to the extent that they can accurately recall them. Yet, as Brown demonstrates, these histories and stories are subject to shortcomings, interruptions, contradictions, (un)conscious omissions, and other constraints, thereby alerting readers to the importance of exercising sound "judgment" when recollecting and relating the past. Thus, beyond having female characters enact the historian role, the novel places emphasis on "memory" as a function of "time," historical or otherwise, a theme that becomes even more pronounced in *Jane Talbot* and a factor, later, in his annals of history.

Jane Talbot

Finally, if Brown's earlier novels move, generally, from historical incidents and historically accurate representations of religious fanaticism, Indian displacement, and yellow fever in Philadelphia, especially as it concerns the lives of men such as Wieland, Ormond, Edgar Huntly, and Arthur Mervyn, to plots more narrowly focused on family relations and the lives of women like Clara Howard and Jane Talbot, they continue to also inquire into the past lives of individuals and into issues of historical representation at the level of memory, narrative, and truth. Nowhere is this more true than with Brown's last novel, *Jane Talbot, A Novel* (1801), which, as Martin Brückner observes, seeks to reclaim romantic love—the ways in which Jane's "memories" are "shaped by 'the fancy and the heart'"—as an important subject for society and the self.[102] Brown's examination, in other words, of female interiority in domestic situations may make for less consideration of the differences between "history" and "romance." But it enables his novel to focus on the manner in which "memory" or the "past" relates to one's construction of the present. Amid social instability and recollection of the past, readers, like Brown's characters, must exercise individual and sometimes collective judgment about the actions and motives of others.

The novel begins with Jane, young and widowed, who falls in love with Henry Colden, a follower of Godwin. Mrs. Fielder, Jane's aunt and guardian, opposes the marriage on the grounds that Colden has written letters that espouse radical ideas about suicide, revelation, marriage, and sexual liberalism derived from Godwin's *Political Justice*. Mrs. Fielder is disgusted by Henry's moral rationalism and dissenting beliefs, saying that he is "the advocate of suicide; a scoffer at promises; the despiser of revelation, of providence and a future state; an opponent of marriage . . . nay, of intercourse without marriage, between brother and sister, parent and child!"[103] She also believes, on the basis of a letter, that Colden had previously seduced Jane one night during a storm while Jane's husband, Talbot, was away, and she urges her to stay away from Colden. The letter, we later learn, was forged by a Miss Jessup, who was in love with Talbot and sought to separate the pair. Colden goes to sea and Miss Jessup confesses her underhanded efforts to secure Talbot's love and dies, which later clears the way for Jane to marry Colden upon his return.

As in the other novels, the epistolary format serves to relate the history of various characters and propel the plot. In Jane's case, as she indicates in an early letter to Colden, her desire to tell him the "story" of her life can only be accomplished if she is able to conduct a "deliberate review of the past" and is able to "refresh . . . [her] memory and methodize . . . [her] recollections." She relates the history of her childhood, for instance, which is based in part on incidents she can remember. Cherishing the remembrance of her mother before she died, and explaining how time has clarified misconceptions about gender, she writes: "My brother, who was three years older than myself, behaved in a very different manner. I used to think the difference between us was merely that of sex; that every boy was boisterous, ungrateful, imperious, and inhuman, as every girl was soft, pliant, affectionate. Time has cured me of that mistake, and as it has shown me females, unfeeling and perverse, so it has introduced me to men full of gentleness and sensibility."[104] Brown blends domestic history, biography, and cultural observation here and comments astutely on gender relations of the time by positioning Jane as an observer of social manners and gender differences—and similarities. He suggests that women can exhibit less desirable masculine traits, and men can exhibit characteristically feminine ones. "Time" and maturity, in other words, enable Jane to appreciate the ways that men and women share certain domestic traits or manners, opening the door for later remarks by Jane in the novel that assert female agency and autonomy in the context of epistolary history, memory, and sentiment.

Jane's narrative continues to detail for Colden her familial history and personal memories as well as a range of sentiments about her past experience and relationships. And even as she relates "the history of Mrs. Henning and her boarder," so other characters such as Mrs. Fielder also relate past events and biographies accompanied by various sentiments and moral judgments. Colden, for example, reflects on and confesses the "errors" of his "past conduct" to Mrs. Fiedler, and likewise presses Miss Jessup to remember her conduct. Stating that he knows that in her "heart" she is asking herself questions such as "Why should you be called upon as a counselor or umpire, in the little family dissentions of Mrs. Talbot and her mother?" he remarks: "And do indeed these questions rise in your heart, Miss Jessup? Does not memory enable you to account for conduct which, to the distant and casual observer, to those who know not what you know, would appear strange and absurd. Recollect yourself. I will give you a moment to recall the past."[105]

Characters, then, interact with other characters in ways that rely on the "memory" and recollection of past histories in order to clarify domestic manners or moments. In this case, Colden asks Miss Jessup to "solemnly and truly" reflect on her role in ruining Talbot's reputation.[106] His desire for an honest remembrance of the past becomes a means of finding out the truth and sorting out fact from fiction. And as in his earlier novels, Brown returns to individual and even collective memory as a way of determining and judging past conduct, moral or otherwise.

While not as action filled, then, as his earlier novels, *Jane Talbot* is focused on issues of interiority and subjectivity. Amid an ever-changing backdrop of social instability, the reader encounters a series of social, philosophical, and epistemological questions concerning the past, human happiness, faith, reason, and personal identity; and, like Brown's characters, the reader is asked to independently reflect on and judge the actions and beliefs of others. Influenced by sentiment and sensibility rather than the Godwinian rationalism of Colden, Jane, for instance, is asked to exercise independent judgment in the story and remarks to Colden's sister, Mrs. Montford, that "memory" is often connected with "the fancy and the heart." In relating how she gravitated toward maps, charts, and books on voyages—outward forms of knowledge—as a way of coping with Colden's departure and imagining his travels, she confesses that her interest in geography has led her to consider alternative views of the world. Miss Betterton, she says, "must have been puzzled to conjecture what charms one of my sex could find in the study of maps and voyages. *Once* I should have been just as puzzled myself."[107]

Conversely, just as Jane changes and develops a sense of intellectual agency and autonomy as a result of travel materials, so Colden travels widely around the world and also changes as a result of recollecting the past and reconciling it with the present. Shipwrecked on the shores of Japan, for example, he relates how he encountered a "new world; a world, civilized, indeed, and peopled by men, but existing in almost total separation from the other families of mankind; with language, manners and policy almost incompatible with the existence of a stranger among them." And although Colden's encounter with cultures, manners, and values other than his own, as well as with Holtz, a European abroad, enables him to learn "humanity and curiosity," his chance meeting with Cartwright, who is also seeking Jane's hand, combines to spark a transformation—greater appreciation for life and knowledge of himself.[108]

He remarks: "The incidents of a long voyage, the vicissitudes through which I have passed have given strength to my frame, while the opportunities and occasions for wisdom which these have afforded me, have made *my mind whole.* I have awakened from dreams of doubt and misery." Colden's "process of reflection" over the years, his reconstruction of the self relative to lived experience and subjective reflection, prompts him, then, to more clearly understand his shortcomings and his place in the universe and enables him, like Jane, to change. While the novel clearly has a sentimental and didactic element at the end in regard to one's faith, "restoration," and happiness, it also seeks to reconcile domestic differences and to encourage a "union" of individuals of similar "hopes," "hearts," and "opinions." In this way, *Jane Talbot*, like Brown's other novels, weaves together "domestic" or familial concerns, the status of women, and various forms of remembrance in order to foster mutual understanding, "compassion," and "respect."[109]

That is, when examining the larger trajectory of Brown's novels from 1798 to 1801, it becomes clear that his representation of "domestic history," especially as it pertains to personal biography and family histories, increasingly focuses on the lives and subjectivity of women, feeling, and the role of collective and individual memory in constructing the past. His novels also inquire into the relationship between history and identity and how historical inquiry and moral accountability are connected. Beyond the historical realism that Brown's novels evince, their focus on how people are constructed, and construct themselves, as historical subjects positions the reader to reflect on a range of philosophical, political, or social issues—to intuitively, and even self-consciously, register knowledge and change rather than being the passive recipients of didactic novels. Brown's interest in, and representation of, the lives of women, especially in a novel like *Jane Talbot,* is intimately connected with his own developing sense of historical time and narrative and the ways one assesses the past relative to the present.

In sum, Steven Watts's observations about Brown, the novel, and his "ideological radicalism" relative to contemporary culture help articulate the ways Brown's Quaker upbringing and liberalism mingled with late Enlightenment ideas about reason and political rights, especially in regard to the historical treatment and representation of women:

> With several forces—the Enlightenment, the novel, Revolutionary republicanism—challenging long-standing patterns of cultural authority, and with a market revolution transforming traditional and social life, Brown entered a maelstrom of controversy. He began to attack the tenets of organized Christianity, to question male dominance of women in Western society, and to offer a brand of political and social utopianism. These "radical" writings, occurring midway between his adolescent scribblings and mature novels, served as an intellectual and emotional bridge. . . . In many ways, Brown's struggle with Christianity drove an entering wedge for other kinds of radical influence.

While Watts limits Brown's radical thinking to the mid-1790s, when he was a young man, and claims that Brown was "no pioneer of religious dissent," he does acknowledge that Brown's skepticism about religion was consistent with that of Enlightenment figures like Voltaire, Thomas Paine, and William Godwin. He also confirms Brown's radicalism, saying that "Brown ventured beyond all but the most daring intellectual contemporaries" when it came to gender relations. "By the mid-1790s," he writes, Brown "began to question the entire structure of gender relationships in the society of the Atlantic world," displaying "a fascination with female status, proclivities, and talents which persisted throughout his career." Indeed, "more broadly, his inquiries into social definitions and structures based on gender brought into question male domination of Western cultural tradition."[110]

Brown's novelistic efforts with the writing of history amid other republican novels reveal a sustained and developing interest in "domestic history," particularly as defined by family histories, the lives and experiences of women, and historical epistemology. This interest contributes to his evolving historical sensibilities and understanding of the past. His efforts, from *Alcuin: A Dialogue* (1798) to when he published his last novel, demonstrate a consistent and, for their time, unparalleled focus on "domestic" issues as they relate to a range of female characters and situations in America. From sympathetic portraits of physically abused and pregnant women to women without property or who are the prey of men, to women who seek to marry for love or openly challenge, and sometimes physically overcome, female oppression in regard to educational, marital, and sexual norms, Brown represents in his fiction a range of women's lives and prerogatives.

For this reason, the sympathy that informs his representation of women and enables him to interrogate the cultural status quo, and advocate a feminist politics, is in its clearest and most provocative form a cumulative or composite one—one that can be fully identified and appreciated as part of a larger whole and one that would importantly prepare him, especially in his historical sketches and, later, his annals, to interrogate patriarchal structures of power and oppression in political spheres of the day. With few exceptions, men such as Benjamin Franklin, Thomas Jefferson, and John Adams did not demonstrate the same sort of provocative inquiry into women's lives, nor did they advocate similar radical "reflection" and action as Brown. Likewise, with the possible exception of Susanna Rowson, few or no women advocated the cause of women's rights or female agency in their fiction in the ways Brown did. In that respect, his representation of women compares with Abigail Adams and Judith Sargent Murray. Brown's curiosity about, and sensitivity toward, "domestic history" in his novels, and the status and subjectivity of women within patriarchal power structures in particular, never really ended. His inquiry into the constructed nature of history—the dynamics of historical representation as well as "memory," "truth," and time—in his novels informed his periodical reviews and theoretical essays, and vice versa; it also enabled him to shape the period's debates about the relationship between history and romance.

Part 2

✳

Historiography and the
"Art of the Historian"

Chapter Three

Historical Representation in the *Monthly Magazine and American Review* and the *Literary Magazine and American Register*

Romance then, strictly considered, may be pronounced to be one of the species of history. The difference between romance and what ordinarily bears the denomination history is this. The historian is confined to individual incident and individual man, and must hang upon that his invention or conjecture as he can. The writer collects his material from all sources, experience, report, and the records of human affairs; then generalises them; and finally selects, from their elements and the various combinations they afford, those instances which he is best qualified to portray, and which he judges most calculated to impress the heart and improve the faculties of his reader. In this point of view we should be apt to pronounce that romance was a bolder species of composition than history.

— William Godwin, "Of History and Romance" (1797)

In *The Open Boundary of History and Fiction: A Critical Approach to the French Enlightenment,* Suzanne Gearhart remarks that the relationship between history and fiction is "not peripheral but rather the central question in the philosophy of history of that age." She argues that while differences have metamorphosed into "a modern opposition between history and literature," it was common in the eighteenth century to view history as a form of literature. The "distinction between history as a category of literature on the one hand and fable, fiction, or the irrational on the other" was constantly being contested. Writings, for example, by Voltaire, Montesquieu, Diderot, and Rousseau were not easily classified as either "history" or "fiction"—as is evidenced by Voltaire's *History of Charles XII,* which makes frequent use of more than "one style, one narrative technique, or one mode of argument."[1] Voltaire's struggle, observes Gearhart, to hierarchize and to integrate a plurality of genres underscores the philosophical and rhetorical complexities associated with attempts to classify language as either "history" or "fiction."

Everett Zimmerman concurs in *The Boundaries of Fiction: History and the Eighteenth-Century British Novel,* saying that the novels of Samuel Richardson, Henry Fielding, and Lawrence Sterne "mediate . . . between figural and empiricist discourses" and use the "emplotment of human actions" to "place themselves in a complementary as well as critical relationship with history."[2] Using Paul Ricoeur's conceptions of "emplotment" and "trace," Zimmerman documents the extent to which their novels "simulate the more private forms of history"—biography, for instance, in *Tom Jones,* autobiography in *Robinson Crusoe,* or family history in *Clarissa* and *Tristram Shandy*—and how they sometimes include "sustained references to public historical events." It was an approach, as Zimmerman demonstrates, that would be popular in the nineteenth century with Sir Walter Scott and other writers of the historical novel.

As Zimmerman notes, William Godwin's unpublished essay "Of History and Romance" is especially useful for understanding the transatlantic context—and "contestations of history and fiction"—that informed early national ideas about the boundaries between history and romance. Prepared in 1797 for the *Enquirer* in the event that another volume was needed, the essay "reflects arguments made piecemeal in a multitude of prefaces to earlier eighteenth-century fiction." It acknowledged, in other words, that while the truths claimed in historical narrative may be few, consistency and accuracy favor the historian, not the novelist. Further, it remarks on the deficiencies of ancient and Enlightenment histories, the relationship between history and romance, and the ability of the novelist to render human motivation and truth. Unlike the historian, asserts Godwin, "the writer" is not restricted to "individual" incidents; instead he engages a range of sources and evidence from which incidents are chosen for moral edification. In that respect, the novelist renders human motivations and action more fully or truthfully.[3]

While American novelists also engaged this debate, they did so not to the extent Brown does in his prefaces and novels and certainly not in his periodical publications during the same period. Like Godwin, Brown wrestled with the relationship between history and fiction in his early periodical editing and writing, namely his *Monthly Magazine and American Review* (1799–1800) and the *Literary Magazine and American Register* (1803–07). In this chapter, I examine the manner in which history emerges as a subject in his early periodical publications and how Brown's reviews of contemporary histories by Benjamin Trumbull, Hannah Adams, and others as well as a series of essays he selected and edited in 1806 enabled him to simultaneously be critical of and conceptualize historiographical principles and practices—an aesthetics of history. In tracing Brown's engagement with the generic boundaries between history and romance, the use of rhetoric and judgment in historical method, and the value of history as moral instruction, these reviews and essays map evolving ideas about objectivity, reflection, and "truth" he would implement in his novels and his later historical writing.

Moreover, as Brown continued to wrestle with a separate-spheres mentality that identified women's intellectual contributions as inferior, so he began the process of reimagining gender—and generic—differences, making his periodical writings on the subject of history as much about rethinking gender norms as they are about the role of bias and subjectivity in representing the past.

The larger, singular implication and claim, however, related to analysis of these materials is that if Brown and other figures of the Enlightenment, such as Godwin and Bayle, were in their own ways conscious of the "uncertainty of history" and the role of bias and subjectivity, political or otherwise, in re-presenting the past, then our own debates about the meaning and function of "history" are themselves ahistorical and neglect an earlier site of historiographical inquiry. Scholars can no longer assume or claim that late Enlightenment intellectuals lived in a flat, rational universe, devoid of historical self-consciousness and, equally as important, that "romance" shaped the "grand narrative of history" and, by default, today's historiographical debates about historical representation, objectivity, and truth. In this way, Brown's periodical writings about history, and those of his contemporaries, raise serious questions about how we regard late Enlightenment historiography relative to postmodern debates about fiction and history and contemporary claims about historical self-consciousness and objectivity.

The Monthly Magazine and American Review (1799–1800)

To begin, in his recent study Scott Slawinski observes that Brown's essays and articles not only "set an important context for examining the fiction that appears in the *Monthly Magazine* and the novels that chronologically surround the magazine," but they open up "interpretive opportunities" for reassessing all of Brown's major and minor fictional writings. Brown's periodical, in other words, is a rich repository of columns, letters, features, essays, reviews, dialogues, fiction, and poetry, which disseminated information and knowledge to an educated readership. Brown may or may not have considered men, or, as Slawinski argues, "bachelors," as his primary audience, but the periodical did devote much of its contents to "works dealing with science, business, and social commentary," and it did address gender relations, especially as they pertain to women.[4]

Brown's early forays into the meaning of historical representation indicate that if he initially conceived of history as a vehicle of moral benefit and idealized its usefulness, he had—by the early 1790s—only moderate interest in inquiring into the sequences of cause and effect. He embraced neoclassical values and came to see history as having limited value—as being of limited use in transmitting moral values. For him, history was more of an antiquarian matter concerning the recording of how "general events" flow from "general causes"—no more, no less.

Brown, of course, was always reading and reflecting on material of a historical nature, and over the years—especially as he began to write novels and reviews of historical publications, to experiment with fictional history writing, and to contribute essays and reviews to the *Monthly Magazine and American Review*—he developed more self-reflexive and sophisticated ideas about the relationship between history and romance—attitudes that began to question the meaning and function of history.

After the Revolution, in other words, historical writing became increasingly popular in the early Republic, and Brown read and reviewed numerous historical publications from roughly April 1799 to January 1806. The bulk of his more substantive reviews, however, were published in his *Monthly Magazine and American Review* (1799–1800) and highlight his developing attitudes toward history. These reviews and essays record not only Brown's increasing interest in history writing per se but his explicit call for a historian of American stock who could write American history. They begin to chart Brown's lifelong interest in issues of historical representation and, more importantly, indicate his growing awareness of the strengths and weaknesses of early American historiography. Thus, if Brown's early writings, for instance, affirm the instructive value of historical writing, his reviews of histories by Benjamin Trumbull, Abiel Holmes, William Robertson, Hannah Adams, and others and his essays on the relationship between history and fiction offer an increasingly defined and revisionist view of the cultural importance of history and how it should be written.

In the first of these reviews, published in April 1799 in the *Monthly Magazine and American Review,* Brown critiques Benjamin Trumbull's *Complete History of Connecticut, Civil and Ecclesiastical, from the Emigration of Its first Planters from England in 1630 to 1713* (1797).[5] He begins by remarking generally on the "progress of the American States" and why in the "history of human society" the United States is a just subject for study and contemplation. And specifically of Trumbull's *History of Connecticut*, Brown writes:

> Though Connecticut is far from being one of those States which have been most famous for great national events, brilliant enterprizes, and what are usually esteemed magnificent subjects for the historian to dwell upon; yet there are few parts of our country which furnish matter for more instructive history, or more lucid examples and proofs of the importance of virtue and religion to the preservation of public tranquility, and the promotion of public happiness. In this point of view, a good history of Connecticut, has, for some time, been a desideratum in the literature of America; none having appeared deserving to be mentioned in this place. We rejoice that this deficiency has been so well supplied.

Similar to his earlier views of the "instructive" value of history, here Brown elaborates more fully on rationalist historiographical principles, and endorses history writing as a means of promoting moral "virtue" and "public happiness." He points to the manner in which the history of Connecticut illustrates the importance of "virtue and religion" in shaping social values and behaviors. In this respect, his review suggests that he saw history writing as a subject, and Trumbull's historical narrative in particular, as providing a much needed cultural directive and moral benefit. "The author," he continues, "seems to have derived his materials from the most respectable sources, and to have discriminated, with a very judicious care, between vague tradition (which, young as our country is, has been too often relied on) and well-attested facts." Trumbull's narrative, observes Brown, ought to be "followed by the future historians of America."[6]

While Brown admits that Trumbull might occasionally "fall into a style of eulogism rather too warm and indiscriminate" and demonstrate a particular bias, he also acknowledges that "the marks of indefatigable industry, of great fidelity in investigating and exhibiting facts, and minuteness of detail, form the leading features." This concern with method and literary style is another characteristic of late Enlightenment historiography. Importantly, as Dunlap notes in his assessment of Brown's critical abilities, Brown critiques Trumbull's history and makes distinctions between the writing of "meagre annals" and a historical narrative, which is characterized by careful investigation and attention to detail. Brown observes, for example, that Trumbull's structure and style could be more substantive and "there are, probably, few things relating to the *method* of historical composition, more important than a careful attention to areas, and making principal and subordinate divisions corresponding to them." Brown, in other words, had much praise for Trumbull's history, particularly its rationalist elements, and his judicious use of sources and "facts." He saw Trumbull's work as a model for "future historians."[7] But he also displayed an acute interest in the nature and effect of its composition—something that would be central to his own later self-consciously critical and dialogical form of history writing.

Brown's interest in historical methodology is briefly developed in a review, which immediately followed the one on Trumbull's work—Abiel Holmes's *The Life of Ezra Stiles,* printed in April 1799; but it is "Parallel between Hume, Robertson and Gibbon," published in May 1799 in the *Monthly Magazine and American Review,* that provided readers with a rich set of observations concerning historical method and style.[8] A comparative analysis of David Hume, William Robertson, and Edward Gibbon as historical writers, Brown's essay primarily explored how the "eloquence and skill of an historian" affect the reader. Brown began by explaining that "logical deductions and comprehensive argumentation" are *not* appropriate to history writing, noting that Gibbon, who used the "dangerous weapons of sarcasm and irony" against religion, did not employ these. At its worst, for Brown, Gibbon's historical writing reflects a shockingly "polluted taste and debauched imagination" in the manner it introduces obscene allusions or perverts the past. However, Brown admits to some amusement when he contemplates Gibbon's inconsistent use—and citation—of historical sources, such as his use of "La Pucelle d'Orleans."[9]

By comparison, he observed that a historian like Hume notes "the effects of superstition and priestcraft; but he is, at least, open and explicit in the avowal of his sentiments" or biases. Unlike Gibbon, said Brown, Hume avoided the "preposterous exaggerations of the satirist" and was not an enemy of Catholicism but "of religion itself." Even Christian readers, suggested Brown, will appreciate Hume's handling of "enthusiasm and hypocrisy" in the chronology of Christian history. While some readers would not necessarily agree with Hume's handling of "religion" in his history writing, those who believed in the "truth and excellence of religion in general" recognized certain historical truths.[10]

By contrast, says Brown, Robertson illustrated an admirable degree of "dignity, moderation and candour"; he avoided the use of artifice and jest in his narrative, and in his best historical writing he "deduced" the history of the Reformation and its effects on people. There is little room for criticism, he remarks, by either Christian or enlightened readers. Robertson took a balanced approach to history writing: his distinctions, observes Brown, between the "substance and the semblance of religion," as well as between the "deductions of reason and the dictates of self-interest" and the "illusions of fanaticism," were fair and accurate.[11] While Brown says little in the essay about any weaknesses in Robertson's history writing, in the remainder of the essay he locates himself philosophically by commenting on why Hume excels as a writer of history.

Remarking that Hume's skill in "deducing one event from another" with relative objectivity was his great achievement, Brown suggests that if Hume best exhibits those rhetorical skills that make for successful historical writing, he also excelled in engaging the reader—in stimulating his or her imagination. On the relation between historical writing and reading, Brown writes:

> The eloquence of any narrative relates to that property in it by which it fastens the attention, awakens the passions, and illuminates the imagination of the reader. That writer is eloquent who creates distinct images of characters and objects, who snatches us away from external things, and makes us spectators of the scenes which he describes. This is effected by selecting and arranging the parts of objects and the circumstances of events which are requisite to constitute the picture, and by clothing them in language always perspicuous, and *sometimes* ornamental. . . . Hume excels all men in portraying the heroes of the scene. His narrative is coherent and luminous.

It affords pleasure to the old and the young, and fiction itself is outdone in
its power to command and delight attention by the seductions of his tale.

Brown's discourse clearly reflects his background as a novelist, yet his analysis
here is directed at the literary qualities of particular historical narratives. The
"clear, flexible, simple language" of Hume, remarked Brown, is a marked contrast
to the "obscurity and pomp" of Gibbon and the "verbose" and sometimes awk-
ward phrasing of Robertson. Hume had his defects also, but his historical narrative more ably incorporated "distinct images" or detailed pictures and "illuminates the imagination of the reader." Hume's "tale," according to Brown, surpasses
fiction itself in the way it captivates and delights the reader. While the review also
identifies shortcomings, such as being "verbose" or lacking clarity of expression
in their narratives, its significance lies in the way it records Brown's emerging appreciation of different historical modes and styles of representation, a sensitivity
toward rhetoric that would later inform his own historical writing in the "Annals
of Europe and America."[12]

Brown's next review—in May 1799, signed "B" and devoted solely to William
Robertson's popular *The History of America, Books IX. and X. Containing the History of Virginia to the Year 1652* (1796)—is another marker of his evolving conception of history and historical writing.[13] It records his engagement with America
as a "subject" of history. However, in addition to identifying the "history of our
native country" as always being of central importance to Americans, he says that
Robertson is the "most eloquent historian of modern times." Robertson's work is
limited in scope, writes Brown, but it is characterized by a "general adherence to
truth, by judicious selection and arrangement, and by the charms of perspicuity
and elegance." In fact, he writes, "Of the various periods in American history, that
of the original colonization of these shores is, in many respects, of more importance than the revolutionary period."[14] The early history, he suggests, of Virginia
and other parts of New England is perhaps the most important or compelling.

Brown then praises Robertson, saying that he accurately deduces or traces
"general causes" behind the colonization of Virginia and identifies the "perverse"
reasons associated it. Circumstances such as the European quest for a new passage to the Far East and the massacre of natives by "the refuse" or dissenters of
England comprise "a diversified and humiliating tale."[15] Robertson, Brown suggests, faithfully recorded the less noble motives for settling in the New World, and
in doing so makes good use of materials by Hutchinson, Mather, Chalmers, Neal,
and others. Such favorable comments on Brown's part suggest that he not only
valued a more secular approach to history writing but that he endorsed its more
skeptical dimensions. Indeed, his agreement with Robertson about the less noble
aspects of English colonization foreshadows his own historical analysis, later, and
his sympathetic portrayal of natives under British rule in India.

For instance, Brown remarks that the "true causes" of early settlement can be traced to the "spirit of emulation" in English history, especially as excited by Spanish success in the New World. And while Brown concedes that the settlement of America is the "greatest event in the history of mankind," he also remarks that it arose from motivations that were less ambitious—Columbus, for instance, aiming mainly for a "new road for the passage of nutmegs and pepper from Malabar to Europe." Further, similar to Cortez and Pizarro, English explorers such as Willoughby, Drake, Gilbert, Ralegh [sic], and Greenville also pursued "exploits," but their "avarice and cruelty" were either "frustrated, or limited to a narrower sphere." The founders of Virginia also "massacred the natives" and experienced hardship because of "pestilence and famine"; Brown writes that despite the "extermination of the natives" the "evils" the early colonists experienced were no different from elsewhere in the "history of the world." In fact, he says provocatively, the "judicious recital" of these would "benefit mankind as much as those greater revolutions which have shaken the nations of the Old World."

However, after more closely considering the "instructive" value of history and reason, historical or teleological progress, and other rationalist historiographical principles, Brown continues and makes a provocative statement about the state of early national historiography. At the end of his review of Robertson's writing and how it compares to Trumbull's, he writes: "It would be no unprofitable exercise to compare the works of the two writers, and to estimate their respective claims to excellence in reasoning and composition. How much it is to be wished that a third historian would arise, combining the accuracy and minuteness of one with the rhetoric and judgement of the other!"[16] Brown identifies Trumbull's "accuracy and minuteness" and Robertson's "rhetoric and judgement" as components of sound historical writing but is unable to find a harmonious balance between the two. Such commentary parallels that in his essay on Hume, Robertson, and Gibbon, which emphasizes Hume's capacity for comprehensiveness, judicious analysis, and rhetorical eloquence. Yet similar to Emerson and his call for a national poet, Brown appears to desire a historian of American stock who compares with Hume and can combine the virtues of Robertson and Trumbull. Unlike his earlier writings, then, Brown's review pays particular attention to writers of American history and implies that a vacuum of sorts exists within the profession—an observation Samuel Miller would confirm in 1803 when he lamented that most American historians are "respectable writers" but "America has not yet produced historians who can vie with the first class."[17]

If in his reviews of Trumbull's and Robertson's historical writings Brown appears to assess the health of American historiography, he made an even more pronounced prognosis of American history writing in his 1799 review of Robert Proud's The History of Pennsylvania (1798) and an essay entitled "Walstein's School of History. From the German of Krants of Gotha," published in August

1799, in the *Monthly Magazine and American Review.*" Brown's review of Proud's work was published in the *Monthly Magazine* in June 1799, and although Proud was Brown's former teacher, the review contains both criticism and praise for his history.[18] What is important here—and this is central for gauging Brown's historical writing—is Brown's early distinction between the "genuine historian" and the "humble, honest, and industrious compiler."[19] His analysis on this point foreshadows the methodological self-consciousness he would later bring to his own historical writing.

Brown begins, for example, by stating that the value of Proud's book "lies not in the elegance of its style, the profoundness of its reflections, or the accuracy of its method." A wealth of facts, he says, are collected, but they are put together by an "old man, uninstructed in the arts of selection, arrangement and expression," who prefers "reciting the deeds and papers which he has gleaned from public offices and private libraries, to the more arduous province of stating their contents in his own words."[20] Anticipating Michael Kraus's observation that "Proud's sentences appear to be threads connecting passages of documents in chronological sequence," Brown says Proud's work "is little more than a series of transcripts, arranged in chronological order, and occasionally connected by a few remarks."[21] One should not look, he concludes, for "any traces of the genuine historian" in Proud's history.

At the same time, just as Brown regards Proud's work as containing a "bias" toward the Quaker religion, he also does not question the "genuineness of the records" and defends the office of the "industrious collector," saying that Proud has provided a useful service for future historians and that the "industrious collector" should not be held in "derision." His great accomplishment is that he systematically collected from "laws, charters, patents, treaties, records of legislation, official and judicial proceedings, private letters, journals, and gazettes" the state of Pennsylvania's history, thus making his history the "first publication" of its kind in the country and of historical significance, especially for future historians.[22]

As already indicated, Brown attempts to provide a balanced assessment of Proud's *History of Pennsylvania* and perhaps faults the author in somewhat disparaging ways. But in identifying Proud's use of "copious extracts" documenting Quaker history and favorable "bias" toward that group, of which he was a member, Brown also communicates his interest in seeing a greater degree of objectivity associated with Proud's representation of the past. Brown demonstrates, then, an early and acute awareness of the historian's obligation to locate suitable historical materials and to render analysis of those materials in ways that are objective and unbiased. In the case of Proud, he asserts that the historian or "artist" cannot render the past accurately without the materials and "mortar" supplied by the "industrious collector." Having such a base allows the historian to liberally follow "the deductions of their reason, or the suggestion of their fancy."[23]

Like Brown's many book reviews, "Walstein's School of History" also provides a key marker of Brown's thinking about historical issues. Though German scholar Alfred Weber has observed that late Enlightenment historiography played a central role in Brown's literary aesthetic or novel writing, Wolfgang Schäfer points out in *Charles Brockden Brown als Literaturkritiker* that Brown wanted both his novel writing and his historical narrative to promote "Nachdenken und Erkennen" in the reader: he knew the limits of his own judgment and preferred that the reader use reflection as a means of gaining insight. Because terminology, such as "story" and "history," was inconsistent during Brown's time, Brown's essays do not necessarily demonstrate an awareness of conceptual continuity. Brown does not always present a fully developed idea in his essays but uses his text, like his novels, for free reflection and associative connections—for, as Warner Berthoff has observed, dialectical exploration and discovery. Thus, because Brown is fascinated not with synthesis but with what Schäfer calls the "Aufzeigen von Gegensätzen" or the contrasting of opposites, one can begin to see, especially in light of the didactic purpose of literature at the time, why Brown valued the ability of "any narrative" to awaken the passions and illuminate the "imagination of the reader."[24] This becomes clear in Brown's fictional essay "Walstein's School of History"—which elaborates in several ways on the historian's role as a "moral painter."

A fictional memoir by the German author Krantz of Gotha, "Walstein's School of History" consists of two parts: the first outlines Walstein's principles for writing history, including his teleological approach to the past and his belief that the artful rendering of models of "right conduct" can promote virtue and the "happiness of mankind"; and the second focuses on Walstein's student, Engel, and his belief that common individuals, not great figures, make for more effective moral exemplars.[25]

As Steven Watts points out, this essay is the most "coherent expression" available of "Brown's intent and focus as a novelist," but it also yields insight into Brown's theory of history.[26] On how Walstein's works on the lives of Cicero and the Marquis of Pombal illustrate the ways individuals affect "human society," Brown writes:

> Walstein was conscious of the uncertainty of history. Actions and motives cannot be truly described. We can only make approaches to the truth. The more attentively we observe mankind, and study ourselves, the greater this uncertainty will appear, and the farther shall we find ourselves from the truth.
>
> This uncertainty, however, has some bounds. Some circumstances of events, and some events, are more capable of evidence than others. The same may be said of motives. Our guesses as to the motives of some actions are more probable than the guesses that relate to other actions.[27]

In emphasizing that "Walstein was conscious of the uncertainty of history" and that one "can only make approaches to the truth," Brown not only reflects philosophical concerns of his time regarding historical representation and the relationship between "history" and "truth" but exhibits an epistemological self-consciousness that resembles elements of our own inquiry into the nature and meaning of historical truth. That is, although he admits that some actions and motives may be better understood, or are "more capable of evidence," than others, his assertion that "actions and motives cannot truly be described" implies a knowledge that history, like fiction, is constructed and, therefore, subjective, if not completely, then to a great extent.[28]

Although I address it more fully in subsequent chapters, it is also useful to point out that Brown's analysis here of the relationship between history and romance and the "uncertainty" of history itself relative to the past and one's historical representation raises epistemological issues associated with the study of history since the rise of poststructuralist thought and the "linguistic turn." Brown, in other words, articulates a consciousness about historical construction and subjectivity that is not only in line with Godwin's meditations on the subject in "Of History and Romance" but also acknowledges more fully, in a postmodern way, that we make "approaches to the truth" based on a variety of empirical and epistemological circumstances. Brown's questioning of the processes and objectivity by which historians or scientists obtain knowledge, especially about the past, and the ability to represent absolute historical truth through the medium of language, is consistent with how Foucault, Jean-Francois Lyotard, and others, including Nietzsche, have characterized the process of historicizing the past.

Brown's observation, then, that the "lives of Cicero and Pombal are imperfectly related by historians" leads him to remark more generally on Walstein's desire to render models of "right conduct" and the success with which Walstein renders the life of Cicero. Events, he writes, are "artfully" connected and "displayed" and human "motives" accurately related. While certain errors and "incongruities" might be expected in this "imaginary history," none were present. Instead, Walstein successfully produced a "whole system of Roman domestic manners" and of "civil and military government." "Pure fiction," says Brown, was "never employed but when truth was unattainable." Their histories "teach us, that a change of national opinion is the necessary prerequisite of revolutions."[29]

In the second part of the essay, Brown associates history with some form of moral instruction or virtue for the public good. Using Engel, Walstein's oldest pupil, to explore issues of historical representation, Brown relates why the "narration of public events, with a certain license of invention," is the "most efficacious of moral instruments." "Mere reasoning," he says, is "cold and unattractive" and is only effective in a limited or "narrow sphere." It is an insufficient method for historicizing the past; rather, the use of detailed "actions" that appeal to certain "affections" is more desirable. According to Engel, "To exhibit, in an eloquent narration, a model of right conduct, is the highest province of benevolence."[30] This is the substance of history—and truth.

While it is difficult in this essay and sometimes in his political pamphlets and other materials to discern where Brown's fictional "persona" ends and his own attitudes begin, Engel's, and by implication, Brown's observation that "fictitious history has, hitherto, chiefly related to the topics of love and marriage" and is frowned upon because "the historian was deficient in knowledge and skill" points to Brown's developing interest in writing fictitious history and, later, actual historical narrative. In fact, Engel's story about Olivo, a "rustic youth, whom domestic equality, personal independence, agricultural occupations, and studious habits," offers, says Brown, a lesson in how "temptation" may be thwarted and individuals can succeed in society despite a background of poverty. As with Richardson's rendering of Clarissa and her demise, with this story, Engel has been successful in telling a tale that appeals to one's "curiosity and sympathy" and produces a "moral benefit."[31]

Significantly, therefore, according to Walstein, the lives and stories of Cicero and Pombal, while "imperfectly related by historians," can effectively reform or enlighten readers, and public events or history must be combined with varying degrees of imagination and affect. Only at that point can readers acquire moral instruction and receive the edification the text offers. Likewise, Engel's relation of the history of Olivo demonstrates that it is productive to relate a tale with "some degree of moral benefit."[32] However, unlike his previous critique of Hume, Robertson, and Gibbon, Brown's theoretical musings in "Walstein's School of History" relay an increasing "uncertainty" about the extents to which actions and motives of individuals can be identified and historians of any sort can relate "truth." It yields insight into Brown's increasingly self-conscious assessment of how he understood the use of a historical imagination—and the role of sympathy—in regard to the past.

As Slawinski rightly observes about Brown's *Monthly Magazine and American Review*, except in reference to isolated essays like "Walstein's School of History," most critics have passed over Brown's editorial work and have not fully understood the dynamics of gender at play in his selection and editing of materials. While Slawinski contends that Brown was antagonistic toward women, discouraging a "female readership," and addressed "bachelor stereotypes and the cultural hegemony of married men," I want to argue that Brown used his periodical to directly address women and women's issues and to comment forcefully and unequivocally on the attempts by one female historian to write contemporary history.[33] The *Monthly Magazine and American Review* contains substantial materials that were edited or authored by Brown and that were sympathetic to, or understanding of, the condition of women.[34] And nowhere are Brown's remarks about history and women's intellectual capacities more clear than, for instance, in his review of Hannah Adams's *A Summary History of New-England* (1799), which highlights his ability to reconsider gender stereotypes regarding women, "objectivity," and the writing of history.[35]

The review itself is both an insightful analysis of a particular piece of history writing and a valuable mirror of early national historiography, culture, and gender.[36] Similar to earlier reviews and writings on the instructive value of history and preserving primary source materials, Brown's review of Adams's history relative to debates about writing history about nations or families, and detailing the lives of individuals as opposed to larger communities, provides insight into the period's notions of historical representation and the role of women in preserving the nation's past. It stands out (like material on Hannah More and Mary Wollstonecraft) as a positive representation of women's intellectual abilities, particularly in regard to selection of historical materials and representation.

Brown's review of Adams's work begins by calling attention to the "instructive" value of history:

> The history of our native country justly merits the highest place in our regard; if not on account of the magnitude and singularity of its revolutions, yet for the unbounded influence of these revolutions on the happiness of us and our posterity. It constitutes an instructive and inestimable spectacle, because it relates, in some sort, to ourselves; because we are fully qualified to understand it; because its lessons are of indispensable use in teaching us our duty, as citizens of a free state, as guardians of our own liberty and happiness, and of those of that part of mankind who are placed within the sphere of our activity, and are best entitled to our affection and beneficence.[37]

As with his earlier writings about history and its value, Brown reaffirms the private and public value history has for free as well as the not-so-free citizens of the early Republic. Although he does not address the implications and potential contradictions inherent in such a statement, later in his annals proper he does offer more explicit commentary about the historical condition of black slaves and their potential for effecting revolution. Here, however, it is important to note Brown's continuing interest in seeing history—when written well—as a model of proper conduct.

Brown continues his review, offering an overview of American history writing and assessing the degree to which U.S. history has been successfully recorded.

> Several domestic writers have undertaken to discuss our history. Some foreign ones (Robertson, Stedman, Gordon, &c.) have pursued the same tracks; but both foreign and domestic historians have hitherto confined themselves, either to a limited period, or to narrow local boundaries. The colonial transactions of most of the American states, have been separately

discussed, with different degrees of skill. The revolution, an event in which all were somewhat, though unequally, concerned, has been copiously related by several writers. National occurrences, since that period, remain, for the most part, still dispersed in public offices, fugitive pamphlets, diurnal gazettes, and in private manuscript collections; and an historian of the United States, in the fullest sense of that term, is still wanting.[38]

Similar to earlier reviews, Brown comments here, but in greater detail than before, on the status of American history writing at the turn of the century. He cites a lack of comprehensiveness and a historical nearsightedness as reasons why a historian of the United States is "still wanting." His concern about the absence of a first-rate American historian does not carry quite the same weight as Emerson's plea for an American bard, but it is legitimate. American histories, as Callcott notes, indeed suffered from being "too biased, too local, too lacking in coherence and style."[39] While Brown admits that "minute details and intricate inquiries" are absent from Adams's history, he also acknowledges that they were not part of her plan. For this reason and others, observes Brown, Adams's *A Summary History of New-England* is "a narrative more comprehensive than any we have ever seen."[40]

As Brown notes, her history examines five of the most significant states and covers revolutionary and "*post* revolutionary events." She takes a "succinct, clear, comprehensive, and judicious view of the subject she has chosen" and has selected and connected "links of the historical chain" to create a "harmonious and useful whole." Although Brown goes on to say that Adams displays "a masculine rectitude of judgment," he also remarks that

> in estimating the merits of writers, we must sometimes look beyond the volume, and consider many circumstances tending to enhance or lessen the merit of their efforts. It is surely no small addition to the credit that belongs to the present writer, to observe that she is a *woman*. So many causes beyond what are incident to the other sex, combine to divert female industry and ambition into frivolous or improper channels, that the same attainments are unspeakably more meritorious in women than in men. They are encompassed and besieged by so many inducements to indolence, so many perverters of the taste, so many encouragements to prejudice, that, to repel, to shake them off, to rise above them, argues an uncommon force of mind. . . . By their rigorous exclusion from all political offices, and by that prejudice in the other sex which banishes political discussions from mixed circles, it is extremely rare that they form any opinions in relation to national transactions.[41]

Although Brown measures "judgment" in masculine terms of the day, he also, quite rightly, acknowledges the historical and social "circumstances" that have oppressed women and made Adams's history writing all the more exceptional. According to Brown, not only has she risen above patriarchical bias and exclusion, but, as a "*woman,*" she has surpassed her male contemporaries in writing comprehensive and judicious history.

This claim on behalf of Adams and, implicitly, to some extent all women, is a radically feminist statement, especially for a man in this period and especially in the context of his reviews of other male historians. It is not anachronistic but rather a claim on Brown's part that is consistent with his Quaker upbringing and respect for the intellectual abilities of women and consistent with his thoughts on the subject in various periodical writings. It is also consistent with material he edited or personally commented on in the *Monthly Magazine and American Review* itself, including an article on Hannah More, a favorable review of Mary Wollstonecraft's *A Vindication of the Rights of Women,* and his editorial comments on Dalloway's *Description of Constantinople* and the historical kidnapping, prostitution, and murder of young women in the Middle East. Finally, it is consistent with his representation of women from his publication of *Alcuin* to his various novels, few of which have any positive or redeeming male characters, and his historical writing.

Brown, to be sure, observes that histories about families or individuals have been written more frequently by women and asserts that the "greater number of female productions, in this kind, are sadly wanting in proofs of good sense and the qualities of good writing," but he identifies Adams as one of the few women who have "raised their view to the contemplation of national events, and the province of instructing mankind in the sciences of policy and government." He points out, in other words, that the great mass of women are conditioned by educational circumstances and "rigorous exclusion" to write poetry "full of rapturous sensibility and tender woe" or, now and then, "moral" instruction in "drama and narration" and other domestic types of writing. He concludes by encouraging Adams to continue with her work and by including—apparently for the first time—an extract of her narrative, which he says is reflective of its "propriety of language, and clearness of arrangement."[42]

Without question, Brown's assessment of Adams's accomplishments as a historian is enmeshed in patriarchal assumptions and stereotypes about women common for the period and quite alive even in our own. Yet, Brown's feminist sympathies and interest in validating and promoting Adams's work speaks to these biases in progressive, liberal ways. By boldly identifying the cultural circumstances and educational restrictions designed to constrain women to a domestic sphere and limit their intellectual development, Brown, like Judith Sargent Murray, indicts a system of education and social upbringing that assigns women "inferior capacities of imagination, reason, memory, or judgement" and instead suggests that Adams exercises intellectual judgment that is equal to that of men.[43]

Indeed, for Brown Adams's "uncommon force of mind" and ability to write history despite such obstacles argue for an "uncommon portion of praise" and affirmation of women's abilities that itself was bold and daring for its time, especially for an unmarried man, or, as Slawinski argues, "bachelor," whose own identity as an author within a masculine hegemony was anything but stable.[44]

Further, beyond identifying the "prejudices" of the age, Wollstonecraft spoke of in *A Vindication of the Rights of Woman* (1792) concerning women's use of "reason" or "intellect" and the ways female education promotes "ignorance and slavish dependence," Brown's review of Adams further historicizes Nina Baym's claim that "women were one in resisting secular history." To be sure, the vast majority of female historians did define themselves "either as students or transmitters of the millennial historical narrative," and they were telling the story of republican history with "gendered significance" and "more fervor" than men.[45] But Brown's review shows the extent to which he admired her comprehensiveness, judgment, and language and the ways, perhaps, her history did not always fully subscribe to a millennial "fervor." It also seems to indicate Brown's intellectual position in regard to the conflict between Calvinist-Congregationalist representations of the past and the more liberal historical perspective of Arminian-Unitarians. For if in her theological and historical writings Adams "necessarily ran up against Calvinistic filiopietism" of the sort Jedidiah Morse defended, Brown's willingness to recommend Adams's work suggests an intellectual sympathy of sorts.[46] In endorsing a historical narrative that attempted to convey a secular or "impartial" point of view and to discount an overtly providential or partisan interpretation of historical events, Brown arguably supports a liberal or unorthodox view of the past.

Importantly, the fact that Brown chose not to review Morse and Parish's highly orthodox history is itself revealing: it highlights how Brown's critique of Adams reflects his liberal position in regard to the existing debates over "authority" and ideological constructions of the past.[47] Like Richard Hildreth's "set[ting] out in avowed opposition to filiopietism," Brown's understanding of historical bias and the uncertainty of history as well as his reluctance to review conventional filiopietistic histories—male or female—testifies to his more rationalist or liberal point of view.[48] It also highlights his misgivings about American histories written from a divine or "exceptionalist" point of view, a position he further develops in his own historical writing several years later.

Finally, just as Brown's historical reviews argue for a sense of historical objectivity and essays like "Walstein's School of History" document Brown's emerging interest in, and capacity for, meditating self-reflexively on historical matters, so his last essay during this period in the *Monthly Magazine and American Review*, "The Difference between History and Romance" (April 1800) continues, as Alfred Weber, Wolfgang Schäfer, and John Holmes astutely point out, "Brown's reflections on prose theory and the theory of historical writing developed in 'Walstein's School of

History.'"[49] In particular, its commentary on how one makes distinctions between historical actions in the past and the "motives" associated with such events provides further insight into the fictional aspects of history writing. It identifies specific differences and similarities between both the historian and the romancer.

Published after *Wieland, Ormond,* and *Edgar Huntly,* and while completing the second part of *Arthur Mervyn* during the summer of 1800, Brown begins by commenting on what supposedly distinguishes "history" from "romance." He writes:

> History and romance are terms that have never been very clearly distinguished from each other. It should seem that one dealt in fiction, and the other in truth; that one is a picture of the *probable* and certain, and the other a tissue of untruths; that one describes what *might* have happened, and what has *actually* happened, and the other what never had existence. These distinctions seem to be just; but we shall find ourselves somewhat perplexed, when we attempt to reduce them to practice, and to ascertain, by their assistance, to what class this or that performance belongs.

If the historian, writes Brown, is one who will write of "the noises, the sights, and the smells that attend the eruption of Vesuvius"—"what is known by the testimony of our senses"—he or she depends on linking facts or events together by circumstance and the "evidence of others," evidence that can never be linked to certainty. A romancer, however, will relate the "*contemporary* ebullitions and inflations, the combustion and decomposition that take place in the earth." He or she will also delve into the "origin of things" as the volcano relates to the composition of the universe and will "paint the universal dissolution that is hereafter to be produced by the influence of volcanic or internal fire." In short, historians will "differ in degrees of diligence and accuracy," while a romancer will "have more or less probability in their narrations."[50]

At the same time, Brown's questioning of the dichotomy between history and romance indicates his, like Godwin's, theoretical awareness of the fictive nature of history—of how boundaries between history writing and romance also blur or overlap. In detailing, for example, how the "observer" who empirically records appearances performs a different sort of analysis from he who "adorns these appearances with cause and effect, and traces resemblances between [the] past, distant, and future, with the present," Brown argues that the writer of history is a "dealer, not in certainties, but probabilities, and is therefore a romancer."[51] Both the historian and the romancer, in other words, deal with "truth" at some level; at the same time, however, they also partake of memory and the imagination. In this respect, suggests Brown, the barrier between "history" and the "novel" as narrative forms evaporates and is permeable.

Although Brown is of the view that those who are not "content with noting and other. - It should seem that one dealt in fiction, and the other in truth; that one is a picture of the *probable* and certain, and the other a tissue of untruths; that one describes what *might* have happened, and what has *actually* happened, and the other what never had existance.

These distinctions seem to be just; but we shall find ourselves somewhat perplexed, when we attempt to reduce them to practice, and to ascertain, by their assistance, to what class this or that performance belongs.

Narratives, whether fictitious or true, may relate to the processes of nature, or the actions of men. The former, if not impenetrable by human faculties, must be acknowledged to be, hitherto, very imperfectly known. Curiosity is not satisfied with viewing facts in their disconnected state and natural order, but is prone to arrange them anew, and to deviate from present and sensible objects, into speculations on the past or future; it is eager to infer from the present state of things, their former or future condition.

The observer or experimentalist, therefore, who carefully watches, and faithfully enumerates the appearances which occur, may claim the appellation of historian. He who adorns these appearances with cause and effect, and traces resemblances between the past, distant, and future, with the present, performs a different part. He is a dealer, not in certainties, but probabilities, and is therefore a romancer.

An historian will relate the noises, the sights, and the smells that attend an eruption of Vesuvius. A romancer will describe, in the first place, the *contemporary* ebullitions and inflations, the combustion and decomposition that take place in the bowels of the earth. Next he will go to the origin of things, and de-

The Difference between History and Romance.

HISTORY and romance are terms that have never been very clearly distinguished from each recording the *actions* of men" and who inquire into the "motives" behind the actions "are not *historians* but *romancers*," he also acknowledges that it is possible to be both a historian and a romancer and complicates this dichotomy by remarking:

> These principles may be employed to illustrate the distinction between history and romance. If history relates what is true, its relations must be limited to what is known by the testimony of our senses. Its sphere, therefore, is extremely narrow. The facts to which we are immediate witnesses, are, indeed, numerous; but time and place merely connect them. Useful narratives must comprise facts linked together by some other circumstance. They must, commonly, consist of events, for a knowledge of which the narrator is indebted to the evidence of others. This evidence, though accompanied with different degrees of probability, can never give birth to certainty. How wide, then, if romance be the narrative of mere probabilities, is the empire of romance? This empire is absolute and undivided over the motives and tendencies of human actions. Over actions themselves, its dominion, though not unlimited, is yet very extensive.[52]

Unlike many of his contemporaries, Brown asks about the authenticity of historical "evidence" itself—about the roles bias, "probability," and even selective memory play in historicizing the past. That is, just as he expressed a degree of historical self-consciousness in "Walstein's School of History," saying that "actions and motives cannot truly be described," so in this passage he explores the implications of such a remark, especially in regard to the "evidence of others" and traditional distinctions between fictional and nonfictional sources. More important, his comments about the "empire of romance," or "narrative of mere probabilities," and its extensiveness in human thought and action suggest that no one can claim complete "objectivity" or access to the truth. His historical self-consciousness here even implies that what he had written was a "construction," a narrative colored by his own bias and intellectual interests. For this reason, Brown's observations about narrative truth—and relativism—curiously echo elements of the "linguistic turn" in history. Indeed, as I suggest later, they resemble or anticipate the thinking of Ferdinand de Saussure and other linguists and philosophers who suggest that narrative meaning is arbitrary or relational, *not* the reflection of some absolute and reliable truth or certainty.

Facing page: The opening page of "Difference between History and Romance," published in the *Monthly Magazine and American Review* (April 1800), signed "X." The essay addresses the boundaries between history writing and imaginative tale or story, suggesting that distinctions between "fiction" and historical "truth" are not always clear. Like his earlier "Walstein's School of History," this essay charts Brown's evolving historical sensibility. Courtesy of the Library Company of Philadelphia.

As mentioned earlier, Brown did not restrict his reflections about history and fiction to book reviews and essays in his periodicals. The novels he published individually and collectively track his evolving reflections on history as a subject and the subjectivity of history relative to fiction. His novels document, with their numerous references to and digressions on "the past," "history," "memory," or "story," even "romancers and historians," how his fiction writing informed his theorizing of history, and vice versa, and enabled him to develop an understanding of representation and a unique theory of the novel that empowered its readers with intellectual and moral agency.

Likewise, however, Brown's publication of several essays—many from British periodicals—in the *Literary Magazine and American Register* during 1806 marks his continued immersion in a philosophical literary debate about the meaning and function of history writing in the early Republic. Brown's serial publication of essays like "Comparisons of Memoirs and History" and "Modes of History Writing" signal that his critical synthesis had reached yet another level of understanding, one that would exhibit itself in his historical sketches and, shortly thereafter, his actual history writing. In the *Literary Magazine,* his editing and publication of essays from Isaac D'Israeli and others on history and historical methods document the dialectical nature of his historicism.

The Literary Magazine and American Register (1803–1807)

At the request of Cornelius and Andrew Conrad of Philadelphia in October 1803, Brown started a literary periodical, *Literary Magazine and American Register.* In his detailed study, Michael Cody writes of Brown's intentions as an editor:

> The material in the *Literary Magazine* shows Brown in his most direct participatory role in what was already a fading republic of letters and represents his most mature literary service in the name of a nascent American cultural nationalism. Analysis of his magazine reveals that, despite criticism portraying him as having disengaged himself—after finishing *Edgar Huntly* and *Arthur Mervyn*—from those vital transformations taking place in the early Republic, Brown used the *Literary Magazine* to remain active in America's shifting ideological and cultural life between 1803 and 1807. He was more serviceable to his country in his capacity as editor than he had ever been before.

The periodical, asserts Cody, reflected Philadelphia's "liberality" and the "mixture of voices and ideas that come to inhabit his miscellany between 1803 and 1807." "Useful information and rational amusement" were Brown's main objectives, and he would fill the magazine with literary essays, biography, political reflections, poetry, history, geography, travel reports, and historical fiction, among other kinds of writings.[53]

If Brown's reviews and essays in the *Monthly Magazine and American Review* represent his initial efforts to understand the differences between history and romance, then his essays, accounts, and other materials he selected for inclusion in the *Literary Magazine and American Register,* especially in 1806, signify an increasingly clear transition toward "political history" and the kinds of historical writing he would undertake more fully with his "Annals of Europe and America" in the *American Register; or, General Repository of History, Politics, and Science.* That is, like his periodical reviews, Brown's own essays contain significant commentary about history and historical writing.[54] But between the periodical essays he published in the *Monthly Magazine and American Review* and the several he edited and included in the *Literary Magazine* in 1806, the latter ones clearly indicate a more sophisticated or advanced view of history writing.

Specifically, although "Comparison of Memoirs and History" (January 1806), "Historical Characters Are False Representations of Nature" (February 1806), and "Modes of Historical Writing" (December 1806) have been mistakenly attributed to Brown, they reflect his continued concentration on and assessment of historians such as Voltaire, Hume, Robertson, and others relative to the popularity of biography and memoirs and his engagement in a debate about the meaning and function of history. Equally as important, they also engage in debates about rationalist historiography and the use of "'empathy' as a method of historical inquiry" and illustrate the manner in which Brown begins to process, conceptually, romanticist attitudes.[55] These essays, in particular, along with Brown's editorial efforts to attend more closely to European and domestic historical events, record his evolving engagement with contemporary debates about the epistemological limits of history and his increasing awareness of the constructed nature of historical writing.

That is, Brown's selection and editing of periodical publications on history and historical method in the *Literary Magazine and American Register* argue not only for a reevaluation of his contributions as an author and editor but also the philosophically self-conscious ways he continuously negotiated early American historical writing. His various essays on the meaning and function of history and the role of the historian demonstrate how his ideas about historical representation developed and simultaneously surpassed his fictitious histories, gothic and sentimental novels, and earlier periodical writing and point toward his actual contributions as a historian of the early Republic. The essays also raise important questions about the history of the romantic historian in nineteenth- and twentieth-century historiography.

First, as remarks in his October 1, 1803, "Editor's Address to the Public" indicate, Brown not only wanted to give a "critical account" of "*domestic* publications" and provide a "history of our native literature," but he also wanted to pay closer attention to historical matters. As in his earlier periodical publications, he continues to establish himself as a literary theorist and critic of early republican literature. But he says he will "pay particular attention to the history of passing events" and announces that he will gather both foreign and domestic news and that other material, such as poetry, will aim for "the promotion of public and private virtue." Further, in addition to declaring that he will be "the ardent friend and willing champion of the Christian religion," he stresses that "as a political annalist [*sic*], he will speculate freely on foreign transactions; but, in his detail of domestic events, he will confine himself, as strictly as possible, to the limits of a mere historian." "There is nothing," he continues, "for which he has a deeper abhorrence than the intemperance of party, and his fundamental rule shall be to exclude from his pages, all personal altercation and abuse."[56]

Similar, then, to his expanding interest in "domestic history" and manners in his novels, Brown continued to edit materials in the *Literary Magazine and American Register* related to domestic "manners" and geographically diverse areas well through 1807. Publications such as "Account of the Present State of the Province of Buenos-Ayres, in South America" (January 1804), "Manners and Characters of the Different Inhabitants of Egypt" (November 1804), "State of Women among the Arabs" (December 1804), and "Some Particulars Respecting the Manners and Customs of the Russian Peasants" (August 1807) all speak to Brown's abiding interest in the behaviors of people, as divided along class and gender lines, and their patterns of social organization and interaction.

For instance, one might compare the content of the *Literary Magazine and American Register* with that in earlier publications. Brown's lingering interest in domestic materials is evident in essays like "The Women of the Romans" (May 1805), signed "R," which tests the "axiom, that the real civilization of a nation may be estimated by nothing more accurately than by the condition of its women." While the essay is by James Pettit Andrews, it nevertheless, argues that the "moral, intellectual, and political refinement of the Greeks and Romans" needs to be reconciled with "the debased condition of their women" and the "vulgar and smutty" ways poets like Ovid and Tibullus represented them.[57] Likewise, if, as mentioned earlier, "The Romance of Real Life" (November 1805) focuses on the past history "of one of the noblest families in Great Britain," "Remarks on the Russian Empire," published by "R" in December 1806, examines the "progress and condition, political and geographical, of that empire."[58]

At the same time, just as Brown continued to inquire into and publish material on domestic manners, so he also, as editor, accepted for the *Literary Magazine and American Register* reviews, essays, and fiction on explicitly historical subjects. In November 1803, for example, he edited and published Abraham Upright's "History of Philip Dellwyn" and Robert Thomas Wilson's "History of the British Expedition to Egypt." In 1804, he published anonymous materials such as "A Sketch of the War of St. Domingo. From the Invasion of Leclerc to the Death of Toussaint," and in 1805, he published "State of France under Louis the Fifteenth" and "Doubts Concerning Roman History." In 1806 he printed "Horrors of West India Slavery," "Conduct of England towards Ireland," "On the Independence of Spanish America," and several essays on the French Revolution, including "Whether France has Gained or Lost by the Revolution," "On the Merits of the Founders of the French Revolution," and "French History." As late as 1807, Brown published "Observations on Military History," which admits to being "too near the scene of action" of the French Revolution to see events with "distinctness, or judge them with impartiality," "Remarks on French History," and "History"—which argues that the histories of individuals and nations are interrelated.[59]

Of unusual interest, because it foreshadows Brown's use of irony in his historical fiction and, later, in his historical annals, is his May 1805 publication of "The Law of Nations," signed "R," which opens by examining the usefulness of recent "treatises" that seek to impose uniformity and laws on European nations.[60] He remarks that some men, like Vattel and Puffendorf, have attempted to devise a "system of conduct" for all nations and that their representation of "the manners of the age . . . are valuable and instructive" to a degree. However, he continues, insofar as they "propound a system of law, drawn on historical precedents, or from their own reasonings upon right and wrong, they are frivolous and nugatory." Further, he (or the author of Brown's text at this point) questions, ironically, the consistency of the "English historian" who is in a position to "reprobate the conduct of the Spaniards towards the natives of America; and the hunting of them with dogs" but who then neglects to record similar motives and actions in regard to the use of "the same species of dogs against an independent people, with whom it had entered into a treaty."[61] For Brown, at least in 1805, "domestic manners" and history, and how they were represented, were sometimes quite similar—and sometimes quite different.

Brown, also, may or may not have written a review of John Burk's *The History of Virginia, from its first settlement to the present day,* and observed how, despite the loss of historical materials on a daily basis, Burke's history offers a "valuable addition to our domestic literature."[62] Likewise in the August 1805 essay "On 'the Enlightened Public,' and 'the Age of Reason,'" signed "W," the speaker comments self-reflexively and insightfully on the "progressive state" of Enlightenment thought and the claims some "speculative moderns" have made concerning the acquisition and construction of knowledge. Without doubt, says the writer, "radical vigour" of thought has been present in the human mind from the earliest periods, and enough writings have survived from ancient Greek and Roman cultures "to serve as models for our greatest poets; to instruct our orators in the arts of eloquence; our historians in the composition of history, and to leave nothing for our moralists, but an amplification of the observations of Seneca and Epictetus." Beyond considering, though, how to judge the human mind and what constitutes an "enlightened public" in an "impartial manner," the essay argues that knowledge eventually passes on from one generation to the next, making what were once "novel discoveries" familiar or even forgotten.[63] Thus, similar to the kinds of metahistorical reflections his earlier writings articulate, Brown's sense of the past and history writing itself— as evidenced by his editorial selections and occasional appropriation of textual content—continued during 1804 and 1805 to engage questions about the construction of history, historical representation, and truth.

As his editorial selections for the *Literary Magazine and American Register* indicate, Brown's historicism continued to evolve, and by 1806 he was also developing clearer and more coherent ideas about the methods and responsibilities of a historian. It is, in other words, in essays like "On Anecdotes" (January 1806), "Comparisons of Memoirs and History" (January 1806), "On Literary Biography" (January 1806), "Historical Characters Are False Representations of Nature" (February 1806), and later, in "Modes of History Writing" (December 1806)—after he had started composing his "Annals of Europe and America"—that one can trace Brown's interest in issues of a historical or historiographical nature. While not Brown's, these essays, along with his historical fiction, provide a major historiographical and theoretical link between Brown's reflections on history, narrative, and truth in his novels and early periodical writing and his more substantive treatment of history in his "Annals of Europe and America" in the *American Register; or, Repository of History, Politics, and Science* (1807–09).

First, the appearance in 1806—almost six years after the first set of essays—of several historiographical essays documents Brown's continued inquiry into the nature and meaning of historical writing and the influence of "empathetic" or romantic attitudes about the past on his own theory of history. As has already been suggested by Brown's use of D'Israeli and other European sources, Brown, of course, was not alone at this time in his reflections on the subject of history. In addition to Abiel Holmes's *American Annals; or, A Chronological History of America* (1805) and his self-reflective commentary about historical narrative and bias, an anonymous article, "History," appeared in 1805 in Stephen Carpenter's *Monthly Review and Literary Miscellany of the United States* and *Monthly Register, Magazine, and Review of the United States,* which echoed Brown's interest in history, objectivity, and truth.[64]

Using discourse similar to Brown's, the author begins by remarking, "Of the many who read history, few are aware of the difficulties which beset the historian." While "to record truth is his business," the historian must also make it "attractive" and contend with the excesses of one's imagination. Because it is difficult to relay historical truth in a way that appeals to the reader's imagination, to "steer a middle course between dry narrative and frothy relation" is ideal. While the author shares Brown's search for historical truth and candor, unlike Brown, he asserts that the novel is "calculated, only to entertain in perusal" and then be forgotten or "consigned to oblivion." Also, in addition to asserting that "frankness, boldness, and impartiality" are essential to accurate historical representation, the author also believes that historians should avoid political partisanship and public censure of individuals and in collecting material "postpone reasoning, and inferences till a future day." An exception is provided, though, for the historian of passing or recent events: "It must, nevertheless, be acknowledged, that there are particular cases in which, from motives of prudence, of decency, or of benevolence, the historian ought to wave many of his privileges, and the world to dispense with his observance of some of the strict laws, to which, generally speaking, he owes obedience. When writing the history of the present time, there are considerations of a peculiar kind which force themselves upon his reason and feeling." While he remarks further that "boldly to censure living characters, and to expose corrupt motives of their political conduct, may, perhaps be thought imprudent," especially as it concerns relatives of the deceased, there are times when closeness to events or living people dictates reserve or patience, of which "the historian will still have a very strong foundation on which to ground his defence." Still, he asserts, "history" should strive to address the "difficulties which beset the historian," specifically the role of exuberant "fancy" in the "composition of history" and the extent to which "prejudices" should be banished in the pursuit of "Truth."[65]

The author concludes that if a historian "scrupulously maintain fidelity to the facts, and, as has already been said, swerve not from truth to please one party, or oblige another; and if he deliver his sentiments with amenity, candour, impartiality, and frankness, he will do all the God requires at his hands." Brown would have endorsed this approach, with certain qualifications. The author also addresses the difficulties of objectively writing history while tracing the "chain of human affairs" and the causes of events before they are forgotten or lost, closely examining the role of "bias" in historical writing and commenting on why so few historians are "strictly impartial." He remarks, near the end, that "history, therefore, is now considered one of the most important branches of polite literature" and that history is only useful to the extent that it is able to "exercise the imagination, amuse the fancy, and afford gratification to the curious." Similar to Brown's inquiry into the differences between history and romance, the author of "History" also calls for close inquiry into history's "motives and causes."[66]

Carpenter's essay is especially useful for what it reveals concerning the romancer or sentimentalist and the "true historian." For instance, in contemplating the "business" of the historian and how to "record truth," he writes that "to render history generally useful, therefore, it must be made attractive, and, to that end, decorated with the finest, but most simple drapery, which judgment can select from the stores of imagination, to embellish truth, without concealing her natural form." While he notes that the historian must be careful to control his fancy and

to "banish all prejudices," he acknowledges that impartiality and bias are pervasive. Indeed, he suggests, "a multitude of inferior writers have laid hold of [his-
tory], and swelled to an enormous size, the catalogue of volumes, without, in the
smallest degree, increasing the sum of human knowledge, or contributing any
thing to the instruction of mankind."[67]

However, similar to plans Brown would put forward a couple years later in the
American Register; or, General Repository of History, Politics, and Science, Carpenter's plan for the *Monthly Register, Magazine, and Review of the United States* (1805)
lays out an editorial and historical plan that is modeled on the "English Annual
Register" that aims to collect "important state papers," as they illustrate "historical
facts," and to analyze the "business" and the "duties" of the historian as they relate
to existing models of history. Concerned, unlike Brown, with the influences of
"Deism" and the "immorality" and "atheism" of books, Carpenter aims to select
more appropriate materials for display. Toward this end, he aims to divide materials into those that are "HISTORICAL" and those that are part of the "LITERARY
REGISTER," ever being conscious, like Brown, of the "great difference there is between the office of the *historian* and *partisan.*" In remarking further that the "business, and consequently the duties of an historian, are wholly dissimilar," Carpenter
provides insight into cultural perceptions of "history," writing:

> The Editor is aware that there are two distinct species of history, each
> of which has been warmly applauded and warmly condemned. The one
> founded on the Grecian model, in which facts are stated with very little
> of the historian's own remarks or disquisitions; the other formed by Livy,
> and since enlarged by Voltaire, Robertson, Hume and Gibbon, which gives
> greater scope to the powers of the historian's mind; permits him fully and
> minutely to describe the manners and morals of the varying ages; to trace
> every event through the windings and mazes of public or private intrigue;
> to exhibit his knowledge of man in splendid portraits of distinguished char-
> acters; to expatiate in moral and philosophical observations on each passing
> scene; and to distinguish each remarkable actor according to his defects, in
> the language of eulogism or reproach.

While he doesn't think it's necessary to decide at the moment which of these two
approaches is the most instructive or entertaining, the "first is more suitable for
histories in our own times," especially since it is difficult to understand and analyze
the actions and motives of living people.[68] For him, political interests and closeness
to events preclude proper historical perspective. Indeed, he confesses in his preface
to the magazine that if his prospectus lays out his intentions as an editor, he is satisfied in being a "good compiler," since "to select judiciously requires some share of
penetration, judgment, and taste"—no small service, he hopes, for his readers.[69]

By 1806, when Carpenter was in New York and publishing the *Monthly Register, Magazine, and Review of the United States,* his "Address to the Public" expressed his appreciation for the patronage of friends and promised future punctuality. He also made clear that the "first and great aim" of his publication was to contribute to the "happiness" of his fellow man by "a vigorous defence of the principles of truth and morality, and by rallying with all their forces, round the sacred ALTARS OF CHRISTIANITY."[70] His "Retrospective History of America" comments self-reflexively, and insightfully, on contemporary modes of historical writing, saying that "the general tendency of historic writings" is to "encourage a wild spirit of military adventure," and rather than considering "the *manners,* and *condition* of the *great mass of the people,* at different periods of time," historians focus instead on instilling "admiration and envy of the honour and glory of *warlike* nations; that is, in other words, the *butchery* and the *murder* of mighty empires." And while he was able to continue it briefly, he is compelled to omit it after February 1807 because, he says, "the history of the times that now are, must, and shall claim a greater portion of our attention and care"—because "we now live in more feverish, and more trying times, and, because we witness more portentous, and more awful events, than have ever shaken terribly the womb of existence, since that hour, when the Lord God Omnipotent, first called the heavens and the earth from out of silence, and of night, into being."[71] Carpenter managed to address elements of Jefferson's Embargo Act in his "History of the Passing Times," and, at less length, events such as the Battle of Austerlitz, remarking that there has always been a "collision of interests" between nations.[72] He discontinued his "History of the Passing Times" by September 1807, and the periodical itself folded in December of that year.

Brown's historical writing makes for a useful comparison. If Holmes's reflections on history writing continue to register a filiopietistic set of assumptions, that is, that he was writing under "divine patronage," Carpenter's periodicals document a similar set of providential assumptions regarding history. At the same time, they record the desirability of historical objectivity and truth and highlight the increase in the production and consumption of history writing—a topic Brown would also engage.[73] While Brown acknowledges similar opinions regarding the value of historical impartiality, he deliberated on the ways histories glorified battle or the rise of empires in other ways. Essays he selected for publication in 1806, however, do reveal a continuously evolving historical self-consciousness, a sense of history that is informed by his awareness of the increasing popularity and commercialization of history writing. That is, these subsequent essays not only confirm the extent to which 1805 marks, at least in the United States, a moment where intellectuals were deeply concerned with the function and meaning of historical narrative—and the novel—and its importance in shaping the cultural memory and identity of the early Republic, but they record ongoing debate about the utility and limits of history writing. These writings, then, may or may not have

prompted debate in certain circles over truth, objectivity, and the role and responsibilities of the historian in the early Republic, but they nevertheless locate a moment where rationalist views of the past and history writing clash with romantic
ones, and Brown's *Literary Magazine* took a cutting-edge interest in addressing
changing economic and cultural motives for writing "history" and "fiction."

To appreciate the importance of these reflections on historical and literary
boundaries, it is useful to examine how an essay like "On Anecdotes" (January
1806), which Brown extracted from Isaac D'Israeli's *A Dissertation on Anecdotes*
(1793)—although identified as Brown's by Alfred Weber, Wolfgang Schäfer, and John
R. Holmes in *Charles Brockden Brown: Literary Essays and Reviews* (1992)—places
even less emphasis on deductive reasoning as a method for understanding the past
and more weight on an empathetic approach to writing history.[74] It provides a different focus on domestic history—one that affirms the lives of individuals.

The essay begins, for instance, by remarking on the literary value of anecdotes,
especially as a form of entertainment, and then turns to the ways anecdotes can
cumulatively instruct the human mind. Saying that "history itself derives some of
its most agreeable instructions from a skillful introduction of anecdotes," D'Israeli
further asserts, "We should not now dwell with anxiety on a dull chronicle of the
reigns of monarchs; a parish register might prove more interesting."[75] The focus
that emerges here is clearly directed more toward the lives of common people
than to the accomplishments of kings and queens.

While D'Israeli continues by remarking that "romancers have existed in all
nations, under the names of historians" and then listing those who have written
under French and Irish reigns, he also argues for reading history more empathetically, in the mode of reading "memoirs." He writes: "Our hearts should learn to
sympathize; and we should consult the annals of history as a son and a brother
would turn over his domestic memoirs. We should read history, not to indulge the
frivolous inquisitiveness of a dull antiquary, but to explore the causes of the misery and prosperity of our country. We ought to be interested in the progress of the
human mind than in that of empires."[76] In saying, for example, that the readers'
"hearts should learn to sympathize" and that rather than dwelling on the reigns of
monarchs one should seek to understand other histories, D'Israeli articulates romanticist attitudes toward history writing, attitudes that value individual character and emotional detail. In fact, by quoting Johnson's remarks on the importance
of "civil," "military," and "religious history" in works like Robert Henry's *History
of Great Britain, from the First Invasion of It by the Romans* (1789) and his desire
to have one branch of history well written—"*the history of manners*, of common
life"—D'Israeli underscores how the "history of manners" has become a topic of
interest among philosophers and other intellectuals. Indeed, as Brown's fictitious
history "Sketches of a History of the Carrils and Ormes" testifies, he places em-

phasis on the Carril family and the lives of common men and women and appears
to embrace a less rationalistic approach to the past.

The "skillful introduction of anecdotes," continues D'Israeli, is particularly useful
for the historian who wishes to integrate private details or "manners" into historical
narrative. "The historian," he remarks, "should assiduously arrange the minute anecdotes of the age he examines; and oftener have recourse to the diaries of individuals
than to the archives of a nation. Nothing should escape his researches, though every
thing he finds is not to be reported."[77] While Brown underscores such commentary
by including an anecdote about the unfair treatment of Jews in the ninth century,
what is significant here in terms of his historicism is that he seems open to a view
of history and history writing that is more romantic. Brown's decision to publish
D'Israeli's "On Anecdotes" under the pseudonym "X" and its "sympathetic" sensibility toward the past and on embracing the "little particulars" in the lives of common
people illustrate his interest in changing European attitudes toward the past.

"Comparison of Memoirs and History," and "On Literary Biography," both published in January 1806, after "On Anecdotes," is also not Brown's but illustrates his
editorial and thematic focus on historical methodologies.[78] It focuses on "memoirs"
of individuals, and remarks that the "historian" cannot always be "impartial" and
that in some respects he is "prejudiced," especially when it comes to rendering "eminent personages in history." In fact, the essay asserts, a historian can acquire more
information or "knowledge of individuals" by reading "memoirs than by histories."
In histories, there is a "majesty" or elevation that prevents the reader from getting
close to the lives of "great men." Memoirs, however, allow for a "familiarity" with the
lives of individuals. This distinction, it is said, enables readers of memoirs to feel as
if they are "concealed spies," rather than outside observers of someone's life.[79]

Further, just as readers are sometimes inclined to read history as if they were
reading "the marvellous of romance," so historians often cannot reproduce or represent the "spontaneous ardour" behind actions and instead must compose a "regular
plot" out of the "accident combinations of fortune" and other particulars. This dis-
crepancy, says D'Israeli, explains why every "statesman who comes down to us as a
Nestor" is not "the sage" readers think he is; likewise, "the most eminent personages
are not so remote from the ordinary level of humanity, as the vulgar conceive." For
these reasons, says D'Israeli, he is more inclined to inquire into a person's character
by reading their "domestic privacies" than their public statements, and he prefers
the "artless recitals of the valet de chamber of Charles I, to the elegant narrative of
his apologist Hume."[80] The essay, in short, lays out the advantages and disadvantages of each genre in regard to learning about important historical personages and
their lives, but clearly expresses a preference for memoirs as a way of understanding
the private lives, conflicts, and motivations of individuals—something Brown could
appreciate.

Despite being signed "R.," "On Literary Biography," just a few pages after "Comparison of Memoirs and History," is also not Brown's; it is a passage from Isaac D'Israeli's 1793 *A Dissertation on Anecdotes* and continues the focus on "domestic privacies" in "Comparison of Memoirs and History."[81] It examines the ways a "man of genius" develops relative to "domestic persecutions" or difficulties and offers instruction on the use of memory in history. Bacon, for example, generally reflected on philosophical questions at one end of the family table while relatives "cheated, ridiculed, and loaded him with infamous aspersions" at the other. And while Hume, Descartes, Rousseau, and others all contended with domestic difficulties of various kinds, men like Burnet in the "History of His Own Times" "appealed to God and his conscience for the veracity of his work" so that he might tell "the truth" and avoid turning it "into a lie." Varillas, as well, was familiar with numerous "original memoirs" but in writing his histories could not document anecdotes and related information. His reliance on "memory" and his subsequent inaccurate rendering of "facts" lead one to consider one important maxim: "that a historian must not write as facts what he only collects from memory" and that he who "relies on his memory is frequently the dupe of his imagination."[82]

The essay ends with remarks on various literary authors, the benefits of access to their conversations, and the importance of a biographer being able to display "the genius of the man whose history he writes, than his own."[83] However, although D'Israeli's "On Literary Biography" delves into issues of historical representation, memory, and subjectivity, Brown's exposure to the role of the imagination in history seems most explicit in the essay "Historical Characters Are False Representations of Nature," which articulates serious misgivings about the intentions, subjectivity, and impact of romantic historians.

Published in the *Literary Magazine* in 1806, the essay, say Alfred Weber, Wolfgang Schäfer, and John Holmes, is a composite of Brown's earlier essays and "focuses on Brown's theory that the reader could gain more instruction from accounts of the private lives of historical greats and from the knowledge of their 'domestic sorrows' than from pure histories."[84] But it is not Brown's—it is, as Philip Barnard observes, another Isaac D'Israeli essay from his *Miscellanies; or, Literary* Recreations (1796).[85] Without doubt, an essay like "On Literary Biography" does acknowledge the value of biographies, especially of literary greats, but "Historical Characters Are False Representations of Nature," signed "R.," appears to do more than celebrate the "great man" biography. The essay, if read in the context of the "On Anecdotes," or even on its own terms, critiques this element of romanticist historiography and focuses attention on the lives of "obscure individuals."[86] D'Israeli's continual questioning of historical and literary boundaries suggests that seemingly democratic concerns about reclaiming the common man and woman were now superseded by problematic motivations for reading and, more specifically, writing historical narratives.

Reflecting, arguably, Brown's own interest in the romantic excesses in history writing, the essay begins:

> We accustom ourselves to paying too liberal an admiration to the great character recorded in modern, to say nothing of ancient, history. It seems often necessary to be reminded, that the most interesting history is generally the most elegantly written, and that whatever is adorned by elegance is the composition of art. Charmed and seduced by variegated tints of imagination, the scene is heightened, and the objects move into life; but while we yield ourselves to the captivating talent of the artist, we forget that the whole representation is but a picture, and that painters, like poets, are indulged with a certain agreeable licentiousness. Hence we form false estimates of the human character, and, while we exhaust our sensations in artificial sympathies, amidst characters and circumstances almost fictitious, for the natural events and the natural calamities of life, we suppress those warmer emotions we otherwise should indulge.[87]

In observing how "interesting history" is often related to how well it's written and the quality of its "composition" or "art," D'Israeli continues inquiry into the relationship between history and romance. He acknowledges up front that historical scenes and characters are often influenced by the historian's "imagination" and efforts to relate a captivating history. For this reason, he says, the whole "representation" of the past is but "a picture," where the historian has most likely taken some liberties with the past or the truth to render a more coherent and interesting picture. And to the extent that we readily believe such representations of the past, we "form false estimates of the human character." Indeed, readers exhaust their "sensations in artificial sympathies, amidst characters and circumstances almost fictitious," leaving people less sensitive to "the natural events and the natural calamities of life."

In fact, he continues, a historian is often as eager to display the talent or "miracles of his art" as he is the historical scenes and circumstances before him. "Let us also reflect," he writes, "how often a shameful partiality dictates to the historians who possess the best information." "Every historian communicates his character to his history," and if he has a "romantic turn" or aptitude, all human subjects become heroic figures like Arthur and perform superhuman accomplishments that overshadow the accomplishments of real personages: "No writers more than the historian, and the professed romancer, so sedulously practice the artifice of awakening curiosity, and feasting that appetency of the mind, which turns from simple truth to spirited fiction. We scarce glance at the glittering of a star, but we gaze with delight on the coruscations of a meteor." This appetite for the sensational and habit of indulging the fantastic at the expense of what's real, will "disappear" or dissipate when individuals are confronted by "those few facts in history, which the art of the historian can no longer disguise, and which, refusing the decorations of his fancy, present the sublime personages of history in the nudity of truth." That is, historical truth can and will present itself in those moments when the monarch, the minister, and the hero are humanized by historians and "speak in the voice of distress," minus the "romantic gilding of the pencil."[88] At that moment, when human sympathy is engaged, historical understanding can occur.

Brown may or may not have agreed on the point of seeking to reign in historical representation or the "art of the historian" that is merely sensational or inflated. But he was clearly processing the idea that history can promote human sympathy, a methodology used in his novels. Just as William Wordsworth made a radical departure from poetic norms in *Lyrical Ballads* (1799) and focused on the lives of common men, not the classical subject matter of the past, so Brown arguably considered how the lives and voices of "obscure men" might also be valued as part of the historical record, an ethos that may be said to inform his later dramatic concerns.

Moreover, just as Mary Wollstonecraft argued for women's equality and domestic rights, and Wordsworth validated the lives of female vagrants and the poor in his poems, so D'Israeli argues for remembering the lives of women as part of a larger historical and moral fabric, thereby underscoring for Brown the idea that history is more than just the "great man" biography. "The sympathy," says D'Israeli,

we give to a princess ravished from her throne, and dragged by traitors to wet with tears the iron gates of her dungeon, we may with no less propriety bestow on that unfortunate female, whom unfeeling creditors have snatched from maternal duties, or social labours, to perish by the hour, in some loathsome prison. If we feel for the decapitation of a virtuous and long persecuted statesman, we are not to feel less for that more common object, a man of genius, condemned to languish in obscurity, and perish in despair. . . .

Katharine, the queen of Henry VIII, is an object of our tenderest sympathy; but why should our sensibility be diminished, when we look on those numerous females, not less gentle, nor less cruelly misused, who, without the consolations of sovereignty, are united to despots, not less arbitrary and brutal than Henry? The sorrows of the Scottish Mary, the refined insults of a rival sister, the grin of scorn, and the implication of infamy, may penetrate our hearts; but we forget that there are families, where scenes not less terrible, and sisters not less unrelenting, are hourly discovered; and that there are beauties, who, without being confined to the melancholy magnificence of a castle, or led to the dismal honour of an axe, equally fall victims, or to fatal indiscretion, or to fatal persecution.[89]

Similar to Brown's novels and earlier periodical writings, where the domestic lives of women are consistently examined or represented in sympathetic ways, D'Israeli appears to advocate a progressive agenda for women's equality, dignity, and respect no less radical than Mary Wollstonecraft's or Judith Sargent Murray's. He examines the status patriarchal institutions and the assumptions about gender difference that are in play and that support them. Just as Murray's "On the Equality of the Sexes," for instance, calls for women's equal rights, especially in regard to education, so D'Israeli argues for more sympathetic laws and legal policies for female debtors and victims of domestic abuse and for a more humane treatment of women, not as property, "victims" of persecution, or agents of moral depravity, but as human beings with the right to life, liberty, and social equality.[90]

The essay closes by restating concerns about the "artifice of the historian" and the bias toward "great characters," saying:

> Familiar objects of distress, and familiar characters of merit, want only, to form a spectacle as interesting as the pompous inflation of history can display, those powers of seducing eloquence, which disguise the simplicity of truth with the romantic grandeur of fiction. Nations have abounded with heroes and sages; but because they wanted historians, they are scarce known to us by name; and individuals have been heroes and sages in domestic life, whose talents and whose virtues are embellished in no historical record, but traced, in transient characters, on the feeble gratitude of the human heart.[91]

The view of historical writing that Brown includes here in his periodical is one that is "romantic" yet modern to the extent that it reevaluates the meaning of history along the lines of individuals or marginalized others, regardless of gender or class, and seeks to validate its more subjective elements. The focus here on nations expands to "domestic life," family and home, and highlights how in both arenas individuals have contributed to society and its improvement. In this respect, D'Israeli takes the unorthodox view that the most instructive lesson of history involves an awareness of its fictive or romantic elements—that is, of the manner in which contemporary history writing communicates "false representations" of the past and denies not only the histories of "obscure individuals" but diminishes one's capacity for human "sympathy" in everyday life. This, one could argue, enriched Brown's emerging synthesis of history and aesthetics as it existed at this time.

As I indicated, though, at the beginning of this chapter, Brown's theory of history, as expressed in his *Monthly Magazine and American Review* essays and 1806 periodical selections, would continue to develop, especially as he composed the first two volumes of his "Annals of Europe and America," and he would begin to more self-consciously critique even the romanticist reaction to rationalist historiography. While not Brown's own composition, "Modes of Historical Writing," which was published in December 1806, within weeks of January 1, 1807, he published his first volume of the *American Register; or, General Repository of History, Politics, and*

Science, and his "Annals of Europe and America" must be read contrapuntally or as informing Brown's history writing and vice versa. While the essay itself is not necessarily any more comprehensive or conclusive than some of the earlier pieces, Alfred Weber, Wolfgang Schäfer, and John Holmes insightfully observe that it stresses "the importance of the arrangement of historical material" in conjunction with Brown's "reader-oriented literary theory."[92] In that respect, Brown's theorizing about history and the practice of history writing reflect his constant engagement with historical processes and procedures, especially as theorized in his novel, and practiced later in his historical sketches and annals.

The essay begins by suggesting that there are three methods by which a historian can raise his writing above the level of "a mere narrative of transactions" and fully engage the subjects of laws, manners, and "civil transactions." First, a historian may interweave such material incidentally with the body of his narration (as Herodotus, Froissart, and writers of contemporary history have done); second, he may station such records in preliminary books or in appendixes, "wherever they bear only a general connection with the main body of the work" (as Robertson did in *Charles V* or Hume did in *History of England*); and, last, he may follow the scheme of Dr. Henry and allow "every distinct subject" to form a separate chapter that is continued in successive volumes.[93]

Of these approaches, the second method is the "best suited to the greater part of histories." The first, he says, provides a welcome relief to the reader from the fatiguing monotony of battles and sieges in war, [and] cabals and negotiations in peace," which so "palls on the mind in almost every historical work."[94] Passages that intermingle and illustrate laws, literature, or manners are rare and so make for historical narratives that are only occasionally interesting or effective. Not "until lately" have the "leading uses of historical knowledge" been understood, nor have Montesquieu's ideas about the "progress of the species" been readily accepted.

The third plan is the "very reverse of confusion": "every genus has its chapter, and every species its section." Here there is a problem because "facts" cannot always be cleanly compartmentalized into "civil or ecclesiastical departments, to the history of science or of art," and moreover, "there is a great danger that too rigorous an adherence to the systematic division may produce a jejune spiritless performance, a mere anatomy of history, more resembling the dry precision of an index or chronological table, than a skillful and harmonious combination of the several parts of the work." Because such a mechanical approach also causes one to spend time on material that might properly be the inquiry of another discipline and the history of language or church schisms, for example, might more profitably be taken account of in another context, the second method, then, appears to be the most desired approach. With it, narratives like Hume's and Robertson's relate a chain of events, discussing the causes and "elucidat[ing] the circumstance[s] of particular events" but do not allow it to be broken by a burdensome dissertation. Rather, "the narrative is agreeably varied and perspicuously illustrated by occasional digressions, and general views of the state of society are introduced in proper places, without tedious accuracy, or an attempt to exhaust materials of an indefinite extent."[95]

The style of history writing Brown is advocating here, in other words, is, one of a balance between general analysis of causes and effects and specific facts, illustrations, and related historical details. Brown argues that it is more effective to balance in a historical narrative accuracy and analysis with "intermingled passages" of cultural history or records. Just as he examined rationalist approaches to history, he closely examines romantic attitudes, finding in both cases that neither offered a pure way to write history. The compromise—"occasional digressions, and general views of the state of society"—is neither comprehensive nor fixed, but it does represent the approach Brown would take as he began composing his own historical annals. Among essays Brown has chosen to include at this point in his periodical, "Modes of Historical Writing" is significant because it seeks to identify a style or approach to historical representation that integrates passages that "illustrate laws, literature, or manners" more effectively, and arguably engages the attention of the reader.

As Weber, Schäfer, and Holmes remarked early on about these essays, Brown "studied the nature and interrelationship of historiography and fiction and developed his own narrative theory," and while he never managed to formulate a systematic literary theory," he approached literature from many angles.[96] However, the cumulative importance and impact of these essays, especially in Brown's capacity as an editor and critical observer of culture, lie in the way they map principles and methods that would later become evident in his writing history— his dialectical assimilation of rationalist and romantic ideas about history writing. They both trace and imply the highly self-conscious nature of his thinking about history and historiography and suggest how Brown was thinking about the dynamic tensions between late Enlightenment and romantic ideas about the past. These essays help account for Brown's eventual preference for a sympathetic inquiry into the historical record, and especially the lives and actions of obscure individuals and women, and a mode of historical representation that, despite the "uncertainty" of language and truth, balanced minimal subjectivity with the use of historical records. While Brown's earlier fictitious histories, the "Sketches of a History of Carsol" and "Sketches of a History of the Carrils and Ormes," no doubt inform his essays, they also help chart his theoretical development of historical narrative and his actual history writing.

Brown's inquiry into critique of historical impartiality and subjectivity has larger implications, however, beyond the context of these particular historiographical or cultural developments. As Philip Gould has observed, for example, Brown's negotiation of rationalist and romanticist ways of historicizing the past may also be seen relative to the "cultural negotiations of the political and psycho-logical borders between reason and the imagination, or social order and popular politics." The culture of sentiment, in other words, may not only be seen as connecting categories of "Enlightenment" and "romantic" but also as collapsing them, calling attention to the writings of the Earl of Shaftsbury as well as Scottish philosophers such as Francis Hutcheson and Adam Smith. Hutcheson's *Inquiry into the Original of Our Ideas of Beauty and Virtue; In Two Treatises* (1725) and its focus on moral philosophy and sense relative to the ancients complements Smith's thoughts on moral epistemology and language in *The Theory of Moral Sentiments* (1759). Arguably, attempts such as Brown's to sort out the overlapping characteristics of history and fiction may, in fact, be viewed relative to a history of moral thought—an emerging faculty psychology that involved unstable tensions between reason, affectation, and imagination for both readers and writers.[97]

More significant, however, Brown's interrogation of narrative meaning—from his own "Walstein's School of History" to 1806 essays like "Historical Charac-ters Are False Representations of Nature," which he selected and edited for his periodical—may also be contextualized relative to eighteenth-century inquiries into the philosophy of language. That is, if Brown's interest in comparing romance and history was not an isolated inquiry, his acute awareness of the uncertainty of linguistic representation and abiding interest in the cultural implications of narrative subjectivity also was not an isolated or insulated intellectual exercise. In 1787, for example, James Madison voiced linguistic skepticism in *The Federal-ist Papers* "Number 37, Convention's Problems in Designing Stable Government" when he discussed the inability of language to consistently and completely repre-sent meaning. Addressing the problem of composing laws that clearly communi-cate their intent, he wrote:

> But no language is so copious as to supply words and phrases for every complex idea, or so correct as not to include many equivocally denoting different ideas. Hence, it must happen that however accurately objects may be discriminated in themselves and however accurately the discrimination may be considered, the definition of them may be rendered inaccurate by the inaccuracy of the terms in which it is delivered. And this unavoidable inaccuracy of the terms must be greater or less, according to the complexity and novelty of the objects defined.

When, he continues, God himself "condescends to address mankind in their own language, his meaning, luminous as it must be, is rendered dim and doubtful by the cloudy medium through which it is communicated."[98] Even Thomas Jefferson, in explaining in his *Autobiography* (1787) how passages were struck out of "The

Declaration of Independence," would note that "the sentiments of men are known not only by what they receive, but what they reject also."[99]

Although Brown's self-consciousness about historical narrative and linguistic representation in his own material as well as in various periodical selections may be linked with developments in sentiment and shares a degree of linguistic scrutiny with Madison and Jefferson, it more importantly points to a neglected tradition of philosophical and linguistic skepticism, which can be traced back through David Hume and Lord Bolingbroke to John Locke and Pierre Bayle.[100] Locke, for instance, writes in "Of Signification of Words," his second chapter in *Essay Concerning Human Understanding* (1690): "Thus we may conceive how *Words,* which were by Nature so well adapted to that purpose, come to be made use of by Men, as *the Signs of* their *Ideas;* not by any natural connexion, that there is between particular articulate Sounds and certain *Ideas,* for then there would be but one language amongst all Men; but by a voluntary Imposition, whereby such a Word is made arbitrarily the Mark of such an *Idea.* The use then of Words, is to be sensible Marks of *Ideas;* and the *Ideas* they stand for, are their proper and immediate Signification."[101] Observations such as these about the unstable nature of discourse, historical or otherwise, anchor the eighteenth century's and even Brown's own interest in the dynamics or deep structure of discourse. Such remarks even bear a striking resemblance to how Saussure and modern philosophers of language define the arbitrary nature—and meaning—of language. Locke provides perspective, in other words, on Saussurian linguistics and philosophy when he remarks that a word does not represent an objective referent or reality; rather, language is in an ultimate sense arbitrary and created, whether it is a single utterance or an extended narrative.

Nowhere, though, is such philosophical inquiry or linguistic self-consciousness more suggestive or revealing than in the footnotes of Pierre Bayle's *Historical and Critical Dictionary* (1696), parts of which he articulated as early as 1675 in his letters. In his remarks, for example, on the difficulties of being a historian, Bayle writes, "A man must be entirely divested of passions, he must be the wise man imagined by the Stoicks, such a one as will never be found, and who exists only in the fancy. . . . These all are obstacles to the perfect impartiality of an Historian, and the medium he ought to observe." And Bayles remarks further on the writings of Carneades, a famous Grecian philosopher, that Carneades "was as vehement a defender of uncertainty as Arcesilaus" and that "this method of disputing against all things, and determining nothing openly . . . proceeded first from Socrates, and was afterwards taken up by Arcesilaus, and confirmed by Carneades, flourished till our time."[102]

If Bayle's philosophical skepticism about narrative truth and Locke's linguistic self-consciousness further historicize a neglected aspect or lineage of historiographical inquiry, Brown's interest in the imagination or "art of the historian" is central to any sort of historiographical genealogy that self-reflexively critiques rationalist or modern history writing. That is, if, as Hayden White observes, late Enlightenment history writers had a limited awareness of the "'fictive' nature of historical reflection," Brown's dialectical assimilation of rationalist and romantic ideas about history writing suggests otherwise.[103] Brown's works and editorial decisions record a highly self-conscious approach to history and historiography that has its roots in Bayle and other religious skeptics of the seventeenth century. Brown's ongoing negotiation, in other words, of the dynamic tensions between late Enlightenment and romantic ideas about representing the past place him at a unique historical and historiographical juncture. He questions rationalist or empiricist approaches to the past and, equally as important, makes astute contemporary analysis of later motivations, commercial and otherwise, associated with the production and consumption of history.

Without doubt, such a dialectic in his periodical materials was grounded in part by his experience as a struggling novelist, his reviews of contemporary histories, and his simultaneous writing of fictitious history. But, if as David Levin stated many years ago, "one might like to know just how deliberately the historians imposed the romantic formulas on the historical record," Brown's inquiry and that of others into the fictive nature of history writing not only informs us of the dynamics of late eighteenth-century and early national history writing but, I want to suggest here, has provocative implications for how we understand Enlightenment historiographical self-consciousness and our own postmodern inquiry into the constructed nature of historical history.[104]

Take, for instance, *Telling the Truth about History,* by Joyce Appleby, Lynn Hunt, and Margaret Jacob, which goes as far as any study has in the last twenty years in "addressing the controversies about objective knowledge" as it relates to democratic institutions and cultural diversity. Arguing that "skepticism and relativism about truth" is tied to the continued presence of a democratic ethos and that "a single narrative of national history" is increasingly accompanied by a "deep skepticism about whether the narrative of America's achievements comprises anything more than a self-congratulatory story masking the power of elites," Appleby, Hunt, and Jacob shake up modern and postmodern assumptions about history, narrative, and truth. While they reject the "cynicism and nihilism that has accompanied contemporary relativism," they believe that "truths about the past are possible" or at least "worth struggling for," and that an "openness to the interplay between certainty and doubt" is essential for acquiring knowledge about the past.[105]

However, their account of Enlightenment history and philosophy and the "story of improvement and then of progress" relative to the early Republic and debates about history, objectivity, and truth also repeat constructions about early national and even nineteenth-century historiography that are, in fact, inaccurate or untrue. Saying, for instance, that Hegel's German historicism "prepared the way for relativ-

ism" but that "none of the leading figures of nineteenth-century European intellectual life embraced either moral or epistemological relativism before the 1880s"
neglects the philosophical, moral, and linguistic inquiries of Vico, Pierre Bayle,
Locke, Godwin, Brown, and other seventeenth- and eighteenth-century intellectuals. Likewise, while after the American Revolution historians did generally construct a "common past which projected the national distinctiveness of the United
States into the future," it is inaccurate to say that the "fundamental assumptions"
of American "nation-building" were "not challenged for over a century." The vast
majority of nineteenth-century American historians did, indeed, provide "the
imagined community of the new nation with a history that was both patriotic and
scientific," but alternative marginalized constructions of the past, such as Brown's,
also existed.[106]

That is, just as Brown and his contemporaries' inquiry into the material and
epistemological dimensions of late eighteenth-century history writing is philosophically and culturally reflexive, so studies since the late 1980s have increasingly
focused on and recognized the cultural and constructed nature of history writing. Beyond the groundbreaking work of Hayden White, David Levin, Dominick
LaCapra, and others, publications such as Joyce Appleby, Lynn Hunt, and Margaret Jacob's *Telling the Truth about History* and Robert Berkhofer Jr.'s *Beyond the
Great Story* seek to understand the implications of the "linguistic turn" on history
writing. Berkhofer, in particular, has stated that "analyzing histories as literary
and rhetorical texts according to the ways of understanding embraced by literary
and rhetorical theory, poetics, and discourse analysis today reorients historians'
evaluations of one another's works, opens new areas of historical criticism, and
ultimately" points to the possibility of a new rhetoric and poetics of history." In
this respect, Berkhofer challenges historians to think more reflexively and openly
about the construction and meaning of historical narrative. He challenges us to
not only "surmount the dilemma of representationalism or the semiotic absolute"
but to also deal with issues of multicultural representation and anachronism as
well as new ways of representing the past.[107]

Importantly, if Brown and other figures of the Enlightenment, such as Godwin
and Bayle, were in their own ways conscious of the "uncertainty of history" and
the role of bias and subjectivity, political or otherwise, in re-presenting the past,
then our own debates about the role and impact of "postmodernism" on historical
writings are themselves ahistorical and neglect an earlier site of historiographical
inquiry. Our own dialogue, in other words, needs to address an earlier one and to
determine how the self-conscious insights of earlier intellectuals such as Brown
were supplanted by a romantic or modern tradition of history writing. If this is
true, then we would also need to reconsider when exactly scholars established
a "scientific" or "rational" approach to the past and the degree, for example, in
the 1890s—when the historical profession was gaining its footing in the United

States—to which they helped institutionalize the creed of historical objectivity. Accounts such as Dorothy Ross's, which claim that "romance" shaped the "grand narrative of history" and today's historiographical debates, need to be put in dialogue with a reassessment of how and why Brown, as well as seventeenth-century English philosophers and religious skeptics such as Pierre Bayle, are able to articulate principles of a seemingly "postmodern" historical sensibility, especially about historical objectivity and the "uncertainty" of history.[108]

Whatever one thinks about how essays in the *Literary Magazine and American Register* engage questions of historical representation, truth, and subjectivity, or "the art of the historian," as they relate to historiography or contemporary debates, the essays played a crucial role in Brown's study of historical impartiality and construction of historical method, a method that would play itself out in ways more radical or "novel" than he imagined. But before Brown took on the subject of contemporary history in his "Annals of Europe and America," he immersed himself in historical fiction, an effort that not only mirrored his periodical meditations on history and romance but would also serve as a philosophical and practical bridge between his novels and late historical writing.

Chapter Four

The Historical Sketches—and "A Government, Ecclesiastical and Civil"

If Religion be not within cognizance of Civil Government, how can its legal establishment be said to be necessary to Civil Government? What influence in fact have ecclesiastical establishments had on Civil Society? In some instances they have been seen to erect a spiritual tyranny on the ruins of Civil authority; in many instances they have seen the upholding of thrones of political tyranny; in no instances have they been seen the guardians of the liberty of the people. Rulers who wish to subvert the public liberty, may have found an established clergy convenient auxiliaries. A just government, instituted to secure and perpetuate it, needs them not.

—James Madison, "A Memorial and Remonstrance, presented to the General Assembly of the State of Virginia" (1785)

Although not published in his lifetime, Brown's "Sketches of a History of Carsol" and "Sketches of a History of the Carrils and Ormes"—some nine, maybe ten, fragments of historical fiction over 100,000 words that detail the history of an English family from ancient times to Brown's own—qualify, like Madison's and Jefferson's writings, as an exercise in secular liberalism and freethinking.[1] An objective correlative to the era's turbulent political climate, Brown's historical sketches imaginatively replicate the problem of authority—its meaning and implementation—in modern society. In doing so, they bridge his earlier novels and his later "Annals of Europe and America" by using family or "domestic history" to simulate, and as a means of understanding, tensions between ecclesiastical and civil power and the various forms of resistance to institutional and individual oppression.

That is, just as Brown made inquiries into "domestic history," or families, in his novels, so he used historical fiction to take up James Madison's question "What influence in fact have ecclesiastical establishments had on Civil Society?" and the period's struggle to understand relations between religious and civil authority at the state and federal levels and the limits of individual liberty. In this respect, the sketches clarify our understanding about the tensions between sectarian beliefs and secular thought and the roles of reason, deism, and a freethinking movement, headed by Thomas Paine, Elihu Palmer, and others, in understanding the religious and political suppositions of the early national period. And in using the history and family to work through a position on religious authority and civil government, and even a position on religion in family terms, Brown's historical fiction illuminates sociopolitical tensions during the Adams and Jeffersonian period—tensions about the boundaries between civil and religious authority that Brown was deeply interested in and that are still with us today.

Also, in drawing from the historically self-conscious, antipatriarchal elements of Brown's novels—and the philosophical inquiries of his periodical reviews and essays—and pointing to the politically ironic aspects of his later history writing, "Sketches of a History of Carsol" and "Sketches of a History of the Carrils and Ormes" serve as a unique transition between his earlier fiction writing and his later "Annals of Europe and America" in both content and form. The sketches not only address the domestic histories of families and their ecclesiastical ties to power over centuries but also foreshadow Brown's method of writing history both as a representation of the past and also as means of later remediating the present. As a historiographical move, in other words, between his earlier novel writing and self-reflexive use of memory and the increasingly heteroglossic nature of later historical annals, Brown's historical sketches, like his periodical publications, enabled him to develop his historicism and a specifically ironic posture toward history and the institutional authority structures that shape it.

Thus, the sketches provide a pivotal workbench upon which Brown could liberally and imaginatively pursue his interest in "domestic history" and inquire, at the same time, more closely into the ways familial structures inform religious and political ones and vice versa. The political stance that emerges in the sketches, especially as it concerns Brown's Quaker heritage and the boundaries between "a government, ecclesiastical and civil," positions Brown alongside Madison, Jefferson, and other freethinking intellectuals in the separation of church and state debates of the 1800s and has a direct bearing later in Brown's career on his historical writing about the Napoleonic wars, despotism, and his Godwinian focus on the use and abuse of political power.

The Republican Family, Religion, and Freethinking

As Shirley Samuels demonstrates in her study *Romances of the Republic,* domesticity in general, and women and the family in particular, comes to represent elements of national identity in the United States between 1776 and the Civil War.

The "concept of a republican family," she says, "implied neither absolute separation nor absolute joining of the state and family, but unstable relations with permeable and unfixed boundaries." In the state as well as with the family, patriarchal assumptions about authority were in place and vital to both institutions. In a novel like *Wieland,* she continues, threats to the structure of family order may also be seen as a potential crisis in terms of national identity. While few studies explore the relationship between familial and religious structures as they pertain to formation of the state, especially the early American republic, Samuels insightfully delineates how the "patriarchal system of familial and state governments was challenged when the eighteenth century began to explain power in terms of the rights of all members of a family rather than justifying it, as in medieval times, by the divine right of kings, a nearly irrefutable buttress of the patriarchal system."[2]

The institution of the family, as Brown and his peers knew it, was, in other words, undergoing fundamental change, especially as it related to the state and the manner in which republican ideals were increasingly part of a public, institutional structure rather than an infrastructure related to religious organizational principles. Brown's fascination with "domestic history" and family, in his novels and especially his historical sketches, tracks the evolution of family and society in American history precisely at the moment near the end of the eighteenth century and beginning of the nineteenth century when that particular institution was being transformed relative to changing notions of women's rights and roles, family law, and the responsibilities of public institutions in a democratic republic.

Steven Mintz agrees with Samuels on the changing composition of the family, saying that "the late eighteenth and early nineteenth centuries witnessed a fundamental redefinition of the boundaries of private and public spheres." It moved from the preindustrial supposition that a family was a "little kingdom" or hierarchical unit, under the authority of patriarchal husband or father to a situation where families began to "assign some of their functions to external institutions," for example, schooling and hospitalization. Although, along with the emergence of republican motherhood and the responsibilities of moral socialization, as families increasingly became more private and their members more individualized, they did not always serve the political order.[3] Parents failed to educate children, drunkenness and domestic abuse occurred, and violence, in both urban and rural areas, took place. The rise of democratic elements in society, then, might be characterized by anxiety and uncertainty, especially about the social and religious implications of political change.

At the same time, however, the constitution of the family was being subjected to change, so too efforts were being made to understand the implications of political change, and the ideology of republicanism, for the church. This largely gets played out in sermons and debates with, or responses to, deists such as Thomas Paine and Elihu Palmer. But in a conservative periodical called the *Churchman's*

Monthly Magazine (1804–05), a serial treatise appeared entitled "On the Church," which records views of how God constructed the Christian church and intended its governance by men. Unlike Madison's liberal view of ecclesiastical and civil government, which associates "authority" and the church with "tyranny" and seeks to separate religious from political institutions, the author of this article argues for seeing the ideologies and discourses of republican family and Christian church as one, or consolidated, saying:

> As the Holy Scriptures are the rule of our faith and practice, it is from them we are to learn the nature and constitution of the Christian Church, the form of its government, the extent of its powers, and the limits of our obedience.
>
> I. From the account which the Divine Records have given us of the *Christian Church,* it appears to be no confused multitude of men, independent of one another, but a well-formed society. This is evident from the names and allusions by which it is described. It is called a *family,* where Christ is the Master, of *whom the whole family is named.* (a) It is said to be the *city of the living God*; (b) whence Christian people are *fellow-citizens with the saints.* (c) And it is often mentioned as a *kingdom,* of which *Christ* is the king. Thus, in our *Lord's* words, *Thou art* Peter, and upon *this rock will I build my Church, and I will give unto thee the keys of the kingdom of Heaven;* (d) where the *Church* and the *Kingdom of Heaven* mean the same thing. As a *family,* a *city,* and a *kingdom,* are societies, and the Christian Church is represented by them, that must likewise be a society.[4]

For religious conservatives and others, the Bible is seen as articulating rules of governance within the Christian church, and that structure may be seen as similar to a "family" where Christ is the head. The church is also depicted as being analogous to a "city" with fellow-citizens, and "kingdom" where Christ is the "king" and his followers are his subjects. The church is, in other words, a "society" with various qualities and responsibilities.

Although the article goes on to delineate the "subordination" among church officers and the "powers which he has committed to his Church for its good government," its value here is in the way the text simultaneously outlines principles of authority and governance and registers political rhetoric usually associated with a republican ideology of "independence," "fellow-citizens," and "family."[5] It articulates the extent to which individuals other than Brown understood religious tenets or institutions in "family" and even political terms, thereby making Brown's own inquiry into "a government, ecclesiastical and civil" part of a larger debate about the principles that would inform republican governing structures at the turn of the eighteenth century. It identifies the ways one element of orthodox Christianity sought to reconcile a patriarchal and hierarchical past with republican ideals of freedom, equality, and democracy.

By contrast, while Brown's novels tend to historically document incidents of familial change, gender roles, autonomy, and even social breakdown, his historical sketches further contextualize the patriarchal organization of family relations as they relate to historical religious and political structures and the ways that authority and power are institutionalized. His historical fiction occurs exactly at the point where "the blurring of boundaries between public and private life" had begun to appear and started to initiate "the transference to public agencies of moral prerogatives and of presumed benevolence and goodwill that had grown out of kinship bonds."[6] Thus, Brown's inquiry into the relations of medieval family history and ecclesiastical government is at once an examination of the status quo—of how such structures were affected, or not, around 1804 or 1805 by late Enlightenment moral and political debates on this side of the Atlantic—and a liberal, Deistic treatise in its own right.

However, if the role and formation of the family in the early republic has been documented by scholars, the history of freethinking in early American history and culture as it relates to mainstream Protestant Christianity in post-Revolutionary politics has been neglected, especially as it pertains to Brown and their lesser-known contemporaries. As popular historian Susan Jacoby observes in *Freethinkers: A History of American Secular Thinking,* "The only freethinkers who have received their due in American history are Thomas Jefferson and James Madison, in spite of the fact that they were denigrated by their Calvinist contemporaries as atheists, heretics, and infidels."[7] Despite efforts before, during, and after the American Revolution to separate civil and religious principles and to more fully distinguish the authority of Christian churches from civil government, conservative forces repeatedly attempted to align the secularism of the Constitution with the evangelical, protestant belief that governmental authority and power came from God.

Clergymen, for instance, like the Reverend John. M. Mason, a New York Federalist, decried the "omission of God" from the Constitution. Such was the religious conservative backlash to Thomas Paine's *The Age of Reason* (1793) and related deist thinking by 1802 when Paine returned to America that, says Jacoby, "had the Constitution been written in 1797 instead of 1787, it is entirely possible that God, not 'we, the people,' would have been credited with supreme governmental authority."[8] This is an important yet ignored point about early republican political culture, and one that helps explain Brown's motivation for writing the sketches when he did, when religious conservatism, in response to Jefferson's election, began to surge.

As noted earlier, James Madison's remarks in 1785 on the influence of religion on "Civil authority" and individual liberty not only anticipate secular principles in the Constitution in 1787 but also point to the ongoing controversy as it existed on the eve of Jefferson's election. It was no coincidence, for instance, that in 1799 the *National Magazine; or, A Political, Historical, Biographical, and Literary Repository* reprinted "An Act of the Legislature of Virginia, passed December 16th, 1785, for establishing 'religious freedom,'" calling attention to presumptions both "civil and ecclesiastical" and the legislative ruling that "no man shall be compelled to frequent or support any religious worship, place, or ministry whatsoever, nor shall be enforced, restrained, molested or burdened in his body or goods."[9] After publishing Jefferson's extract from his *Notes on Virginia,* "The Different Religions Received into the State of Virginia," and its view of the "religious slavery" and "systems" American colonials supposedly sought to escape, it is no coincidence that the *National Magazine* reprinted, yet again, in May 1800 (and immediately after Jefferson's extract) "An Act, for Establishing RELIGIOUS FREEDOM, passed in the Assembly of Virginia, in the beginning of the Year 1786." Publication of Virginia's legislative act twice within the same periodical in such a short time clearly reveals a sense of political interest and urgency.[10]

Similarly, publication of a letter, from a member of the Protestant Episcopal Church, "To the PEOPLE of the UNITED STATES" in the next issue of the *National Magazine,* further illustrates the intense nature of the debate. Its focus on "the great clamor" caused by "one or two designing and ill-conditioned clergymen in Philadelphia and New-York" concerning Jefferson's remarks is underscored by the assertion that Washington and Adams, like Jefferson, affirmed in the Constitution "that no religious test shall ever be required, as qualification to any office or public trust under the United States." Moreover, the letter's repeated injunction that "the Government of the United States of America, is not *in any sense* founded on the Christian Religion" clearly seeks to address claims by opponents that a republican government needs "men of virtue" and the "aid and supportive energy of Religion."[11] Although, says Jacoby, those who framed the Constitution had chosen Virginia's law as its model, other states took decades to follow suit and sort out the separation of church from state.[12]

As political events unfolded and a print medium afforded greater accessibility, especially after 1800, when religious conservatism surged and revolutionaries like Thomas Paine and Thomas Jefferson were attacked, it is no surprise that individuals also began to argue more fervently the idea that American domestic policy and providential design were one and the same—that in America not only did God have special purpose for his New Israel but that he was the basis for governmental authority itself. Like Otis Thompson's "An Oration Urging the Necessity of Religion as the only Permanent Basis of Civil Government" (1798) in Rhode Island and the anonymous "Address to the Friends of Religion on Civil Government" (1802) in Georgia, Joseph Dennie's Federalist periodical the *Port Folio* (1801–09) is typical of the period's resistance to a secular interpretation of governmental authority.[13] Calling Paine a "drunken atheist," it exemplifies the intensifying battle, much like that which occurred after the 1990s in modern America between American secularism, or freethinking, and religious conservatives who increasingly desired minimal separation of church and state—of political access and ecclesiastical authority anchored in Baptist, Methodist, and Presbyterian theological conservatism.[14]

In his study *Religion of the American Enlightenment,* G. Adolf Koch remarks that "openly declared Unitarianism was regarded as deliberate blasphemy and a crime" and that liberal deists like Elihu Palmer frequently challenged the forces of civil and religious tyranny by calling attention to "superstition and despotism" and the ways Christianity promoted human "self-insufficiency." In America after 1800, he observes, it took "an extraordinary person" to publicly espouse a "Gospel of liberty, reason, and belief in human dignity." And while deists in Philadelphia at this time would form themselves into a society of Theophilanthropists, meaning "lovers of God and Man," and until February 19, 1803, publish the *Temple of Reason,* their cause sputtered. Still, as late as 1810, after Paine's death in 1809, publications like the *Theophilanthropist* urged resistance to the slavery of "superstition" and religious tyranny, cautioning that "America is the only country in which 'reason is left to combat error'" and that to remain so, or to enjoy any measure of happiness, it is incumbent to "think freely, and express our thoughts like freemen."[15]

Herbert M. Morais concurs, saying that "From 1789 to 1805, deism assailed more vigorously than ever before the supernatural revelation of Christianity. Paine, Volney, and Palmer, though not typical of the American movement, were nevertheless examples of the rising militancy." Even among the Federalists, Timothy Pickering engaged the latitudinarian beliefs and eventually became a Unitarian. John Adams, though, questioned Biblical miracles but also viewed Christianity as necessary for government. By the early nineteenth century, remarks Morais, it was clear that the emotionalism of the Awakening had helped put into place "a more vigorous orthodox movement designed to check the progress of deism" and that "missionary societies, religious periodicals, Bible associations and educational institutions" had become effective weapons in that era's cultural and political war.[16]

In this climate, Jeffersonians were often associated with deistic thinking and Federalists with defending orthodox beliefs, but freethinking deists could be found in both parties.[17] And while supporters of deism would eventually be drowned out by increasingly vocal evangelical forces, this is the theological and political arena—the ongoing struggle between religious orthodoxy and militant deism—Brown witnessed during the early 1800s. It is amid this flood of periodical publications and philosophically charged atmosphere of changing ideals related to the family; intensifying evangelical revivalism; emerging visions of Jeffersonian expansionism; and, across the Atlantic, Napoleonic rule, that Brown, in Quaker fashion, was independently and imaginatively reflecting on the relationships among familial, religious, and state structures—and the ramifications of an emerging republican identity influenced by the imperial impulses of divine right.

He, like Madison and others, attempted to discern what "influence in fact have ecclesiastical establishments had on Civil Society" and what impact could they have in post-Revolutionary America.

In fact, as his "Sketch of American Literature for 1807" in the *American Register; or, General Repository of History, Politics, and Science* reveals, by 1807 publications on theological matters were "very numerous." And while he thought that Paine's "Examination of the Passages in the Old Testament" would probably be unread by the "majority of the reading and enlightened world," Brown closely tracked publications on "religious subjects," noting how few religious publications there were south of the Chesapeake and how a member of the First Unitarian Society of Philadelphia published "a discourse on the right, duty, and importance of free inquiry in matters of religion."[18]

In addition to publishing the titles of numerous sermons, Brown remarks that "in a periodical work, called the Christian Magazine, published at New York, a criticism by the editor, Dr. Mason, on some controversial pieces on the subject of ecclesiastical government, brought forth, in the form of letters, addressed to Dr. Mason a publication entitled 'An Apology for Apostolic Order and its Advocates,' by the Rev. J. H. Hobart." After mentioning another publication that addresses the "government of the Church of England," Brown editorializes on the "*purpose* of all controversy" and the reasons he thinks Archdeacon William Paley "is the best."[19] After applauding his candor and praising him as "the acutest controversial writer this age has produced," Brown says that unless "previously neutral on the subject" few readers will agree with Paley "that Christians were left by their great Teacher to the guidance of their own judgment, in the choice of modes of ecclesiastical discipline and government; that this judgment is to be swayed by considerations of utility alone, and is not to be regulated by authority or former practice, and is to consult no other end than the preservation and diffusion of religious knowledge."[20] For Brown, it seems, religious controversy was still of great interest, and that while his religious belief system was perhaps not as radical as it had been in his personal letters to Joseph Bringhurst in 1795, he was still quite familiar with sectarian beliefs and the ways secular freethinking engaged orthodox Christianity. As his remarks about Paley's interpretation of human judgment indicate, Brown was prepared to imaginatively, and critically, tackle questions about institutional authority and individual agency in his historical sketches, especially as they pertained to "government, civil and ecclesiastical" and the role of the family in maintaining such structures.

Thus, similar to, and even building upon, Brown's fiction and elements in his political pamphlets on the Louisiana Purchase in 1803 and the ways those texts stage or represent historical and political contingencies, the historical sketches may be read as providing a unique vantage point on Brown's era and its struggles with religious belief and political authority. Contrary to Steven Watts's assertion that Brown's "religious radicalism" dissipated as the "youthful author" matured, these fragments and their focus on family histories may be seen as a series of free-thinking inquiries into ecclesiastical and civil government as well as interrogating, often ironically, the dynamics of power and cultural hegemony between religious institutions and the state in an era of colonial expansion, ideological instability, and empire—and fundamental change in the dynamics of the republican family.[21]

The Historical Sketches

Just as Brown's novels inquire into "domestic history" and his political pamphlets address, through the use of a fictional persona, issues of national import, so "Sketches of a History of Carsol" and "Sketches of a History of the Carrils and Ormes" imaginatively use the past to articulate a position on the excesses of political authority and power. Focusing loosely on two families and their histories, one on the island of Sardinia and the other in England, from the medieval period to Brown's own time in the early 1800s, the plot of the first set of sketches, if following the sequence of fragments as arranged by William Dunlap, Brown's biographer, examines the wealth and history of the island of Carsol and its ecclesiastical infrastructure. Using his authority, Sir Arthur Carril attempts to mediate abuses, such as the pious sale of calendars, and to initiate various reforms. The biographical backgrounds of individuals like Charles Martel are interwoven in the narrative as are historical events such as the Reformation. The history of a religious and civic tribunal under the despotic Michael Praya reveals much about the treatment, often oppressive, of ethnic groups such as Jews. As the narrative moves toward the renaissance and details how alterative systems of belief, some more political or absolute than others, emerged, Brown also outlines the rise of families led by women such as Alexandra. "Sketches of a History of Carsol" concludes with the reigns of succeeding family members and their struggles to avoid various calamities or "evils."[22]

"Sketches of a History of the Carrils and Ormes," though, opens with reference to Arthur, "earl of Orme," and his birth in 1702 and then moves quickly into his management and enhancement of particular family properties. We learn about his failed efforts to marry Miss D'Arce, the sister of a childhood friend; the history of Arthur's family; and his eventual death. Brown then chronicles the life of Ambrosius and his stature as a hero and the ways Earl Vincent sought to locate the remains of Ambrosius. The lives, intimate affairs, and illegitimate children of various in-laws follow, along with particulars on the importance of virtue. The narrative then focuses on the life of "St. Arthur Carril," the impact of the Reformation, the reputation of the Carthew family, and the writings of Beda as they detail ecclesiastical history. The illustrious life of the "countess Pamphela" and her "singular opinions on religious topics" come alive as do the histories of various churches such as that of St. Ulpha in Rome. Brown brings the story, particularly of women in the Orme family, to present-day America and relates their interactions up to 1804 with Philadelphia contemporaries before returning to family developments and politics in Europe. These sketches close with further descriptions of various families and estates, with particular emphasis on the history, papal authority, and benevolence of Pope Felix Carril and his understanding of "government."[23] The sections or sketches that appear in the *Literary Magazine and American Register* in 1805 alternatively focus on the agricultural improvement of Sir Arthur's properties as well as the ways the lives of tenants and their families are subject to financial strain and the authority and abuses of landlords.

Before claiming that the sketches enable Brown to meditate on, and work through, questions of civil and ecclesiastical authority in familial and other terms, it is necessary to address previous assessments of this material and to address questions about their composition or structure. Clarification on how these fragments were constructed provides, I believe, for a more precise understanding of their historical and political value, especially as it concerns debates in Brown's time regarding the meaning of, and the proper relationship between, civil and ecclesiastical authority in the early Republic.

William Dunlap first initiated criticism of this body of work when in his biography on Brown in 1815 he refers to the tales as "works of imagination in which historical facts are mingled and the air of history imitated."[24] Brown, he says, was not only passionate about "architectural study," but he left some parts of the sketches more complete than others. Apparently, he was also of the belief that Brown planned to write "an Utopian system of manners and government [that] was to complete the whole." While later critics would qualify his assessment of Brown's utopian aspirations, Dunlap nevertheless accurately identifies Brown's use of the historical and the imaginary in the sketches.

In the twentieth century, David Lee Clark was among the first to comment on Brown's historical sketches and asked what "was Brown's purpose in all these performances?" Was Brown "merely getting practice in the historical writing which was eventually to become his main interest?"[25] As he points out, Brown deliberately "mingled history and fiction, real persons and imaginary ones" to the point that one wants to "turn to a history text" to learn what really happened in the past. He, observes, for instance, how Catherine Tudor, the youngest daughter of Henry VII, who actually died when an infant, grows up in Brown's sketches and marries a descendent of the Ormes. This blending of real historical characters with fictional ones drives Brown's representation of two imagined families. Further, remarks Clark, "Next to religious matters, Brown was interested in economics and government."[26]

Similar to Clark, Donald Ringe also provides a somewhat general analysis of Brown's fragments, stating that "episodes follow one another with little explicit connection between them," almost as if they happened to have been printed in their existing order by chance. More so than Brown's novels, he says, the sketches focus on "political and religious matters." And although they appear conservative, Brown seems to make no judgments about the systems he examines, retaining "the mask of objective chronicler throughout."[27] Steven Watts concurs, seeing Brown's historical fiction as a reflection of his "developing ideological sensibilities" and as providing "more fertile ground for the nurture of a unified cultural vision of stability and self-restraint." Attempting to overcome the "isolation and strife that often colored the social relationships of emerging liberal capitalism," Brown "envisioned the creation of an efficient, rationalized social order melding productivity and security." He sees Brown as espousing a form of "enlightened totalitarianism," a system that "crush[ed] diversity and dissent" and "revealed the author's lingering alienation from the separations and competition of a liberalizing market society, a society that he ostensibly accepted." Aside from right reason and "religious uniformity," Brown's "reform program," says Watts, relied on the effectiveness of a "benevolent dictator"—a man who had "absolute power" and was "above all restraints."[28]

More recently, Philip Barnard has put forward a less literal interpretation and insightfully argues that Brown's fragments are more ironic and critical in nature than they are conservative or reactionary. To be sure, he says, the narratives "dramatize the multiple systems and institutional forms of political, ecclesiastical, and cultural power with which the Carrils and other rulers create and legitimate their authority." Yet, at the same time, the sketches represent various "designs" or "schemes" for authority and control, these "repressive regimes" serve as "negative counterexamples" of suppression. For example, Brown's supposed anti-Semitism in these texts, he says, is not an affirmation of Jew-bashing and repression; rather, it is a critical portrayal of Federalist scapegoating and demonization of Jews, what David Fischer calls "'the wide and fetid stream of anti-Semitism in Federalist thought' during the 1790s." In this light, Brown indeed writes a history that is satirical or ironic, like that of Edward Gibbon. What Brown provides us with, argues Barnard, is "a history whose claims are essentially critical in nature and which emphasize history's status as an interpretive and constructive medium" rather than, as with previous generations of historians, a "representative one." Thus, concludes Barnard, Brown's historical sketches and his later years record a "deep-rooted and principled antagonism toward the period's *status quo* rather than any endorsement of it."[29]

Like Barnard, I interpret Brown's historical sketches as anything but "conservative" or an embrace of "enlightened totalitarianism." Instead, similar to his earlier novels and his interest in "domestic manners," the historical sketches offer (see Bennett) the history—sometimes fictional, sometimes not—of a family through multiple generations of political, institutional, and cultural change. As Daniel Edwards Kennedy points out in his unpublished biography of Brown, "The whole work confines itself to ecclesiastical history, family history, individual history," and the sketches are not any sort of "ideal geography or Utopia" or even anti-Catholic propaganda, but rather a representation of cultural "prejudices that were historically true of the time and the people." He argues that there is really nothing in the fragments that advocates any kind of ideal republic and that except for a few occasions it is unlikely that Brown was sharing his personal beliefs.[30] While I differ with Kennedy on the question of Brown's beliefs and argue that Brown interrogates, often ironically, the dynamics of power and cultural hegemony between religious institutions and the state in an era of colonial expansion, ideological instability, and empire, I believe that Kennedy, like Barnard, is fundamentally right in seeing the sketches as inquiring into the historical intersections among religion, politics, and institutional power.

As Charles Bennett points out then, the publication in 1799 of "Thessalonica," "Walstein's School of History," and "The Death of Cicero" all show Brown's movement toward "historical fiction *per se*," a movement that led to his composition of the historical sketches.[31] Such works deal with ancient Roman history, politics, or "domestic manners" and the ways individuals such as Cicero and Pombal influenced historical events.[32] Along with scenes of Philadelphia and yellow fever in his novels, in other words, Brown had begun early on practicing historical fiction.

Beyond that, though, the sources of Brown's sketches are, as Kennedy indicates, difficult to trace. In the sketches themselves, Brown admits to using Bede's writings on England's church history *Historia ecclesiastcia gentis Anglorum* or *The Ecclesiastical History of the English People,* saying, for instance, "Beda relates, that, according to a British chronicle which he had seen" a belt "or girdle was originally given, by St. Paul, to a British chieftain, once of Artland, by the name of Arthur."[33] He also says a little bit later, "Beda professes to have drawn up this part of his prolix annals of Carthew, from certain chronicles compiled by monks of the convent, which the Eleventh Arthur founded here in 296."[34] Kennedy remarks that J. Batley's *Ecclesiastical History of the English Nation* (1723) was an English translation of Smith's Bede in 1722, but he doubts Brown had access to it. While it is difficult to document the influence of such sources, they suggest that Brown, at least in part, consulted with historical works on England's religious history.[35]

Just as Brown's historical sources are unclear, so the dates of the fragments themselves, especially as arranged by Dunlap, are less than concrete and in need of revision. Although Warner Berthoff concluded on the basis of historical dates mentioned in the material that "a major part of the 'Sketches' was composed between 1803 and 1807," with dates as early as 1803 and late as 1810, the majority of dates cohere more accurately around the years 1804 and 1805—after his publication of the Louisiana pamphlets but before his writing of the "Annals of Europe and America" in 1806.[36] Such dates, I believe, align more accurately with internal dates in the texts themselves and the reality of Brown's workload at that time as novelist, editor, pamphleteer, translator, and historian. In fact, as the following digression on the sketches, their internal dates, and their individual, familial, and ecclesiastical histories suggests, the sequence of fragments usually associated with Allen and Dunlap might more accurately be revised so that the "Sketches of a History of Carsol" is positioned after, not before, material on "Arthur, earl of Orme" in Paul Allen's *The Life of Charles Brockden Brown: A Facsimile Reproduction,* or what Dunlap calls "Sketches of the History of the Carrils and Ormes."

First, the internal date that dominates the opening sections of Allen's and Dunlap's versions of the biography is 1805 and, possibly, 1810. Within the first few pages, for instance, of "Sketches of a History of Carsol," Brown, while describing the funds of the island of Carsol, remarks, "These funds have been reduced to their present state, since 1725, that is for 85 years." He then goes on to say that the "whole amount has been (up to 1805) 125,000; which gives a principal, at only 5 percent. of 2,500,000 ducats."[37] I concur with Kennedy's observation that the "eighty-five years 'since 1725' (total 1810) is very likely an error for eighty," since Brown would have referenced 1810 as the present a few sentences later; instead, he refers to "1805," which would be consistent with other references in this part of the text.[38]

For instance, when relating the political conditions of the island during the times of Charles Martel and the succeeding family line, Brown remarks, "By the marriage of this heiress to Arthur Carrol, a third son of Carrol, lord of Halloway, and Lodowick, in England, a new line was established. For 125 years, that is from, 1680 to 1805, the Island has been governed by this Arthur and his son." The internal dating, in other words, of what Dunlap calls the "Sketches of a History of Carsol" leans strongly toward 1805 as the period of time in which Brown, like his persona in the sketches, was most likely making a conscious "contrast" of "the past" to "the present."[39] Such internal dating, then, suggests a closer alignment between the first part of the sketches and the three, possibly four, fragments that were published in the *Literary Magazine and American Register* beginning in February 1805 with "A Specimen of Agricultural Improvement" and continuing through December of that year, one year before Brown published the first two volumes of his massive *American Register; or, General Repository of History, Politics, and Science.*

The question then becomes "What kinds of internal dating are present in the fragments that largely consist of the 'Sketches of the History of the Carrils and Ormes'?" Aside from the initial reference to when Arthur was born, in 1702, dates dealing with the past are mostly medieval or having to do with eighteenth-century family marriages, deaths, and alliances until about midway through the fragments, when the story focuses on the home and "domestic privacy" of lifestyle of Lady Mary Carril shortly before a member of her family moved into the house in "the year 1786." The history of the "family alliance" between the "Ormes and Martils" is yet another instance where the present is alluded to in the text. "Philibert and Bertrand," two sons, "were at first friendly to the [French] revolution of 1788, but their sentiments soon changed with events." Brown's tale continues: "They remained however, in France, as long as there was safety in a quiet and neutral department. At length they narrowly escaped judicial murder under Robespierre, and took refuge in England, where they still remained (in 1803.) They are between forty-nine and fifty years of age." This type of internal historical dating, here to "1803," continues later in the text when Mrs. Boyle and her children embark for America, and specifically Philadelphia, and the reader learns about their experiences as members of the Orme family.[40]

Becoming "acquainted with the history of their family," we learn, was one of the objects of Arthur and Herbert, the Ormes from Sudley, especially when Herbert arrived in Philadelphia and met Elizabeth, his cousin. After their marriage and, later, the marriage of her sister, Mary, and Sale in September 1798, we learn that Sale dies on his way to the West Indies in August 1799 and that Lady Jane also dies in August 1799 and leaves her estate to the two granddaughters. The grandmother's will contains various conditions, one of which is that Mary should never marry Coulthurst, a previous lover. The plot moves closer to the present when we learn of Mary's return to England, at the request of the ninety-five-year-old earl of Orme, and Arthur's attempts to woo her. His rejection by Mary and the deferment of her reunion with Coulthurst in "the year 1804" because of the earl's interest in seeing the "perpetuation of his race by the marriage of his two nephews with his two nieces" is followed by the earl's death. The fragment ends with the "impediment" of the earl gone, and with Coulthurst leaving in "August 1804 for England." After a three-month voyage, he arrives in London on "the 10th of December 1804, exactly seven years and two months after the first interview of Coulthurst and Mary in 1797."[41]

This kind of familial and genealogical dating is common throughout Brown's sketches, and the repeated reference to the dates in the late 1790s and particularly 1804 in the "Sketches of the History of the Carrils and Ormes" is significant because it suggests that at least a portion of these sketches were composed around dates leading up to 1804. Such internal dating, when placed alongside other parts of the sketches, suggests that what has come to be known as "Sketches of the History of the Carrils and Ormes" might reasonably have been composed before "Sketches of a History of Carsol" and the fragments that appear in the *Literary Magazine and American Register* in 1805. I assess the sketches in light of this revised chronology and its implications for understanding Brown's rendering of individual, familial, and ecclesiastical histories as well as the subject of historical representation itself and argue that even as Brown wrestled with the differences and similarities between history and romance, and the uncertainty at times of knowing historical truth, he worked through a position on religious authority and civil liberty by thinking about it in familial terms.

First, Brown's use of individual histories—some real, some not—is evident in most of the fragments, as can be seen, for instance, in "Sketches of the History of the Carrils and Ormes." As mentioned earlier, the fragment begins with the story of "Arthur, earl of Orme, eldest son of earl Vincent, and Miss Tenbrook" and then launches into his family history. The "history of Ambresbury," a leader or king of the South Britons between the years 460 and 508 is woven into the story and traced, as is that of Sir William D'Acre, who inherits the Isle of Vackland, which was originally granted to Sir Egbert D'Acre by Henry V.[42] St. Arthur Carril is mentioned several times, first in reference to his death in 1711 and King Arthur of England, and then relative to various historical jubilees and succeeding Arthurs. St. Ulpha emerges both as a historical personage and an "abbey" or "nunnery" "founded by the earl of Orme in the tenth of Henry IV." Biographical background on "Catharine, daughter of Henry VII," born in 1498, and Catharine Tudor Carril, "countess of Orme," born in 1545, is presented, as are facts about assassination attempts on the life of Henry VIII.[43] While some individual histories contain more detail than others, one that stands out is that of Catharine Tudor, especially in the way it recalls Brown's emphasis in his novels on the domestic history and lives of women.

Catharine Tudor's story is prefaced by remarks about the first Catharine, who became a widow in 1547 and whose husband offended royalty because he dissented from the king's "theological opinions." Catharine Tudor herself, we learn, entertained religious visions and "plunged deeply into the theological studies and controversies of her times," resulting in a "special revelation" that prompted her to build a temple in the name of St. Rhoda. Her marriage to the earl of Orme did not preclude her from initiating a convent of women devoted to the worship of St. Rhoda. Described as a "wise and beneficent mistress" by her peers, she promoted a theological doctrine that reverenced God and Jesus Christ but had "no stated forms of worship"—no "observances, festivals, prayers, dresses and gestures" because they were seen as "superfluous and absurd." Such was her female leadership in regard to religious belief that, says Brown, "the protestant would be nearly as little pleased as the Catholic."[44] The fragment concludes with the architectural description of a home and a return to the history of Arthur Carril.

In many ways, Tudor's immersion in the theological "controversies of her times" may recall Brown's own attention to issues of theology and "religious controversy" in his "Sketch of American Literature for 1807." Her minimalist doctrine of worship recalls elements of deist or individual belief and the Unitarian Church. Likewise, just as the convent provides a familial setting for religious community and worship, so elsewhere in the fragments Lady Mary Carril frequents a chapel of sorts for worship that also houses a portrait of her late husband, raising questions about the precise nature or objects of worship.[45] These and other biographies in the fragments offer, then, alternative ways to understand metaphors about the church being a family, with Christ as its head, and the historical relations between church and family history, thereby suggesting that "religion" or belief can mean different things to different people at different times—and that institutional religion frequently also operates on an individual level. It is not always monolithic, formally organized, or even conducted by men; it often partakes of private meditations and different expressions of spiritual subjectivity.[46]

Similar to how Brown represents "family" histories in his novels, the histories and genealogies, then, of different families, such as the Alexandrines, are central to understanding what the sketches seek to accomplish in and of themselves and in relation to one another. Beginning with the story of Arthur, earl of Orme, marriage is the primary means of uniting "the nobelist families of England." The succeeding reigns of families and lineages in England, such as that of Constantius Chlorus, are explained in terms of how family alliances were "founded on sympathy of language, religion and manners, and on voluntary facts and treaties" and connected to broader historical ties between the Britons and the Saxons during the medieval period.[47] Arthur Carril, for instance, is later described as being "lineally descended from Arthur, a chief of Cambrian extraction, whose family had been in immemorial possession of these lordships, previous to the Norman invasion, and who possessed them at that period."[48] And just as the histories of families are affected by property, politics, and the lives of various family members, so the history of a particular period is mirrored by family histories, especially in "Sketches of the History of the Carrils and Ormes."

That is, beyond the way the history of the Martel family, and Philibert and Bertrand, is depicted during the time of the French Revolution, and the Orme family history locates itself relative to events in post-Revolutionary Philadelphia, one finds a conscious effort in the sketches to record family history alongside period events—or an explanation, in other words, of how Brown's fictitious historians informed his later historical writing. For example, we learn that in 1723 Simon Tuild, the dean of St. Ulpha, "was employed to examine and arrange all the monuments extant of this family, and to compile an history of the house of Carril." As part of his efforts to assemble a "copious history," he visited libraries and identified numerous materials. He even includes information from a 1480 copy of the "Rhodian chronicle" and events that are "detailed in the history." Brown's narrator reports that "a chronicle still extant, of the same age with the last and only copy of the 'Liber Rhodeanus,' relates the history of the convent, which the historian pretends to have collected from the contents of the conventical library at the time." Such is the importance of the domestic history of the Carrils that "historians of the island" identify Ulpha as "the mother of a lineage of ten princes" and, we are told, "no family has made a more conspicuous and illustrious figure in British annals than this." Finally, at the end of one fragment Brown's narrator flatly states that "the history of Brittany, during this period of 150 years, forms a part of the history of the Carril family," and such was the harmony between different branches of the family that intermarrying frequently took place.[49]

If individual histories are often related in connection with the bloodlines of family royalty or in the context of Roman Catholic Church history, it seems that family histories also serve—as a form of "domestic history" and manners—to highlight social ties and broader cultural, political, and religious histories. However, if internal dates and the revised sequence of the fragments are accurate, it is worth returning to the lives and authority of Pope Felix as well as Michael Praya and Alexandria insofar as Brown seems to tie such histories to contemporary debates about ecclesiastical history—and civil governance. In other words, if by 1800, when Jefferson was elected president of the United States, the country, or at least certain states, was still wrestling with secular provisions of the Constitution, particularly its "prohibition of religious tests."[50] As in his novels, here Brown's fictional engagement with, and historical representation of, issues of religious authoritarianism, individual liberty, and political equality mirrored a quite real, and historically intense, political and social correlative.

The history, for instance, of Pope Felix begins with remarks that St. Ulpha, "the reputed mother of Arthur, and, of consequence, the lineal and direct ancestor of the Carril family," provided revelations and guided him in his understanding. With the exception of his falling in love with his sister's friend, his decision to become a bishop, his resistance to changes proposed by Henry VIII, his acceptance of the primacy, his move to Italy, and his resignation as pope were all connected to her "special commands." While many of his decisions were based on religious belief, he also was "governed by a disinterested regard to justice," as in the case of his efforts to resist the machinations of Charles and Philip. His rise from cardinal to pope was supported by the people of Rome and Italy, who admired his "devotion and charity." Trusting to "the protection of providence," he ignored plots to assassinate or poison him, yet, at the same time, trusted his own understanding when serving as governor of Avignon.[51]

During his papacy, Felix strenuously tried to avoid corrupting forces, "embraced no party," took into consideration "the happiness of his people," and sought to establish "order, peace, and prosperity," all in an effort to rule equitably and maintain harmony. And while it was within his power to acquire islands from Spain and Genoa and to expand the "ecclesiastical empire" of Rome, he seems to have developed, relative to his peers, dissenting ideas about the relationship between civic and religious responsibilities. Brown's narrator remarks on this:

> Though the subject was generally viewed in this light, the pontiff reasoned in a very different manner. He considered the union of civil and ecclesiastical functions in the same purpose as a prolific source of corruption and depravity, and as the principal abuse as well as the cause of almost all the abuses with which the court of Rome had been charged. The character and

conduct of the pontiffs had been exposed to ridicule and detestation, by their indecent lust after riches and power, by their ambition and perfidy in acquiring, and their prodigality and weakness in dismembering the lands and territories of their neighbors.

Similar to debates during Brown's and Jefferson's time about empire, authority, and the separation of church and state powers in the early Republic, Brown's historical sketches reenact real-life disagreement about the meaning and function of ecclesiastical and civil power in government and how to balance those competing interests in light of challenges to the Constitution during the early national period. Conscious of the "evils and corruptions inseparable from the civil government of popes" and the "anarchy and misery" of the past as well as the need for his own "safety," Pope Felix keeps such sentiments to himself, indicating that he is quite conscious that his ideas about the "propriety of severing the temporal and spiritual power of the popes" are radical and "would have been branded as the most odious heresy."[52]

The fragment closes with Pope Felix's efforts to establish a kingdom as "distinct as possible" from others, especially in regard to political and ecclesiastical matters. He grants the islands "civil independence" but pursues his "favorite dream" since boyhood—that of seeing "a government, ecclesiastical and civil, perfectly constituted and perfectly administered." He combines his papal powers and, with the help of his nephew, possession of the islands to establish a government that was "only inferior to that which the deity himself possessed." While he renounces certain claims to ecclesiastical power, he also institutes a mode of religious belief and practices consistent with his beliefs in St. Ulpha. As a result, the customs, beliefs, and opinions of the people he rules become subject to his "absolute control, as supreme pontiff," and Felix, by both "virtue of his office" and "special revelation," becomes, in the mode of Wieland, the "messenger and interpreter of Heaven, and his decrees [are] submitted to as the express will of God."[53]

Although, then, Felix believed at one point that the "union of civil and ecclesiastical functions in the same purpose" can become a prolific source of corruption and depravity, his ecclesiastical ambitions slip into political ones, and his "pontifical authority" becomes equated with "divine authority."[54] The resultant institution is one in which political and social "order" is determined by prescribed conduct and the ability of ecclesiastical powers to enforce duties in relation to God or fellow citizens in the same way obedience to civil laws is enforced. Ironically or not, such an arrangement recalls concerns that James Madison, Thomas Jefferson, and others had about the "influence" of ecclesiastical establishments on civil society, and the ways such "spiritual tyranny" can easily impose itself on civil government and individual liberties. Specifically, it recalls the manner in which "established clergy" have compromised "public liberty" rather than protect it from ecclesiastical or political interests. Brown's analysis of "a government, ecclesiastical and civil"—and the downside of a purely religious state apparatus or form of governance in the mode today of Iran's Supreme Ruler—becomes even more explicit in his "Sketches of a History of Carsol," in which he probes, often ironically, relations among ecclesiastical authority, patriarchic power, and paranoia.

Like Dan Brown's best-selling novel *The Da Vinci Code* (2003) and its pseudo-historical focus on the intrigues and power structures of the Catholic church, Brown's inquiry into the island of Carsol's "Senatus Clericus" and the legislative and ecclesiastical authority of its bishops, archbishops, and clergy appears to be critical of organized religion in general and Roman Catholicism in particular. This becomes apparent at the beginning of the sketches, when Brown's speaker remarks that at the "accession of the Carrils" the council's office and appointments were permanent and that "as in all ecclesiastical appointments, the court of Rome had nothing but revenue and influence in view." Likewise, he remarks, the organization of "convents" was also subject to "venality, tyranny and negligence," causing the "administration of justice" to be undermined and "poverty, depopulation and depravity" to flourish.[55]

The scheme, by pontiffs, however, to sell papal calendars to the island's peasant families is more oblique. A combination of distributors and a revenue system, the distribution of calendars could, in the right hands, be an effective means of communicating with and enlightening a populace, and Arthur seems to endorse it, at least in principle. At the same time, one can also interpret Arthur's actions as taking advantage of religious superstition and ignorance, especially in the way each member was socialized to believe it was his "religious duty to purchase copy of this work for each member of his family."[56] The fact that Arthur eventually opposes such abuses seems to suggest that his appropriation of the calendar distribution system may have been the result of good intentions but that it also had some negative consequences or results. One might also argue, however, that in the wrong hands the calendar system distributes and reinforces ignorance but in the right hands it could promote enlightenment.

The Reformation two centuries before, we are told, did not leave Carsol "entirely unmolested." Brown's narrator remarks, ironically, "In the year 1750, some enthusiasts of the neighboring continent conceived themselves impelled by a divine command, to visit and convert Carsol. They were men naturally bold, enterprising and inflexible, and religious zeal had added new force to all these qualities. A bible, carefully concealed in their baggage, was the only weapon of mediated warfare against the peace of the Island." Brown describes the ensuing plot as a kind of spiritual adventurism, led by Hecta, that infected the population before the government became aware of its impact. The result was a "religious war," with the prince, nobles, and clergy on the one side and the converts of Hecta on the other, and the loss of life adding up to "30,000" people. After suppressing these heretical ideas and their propagation, a tribunal was formed that resembled the "odious inquisition" and aimed at outlawing "heresy."[57]

The establishment of a tribunal or "Convicata" by Michael Praya in response to the propagation of alternative religious views earns some of Brown's most distrustful remarks. Saying that the tribunal had the power to arrest, try, and punish all persons "charged with, or suspected of heresy" and that their proceedings "were secret, and their decisions liable to no appeal or controul, from any other jurisdiction, ecclesiastical or civil," Brown compares its excesses to the piety, secrecy, and abuses of the Jesuits.[58] This is similar, in other words, to his observations about religious oppression and Christianity in his 1795 letter to Joseph Bringhurst, where he observes that Christianity has been "pernicious to mankind" and "created war and engendered hatred," and similar to his hard-hitting critique in *Edgar Huntly* of the sordid monks that "persecute" Weymouth, Brown describes a religious police state where some forty "inspectors" were commissioned to report "any thing that favoured heresy or innovation" so that the appropriate punishment could be given.[59] Although torture was not part of the process of the tribunal, one of the maxims of the Convicata was that it was "better for a score of innocent persons to suffer than one guilty escape." Thus, death was routine, and when there was doubt about a person's guilt or innocence, the accused still "lost his life," not as one who merited punishment, but, says Brown ironically, as a "victim offered at the shrine of the public welfare."[60]

Praya, the "supreme judge" of the tribunal, resided in Toro Letza with a "family of ten monks, and the officers of his tribunal," and distinguished himself amidst this religious intolerance and persecution by keeping a close eye on its agents. Such was his authority, secrecy, and power that people, out of fear, held him in fearful reverence for a period of fifty-seven years. Along with being "impregnable" by those with political "interests or passions," Praya, remarks Brown, established a kind of political theocracy and system of religious control:

> He was looked up to as one possessing preternatural powers, and whose decrees were specially dictated by heaven. The lofty and inaccessible walls of his residence, the invisible majesty in which he lived, the utter oblivion which involved the fate of every one who entered these gates, the mysterious and unseen, yet irresistible energy with which every corner of the island, every town and village, and almost every family, were occasionally visited by his power, combined to impress the popular imagination, with the most awful dread, both of the tribunal and of him whose genius and authority animated it.
>
> One is struck with astonishment at beholding so omniscient a scrutiny, so elaborate a system, constructed and directed to no other end than to detect and punish imaginary crimes, opinions relative to points, trifling and ridiculous, or absurd and contradictory. What efficacy would a system like this possess, if directed against the genuine crimes by which human society is afflicted, if this potent engine had been turned against the innumerable

curses of fraud and violence? How could they have hoped to escape detection and vengeance? Place a king at the head of such a tribunal, and make this implicated agency subservient to maintenance of public order, and of royal authority, what despotism can be imagined more absolute and irresistible.

Although Brown's narrator sees some efficacy or positive consequences in having a police "system" that is effective in dealing with "genuine crimes" having to do with fraud and violence and, later, the existence of slavery, Praya's obsessive perfection of this penal system as it concerns religious belief and "points trifling and ridiculous, or absurd" is clearly excessive. A classic illustration of Foucault's Panopticon, where the illusion of power is just as effective and important as its actual implementation, Praya's tribunal and apparatus of control feeds on fear and is seen as the equivalent of "despotism." In this way, says Brown, society as a whole put "their lives" into "the hands of one man," living in dread, and under the iron hand, of "a power, thus apparently without limits."[61]

It is not coincidental that in this part of the sketches Brown also interrogates Praya's attempts at ethnic cleansing, specifically the "banishment of Jews and infidels." "The Jews," remarks Brown's narrator, "had hitherto been merely tolerated at Carsol," had "not been allowed to hold real property," were denied "every municipial privilege," and were subject to various forms of "degradation." Further, he writes, "The consequences of this degradation betrayed itself in the squalidness of their appearance, the knavery of their conduct, and the vileness of their pursuits." Influenced by "an imaginary mandate from heaven," Praya eventually sends them into exile, albeit with a sense of guilt and an effort to make for the "least possible hardship of suffering."[62]

By comparison, Brown's representation of Carsol's slave economy also speaks, with an ironic undertone, to matters of race and ethnicity, power, and control. While "sincere conversion to the Christian faith" often justified redemption or the ability to gain one's freedom at a certain age, slaves were usually "brought to market at Carsol, and sold indiscriminately." Male children raised in Christianity could be set free as young adults; females "easily adopted the religion of their masters." "Every master," writes Brown, "enjoyed, by law, unlimited power over his slave, and might even kill him with impunity." Thus, "chains, stripes, scanty fare, rags and excessive labour, was commonly the lot of this unhappy race."[63]

This type of "abuse" continued until a slave by the name of Achmet Pruli led an insurrection. Although the rebellion is eventually extinguished, Brown slips out of his narrative voice and remarks at this point on the master/slave dynamic as it relates to race, gender, and sexual control; his narrative here is as historically accurate and penetrating as any antislavery or abolitionist discourse of the period. On buying, selling, and using humans like material objects, a historical truth bleeds through Brown's fiction:

The morality current in Carsol, allowed the master to enact what services he pleased from his slave. The latter lived for no end but the gratification of the former, and provided no cruelty was wantonly employed, there was no bounds to the reasonable demands of the lord, but such as mere physical capacities established. The female slave was considered as performing her mere duty, in gratifying her master's appetites, and in bringing forth and nourishing those who will belong to him by the double title of father and master. Intercourse with the slave, was not considered as interfering with the rights of matrimony. No moral, nor ecclesiastical, nor legal cognizance was taken of such transactions.

While Brown goes on to say that the Greeks of Turkish provinces were also treated like "oxen and sheep" and that at the slave market at Carsol "a captive of one nation was generally disposed of on the same terms as one of the other," the conditions he describes are a manifestation of the ultimate despotism and tyranny on the island. Similar to Praya's authoritarian control with religious belief, the system of slavery in place in Carsol, where people of different races are bought and sold like property, is not only oppressive but ultimately sanctioned by political and religious institutions—and the Bible—and "inhuman."[64] Brown's representation, of course, of female slaves and sexual "duty" also resembled the reality of master/ slave relations in the early Republic, whether it be at Jefferson's Monticello or other parts of the American South.

Brown's willingness here to imaginatively interrogate, in the same breath, church hierarchies and the social apparatus of slavery as it existed in his day is an important but often misread element of his later career and recalls his earlier liberal, dissenting impulses as a Quaker and his deistic philosophical principles as a child of the Enlightenment.[65] Decades before Herman Melville serially published "Benito Cereno" in *Putnam's Monthly* (1855), Brown imaginatively tackles the question of biblical morality and social authority as they relate to slavery and human oppression and finds both culture bound, inhumane, and oppressive. And like James Madison and the ways his "Memorial" seeks to separate civil and religious authority and to preserve "pubic liberty" from religious intolerance and the tyranny of a few, Brown also registers concerns about religious authoritarianism and despotic power systems. Thus, just as Madison believed that "ecclesiastical establishments" have been known to "erect a spiritual tyranny on the ruins of Civil authority" and that an "established clergy," under the right circumstances, had the capacity to "subvert the public liberty," so Brown had concerns about the existence of a "government ecclesiastical and civil" and used his historical sketches to play out its political and social ramifications.

Nowhere, though, are Brown's concerns (and those of other secular thinkers of the 1790s and early 1800s) about the history of religious authority and its influence on American governance and politics articulated more clearly than in an exchange of letters between Thomas Jefferson and John Adams in May 1817, in which Jefferson confides to Adams that he was pleased that the Congregationalist Church in Connecticut—a "den of the priesthood"—had finally "broken up" and that a "protestant popedom is no longer to disgrace American history and character." Further, Jefferson remarks that he had thought of Connecticut and Massachusetts as "the last retreat of Monkish darkness, bigotry, and abhorrence of those advances of the mind which had carried the other states a century ahead of them." These states, he laments, "still seemed to be exactly where their forefathers were . . . and to consider, as dangerous *heresies*, all *innovations* good or bad."[66] Brown anticipates Jefferson's remark and even the wry irony of Herman Melville, writing in his sketch of the Convicata, that to be found guilty by agents of the tribunal of "any thing that favoured heresy or innovation" was, indeed, to become a "victim offered at the shrine of the public welfare."[67]

Although Jefferson goes on to support the "doctrines of philanthropism, and deism taught us by Jesus," Adams's response on May 18, 1817, is one of shock and further dismay:

> Oh! Lord! Do you think that a Protestant Popedom is annihilated in America? Do you recollect, or have you ever attended to the ecclesiastical Strifes in Maryland Pensilvania, New York, and every part of New England? What a mercy it is that these People cannot whip and crop, and pillory and roast, *as yet* in the U.S.! If they could they would.
>
> Do you know that The General of the Jesuits and consequently all his Host have their Eyes on this Country? Do you know that the Church of England is employing more means and more Art, to propagate their demi-popery among Us, than ever?[68]

Brown, like Madison, Jefferson, Adams, and other socially progressive thinkers of the Enlightenment, was attuned to historical and contemporary efforts by religious clergy of various denominations to embed the laws of God in American government. If, as Adams emphasizes, religious conservatives aggressively sought to infuse theocratic principles and practices into a foundling American government, Brown and other more secular thinkers responded, sometimes in public and sometimes not. Indeed, as Philip Barnard crucially observes, in a letter to John Quincy Adams on November 30, 1802, Thomas Boylston Adams described Brown as (quoting Adams) "a *small*, sly Deist, a disguised, but determined Jacobin, a sort of Sammy Harison [*sic*] Smith in 'shape and size the same.'" "Scornfully likening Brown," says Barnard, "to Samuel Harrison Smith, editor of the *National Intelligencer*, official organ of the Jefferson administration, Adams's remarks suggest that informed conservative contemporaries of Brown viewed him as anything but one of their own."[69]

On the point of theocratic rule, Praya, under an "imaginary mandate from heaven," also discriminates against and eventually banishes Jews because St. Vesta "could not suffer her particular precincts to be polluted by that accursed race," but such oppression and despotism are contrasted later in the sketches with the "prosperous reign" of Alexandra from 1597 to 1631, who compares favorably with Queen Mary of Scotland and Queen Elizabeth of England and is seen as someone "celestial and divine." She is described as perfectly combining "ecclesiastical supremacy" and "civil authority" and having such "extraordinary felicity" that her being was clearly under "the particular care of Heaven." Similar to her predecessors, though, she is assailed by different pretenders and schemes, and eventually her reign of "benevolence and justice" gives way to successors whose rule is not as successful and leads, finally, to the island's demise.[70]

The sketches, therefore, provide a potent but neglected cocktail of discourses on ecclesiastical and civil government, systems of control and their political rationale, and the implications and immorality of tyranny and oppression. However one classifies the sketches, though, two points are worth emphasizing. First, as an extension of his novels and their historical elements, "Sketches of a History of the Carrils and Ormes" and "Sketches of a History of Carsol" focus on the history and branches of an English family from the medieval era to Brown's present. If the historical sketches represent Brown's acceptance of history as Johann Gottfried Herder understood it—the attempt to trace the progress of a people from the medieval past to the present—to revalue the "individual" in society, and especially the context of a family polity, as an agent of historical change, they are his most ambitious and most expansive fictional representation of his favorite topic—"domestic history" and manners.[71] Unlike his novels, where representation of a family such as the Wielands or the Mervyns and its relevance to the plot is limited both in time and space, here Brown combines family histories and traces family origins and ancestors through several generations in geographically diverse space. He imaginatively commingles historical and fictional personages over a period of centuries in an attempt to depict relationships between ecclesiastical and civil authority—and the rising importance of individual agency.

Second, just as Brown's fragments are mimetic, so, at the same time, they seek, as Barnard points out, to perform a political intervention in the cultural and religious status quo of the present. They are much more than a representation of the past to the extent that they dialogically enter contemporary debates about religion, race, and political power. For this reason, Brown's sketches, like his Louisiana political pamphlets, often embed irony and cultural critique. While the sketches may at times appear conservative, such statements need to be reconciled with Brown's interrogation of European "superstition" and "oppression" elsewhere in his writing. To regard the sketches as some kind of "totalitarian" treatise and to view them as representative of Brown's latent conservatism is to simply or deliberately misread them and ignore the larger context of Brown's later thinking and writing, especially cultural debates about ecclesiastical and civil authority in government, and the views he expressed in his "Annals of Europe and America."

Thus, if Brown's novels and essays informed his fictitious histories and allowed him to test ideas, his "historical sketches" form a historiographical bridge between his novels and his actual history writing. And what seems to be the major phase of his historical fiction, 1804–05, argues for his having moved beyond a simple encyclopedic or fileopietistic stage of historiography and embracing a more sympathetic or revolutionary conception of history. When properly understood in the context of religious and liberal, freethinking political debates, Brown's interrogation of the political and religious status quo vis-à-vis an imaginative historical rendering of European "superstition," "corruption," and "oppression" may be seen as radical—and resisting in principle (and later, in practice) assumptions concerning a teleological construction of history.

Likewise, the form of his historical novel may be seen as marking developing ideas of history and history writing—ideas that crystallize in his 1806 periodical editing and authorship, suggesting that just as Brown's numerous periodical reviews, essays, and extracts may be viewed as a philosophical laboratory for inquiring into the similarities and differences between history and romance, so his historical fiction may also be understood as a practical extension of these materials—as readying Brown to write his annals proper. Indeed, if it seems appropriate to view his interest in "domestic history" and historical fiction as preparation for the actual writing of history, then his political theorizing and use of interrogation and irony in the historical sketches provide a unique context for understanding his "Annals of Europe and America" and the emergence of a historical voice that provides a candid, and sometimes searing, indictment of European and, importantly, American pretensions of empire and power. Brown's radicalism becomes even more overt when he refuses to assign Divine Providence a role in the annals of American or any history, focusing instead, like his novels, on the actions and motives of institutions and individuals.

Brown may not have been ready by 1803 to be a historian who combined the "accuracy and minuteness" of Trumbull with the "rhetoric and judgment" of Robertson, but there is no denying that by 1806 his historical fiction, however fragmented, along with his periodical editing and writing, enabled him to sharpen his understanding about the causes and effects of history and to finally begin his writing and serial publication of the "Annals of Europe and America."

Chapter Five

Empire and the "Annals of Europe"

The years between 1775 and 1815 constitute a crucial episode in the evolutionary history of Europe and America. Between the start of the American Revolution, with the first armed clashes between British regulars and American militiamen at Concord and Lexington, and the closing act of the French Revolution, with the eclipse of Napoleon's dreams of pan-European glory on the battlefield of Waterloo, America and Europe witnessed the rise and fall of radicalism, which left virtually no aspect of public and private life untouched. While the American colonies managed to wrench themselves away from their colonial parent, and while France careered down the stormy rapids of its own Revolution, Great Britain went through the turbulent process of redefining itself vis-à-vis both these emerging nations, and the world at large.

—W. M. Verhoeven and Beth Dolan Kauntz, *Revolutions and Watersheds: Transatlantic Dialogues 1775–1815* (1999)

If Brown's historical sketches and various periodical reviews, philosophical essays, and extracts prepared him for the practical aspects of history writing, his serial publication of the "Annals of Europe and America" in the *American Register; or, General Repository of History, Politics, and Science* (1807–09) was a natural extension of his theoretical forays into history. His coverage of the Napoleonic Wars and British colonization efforts in the "Annals of Europe" and his practice of appending foreign state papers in the *American Register* testify to transnational events in Europe after the French Revolution and introduced his readers to a wide variety of events having to do with the expansion of European empires generally—and revolution, war, nationalism, and reform specifically.[1] Such activities would allow him to see, for instance, that the United States was not the only country to claim divine sanction as part of claims for territorial expansion and that other countries, France in particular, also invoked a "redeemer nation" rationale.[2] Brown's encounter with this kind of rhetoric in various public and private documents relating to the Napoleonic Wars would ultimately contribute, as I contend later, to an altered sense of filiopietistic history writing and American exceptionalism.

In this chapter, I specifically analyze how Brown's Quaker upbringing prepared him in his "Annals of Europe" to analyze the chaotic political, military, and social winds of post-Revolutionary Europe, specifically the aftermath of the French Revolution, Napoleonic rule in Europe; the spread of the British Empire in South America and India; Napoleon's march through the Mediterranean and Eastern Europe in countries like Turkey and Prussia; and, finally, English aggression against Copenhagen and Denmark and the tragedy of Napoleonic pillage in Portugal. Despite his efforts toward, and reflections on, not indulging in historical bias, Brown's historical narrative brings a specifically American perspective to events unfolding in Europe, one not commonly found in the early Republic except in newspapers. Using postcolonial theory, from Edward Said to more recent scholars, I argue that Brown's systematic analysis of Napoleon's military campaigns and English military aggression enabled him to better understand the symbiotic relationship between political and economic self-interest, especially as it related to military imperialism. Moreover, as Brown's historical consciousness evolved relative to his analysis of the events and ideologies of early nineteenth-century European imperialism, colonialism, nationalism, and how colonial assumptions about race and gender construct and subjugate the Other, his history writing itself also changed. He simultaneously began to articulate, sometimes in the form of footnotes, questions about historical evidence, and he began to articulate a resistance to political injustice—a sympathy for oppressed races that recalls his earlier philosophical radicalism.

Napoleonic Rule in Europe

To begin, on October 31, 1807, Joseph Dennie published in his *Port Folio* a review of Brown's *American Register* in general and the "Annals of Europe and America" in particular. The review remarks how Brown's publication is similar to "Dodsley's Annual Register, and has long been wanted in this country" as a means of preserving all the "valuable historical, state, and miscellaneous papers."[3] The annals, the review continues, is "entirely original," "modeled after Burke's historical introductions" and "written with great ability, and in a temper of the utmost moderation."[4] And in the February 27, 1808, issue of the *Port Folio*, the reviewer states that the annals contain "an accurate and impartial history of domestick and foreign politicks" and that if we mistake not, Mr. B. is an admirer of the genius and eloquence of Edmund Burke. We honour both the taste and judgment of any man, who is an enthusiast in his partiality towards that calumniated statesman, who was one of the wisest as well as one of the most brilliant of those generous spirits, who have trolled the tongue, or exercised the pen, in support of doctrines, hostile to the factious humour of mankind. In particular, we honour Mr. Brown for his admiration of Burke, because we know that his partiality is of the purest kind, as in many political opinions we presume they are by no means in unison.[5]

Dennie's reviews point up both the novelty and sources of Brown's *American Register* and his historical annals while highlighting the "original" and "impartial" character of the annals. More interesting and important, they commend Brown's modeling of Burke's historical writing, while stating that Brown's "political opinions" were not "in unison" with the conservative ones of Burke—another reason for not reading the later Brown as a political or social conservative in his later years. Although it is difficult to ascertain which specific opinions he refers to, it is likely that Dennie meant Brown's democratic sympathies—his "Woldwinite," or liberal, political assumptions.[6] While the review goes on to suggest ways to enhance the *American Register*'s departments and utilize Brown's "genius" as a literary "artist," Dennie and other editors applauded the periodical's rich cache of historical documents.[7]

Brown, it seems, paid attention to how to improve the periodical through the judicious selection of state papers and other materials related to "the times." As Brown's prefaces to the *American Register* in volumes one, two, and four attest, he seems to have increasingly seen himself not as a compiler but as "a historian" and had doubts about the construction of history as an insulated, monological enterprise. For instance, in the preface to volume 1, dated November 1, 1807, Brown writes that as the editor of the *American Register* he is "conscious" that the periodical will contain "many omissions and errors" and that these are owing to "his own incapacity or ignorance." He further admits that as a "compiler" he can only be guided by "experience" before the format of the magazine has settled into regularity and that he had collected more materials for each department but press limitations caused him to forgo obituaries, "carefully translated and digested" French war bulletins, and other domestic documents.[8] While such remarks are, in part, standard for the period's fledgling periodicals, they also point to Brown's initial conception of how he would handle print materials of historical importance and the kinds of obstacles that forced him to alter his plans.

By contrast, the preface to volume 2, published in 1808, announces Brown's efforts to "relate the last half year of 1807" and contains at least ten references to "history" or the role of "the historian." In explaining, for example, how he is conscious of the "present popularity" of partisan journalism and how "this spirit extends to the transactions of foreign nations," especially as it concerns France and England and their respective advocates, he writes:

> What indulgence, therefore, can be hoped for a work which bestows censure and praise without respect to persons or nations; which considers political events merely in relation to justice and truth, and distributes blame sometimes to one party, and sometimes to the other, and sometimes to both on the same page? who, in writing the history of a war between France and England, never forgets that he is neither Frenchman nor Englishman, nor is bound to shut his eyes upon the faults or merits of either?
>
> Of those, therefore, who are dissatisfied with his history, he can only cherish the hope that they will forgive the faults of this part of his volume for the sake of the manifest utility of the rest. A collection of public and official documents in this convenient form, together with what we may call the private or internal history of the nation, in the Chronicle, is no where else to be found, and may hope to gain consideration from the enlightened part of the community.

Brown articulates here a desire to be impartial or objective in regard to historical events abroad and at home and suggests that even if his historical narrative is deficient in some way readers will still find value in the "public and official documents" he has collected. He continues to wrestle with the sheer bulk of pertinent materials and goes so far as to suggest that perhaps a plan of "greater simplicity" is needed and that reducing the magazine to "a mere depository of history and politics" might be a solution.[9] It is a plan he comments on again in volumes 3 and 4 and, eventually, implements, with some modifications, in volume 5.[10]

While the various coalitions that were formed against Napoleon were interrupted by treaties like that signed at Pressbourg (1805) and Tilsit (1807), the Continental System effectively extended Napoleon's capacity for warfare to an economic front. By not allowing the English to export their products to the Continent, Napoleon sought to drain England's economic lifeblood, an effort that backfired when he tried to enforce his Continental System in Portugal and Spain. Granted, by the peak of Napoleon's power in 1808, Europe as a whole had adopted his revolutionary ideas and reformed its own social and economic institutions. However, nationalism of the brand that fueled France for so long spread to countries like Spain and Austria (courtesy of the Napoleonic Code) and led to Napoleon's military and political undoing.

As French historian Georges Lefebvre observes, after the French Revolution the "great Napoleonic achievement—the establishment of a new dynasty and the building of a universal empire—ended in failure." And although the empire Napoleon built eventually unraveled, his political and administrative initiatives left a lasting impression on the modern European nation state. Despite his regime's restrictions on civil liberties, Napoleon's "rearrangements and reforms" in various territories encouraged the rise of the middle class, the expansion of capitalism, and the emergence of modern institutional practices and nationalism.[11] Stuart Woolf agrees with Lefebvre's point, saying that in "most states or regions that had experienced French dominion, the Restoration monarchs retained the structures, if not the names, of the Napoleonic administrative, fiscal or juridical reforms" and that the Napoleonic model of administration was retained by the governments of European states after the "collapse of the Napoleonic Empire" and by many of those states that later achieved independence in the nineteenth century.[12]

Although Napoleon's regime was generally seen as a threat to English national identity, complicating British loyalist views and, arguably, British colonial interests in India and elsewhere, was the fact, says Stuart Semmel, that a "radical sympathy for Bonaparte" as well as "outright endorsement" was an integral "element of British political culture during and after Napoleon's empire." "The radical upheaval," he observes, after Napoleon's abdication was characterized not only by an "efflorescence of radical journalism" but also by "mass meetings advocating parliamentary reform and protesting against state corruption." Contributors to periodicals like *Sherwin's Weekly Political Register* regularly defended Napoleon's past actions and highlighted "British economic and political injustice with references to Napoleon's alternative regime." One letter to the paper, dated June 1818, argued that the British government sought "not Bonaparte's overthrow, but the destruction of liberty in France, and the security of despotism at home." Semmel observes that "by overemphasizing loyalist consensus during the Napoleonic wars" and downplaying the existence of British radicalism, "historians may have helped obscure the extent to which Bonaparte retained British admirers during his rule."[13] This is a point worth considering, especially in regard to Brown's own historiographical status.

European expansionism, then, was not only local—focusing on the resources and economic markets of the Continent—but global, and in that sense was colonization.[14] Such a movement is complicated by the beginnings of decolonization, or voices of resistance such as Burke's, and the fact that there was a conspicuous slowdown of Portuguese and Spanish colonization in South America. But, observes Edward Said, for the people of nineteenth-century Britain and France, "empire was a major topic of unembarrassed cultural attention."[15] It was a mainstream focus of political, social, and economic energies.

In the United States, Napoleon's imperial marches were covered in newspapers, various periodical venues, and occasional histories. George Bourne's *The History of Napoleon Bonaparte: Emperor of the French, and King of Italy* (1806) is one of several histories published during the period that speaks to public interest in Napoleon:

He who writes the life of Bonaparte at present, even if he were so inclined, dares not to investigate freely and fully the cause and effect of all those important events in which he has been principally concerned; and that patience of investigation which such a work would demand, will not suit the avidity with which the present generation wish to be informed of the wonderful changes which the French emperor is daily producing on the European continent. In this volume will be found no profundity of disquisition, no excursions of the imagination, no embellishments of fancy, which never should be admitted into historical composition.[16]

While the author also apologizes for any accidental "plagiarism," he is conscious, like Brown, of the difficulties of writing recent history without bias and with adequate means of discerning "cause and effect." Other periodical publications were less interested in historical impartiality and more interested in biblical prophecy. *Political & Theological Disquisitions on the Signs of the Times, Relative to the Present Conquests of France* (1807), by Thomas Branagan, and *Identity of Napoleon and Antichrist; Completely Demonstrated* (1807) are typical of the tracts or periodical publications of the time.[17]

Although it is difficult to trace sources Brown consulted at the time, he most likely had several at his disposal. In addition to Philadelphia newspapers such as *Poulson's American Daily Advertiser,* Duane's *Aurora General Advertiser, Relf's Philadelphia Gazette and Daily Advertiser,* and the *United States Gazette* (1804–18), which reprinted French war bulletins or reported on various battles abroad, Brown also had access to James Thomson Callender's and Edward Baines's works and might have consulted Joseph Petit's *Marengo; or, the Campaign of Italy, by the Army of Reserve, under the Command of the Chief Consul Bonaparte* (1801) and Sir Robert Thomas Wilson's *History of the British Expedition to Egypt* (1803), all of which were either published in Philadelphia by Conrad or sold at bookstores in nearby cities such as Baltimore and Washington.[18] Brown would have also had access to material that was republished in area newspapers from the *London Gazette* or the *London Monthly Magazine; or, British Register.* It is unlikely, however, that he took material from the *British Annual Register,* which was a model for his annals in form but was at least two years or more behind in its own publication of historical events in Europe during the Napoleonic era.[19]

If by 1806 Brown was, for all practical purposes, invested in writing historical narrative in the mode of Hume and Robertson and sought to make "dignity, moderation and candour" the hallmarks of his history writing, his opening remarks in the *American Register* attest to his efforts at writing an impartial narrative. Specifically, in the opening of volume 1, published in November or December 1807, Brown makes one of many comments in his "Annals of Europe" that records his self-conscious efforts at being "impartial" in his rendering of history:

Political transactions are connected together in so long and various a chain, that a relater of contemporary events is frequently obliged to carry his narration somewhat backward, in order to make himself intelligible. He generally finds himself placed in the midst of things, and quickly perceives that he cannot go forward with a firm and easy step, without previously returning to some commencing point. An active imagination is apt to carry us very far backward on these occasions; for, in truth, the chain of successive and dependent causes is endless; and he may be said to be imperfectly acquainted with the last link, who has not attentively scrutinized the very first in the series, however remote it may be.[20]

Just as his reviews, essays, and prefaces to the *American Register* cumulatively articulate an element of self-scrutiny or historical self-consciousness, so Brown's history writing proper also registers a methodological self-awareness or consciousness of the difficulty of writing history. That is, if he earlier questioned the "distinctions" or dichotomies between the terms "history" and "romance" in his essay "The Difference between History and Romance," then his reference in 1806 to an "active imagination" also acknowledges the role of subjectivity in (re)constructing history. It records his developing self-consciousness as a historian—his awareness of the "chain of successive and dependent causes" associated with a given moment in history and how history writing necessarily involves creativity or "imagination."

Brown's view or interpretation of the major events of his day and their significance is consistent with the generalizations outlined above, but unlike many of his contemporaries he also recognized that the "destiny" of the United States was "intimately connected with the situation and transactions of European nations." Trade and opportunities for "commercial dealings almost without limit" have brought countries from all over the world into contact and also provided unprecedented "occasions and incentives for rivalship, jealousy, and war." In particular, the political and economic "interests" of France and Great Britain have been the source of great tension—both past and present. Brown further notes that the "history of France and England . . . is the history of Europe, and, in some measure, of the world."[21] But because the United States also has economic interests and is surrounded by the ships or colonies of France and Great Britain, it is important to recognize that our histories—and future—are intimately connected with the activities and policies of France and England.

In taking account of events that occurred before 1806, Brown remarks that "it is still a matter of doubt whether England commenced hostility, or the first provocation came from France." But it is "well known" how France "defeated, repulsed, disarmed, or subdued" countries such as England, Spain, and Austria, and that the English refusal to surrender Malta (in retaliation for French aggression) rekindled war between the countries and caused France to renew hostilities against Austria.

ANNALS OF EUROPE AND AMERICA.

CHAP. I.

POLITICAL transactions are connected together in so long and various a chain, that a relater of contemporary events is frequently obliged to carry his narration somewhat backward, in order to make himself intelligible. He generally finds himself placed in the midst of things, and quickly perceives that he cannot go forward with a firm and easy step, without previously returning to some commencing point. An active imagination is apt to carry us very far backward on these occasions; for, in truth, the chain of successive and dependent causes is endless; and he may be said to be imperfectly acquainted with the last link, who has not attentively scrutinized the very first in the series, however remote it may be.

An American observer, who proposes to give an account of passing events, immediately perceives that the field before him naturally divides itself into foreign and domestic. It may seem, at first sight, that his concern is only with the latter; but a little reflection convinces him, that the destiny of his own country is intimately connected with the situation and transactions of European nations. As trade is the principal employment of the American people; as their trade is chiefly with the nations of Europe, or their colonies; and as the present state of navigation renders the whole globe a theatre of commerce to more than one people, our situation is deeply influenced through the medium of traffic, by the domestic condition and mutual operations of European states. If they are at war among themselves, those wants which, in peaceable times, were supplied by one another, must now find a supply elsewhere, and whatever influences their manufactures and produce on one hand, and their consumption, or the channel which feeds it, on the other, is deeply interesting to a country like our own, which has both the inclination and the power to extend and dilate its commercial dealings almost without limit. Trade and navigation likewise have the wonderful power of annihilating, in its usual and natural effects, even space itself. They bring into contact nations separated by half the diameter of the globe, and supply them

First page of Brown "Annals of Europe and America," chapter 1, *American Register; or, General Repository of History, Politics, and Science,* 1 (1807). Brown relates the difficulties of writing historical narrative without an "active imagination." This type of historical self-consciousness led him later to question prevailing assumptions about American history and destiny. Courtesy of the Library Company of Philadelphia.

Aside from commenting on debates in England about how to resist an invasion from France, the "motives of jealousy and ambition," says Brown, which have caused the French and Austrian governments to tangle with one another for centuries, have also infected other countries. Turkey, Russia, and Prussia are the only powers that have held onto their independence and still might join an alliance.[22]

Brown's commentary on Napoleon and the French in general is similar. For example, in assessing the influence of the British government in provoking wars on the Continent, Brown comments that it would be "absurd" to say that England has somehow influenced all the wars that have taken place in Europe in recent years. He writes, "The maxims of the French revolutionists, with their conduct in destroying the royal family and abjuring religion and monarchy, were amply sufficient to excite a spirit of hostility in all surrounding nations."[23] Along with the cry for "liberty, equality, fraternity," the French, asserts Brown, also denounced religious orthodoxy and destroyed the political status quo, an action that led to increased instability in surrounding nations.

Brown goes on in his narrative to write about the impact of war between France and other powers on "commerce and industry," saying that both England and France began, over time, to realize the economic "advantages of peace." Although he comments on correspondence between Charles Fox and Talleyrand concerning peace, he also says, in regard to England's efforts to include Russia in negotiations that "the French were not blind to the obvious policy of disuniting these allies, and that dexterity and artifice, in which the French excel all other nations, were exerted for the purpose, but entirely without success." Yet he writes further on succeeding negotiations, and political posturing by both the French and English: "If we take an impartial view of this negotiation, we shall be obliged to acknowledge that the conduct of the English throughout was candid and upright, while that of the French was full of subterfuge and sophistry, equally disingenuous and fruitless." Such remarks are followed by additional observations about the pleas of the British concerning the restoration of Hanover being "plainly nugatory and absurd" and illustrate Brown's efforts to examine circumstances in an impartial or balanced manner, which, though, does clearly indicate his willingness to remark more subjectively on what he thought was "ridiculous" or "folly" in regard to a particular country's motives or behavior.[24]

After observing how England's naval forces acted as an impediment to France, Brown returns to the topic of Napoleon and his effect on the political stability of other European countries, such as Prussia, and makes an interesting observation for his time. Beginning with the observation that France essentially conducted a policy of bribery and gained the "connivance and neutrality" of that country by sharing the spoils of its campaigns, Brown then observes that the offering of Hanover to Prussia was a prime instance of Napoleon's use of territorial acquisitions as gifts to pacify a country while continuing to expand his empire. Consistent with his belief that the "three great powers on whom lesser German states were more or less dependent were Austria, Prussia, and France," he focused his attention less on the dismantling of the German states and more on how the larger powers influenced one another.[25]

But in addition to less-than-favorable representations of Napoleon and stereotypes about the French as masters of "subterfuge and sophistry," Brown's disdain for self-aggrandizement is also evident in his commentary on the manner in which countries besides France relate to one another. One such instance occurs in chapter 6 of volume 1, where Brown offers an opinion about the way countries conduct business: "Nothing can be more absurd than to think that gratitude or justice has any concern in the intercourse or compacts of nations, or rather than to imagine that any nation will be brought to allow that there is any justice in sacrificing the least advantage of their own, to the greatest of another community." The context for this statement about nations and their reluctance to sacrifice their own advantage for the sake of justice is Brown's analysis of French policy toward Prussia and the claim that the Prussian government's neutrality was less valuable than Austria's aggression, the consequence of which was a violation of Prussian territory in October 1805. The "selfish principle," remarks Brown, dictates that "deference and favour" toward someone are sweetest when something is to be gained. Once the favor is given, "gratitude or justice" is no longer a consideration.[26]

Similar to his posture in his historical sketches, despite Brown's interest in and reflections on maintaining historical objectivity and despite penetrating analysis that sometimes reveals his own biases, he occasionally makes subjective remarks that are not completely contained by the veil of "impartiality" and, importantly, comment ironically on history. Such remarks are not particularly extensive in regard to Napoleonic rule, especially as compared to his "Annals of America," but they are present both in that context and elsewhere. For instance, Brown writes quite openly about relations between Fox, the British prime minister, and Talleyrand, the French minister of foreign affairs, and the attempt by the former in the early part of 1806 to include Russia in negotiations, saying that the French outstrip other countries when it comes to political posturing and artifice, especially in regard to England. Brown goes on in later commentary on European alliances and changes to highlight the "intermeddling craft, the tyrannical incroachments, and the irresistible power of France," a remark that sufficiently indexes the belief, dating back at least to Voltaire, that the French excel in political "dexterity and artifice"; this attitude toward the French surfaces again in other volumes of the annals.[27] Similar, therefore, to that of others who became disillusioned with the French Revolution and its excesses, Brown's narrative impartiality slips and he records a reluctance to completely condone their political means and ends, particularly as later instituted by Napoleon.

As Brown relates elsewhere in the annals, countries—like individuals and characters in novels—have motives, and understanding those motives can yield insight into actions. While Brown, who refers to himself here as an "impartial observer," goes on in his narrative to outline French progress into Poland and to give a blow-by-blow account of how Napoleon's forces were checked at the Prussian town of Eylau, the most astute commentary by far is that dealing with Brown's assessment of French aggression and "power."[28]

When taking account of how European nations have acted, says Brown, "in seizing all within our reach, we act like the rest of the world, but in abstaining from the prey, when none can force us to abstain, we display an equity and moderation singular and meritorious. If we apply this impartial standard to the conduct of the French emperor, towards Austria, Tuscany, the Pope, and the German princes, shall we not be obliged to allow the merit of some moderation and forbearance. Has he retained all that was in his power? did he make the most profitable use of his victories?" Brown's analysis of power here as it relates to Napoleon and other European countries documents his continuing efforts at being "impartial" in his history writing. By suggesting that countries like England are also busy with empire building and that Napoleon displays a certain amount of "equity and moderation" when it comes to using his "power," Brown clearly steers his analysis away from a more orthodox or reactionary point of view, one that typically saw Napoleon as an absolute dictator. It is an approach one also finds later in his narrative when he writes of Napoleon's ability to be "the champion of toleration and the catholic faith" in requiring that the "Lutherans and catholics shall be placed exactly on the same footing" and "admitted to the same religious and political privileges throughout the Saxon kingdom."[29]

While Brown recognized and critiqued Napoleon's capacity for empire building, he was also willing to acknowledge that such imperialistic desires were not unique to Napoleon, an important insight for his later views of America, and that there were possibly some "advantages" among the "calamities" of conquest. Such ambivalence appears, at first glance, to embrace a totalitarian ethos, but it is clarified by other aspects of Brown's history writing. For example, Brown offers additional commentary about this principle when he writes about how France and Prussia were guided by the sense of their "own interest" and examines the "pretexts" of Prussia, Russia, and Austria for preying on Poland. All of these countries had the "usual lust for dominion," and an "interest in each other's destiny, merely from the relation which it may bear to their own safety."[30] Similar to the kind of political analysis he rendered about civil and ecclesiastical despotism in his historical sketches, Brown says, "power is their measure of right," and if lessening a neighbor's power preserves one's own, then military aggression is justified. In the case of Poland, its partition by Prussia, Russia, and Austria was countered by a French initiative in the fall of 1806—another round of "pretexts" and power shifting.

Brown's beliefs, or biases, however, concerning French military conquests and the acquisition of property and "plunder" in regard to the English are perhaps

where he first allows himself to be ironic in the "Annals of Europe." In identifying common rules of naval warfare and how the English "assumed the right of
intercepting all commerce," Brown comments on Napoleon's decree that unless
England affirmed that "the rights of war to be the same at sea as on land, and that
these rights cannot be extended to private property or private persons," France
would treat the English on land the same way the English treat others at sea. Such
a decree, he says, encountered many obstacles in regard to the concealment of
property and proving, for instance, that seized property was in fact English. "In
most cases," writes Brown ironically, "the summary expedient was resorted to of
seizing all English manufactures, wherever they could be found, without regard to
the nice and intricate question of ownership." Further, it would be "worthy of curiosity" but almost impossible to confirm the degree to which such "confiscation"
existed and with what degree of enforcement it was carried out. Such factors, he
says, must be known in order to accurately estimate the "misery" to which people
were "exposed by such a system of plunder."[31]

Brown inquires more fully into French successes in Poland in chapter 9, again
seeking to be an "impartial observer" on the subject of soldier "cowardice" and
"disaffection." And he provides extensive detail on the French invasion of Poland,
especially in terms of its history as an independent political state, the impact of the
French Revolution, and Prussian, Russian, and Austrian interests in the country,
promising the Poles that he would make them, in Napoleon's words, *"once more a
nation."* Brown also continues to recount Prussian and Russian army movements
relative to French positions. Napoleonic rule continues to be discussed in volume
2, after Brown writes of English interests in Turkey and the Mediterranean area
and in South America. He pays particular attention to the French defeat at Eylau
and its consequences for taking Dantzig, describing how the Russians and Prussians prepared for Napoleon's attack and how battle unfolded near Gutstadt with
"extraordinary cannonade" and the "incessant fire of musketry."[32]

Brown's historical narrative focuses on France's willingness to yield provinces
and how the nation may be suspect and have some "secret" advantage for doing
so, but then opens up another line of historical inquiry by commenting on French
efforts to compromise England's effectiveness by "diminishing her commerce"
and influencing her allies to follow a similar path. This expedient, remarks Brown
toward the end of volume 2, was a "desperate and dubious one." "Experience," he
asserts, "only can inform us whether this kind of warfare, by which both parties
are injured, is the most injurious to the nation who carries it on or that which is its
object." Such "contrivances," he suggests, act to diffuse "the evils of war" to places
and people beyond the immediate scene, with victory being claimed "by the party
who suffers least."[33] As with previous analysis of the impact of Napoleonic rule on
other countries, Brown comments here on the implications or consequences of
events and the manner in which countries compete for power and prestige.

By contrast, Brown's words on Napoleonic rule in volume 4 are brief, but in the preface to this volume, dated May 20, 1809, he judiciously states that the "brevity of the historical introduction" is due to the "too inconsiderable progress" of events in Spain and especially with Great Britain. Along with commenting on the time between the Treaty of Tilsit and the "attack of the French emperor on Spain," he says that documents like the proceedings of the society of Friends concerning American Indians and sketches of Louisiana's geography have "intrinsic value," so much so that he thinks the *American Register* "would be entitled to no small share of public regard, if it were merely a general depository of papers so valuable as these."[34] As I argue later, Brown's meditations on historical impartiality and the dialogical nature of historical narrative and evidence ultimately persuade him to select and arrange primary documents in lieu of historical narrative.

In this volume, though, Brown returns to the state of Europe after the Treaty of Tilsit. He even appends to the historical narrative "Official State Papers Relative to the Evacuation of Portugal by the French Army." Of Napoleon's rule, specifically, Brown covers the French campaign in Italy, putting forward comparisons between the rule and "imperial trappings and barbarous pomp" of Charlemagne and Napoleon's own "vanity" in calling himself "emperor of the French and king of Italy." As in his novels, where the motives of characters are held up for scrutiny, Brown applies his analysis of individuals to the behavior of institutions and countries. Such "pretensions," regardless of historical period, do not account for "the real motives of the conquerors." "Ordinary, vulgar ambition," asserts Brown, was "as much the genuine inducement, and military violence the instrument, in the revival of republics, as of kingdoms in Italy."[35] The French invasion of Portugal, like other instances of imperial aggression, testifies, according to Brown, to that historical truth.

However, beyond his reflections on political rhetoric and the overt bias or opinion in Brown's singular reference to the ruler of Spain as a "prince verging upon idiocy and dotage, enslaved by the most ridiculous passions and devoted to the most childish pursuits," nowhere is Brown more forthright in his historical judgment than when he criticizes French and English military aggression. Countering the idea that Brown in his historical sketches had been drifting toward "totalitarianism," enlightened or otherwise, Brown's narrative associates France with "that contempt of truth and equity, by which all diplomatic papers, and the conduct of nations" are collectively distinguished. He goes on to say in a footnote how "French rhetoric" "contrives" to represent French ambition as being in the "interests of the continent" and that

Greek and Roman liberty are phantoms which enjoyed their transient hour of idolatry at the opening of the French revolution, but are now succeeded by the imperial trappings and barbarous pomp of Charlemagne, and the iron crown of the Lombards. As a double title, and the union of emperor and king confer an imaginary dignity, which is wanting in a single name; as the emperors whom Napoleon has supplanted, were royal as well as imperial; as Italy when in possession of the Ostrogoths was called a kingdom: the vanity of the conqueror required the revival of those gorgious distinctions in his own person, and he accordingly created himself emperor of the French and King of Italy.

The French Revolution, according to Brown, may have initially glorified "Greek and Roman liberty," but Napoleon's imitation of Charlemagne and his "barbarous pomp" has supplanted such idealism. Brown's ironic depiction of Napoleon's "vanity" suggests a heightened degree of contempt for the egotistical manner in which Napoleon conquered Italy. Any "pretensions" by Napoleon to restore Italy to its "ancient and lawful limits" are a farce, a view echoed later in the "Annals of Europe" when Brown writes that the ability of the French to appropriate land and property "has never been equalled in any former time."[36]

On Brown's use of footnotes in the annals, it is worth digressing briefly. As Anthony Grafton points out in *The Footnote,* "In the eighteenth century, the historical footnote was a high form of literary art," and "no Enlightenment historian achieved a work of more epic scale or more classic style than Edward Gibbon's *History of the Decline and Fall of the Roman Empire.*" Brown, as has been suggested, was familiar with different modes of historical writing, including Hume's and Gibbon's. For both Gibbon and, earlier, Pierre Bayle and his *Historical and Critical Dictionary* (1696), the footnote provided space to contest commonly accepted truths. While it may seem "odd," says Grafton, to see Bayle as a "founder of historical learning," many have come to see his dictionary, with its footnotes and footnotes to footnotes, as a "vast subversive engine, designed to undermine the Bible, Protestant orthodoxy, the very notion of exact knowledge." In this last respect, especially, Brown and Bayle are similar. And if Bayle, says Grafton, thought his use of footnotes made his work "radically new," Brown, it seems, also found use for the footnote as an outlet to express historical qualifications or ironic criticisms of his subject.[37] It also became a vehicle that allowed him to reconsider, or reimagine, the role of historical narrative proper relative to primary documents and other historical materials.

Brown's efforts, then, to impartially assess Napoleon's marches across Europe using French bulletins and other original sources enabled him to accomplish a measure of historical objectivity that was rare for the period. Likewise, his efforts to wait until events had unfolded and patiently inquire into the causes and effects of French aggression signals his willingness to impartially examine historical evidence and withhold judgment until the proper time. Brown's focus, in other words, on French aggression relative to other European countries demonstrates his awareness of the complex nature of historical events and his early attempt to be objective in his analysis of historical evidence. His later understanding that the United States did not operate in an economic or political vacuum is informed, in other words, by this earlier perceptive analysis of imperial motives and the kinds of political assumptions that accompanied the Napoleonic appetite for territory, commerce, capital, and "power."

At the same time his narrative illustrates a high level of historical impartiality or moderation, it also registers—in his articulation of various types of "absurdity"— the biases of Brown and his time. Negative commentary about the French and their "intermeddling craft, the tyrannical incroachments" reflects a general, societal loathing of post-Revolution tyranny, and Brown's impatience with the political ambitions and egotism of rulers. Beyond, though, leaving traces of ironic analysis or commentary, Brown developed a clearer understanding of imperial rule—how the personal ambitions and political motivations of someone like Napoleon can become propaganda, or a pretense for military aggression against others, in the name of "liberty" and equality. As I argue later about the "Annals of America," Brown increasingly became attuned to the manner in which some Americans manifested their own imperial ambitions using the political rhetoric and pretense of liberation, thereby making his early historical analysis of Napoleonic rule and the spread of British empire an important feature of his later historicism and capacity for using political irony.

British Empire in South America and India

On the larger world stage, France, of course, was not the only country to engage in policies of empire building or territorial expansion. England was also busy settling Australia, extending its control in India, and annexing territories in Africa and the Caribbean—the acquisition of Sierra Leone in 1808 being a case in point. Despite Horace Walpole's protests after 1771 about the famine of Bengal and Edmund Burke's "Speech on Mr. Fox's East India Bill, December 1, 1783" and his plea for a more humane treatment of colonized peoples, the English "public was not conscious of the idea that the problems of British rule could be surveyed or made the subject of criticism on the basis of so comprehensive a notion as the term *imperialism* implied."[38] By 1805, as General Arthur Wellesley observed, the East India Company had nearly absolute control and power. Despite native unrest and numerous military battles, the company and the British government were "in a most glorious situation, as the sovereigns of a great part of India; the protectors of the principal powers and the mediators, by treaty, of the disputes of all."[39] Karl Marx, writes Allen Edwards in *The Rape of India,* accurately summed relations among the English, Muslim officials, and Hindu capitalists when he remarked of India that the "aristocracy wanted to conquer it, the moneyocracy to plunder it, and the millocracy to undersell it."[40]

In the United States, the most prominent critics of the East India Company and British control of India were Thomas Paine and William Duane. During the 1790s, reports of battles between Earl Cornwallis and Tipu Sultan were regularly reported in newspapers and periodical publications such as Isaiah Thomas's *Massachusetts Magazine* (1789–96) and the *New-York Magazine* (1790–95). In Philadelphia, where Brown lived permanently after 1800, publications such as the *Philadelphia Monthly Magazine* (1798), Duane's *Aurora General Advertiser* (1795–1812), and *Poulson's American Daily Advertiser* (1801–39) all regularly printed news about British military operations, mutinies in India, or the successes of native resistors such as Tipu Sultan, son of Muslim Haidar Ali.[41] But until 1807, it was Thomas Paine and William Duane who were most vocal in their protest of British imperial policy in India. Paine made strong remarks in his "American Crisis" pamphlets in 1778, and Duane wrote about "the injustice of the English government in India" and the "massacres of millions for commercial purposes in India, or Asia."[42] Brown, who made ready reference to the British in India in his novel *Edgar Huntly*, no doubt had easy access to his friend Zachariah Poulson's *American Daily Advertiser* and the latest news from India.[43]

As one reads the "Annals of Europe," then, it becomes clear that Brown was acutely aware that the desire for economic capital and colonial possessions was often the source of political and military controversy in Europe, and he does not hesitate to observe that the British, no less than the French, participated in empire building. Similar to his analysis of French policies and military aggression, he closely examines the interests and actions of the English at this time, especially in relationship to Napoleon's activities and his war with England. As part of his efforts, in other words, to accurately and impartially understand each country's behavior, he juxtaposes their actions, drawing specific attention to England's own brand of imperial expansion and military aggression in South America and India and, to a lesser extent, Denmark.

In the opening part of volume 1, Brown recounts events leading to the current war between France and England and identifies existing alliances and successes, particularly in regard to the English. Because of British naval superiority, England, he points out, was able to grab Egypt and Malta from France, destroying "the navy and commerce of France" in the process. And while the 1802 Peace of Amiens lasted briefly, allowing the English to return Surinam, the Cape of Good Hope, and other territories and the French to relinquish Trinidad, the status of Malta was more complicated. Its safety as a port and location for commerce and naval activities made it much more valuable to the British than Gibraltar.[44] But, remarks

Brown, despite costs to operate the garrison, the English refused to relinquish the island due to renewed aggression by the French against the independence of nearby countries, and the war between France and England continued.

Brown continues in his historical narrative to evaluate the motives of countries and their actions, and in assessing France's and England's "mutual desire for peace," for example, and the attempts by Talleyrand and Fox to negotiate reconciliation, he remarks:

> If we take an impartial view of this negotiation, we shall be obliged to acknowledge that the conduct of the English throughout was candid and upright, while that of the French was full of subterfuge and sophistry, equally disingenuous and fruitless. They were evidently much deceived in their notions of the views and temper of the new British ministry. . . . [The British] not only insisted on retaining all they had conquered, but required the restitution of a province, which it was impossible to wrest from France by force of arms, and which France had given already to an ally, who would never have peaceably surrendered it. . . . The pleas of the British, that Hanover ought to be restored, because it was unjustly attacked, were plainly nugatory and absurd.[45]

As with his earlier analysis of the French, here Brown not only takes a hard look at how the French approached negotiations, but he applies a similar standard of judgment to the English, as when he cites their demand for the "restitution" of Hanover as being excessive or unrealistic. He puts aside any partisanship by saying that both the English and the French "acted in this negotiation as conquerors," and he objectively estimates how the war between France and England was proceeding both on the field and at the negotiation table.

Brown then turns to differences in how France and England have been financing the war. France, he observes, derives most of its funding from heavy taxation, without impairing its sources of revenue in the future. England, however, must continuously increase its taxes to keep pace with the cost of supporting its armies and fleets and, observes Brown, its people are increasingly anxious about reaching a point where taxes would be detrimental to their livelihood and lives. The possibility of the English government suspending payment of interest on its debt became, he says, a major concern, but such was the "national spirit" of the country that it would not allow the enemy to have a superior army. While Brown comments further in a note about the "injury" and "benefit" of debt, he elaborates more fully on the "trade and revenue of the British empire" and the amount of money it costs to support "civil government," collect taxes, and pay interest on the debt. The "most striking feature," he says, of England's financial situation is the amount of money it borrowed, but this was offset by the generation of additional loans and as such presented "no present evil."[46] Before turning to British inter- ests in the Middle East, Brown ends the chapter with British manufacture export numbers and ships for 1803 through 1806.

Of Napoleon's desire to conquer England, and how the English "hitherto con- tented themselves with checking and opposing the French in their distant expedi- tions" where a strong English navy had a distinct advantage, Brown writes that Malta and Egypt were recovered from France, leaving Napoleon with limited access to Sicily and Naples. But it is on the matter of how England used its "naval power and commercial habits" to "attack the colonies and remote possessions" of its en- emies that Brown offers revealing commentary not only about England's imperial designs but about the role of race and gender in regard to a colonial ethos.[47]

He begins by noting that it is "somewhat surprising" that the colonies of Spain in South America have "never been formally attacked by the English" but then states that the territories there abound with riches and food products and that the people are "thought to be discontented with their government, and ripe for any revolution; to be the prey of domestic faction; and disabled, by effeminacy, indolence, and a long inexperience of war, for any effectual resistance."[48] While Brown would later voice stronger views on this topic, what is significant at this point is that he identifies, much like in his novels, the ways colonial motives and stereotypes about subordinate peoples often exist side by side with patriarchal assumptions. Not only are native peoples perceived to be ready for "any revo- lution," but they are stereotyped or Orientalized, as Edward Said has shown, as being lazy, "irrational, depraved (fallen), childlike, 'different,'"—a "subject race" completely exploitable because of their perceived physical inferiority.[49] A gender bias, as Brown's narrative shows, was associated with race; and both ways of defin- ing the other were accompanied by the myth that the resources of non-European countries were ripe for exploitation. If, as feminist cultural scholar Vron Ware suggests, "a historical perspective that takes into account race, class, *and* gen- der is essential in analyzing the highly complex web of social relations found in colonial societies," Brown's narrative about the English in South America seems conscious—at least to some degree—of the relationship between race and gender in colonial constructions of the Other and, like Said, of the "repertoire" of images and stereotypes that inform them.[50]

At the same time, however, Brown observes, "After the revolution in North America, an opinion began to gain ground in England, that colonial establish- ments, were on the whole injurious"—that the diversion of "enterprize, industry, and capital" away from the home soil also seemed to necessitate occasional wars and "enormous public expenses," such as have been seen with the English in respect to the American colonies. This situation, he remarks, generally preserved Spanish colonies from attack and made them "objects of abhorence [sic], rather than of envy to their neighbors." Yet, the British government had begun "to imagine that the Spanish colonies were worth obtaining, not for the sake of their mines or taxes, but merely of the custom which their numerous and luxurious inhabitants would afford to their own work-shops."[51] The possibility, in other words, of acquiring a broader market for the distribution of its manufactured goods now made Spanish colonies more appealing.

Brown goes on, interestingly, to acknowledge that upon more "accurate enquiry" colonists in South America seem to have made certain advancements in regard to population and demonstrated a reciprocal interest in European goods. Whether or not native populations benefited from such trade, Brown does not say. He does comment on a band of British "adventurers" who captured Buenos Aires—a "conquest" the English government quickly moved to sanction—and on the reduced tax the colony placed on British imports. But it is on the matter of trade and the ways the English government dealt with colonists and native customs that he offers a more valuable perspective on the economic and cultural dimensions of colonizing practices:

> The new trade, though not without restrictions, would be boundless liberty to the colonists, when compared with their ancient fetters, and would secure their allegiance by bonds stronger than those of iron or of oaths. As to national and religious prejudices, the time was long past since the English had grown perfectly indifferent to the religion of their subjects. They meddle not with the legal customs, domestic habits, or modes of worship of the conquered people, and are contented with having in their own hands their trade and public revenue.

And he continues, saying that however valid or invalid his reflections may be, "the English government were undoubtedly much mistaken in imagining, that the capture of the chief town was the conquest of the whole province, or that the remaining posts could be as easily subdued as the metropolis had been. Great likewise was their error as to the wonder-working power, which they ascribed to commercial liberty, in dissolving the ties which held the colony and parent country together."[52] Beyond recalling Edgar's bayoneting of a native in *Edgar Huntly* and Brown's remarks about how "perverse nature compels thousands of rational beings to perform and witness" such deeds with "indifference," the above passage shows Brown's awareness of colonial practices of interfering with the "legal customs, domestic habits, or modes of worship" of a native people. Such rhetoric, Daniel Ritchie might suggest, is consistent with Burke's understanding of "Indian oppression" and the need to consider the "welfare of the Indian people . . . before interests of the [East India] Company."[53] However, at the same time as Brown acknowledges blatant forms of cruelty and cultural oppression, he points out the illusions of the English government—its misconception that to conquer a part of a country was to subdue the whole, and its assumption that "commercial liberty" was sufficient to bind a "colony" to its "parent country." While such comments arguably offer only a mild critique of colonial practices, later in the annals Brown tackles their racist elements.

If at one point Brown praises "the conduct and valour of the English" in regard to conflict with European powers like Spain, he again takes up the subject of British activity in South America in volume 2 of the "Annals of Europe." In stating, for instance, that "the empire of the Mediterranean was never so fully in possession of the English as now," he observes that the "three great steps" to England's "naval empire" were the capture of Malta and battles at the Nile and Trafalgar. Despite such acquisitions, though, says Brown, and however "flattering to national vanity," a nation's wealth is measured by its trade, and mere possession of a territory is a "heavy incumbrance" unless local revenue can be generated. Brown's analysis on this point—the relationship between naval developments and sea commerce— prompts him to remark further that while his assessment is "by no means an impartial view," it seemed that despite the "unprofitable nature" of merely inhabiting islands or fortresses nothing at this point would be more devastating to England than the "loss of Malta and Gibraltar." His analysis then focuses further on how naval supremacy can affect commerce of the enemy and how possession of Egypt would afford a "passage to India," but, he says, the British had no desire to acquire the entire country—just strategic harbors like that of Alexandria.[54]

After recounting England's difficulties in capturing and maintaining Alexandria, Brown next addresses the English defeat at Buenos Aires by the Spanish. He examines how the architecture of the city and its surrounding geography made it difficult for the British to mount successful attacks and how after several days of fighting the Spanish officer in charge, Liniers, eventually took enough prisoners to threaten the British with the "danger of a general massacre." As for the prudence of the British surrender in the face of losses and total resistance from the inhabitants of the city, Brown writes: "How far this decision was prudent or rash, cowardly or brave, is at present merely [a] matter of conjecture. A legal review will probably be had of these transactions, and then we shall be able to form a more enlightened judgment concerning them."[55] Brown's reluctance in his analysis to prematurely assess the actions and motives of the British commander suggests a continued interest in being impartial. While Brown does go on to comment less impartially about "some important lessons" that can be drawn from the incident, he also makes provocative comments concerning British activity in Argentina.

For example, of the infamous expedition to La Plata, he comments that "whether the establishment of the British power in this quarter would have proved a benefit or evil to the nation, is a point of much controversy." He finds that one advantage the presence of British power offers is bargaining power with the French in the event of a peace and concessions. While Brown admits that any estimation of the value of territories in South America is mere "speculation," he nevertheless imagines that "the more that England conquers, the more she will have to give at a peace." At the same time, Brown is able to say that it should seem "sufficiently clear, that never to have undertaken this enterprize would have been much better than failure." Military troops and "great commercial capital" would have been preserved as would have been the British reputation.[56]

Brown does not stop there in his analysis: "Yet, if this disappointment preclude a future one, by inculcating a proper caution and distrust with respect to similar projects, it may be an ultimate advantage to the British nation." He speculates, in other words, about the effects of a British success and colony in this part of South America and how it might have led to the "subversion of Spanish power" in the area and the spread of British "language, manners, and people" to both North and South America, an event, he says, that would have been to some degree a "wonderful, yet probable, indeed an invaluable consequence."[57] Brown, of course, sought to avoid "conjecture" in his narrative, but, as his commentary here reveals, his desire for historical accuracy and comprehensiveness, especially as it concerns a British perspective, may give the impression that he condoned British colonial aggression. It is more accurate, though, to regard his reporting from the British perspective as just that—a historical account that attempts to examine British colonial events from an English perspective. Thus, while Brown was interested the global effects of European colonialism, he was equally willing to critique it.

However, it is in volume 4 that Brown's narrative in the "Annals of Europe" is perhaps most impartial and illuminating in a historical sense, especially when he comments on how the "conduct of nations is regulated by their power." While I have suggested that Brown occasionally seems to admire elements of certain colonial successes, he was at the same time capable of stepping back and offering relatively detached analysis of imperialism or colonialism as he knew it. As has been mentioned earlier, Brown closely followed British colonial interests in India as well as Continental efforts to control Turkey and any maritime advantage it might offer, especially in regard to India.[58] On the topic of South America and the English withdrawal from Buenos Aires, Brown not only tentatively associates American expressions of imperialism with British ones, but his narrative also more aggressively and ironically critiques British colonialism.

First, of the ways British colonial expeditions to South America point up American pseudocolonial pretensions, Brown writes:

> The issue of this contest inculcates some important lessons. It overthrows two material errors: first, as to the disaffection of the Spanish colonists to the parent state, arising from commercial restraints; and, secondly, as to the indolence, cowardice, and effeminacy of their character. The habit of imputing our own feelings to others has betrayed us into the glaring folly

of imagining the same impatience of foreign controul in all the American colonies which once actuated ourselves. We have even harboured the gross delusion, that a wretched adventurer, at the head of two or three hundred men, picked up in our cities, could work a revolution in South America, and that the initial spark only was wanting to kindle a rebellion in Peru or Mexico. The grossness of these delusions is now made evident by the failure of so many formidable expeditions to La Plata.[59]

While I examine this incident more closely in the next chapter, Brown's brief coverage of Francisco de Miranda's attempt to liberate Argentina from the Spanish points to his emerging interest in American imperialism or at least those attitudes that espoused its nationalist expression. By pointing up the "habit of imputing our own feelings to others," Brown taps into a line of thinking in the Republic that assumes that "others" have or ought to have the same desire for liberty and political autonomy. Such an assumption, says Brown in a somewhat ironic tone, is presumptuous and has led to the "gross delusion" that a few good men and a lot of bullets "could work a revolution in South America." In addition, Brown's narrative implicitly stresses the ways gender—"effeminacy of their character"—is used to view a cultural or military Other and to justify invasion or conquest. In saying that the English were mistaken in their assessment of the Spanish colonists, he points to the ways gender biases or notions of cultural inferiority influenced perceptions not just of local natives but also of the Spanish colonists.

Last, in what is arguably the most penetrating or politically revealing analysis in the annals of the practice of colonialism and its ties to race and religion, Brown blasts the prevailing or "darling" theme of his time—the idea that the French substitution of "power for right" is unique to France and its selfish motives—and provides a stinging critique of English exploits in India. Brown writes in the provocative tone of his earlier Friendly Club days—the way he used to argue with his friend Joseph Bringhurst about the shortcomings of organized religion—in a manner or tone that once recalls both Godwin and Burke:

> Though it requires no extensive research to discover instances of selfish and iniquitous policy in the history of all nations, and especially in British history, mankind seldom extend their view beyond the present scene, and the recent usurpations of the French in the free cities and small states of Germany, in Switzerland, and Italy*, excluded from the view of political observers the more ancient or distant examples of similar iniquities in the conduct of Great Britain. Even the recent conduct of that power in Turkey was as egregious an instance of political injustice as the imagination can conceive; but it was transacted at a distance, was aimed against infidels and the perpetual enemies of christian Europe, and was not crowned with success†. The

conduct, likewise, of the same government in India was a tissue of bare-faced usurpations on the rights of others, for which the usurper never deigned to allege any other motive than his own interest. But these were likewise afar off, and affected a race of men too much unlike ourselves to awaken our sympathy.[60]

First, just as Brown identified the "evils" of war in Europe, here in his usual candor and effort to be impartial he does not hesitate to point out that France is not the only country guilty of "selfish and iniquitous policy." Britain too, he reminds the reader, has a distinctive history of such conduct. Like India, the example of Turkey provides a recent "instance of political injustice" that recalls Godwin's *Enquiry Concerning Political Justice and Its Influence on Morals and Happiness* (1793) and the impact of political institutions and tyranny on the individual. British dismissal, however, of the "rights of others" in India, recalls Burke's interrogation of the East India Company's assault on the "natural rights of mankind."[61] Both instances of British aggression involved infringement "on the rights of others," "usurpations" that were antithetical to Brown's Quaker beliefs and his earlier, more radical conception of natural rights.

Moreover, in the analysis that immediately follows this passage Brown observes that the English parliamentary style of government occasioned significant debate on the issue of Denmark, with parties trying to destroy each other's credibility by "imputing iniquity or folly" to their projects. It is "power," says Brown, that drives contention between adverse parties. Despite such debates, the times, he says, "were extremely favourable for concealing the true purpose of this expedition." Despite giving the appearance that the armament was aimed at defeating Napoleon, it was the secret design of the British to join forces with the Swedish army in Pomerania or the Russian one in Poland and to dispatch troops to Denmark. Ships and 30,000 troops were ready and in fact embarked in July 1807, lead by Gambier at sea and Lord Cathart by land. Ultimately and, remarkably, quite accurately, observes Brown in a footnote, the "French expedition to Malta and Egypt, and that of the English to Denmark, are striking proofs of the secrecy with which public undertakings, of the greatest magnitude, may be conducted."[62]

Second, just as Brown had written in volume 2 on how the "combination of Christian powers was always sufficient to stop the progress and exterminate the kingdom of the Othmans," so in the above passage his substitution of "his own interest" for the more conventional "her" in regard to England resists the colonial enterprise at another rhetorical level.[63] That is, if the "usurper" can be interpreted as a reference to King George or to England's political "interests" as represented by its navy or the British East India Company, Brown's reversal of the traditional feminine pronoun used to describe England (the substitution of "his own interest" for "her") rhetorically questions the colonial enterprise in a much subtler way.

Such "double-voiced discourse," to borrow from the work of Mikhail Bakhtin, suggests Brown's capacity for resisting both outright expressions of colonialism and its masculine hegemony—the patriarchic infrastructure of the English colonizing system.[64] For this reason, his discourse not only disrupts and challenges a colonial ethos in a manner consistent with a postcolonial subject position but, ironically, also uses sentiment or sympathy to interrogate the hierarchy that sustains it.

Brown's discourse here may not move narrative or postcolonial theory any closer toward resolving the current dilemma of how to construct a "non-repressive, anti-imperialist knowledge of women (and men)," but his rhetoric does index an ideology of racial (in)difference and religious superiority.[65] In identifying racism as a motive for being "indifferent" toward colonial activities abroad, Brown dialogically echoes Burke's willingness, which was progressive for the time, to acknowledge "Indian suffering" and "*the rights of men,* cruelly violated" under East India Company's practices. If Burke, whose depiction of atrocities against natives was the result, primarily, of the desire in "governing India *well,*" Brown never relays similar sentiments about the American Indian, as is evident in his comments attending his translation of C. F. Volney. Like Burke, though, he interrogates the colonial status quo, writing ironically about the lack of feeling or sympathy that fuels indifference and the continued oppression of other peoples. If Burke spoke of the desire for "our feelings" to help "awaken something of sympathy for the unfortunate natives," Brown also is conscious of how racial indifference and distance fail to "awaken our sympathy."[66] He identifies the racial and racist dimensions of colonialism—both in European practices and the disinterested attitudes of people, including himself, in his time.

Along, then, with the appearance of a trimmer narrative and the increased presence of editorial comments in footnotes, Brown's history of Europe and British colonialism in South America and India in particular continues to embody a historical self-consciousness as well as increasingly perceptive insights into European imperialism. However, the historiographical style Brown uses in the annals can also be described as combining what Hayden White calls a satirical mode of emplotment and a "Mechanistic" or causal mode of argument. It is a style that is at once representative in the manner of his contemporaries while also a vehicle of modern ideology and radical political intervention. Indeed, insofar as the historian "must first prefigure . . . the whole set of events reported in the documents," that "*prefigurative* act is poetic," says White, "inasmuch as it is precognitive and precriticial in the economy of the historian's own consciousness. In this respect, history writing is a "*poetic* act" that requires the use of an active, yet critical, imagination.[67]

Napoleon's March through the Mediterranean and Eastern Europe

Just as Brown's annals concentrate on history in Europe relative to French imperial rule and British colonialism, so they also offer, for early Americanists and historians, a rare look at the impact and politics of such aggression in the Mediterranean area and on the countries of Turkey, Russia, and Prussia. He takes into account the impact of Napoleonic aggression in the Mediterranean and Eastern Europe and what motivated countries to act in their own interests or to join alliances and sign treaties. Brown, I contend, continues to strive for historical "impartiality"—though not always consistently—in regard to colonial ambitions and to provide historical context and perspective on the events he covers, but he also becomes more open or critical in his analysis of the Napoleonic wars and their impact in other parts of Europe, and even about his own historical assumptions.

In fact, it is partway through volume 1 where Brown writes more fully on these three countries. After recalling how there was debate in England about the proper way to defend against a French military invasion by sea, he comments on England's history of "sowing dissention between France and her neighbors" and, further, that "the only powers of Europe that retained their independence, and whose alliance or co-operation might be purchased without imminent danger to themselves, were Turkey, Russia, and Prussia." Turkey, he says, was "little valued as a friend, or dreaded as an enemy" and had about the same economic impact or worth as Portugal. By contrast, "the empire of the Russians" seems to have earned the respect of European countries, despite the fact that that its population is spread out geographically over largely uninhabitable land.[68] Even the people of Turkey live in a more hospitable climate.

Prussia, however, is regarded as a country whose stability and independence make it desirable, especially for France at one point, to have an alliance with. Its material gain as a neutral state during the war between France and England testifies, says Brown, to the "general principle, by which all states are governed"—that of "aggrandizing themselves" and looking out only for their own interests. If Brown is accurate, Prussia's neutrality during the war enabled it to annex Hanover to its empire and to benefit politically and economically. Under these circumstances, England began to lose confidence in the possibility of forming alliances with other European powers on the Continent. Brown underscores this observation by remarking later in the annals on how the French bribed the Prussians into "connivance and neutrality" and how that same "selfish principle" permeated the policies and politics of other nations at that time. In fact, Prussia, he contends, "contributed, on all occasions, her wishes and efforts to the depression of Austria, not merely for the sake of territorial security and aggrandizement, but in order to decorate herself in [the] future with imperial honors." Further, he writes, "As the empire would be given to the strongest, her own superiority would be followed inevitably by that splendid consequence, and the empire in her hands would become an empire indeed."[69]

Brown continues his analysis of the Prussian government and its motives for taking military action, observing that France's unwillingness to withdraw troops from Germany, to allow Prussia to integrate states outside the league of the Rhine, and to yield particular towns and districts along the Rhine River all prompted Prussia to arm itself. On the point of persuading France to accommodate Prussia's interests, "pride," says Brown, "will frequently hinder us from revoking an unjust step, when the inducement is conveyed in the form of threats, though our sense of justice might prevent us from advancing any further in the same road." This "crisis," when viewed by an "impartial observer," might first suggest that Prussia was at a disadvantage. More insightfully, he remarks that when evaluating the conduct of nations relative to one another, one should always take into account the amount of power each nation has. All nations, he suggests, are capable of political self-interest and hypocrisy—a "guilt enormous and peculiar" to all, including, he says, in a potentially revealing or historically self-conscious comment, the "judge himself":

> When the Prussians and English revile the French for their encroachments in Italy, Switzerland, and Holland, they are so far inconsistent and absurd, as their own conduct is equally culpable. The English in India, the Prussians, Austrians, and Russians in Poland, and the French in Italy, have equally availed themselves of their superior power to aggrandize themselves, without regard to the claims and inclinations of others, or of the subject of their tyranny. To this species of injustice we must submit as to a physical necessity, knowing, as we do, that nations are always the same in the same situation, and that the sufferer who now complains would have been the tyrant, if fate had allotted to him the superiority enjoyed by his oppressor.

With the phrase "the judge himself" relative to the self-interests of Prussia and other countries, Brown arguably confesses his own biases and slips of historical objectivity—a self-conscious admission, as a historian, that would, crucially, later allow him to push beyond the ethnocentric, patriotic assumptions that girded emerging expressions of American exceptionalism during the Jefferson era. Further, any criticism of France by the Prussians and English on the point of encroaching unfairly on neighboring countries is "inconsistent and absurd" for two reasons: Prussia and Russia, the accusers, are equally guilty of practicing such aggression; and had the "sufferer," a country like Poland, a measure of "superiority," it would commit the same offense. For Brown, it is "absurd" to suggest that countries are capable of placing "justice" over self-interest or that powers like Prussia and England place themselves on higher moral ground when it comes to foreign policy. Remembering how the Marquis of Brandenburg "raised himself, by a long series of Prussian, Polish, Silesian, Westphalian, and Franciscan usurpations," Prussia, in particular, he says, has no claim to political or imperial innocence.[70]

Brown's analysis of Prussian territorial interests and actions continues with observations about the contradictory and confusing accounts of Prussian military resistance to France under the leadership of the Duke of Brunswick and the princes of Hohenlohe, Ruchel, and Kalcreuth. After describing how the French cut off the Prussian army from Saxony and defeated it, he turns to the manner in which the French finally conquered the Prussians at Lubeck and how the city was abandoned to plundering and the "evils" of "poverty, epidemical disease, famine, and despair." Even though random plundering and massacre by soldiers is no longer sanctioned as part of the "operations of modern warfare," the French were able to levy "contributions" in the form of money, clothing, and provisions from the Prussians and other states.[71]

Although Brown offers useful analysis of how the king of Prussia escaped into Poland and attempted to renew alliances with Sweden, England, and Russia and, as "an impartial observer," on the behavior of Prussian officers and soldiers in the face of French aggression, his assessment of relations between the French and "discontented Poles," Russian military maneuvers, and the battle of Eylau in Prussia inform our understanding of military operations relative to geographical terrain, weather, and the accuracy of battle reports. Brown digresses, for example, on how the French and Russians negotiated rivers and "a dreary plain, intersected with lakes and marshes" in the dead of winter and how French forces collected near Warsaw. His account of the Russian retreat to the Prussian town Eylau, the protection afforded by hills and ravines, and the subsequent fighting in village streets is as detailed as any in the military history of the period. The battle at Eylau was "the first great check" that Napoleon received since his military career began in 1796. While Brown continues to remark in footnotes on the apparent impartiality of his sources, he concludes that while Russian resistance to the French was "doubtless honourable to their military character," others may consider their inability to round up large numbers of troops as a reason why the "respect hitherto paid to the empire" would most likely diminish or decline in the eyes of other European nations.[72]

In volume 2, Brown examines the relationship between war and ethnocentrism by commenting on the war between Russia and Turkey at the end of 1806 and noting that the origin of the war "cannot be minutely or satisfactorily explained, from any documents hitherto published." As part of his explanation, he reflects on class differences in the Turkish empire and how such structures engender conflict and power and inquires into why the Turks perceive Greeks and Christians as "slaves," noting that a battle for power between rulers and subjects contributed to a constant tension in various districts.[73]

Brown goes on to observe that the "ancient animosity" between the countries is tied to differences in religion and perceptions of rule and power, especially in regard to the border provinces of Moldavia and Wallachia. The war of late, says Brown, appears on the surface to have for one of its "causes or pretexts" the violation of an agreement regarding the naming of princes. However, further inquiry reveals that the causes of the war stem from the war between Great Britain and France:

> It would be a fruitless task to enter into the question respecting the motives or conduct of the Greek princes, protected on this occasion by Russia. Genuine or satisfactory evidence on that head is wholly unattainable; nor is the enquiry of any importance. It is sufficient to observe, what the nature of things renders indisputable, that the French laboured to arm Turkey against Russia, and that means were good or bad, and adopted or rejected, merely as subservient to that end; that Russia befriended the exiles because a suitable opportunity hence arose for pillaging the sinking empire of the Ottomans; and that the English sided with the Russians in pursuance of the treaty that made them enemies of France.

Evident here is Brown's continued interest in providing an evenhanded perspective on the past. Not only does he admit that "genuine or satisfactory evidence" is lacking when it comes to documenting the "motives or conduct of Greek princes" relative to Russia, but he is careful in not saying that French efforts against Russia vis-à-vis Turkey were "good or bad" as justified by their end. Such comments also testify to Brown's continuing desire for historical accuracy—his interest in investigating such things as why a French narrative of military defeat at Constantinople "omits the mention of winds and weather" and its impact or how British foreign policy and aggression in the Mediterranean, South America, and Denmark make for further thought-provoking comparisons about the colonizing efforts of European countries such as France.[74]

In chapter 3, Brown observes that "the decline of the Turkish empire has long been a topic of familiar observation to the rest of Europe." He says that they are "taught" that this part of the Middle East was at one time a politically stable and prosperous vessel but that now the country is "crazy in her sides and bottom, destitute of tackle and provision," ready to sink, and in a "ruinous and tottering condition." Brown's attempts here at historical accuracy and, importantly, impartiality in regard to Turkey are particularly evident when he questions existing assessments of the area and says that such representations of Turkey are "liable to some doubts," especially when one reflects on the past. If one examines Turkish history carefully, it is difficult to find "traces of that internal declension so frequently asserted." Likewise, he says, military power and "national prosperity" are relative. An increase in Russia's and Austria's military capacity does not necessarily argue for diminished capacity in Turkey's own. In fact, he continues, as long as countries like Russia and Austria "check and counteract" each other in terms of strength, Turkey may be considered as safe from encroachment. At the same time, though, he understands that because of relations among France, Russia, and England, the empire of Turkey was vulnerable, though it was "a danger not arising from the decline of her own strength, nor properly from the increased strength of her enemies."[75]

Brown, of course, also recognized that Turkey was different from the West, that there were distinct cultural differences on the point of religion, and that a structure of class superiority was based on a mingling of "contempt" and "fear"— on the same kind of axis that perpetuated slavery in Europe and America. On the point of religious and ethnic differences and the "mutual hatred with which opposite religions inspire their votaries," he observes: "But the religion of the Turks tended to breed in them a hatred and contempt of christians on account of the division of their own community into these two classes, and the political servitude in which the class of christians was held. The mussulmen are, by this circumstance, habituated to regard the christians as slaves, and consequently as domestic enemies. Thus contempt is mingled with fear, and both these sentiments naturally make them studious of sustaining all their ancient distinctions with peculiar zeal and assiduity."[76] The political and social hierarchy between Muslims and Christians is maintained, suggests Brown, by certain sentiments or prejudices. In particular, Turkish disdain for Christians seems to be anchored by assumptions of superiority and an ethos that promotes exclusion and oppression. Brown's observations are useful here because if accurate they point up a neglected instance of subordination or discrimination in terms of class and culture. Instead of the conventional, by modern standards, cultural encounter where Christian cultures oppress native or non-Christian peoples, here the "might makes right" trope reveals the capacity of a non-European ethnic group to also construct and enforce a cultural hegemony. As a kind of counter to Said's Orientalism, Middle Eastern cultures, in the mode of the Taliban in Afghanistan today, may themselves be seen as effecting cultural stereotyping and oppression based on categories of ethnicity, race, gender, and religious belief. If true, such an assessment further testifies to Brown's efforts at, and success with, historical impartiality.

As already discussed, Brown comments on how the English have come to dominate the Mediterranean area in terms of empire and trade, and he analyzes France's and England's relations with Egypt and British interests in South America. It is worth digressing briefly here, though, on the relationship between Brown's novel writing and historical narrative. If Brown sought to avoid the use of artifice and jest in his historical narrative and to use impartiality and deductive reasoning as a means of approaching the truth, such principles were modified by his knowledge of the fictive dimensions of history writing. Without doubt, Brown's historical narrative differs in obvious ways from his fiction, especially in regard to content, or his use of Gothic themes. But there are similarities, especially in regard to Brown's rhetorical devices or techniques—two of which are his use of sensational action and detail and of moral maxims.

To illustrate: in writing about the confrontation between the French and Russians near Lannau, Brown actively dramatizes the event in ways that recall action in earlier novels such as *Edgar Huntly*: "The right wing of the Russians charging instantly with the bayonet, the French were driven back with great slaughter. . . . The action then continued with an extraordinary cannonade, and an incessant fire of musketry. A little before ten o'clock, information was received by Bennigsen, that the division of Oudinot's grenadiers was again about to storm the advanced battery, presuming to succeed under the favour of prevailing darkness."[77] Brown does not frequently resort to this kind of narrative; however, when he does tell the story of a battle, he makes use of strong verbs and vivid modifiers—language such as "charging instantly," "great slaughter," "extraordinary cannonade," "incessant fire," and "storm the advanced battery"—to render an engaging account. He adapts the "vocabulary of contemporary literature," as David Levin said of William Prescott, Francis Parkman, and other New England history writers in *History as Romantic Art,* in order to give the past "artistic order and contemporary moral significance." Brown did not raise his portrayal of representative types or characters to the high romantic level Parkman did, nor did he indulge excessively in the "conventional imagery" and "trite language" as Prescott was prone to doing.[78] But he was not afraid to use engaging action and historical detail as a means of appealing to his readership.[79]

On the surface, in other words, Brown's historical narrative continues to employ certain rhetorical conventions that he used when writing his novels in the late 1790s. In particular, his eye continued to be attracted to exotic landscapes and to moments of physical and moral conflict as he sought to "illuminate the imagination" of his readers. Warner Berthoff observes that Brown generally "gave his narrative a steady measure of objectivity" and "kept the attitude of the 'romancer,' proceeding from the hypothesis that in politics as in fiction the important study was the realm of motives, of causation, of ideas." For both Berthoff and David Lee Clark, "analysis" of causes or "motives" was a distinguishing characteristic of Brown's writing. At the same time, Brown's attempts at "historical objectivity," admits Berthoff, occasionally reflected his own biases or values—the "continuing dialectic of his long sympathy with radical idealism."[80] Beyond being the result of his earlier reading of Godwin's *Enquiry Concerning Political Justice,* Rousseau, and others, such a sympathy was, arguably, directly related to Brown's Quaker upbringing—an influence Harry Warfel first identified but that others have more fully traced in regard to Brown's novels.[81] As with other battles, Brown provides a blow-by-blow account of French and Russian movements and countermovements, indicating the time in the afternoon, for instance, Napoleon arrived with his army from Eylau in Prussia and rested his troops before advancing again.

In reading the account, one gets a clear picture of cavalry formation, number of enemy canon, the impact of obstacles such as rivers and river banks, and "causes which occasioned the defeat."[82]

Aside from French military advancements and battles in Prussia in the spring of 1807, the remaining chapters in the second volume of the "Annals of Europe"—chapters 5 through 9—concentrate mainly on the circumstances concerning the Treaty of Tilsit and how the neutrality of Denmark was jeopardized by them. Brown's accounting of military maneuvers in Poland, particularly of Russian and Prussian resistance to the French at Gutstadt and the Alle River, anticipates the sweeping narratives of a Parkman or Prescott, where dense woods, steep river banks, thundering cannons, and storms of bullets make up the "theatre of action." Brown uses post-Revolutionary discourse that compares the battlefield to a "theatre of action," but he is also careful to include and comment extensively on an English officer's observation of the Russian army as well as a French narrative of the events.[83]

For example, noting that a "topographical acquaintance with the theatre of war is absolutely necessary" in order to get an accurate picture of what happens on the battlefield, Brown goes on to say that the "testimony of witnesses" is "necessarily partial":

> The above account of the contests between France and Russia is taken from the narrative of an English officer, who surveys the scene with a military eye, but whose observation was confined to the Russian army, and who cannot be considered as an impartial witness. He must, however, be considered as less partial than a Russian historian; and those who question his accuracy will be amused, yet not enlightened, by the narrative of these transactions, published by the French. We cannot judge of the degree in which one narrator deviates from the truth on one side, by noticing the deviations of an adverse witness on the other.

What is apparent here and elsewhere in his attention to historical method and objectivity is that Brown does not rest comfortably with the assumption that "eyewitness" accounts of an event are necessarily impartial or reliable. He recognizes, as he did in his earlier essays, that oral or written sources of historical evidence are subject to the same biases and prejudices as his own narrative. Still, he makes a comparative distinction between the degrees to which the Russian historian might be biased and the English officer might be predisposed to interpret the event.[84] Similar to his reflections on history, memory, and narrative in his novels, Brown's comments here on historical impartiality speak, relative to knowledge of battle conditions, to the differences of perception that can emerge and the difficulties of either side in achieving complete historical objectivity and accuracy.

Even comparing accounts and where they deviate according to events yields, says Brown, no degree of absolute truth.

Although he goes on to compare reports concerning the Battle of Heilsberg, detailing, for instance, the manner in which columns advanced and how "woods and villages were full of straggling Russians, sick or wounded," he also provides casualty counts and, as mentioned earlier, particulars on the Treaty of Tilsit and Napoleon's assault on Dantzig, Poland. The Treaty of Tilsit, for instance, receives considerable attention in his narrative. Signed by France and Prussia on July 9, 1807, the treaty essentially restored to Prussia a number of German territories east of the Elbe River as well as a part of old Prussia; it also relinquished to Napoleon Prussian claims in Poland and the Prussian monarch's ascendancy over the smaller states of northern Germany. Of this change of political power, Brown writes: "History does not exhibit a more remarkable spectacle than the progress of the Prussian monarchy, unless it be the sudden advance of the French." The decline in strength since Frederick the Great, says Brown, is inversely proportionate to the rise of France's military power. And even though the influence of Napoleon is unmistakable, in such a "constitution-making age," political birth and rebirth is evident in governments and laws as well as states and "families of rulers." Brown notes other repercussions of the treaty, such as how England and Russia were prevented from having commerce and the British were forced to keep their ships and manufactured goods from northern Germany and Poland. As seen earlier, for Brown one conclusion was increasingly inescapable: the "conduct of nations is regulated by their power." If Brown assessed Napoleon's family and the distribution of "possessions"—states and cities along the Rhine River, for instance—and remarked on the general rise of Napoleon's family from "indigence, obscurity, and nearly the lowest rank" to such a level that one brother became the "absolute and *consecrated* sovereign of France," he also saw that in an empire-building atmosphere, countries such as Prussia did unto others as they deemed others would do unto them.[85]

But it is on the subject of the peace made at Tilsit itself that Brown meditates further on the subject of writing history and writes, again self-reflexively: "It is not the historian's province to indulge in conjecture with regard to the future, especially when the events of every new year tend to discredit all the conclusions of human judgment and foresight. There is nothing, however, more certain than that the conduct of nations is regulated by their power."[86] As with earlier statements on history writing, Brown attempts to regulate his own subjectivity by commenting on the dangers of "conjecture" and premature historical analysis and judgment. Allowing sufficient time for events and consequences to settle, he suggests, will provide for greater historical accuracy and integrity of judgment. At the same time, he qualifies such remarks by saying, somewhat provocatively, that despite the passage of time the actions of nations are influenced, or limited, by their political, military, or economic "power." That, he says, is a historical constant or truth.

Just as Brown returns toward the end of his narrative to Britain and the effect of the Treaty of Tilsit on its interests, so, he says, the loss of Russia, England's main ally, was cause for "deepest regret and consternation." However, the treaty also allowed France to cut off all trade between England and the Continent, and it made Sweden and Denmark the sole neutral countries with which Britain associated. Beyond the "qualification and exception" Brown attributes to the embargo against England, his major observation or insight is that the Treaty of Tilsit "was more dangerous to Great Britain, in its consequences, with regard to Denmark than to Sweden." The Danish, as he saw it, were now more vulnerable than ever to Napoleon because of their geographical position and the fact that tensions had been reduced among France and Prussia and Russia.[87]

It is in volume 4 of the "Annals of Europe," though, that Brown returns again to the aftermath of the Treaty of Tilsit and various campaigns by the French and English and remarks on how the treaty had been hidden from the British government because of elements in it that compromised English and Russian relations. After observing England's demands for disclosure, especially as treaty conditions pertained to her commercial interests, Brown writes bluntly:

> There is something extremely fulsome and disgusting in the customary language of diplomatic papers. Politeness, on other occasions, is shewn by deference and compliment paid by one party to another, but here we usually meet with little else than solemn and ostentatious encomiums by each party on its own wisdom, moderation, sincerity and justice, though the conduct of each manifests selfish and unfeeling contempt for the welfare of the other, and an exclusive regard to that interest of its own, which consists in the enlargement of power and dominion, and which therefore is promoted only by the injury of others. This odious spirit is plentifully breathed into the present conference, and each party decks himself with the epithets of equitable, generous, faithful and magnanimous, while an impartial sentence involves them both in the crimes of political avarice and national ambition.[88]

Brown finds the discourse of diplomatic papers to often be artificial or disingenuous. He identifies a disparity between the political language of particular countries and their subsequent actions. As a historian, and more interestingly, an individual with legal training, Brown displays an "impartial" judgment or "sentence" that is in line with his Godwinian political ethos and Quaker conscience and candor. He argues that countries such as England and Russia are guilty of "the crimes of political avarice and national ambition." Such greed and self-interest, he suggests, is typical of countries and their governments and contributes to acts of military aggression throughout Europe.

In short, Brown's historical analysis of French imperial rule and English commercial interests in the Mediterranean area takes into account the impact of such ambitions on Turkey, Russia, and Prussia. His inquiry, in particular, into historical political, ethnic, and social differences among nations helps explain the causes behind their actions and subsequent military alliances, conflicts, and treaties. In determining that the "conduct of nations is regulated by their power," Brown identifies a contributing factor to the Napoleonic wars. Likewise, his assessment of the geographical "theatre of war" and the accuracy and impartiality of military reports also leads to a clearer understanding of the meaning of historical subjectivity and what constitutes fact and fiction—and truth—in representing the past. As a result of his sharpened historical sensibilities, Brown also articulates a profound sense of war and the impact of its rhetoric and actions on people's lives, a consciousness that would inform his final assessment of Napoleonic aggression.

English Aggression against Denmark, and the "Miseries of Invasion and Pillage" in Portugal

On May 26, 1809, Harry Croswell's *Balance and State Journal* of Albany, New York, published an essay from the *Federal Gazette* titled "Democratic Impartiality," decrying democratic publications and their treatment of British and French aggression, especially in regard to recent events in Denmark.[89]

It is the observation made by many intelligent persons, that nothing can be more insincere and strikingly delusive, than the affected impartiality of democratic scribblers, with regard to our foreign relations.

Can any man for a moment doubt whether these noisy people would have conducted as now do, if France had rescinded her decrees and Great Britain continued her orders in council? Surely nothing is hazarded in declaring, that far different would have been their conduct.

The constant practice of democratic writers, is to rave at English wrongs, and wink at the perfidies of France. An exception breaks no general rule. If England, apprehending, as she says, hostilities from Denmark, seizes the Danish navy, these crazy politicians and vindictive partizans, denounce the British:—*"O thou horrible monster! for to go and to rob, murder and plunder an independent nation! Die, tyrant!"* But when French rapacity fleeces the allies of France, and having drained them of their cash, seizes on the thrones of Portugal and Spain, burning their dwellings and murdering the people— why then, good reader, these daring dragoons, these *impartial* scribblers, cry out "Well done! Republican Emperor, tear down their Inquisitions! Annihilate their Priests! And proceed, thou *Great Pacificator,* in liberating nations, and meliorating the condition of man!"[90]

To be clear, political conservatives and liberal radicals were at war with one another about historical events and their representation in the media. The complaints about democratic "impartiality" in regard to Great Britain's aggression toward Denmark argue that no similar outcry is voiced when French actions are similarly aggressive in the name of political and military self-interest or self-preservation. In this regard, the editorial accurately documents historical tensions between British and Irish radical democrats in America such as William Duane and John Binns (or those sympathetic to British radicalism) and partisans of Great Britain and the monarchal, aristocratic status quo.[91] It also references debates about history, "impartiality," and how events in Europe entered the public sphere, and provides context for seeing how Brown himself understood English aggression relative to the "affected impartiality of democratic scribblers"—a key factor for gauging the reception of Brown's own democratic or radical inclinations.

That is, in his last volume of the "Annals of Europe," Brown remarks in his preface that while events had unfolded in Spain, too few "materials of a legitimate narration" had reached América to justify historical analysis. However, he could, he says, comment generally on the state of Europe and events as they pertain to the Treaty of Tilsit and Napoleon's aggression toward Spain. Further, he hopes that readers will find materials of "more value and variety than any former volume," and thinks his publication might be valuable to the public if it were "merely a general depository of papers" concerning primary materials, as opposed to a historical narrative.[92] I examine Brown's analysis of Denmark and its role during the Napoleonic wars and argue that his historical analysis increasingly takes account of the impact of Napoleonic aggression in Portugal and the effect on its people.

In his study *The Anglo-Swedish Alliance against Napoleonic France,* historian Christer Jorgensen observes that if 1806 was a year of foreign policy and military setbacks for England and its allies, 1807 "was even worse." Russia pulled out of the coalition, and Britain "had shown the price of defying her when she attacked Copenhagen."[93] The Danes were in a bind. If they surrendered their fleet to England, Napoleon would retaliate by attacking Denmark. While this would preserve Denmark's colonies and relations with Norway, the country's "continental possessions" as well as Fünen would be occupied by France. The decision to maintain neutrality against England would be a costly one, and when the British invasion force of 30,000 men under Generals Cathcart and Wellesley was complete, the bombardment of Copenhagen would destroy some 400 homes and leave 2,000 dead inhabitants. England, he says, captured the Danish fleet and a wealth of naval supplies. It also took Heligoland, an island near northern Germany; Denmark's claim to various West Indian islands; and, in 1808, Danish colonies in India. "Reaction," writes Jorgensen, "to events in Denmark was mixed, but the general European impression of Britain's conduct was very negative. It was felt that the British had emulated French ruthlessness and brutality. In Britain reactions were also very mixed."[94]

Brown understood both the colonial ambitions of, and the political pressures on, a country like Denmark. He tracks these events closely in his annals, paying particular attention to how Denmark suffered because of its policies and geographical position. While Brown understood that European political institutions were imbued with patriarchal assumptions and traditions, his rendering of tensions between England and Denmark appears to be more sympathetic. That is, beyond referring to the King of Denmark simply as a "driveling idiot" and making insightful distinctions between a country's government and its people, Brown's writing about the recent political tension between England and Denmark appears at one point to contain the voice of a Danish speaker—a literal dramatization, one might say, of Bakhtin's notion that in an "utterance" part of the discourse can be identified implicitly or explicitly as someone else's.[95]

According to Brown, in the "eyes of the Danes" every excuse offered by the British could only aggravate "the injury," and heighten the "injustice of their conduct." Brown remarks that "to be invaded and exterminated" solely on the grounds of avoiding aggression from a third party is "a conduct unavoidably followed by our deepest abhorrence and revenge." At first glance, such discourse seems to suggest that Brown is speaking; however, the ambiguity is lessened when one considers the perspective or "eyes of the Danes" (and the attendant bias) shown here:

> It does not moderate these feelings to be told by the injurer that a similar attack was meditated against us by another, and that he seized the spoil merely to prevent one whom he hates from seizing it before him. The interests of these rivals are nothing to me. I regard them both with equal affection or indifference, and perform my duty by maintaining peace with both of them. That they both are willing to destroy me for their separate advantage, only justifies my fear and hatred of both; but he that first resorts to actual violence against me will, of course, incur my first and deepest detestation.

Given the use of pronouns like "our," "me," and "I," one might infer that Brown is paraphrasing or quoting a source here and that he accidentally neglected to insert quotation marks. One might also interpret this as Brown using a universalized or ventriloquized voice where "we" correlates with humanity—a reading that complicates the passage's philosophical tone. Or one can argue that Brown may be unconsciously slipping into another narrative voice, not unusual for someone who wrote novels, and that the ambiguity surrounding the speaker also registers Brown's personal resistance to the practice of military "extermination." This is, this conflation of voices, or lapse of narrative objectivity, communicates to the reader the immediacy and impact of a predatory foreign policy and implies why it "merits censure."[96] Even though such narrative literalizes what Bakhtin calls a "dialogized transmission of another's word," it is still "ideologically meaningful" because it simultaneously points to the frequency of military rationalization and domination and to a gesture of resistance by the objectified Other—"the spoil."[97]

If Brown was willing to challenge the rationale for imperial and colonial action in an empathetic way, a way that partakes of fellow "feeling," such views were under constant scrutiny and subject to change, as when he acknowledges the presence of "contingencies" in the English decision to attack Denmark and writes: "As to the *policy* of *honesty,* the *utility* of *justice,* these maxims have no clear application to human conduct." "If utility be the criterion of justice," he says, "each one will conclude it just to benefit himself." And "if justice has only a metaphysical or argumentative test, a door is opened to eternal disputation." Thus, from the "deepest detestation" one might feel in response to political or personal violation to the ambiguous application of moral abstracts, Brown concludes—in a way that again resonates with the central tenets of Godwin's thought—that personal interests of individuals and the public interest of nations mingle in "peculiar" ways, leading men to encroach on others "as if the sacrifice were made to preserve his peculiar country from pestilence or civil war."[98]

On one level, then, Brown registers throughout the annals an increasing measure of historical self-consciousness and an identifiable measure of resistance to the principle, practice, and rhetorical expression of political domination or colonialism. He not only questions the "impartiality" of eyewitness testimony and documents but also acknowledges his own inability to be free of prejudice. In addition to voicing an overt resistance to the idea of imperial and colonial aggression—the "selfish principle"—or the "pretexts" nations use to justify acts of military or economic force, his narrative or discourse registers a "double-voicedness" or hybrid of speech that criticizes not only the practice of imperial or colonial aggression but also the patriarchical structures and racial assumptions that ignore the "political injustice," or "rights of others," and condone the invasion and extermination of other countries and cultures.

Brown, as I have suggested, was highly critical of the impact of French policy and aggression on Denmark. Although he remarks toward the end of volume 4 on the "miseries of invasion and pillage" regarding Portugal and how this "evil" was exacerbated by the "hostile proceedings of their former ally," France, he reserves his most pungent use of the term "evil" for his analysis of the English attack on Copenhagen:

> The attack on Copenhagen was sufficiently disastrous to the Danish people, in its proper and immediate consequences. This, however, composed a

very small part of the evils with which it was pregnant. By laying that nation under the necessity of accepting the alliance and admitting the armies
of France, it made them virtually its subjects and slaves, and entailed upon
it the evils of a perpetual but hopeless war. In war with England, Denmark
could not possibly gain any thing but new mischief and distress. She afforded a stage for foreign armies to fight their own battles, while her own
real independence was utterly extinguished.

Even this, however, was not the worst evil arising from her present situation. Her neutrality must now, at the pleasure of her new ally, be totally
relinquished, and France, with armies in her bowels, will treat her as an
enemy, unless she declares open war with all the enemies of France. Denmark, accordingly, under this irresistible impulse, united with those furious
passions which the outrages of England had awakened, commenced a war
with Sweden, on the twenty-ninth of February.[99]

Brown did not condone the Danish attack on Sweden or her "public reasons for
hostilities," but he did understand the political vulnerability of Denmark. Beyond
being forced into an alliance with France to protect itself from further invasion
from England, Denmark lost its "independence": its "neutrality" was "relinquished," says Brown, because unless Denmark declared war on the adversaries
of France, Napoleon would consider Denmark its enemy.

Importantly here as well, bodily or gender parallels connected with Denmark
intersect with Brown's political analysis, enacting a double-voiced discourse that
characterizes the "worst evil" as Copenhagen's loss of self-determination. According to Brown, Denmark appeared to have little choice in regard to "her" destiny,
so the country's "irresistible impulse" and "furious passions" drove it to commit
similar hostilities against Sweden. Such discourse reenacts what Josephine Donovan calls the "Enlightenment identification of rationalism with the public sphere,
and the non-rational and the moral with the private sphere and with women" as
well as the view that the "subordination of women" was linked to Lockian notions of private property.[100] Ironically, Brown's casting of Denmark as the victim
whose "independence was utterly extinguished" also links his earlier references
to a masculine or militaristic England with oppression and a whole new cycle of
domestic violation—Denmark's acts of aggression against Sweden.

Whether or not Brown identified strongly with Denmark's "neutrality" because
of his Quaker pacifism or his earlier sympathies for the rights of women as expressed in *Alcuin* (1798, 1815) and his novels is difficult to determine. It is clear,
though, that Brown associated England's military aggressiveness against Denmark
with the oppression and abuse of women and that gender constructions informed
his interpretation of history, political or otherwise. It should also be said that while
Brown never seems to equate the word "evil" with supernatural causation, he does

use the term in a way that denotes more than just a passing misfortune or unfortunate consequence. His labeling of "poverty, epidemical diseases, famine," and so forth as "evils" of secondary importance when compared to the carnage of war suggests that he made explicit distinctions in his definitions of the term. Indeed, Brown's willingness to classify an event in Danish history as the "worst evil" and his frequent use of the appellation at certain points in his narrative suggests he used the word to express varying degrees of judgment, and to decry policies of political and economic self-interest that he found to be morally suspect.

Similar, then, to his representation of English aggression against Denmark, and Copenhagen in particular, Brown's representation of French actions toward Portugal also yields analysis that is at once both bold and sympathetic. In volume 4 he writes, "Thus it was that the opening of the year 1808, beheld Great Britain at open war, or at enmity with every European state but Portugal, Sicily and Sweden," and "the French had subdued Prussia, and converted Austria, Russia, Denmark and Turkey into open and zealous enemies."[101] Although Brown notes that Sweden and Portugal were allies with England and that England was for various reasons unable or unwilling to come to their assistance, the bulk of the last volume of the annals on Europe—chapters three through six—deals almost exclusively with events as they concern Portugal and Brown's efforts to be impartial and eliminate personal bias from his historical narrative.

This is evident in Brown's assessment of Portugal's military force and how it was commonly represented by political observers:

> The political or national weakness of Portugal is a problem which political enquirers find it easy to resolve into the malignant influence of the Romish religion. Its priests, monks, and inquisition are, it is imagined, the true causes of its political infirmities. This notion is adopted by many in defiance of the plainest dictates of history and experience, which informs us that when that religion flourished with most vigour Europe was most turbulent and ferocious, and actuated most by the military spirit; that the greatest political energy and wisdom have been displayed, in all past times by the nations which were most devoted to it; that national strength is most naturally to be expected in countries where religious differences and disputes prevail the least, and that Portugal itself, when she transcended all the European nations in the commercial and military spirit; when she executed the most romantic projects of conquest and aggrandizement, and atchieved [sic] the most incredible exploits in navigation and trade, was as much devoted to that religion as at present, and even sunk much deeper into superstition.

In countering contemporary representations of Portugal as a country weakened by the "Romish religion," Brown offers the view that the nation's "priests, monks, and inquisition" have no more to do with its current military strength than when it was at its "commercial and military" height. In fact, he suggests, when it was at its peak, it was "as much devoted to that religion as at present," if not even more. That is, while Portugal does not have the military strength it once had, especially compared to a modern France or England, its weakness, is overrated when compared to its past or the relative strength of Spain. While such commentary runs counter to Brown's earlier, more skeptical views of Roman Catholicism and its "projects of conquest and aggrandizement," it is consistent with his efforts to be impartial when assessing causes and effects of contemporary events.

Brown goes on to describe how, until now, the political "equipoise" existing between Portugal's neighbors preserved it from foreign conquest. He also comments on the ways Portugal's prize colony in South America, Brazil, may be destined to become the "head and not the subordinate member of that body composed by their union." Although he does claim earlier that too "inconsiderable progress" was made with events in Spain, it is difficult to determine why Brown marginalizes Spain. He makes only a passing comment about the May 3 revolt of the Spanish against the French and focuses completely on the British encounter with the French near Lisbon and the political reasons the French in their defeat weren't given harder terms by General Wellesley and Sir H. Dalrymple. Beyond the manner in which his remarks about the "bickerings" between England and Portugal and the "discontent" of the English make for an interesting insight into national temperaments, his narrative points to how difference in "manners and religion" contributed to tensions between countries.[102]

Brown, however, did not limit his criticism to public documents; he also assessed less public sources of information as well as the historian's own agenda in writing history. For instance, with a blockade in effect on Lisbon and the emigration of Portugal's royal family to Brazil, Brown is cautious in what he says about the circumstances of the escape and to what degree similar "opportunities were seized by the higher classes of the people." While he is only able to determine that "no serious opposition" was made to those who could afford to leave, his investigation of the actual invasion of Portugal allows him to document how Portugal was "suddenly exposed to all the miseries of invasion and pillage," including the obligation of the Portuguese to feed and house French and Spanish troops and to pay excise taxes on everything from horses and mules to rent and the annual incomes of "prelates and superiors of religious orders." Brown finds that over $20 million was raised from the Portuguese people in this way, and he comments on how British and Portuguese trade was affected by such events. On this point, he remarks in a footnote:

Private and anonymous information is so vague and deceitful, that no conscientious historian will venture to rely on it. On this occasion all our intelligence, of this kind, passes through an English channel, and is liable, therefore, to be perverted by the natural prejudices of the enemy. We have, in a printed form, a vast mass of intelligence respecting the conduct of the French in Portugal, and the sufferings of the people. The blockade of Lisbon is said to have even produced a famine in that capital, and the French, we have been told, were ready to depart, on account of the difficulty of subsistence. All this, however, was no less inconsistent with probability than with subsequent experience.

Brown was willing to write about the "miseries" and hardships of the Portuguese, but he also came to believe as a result of his experience that "private and anonymous information" was less reliable than the public or "printed form" (which, as we have seen in the case of the English officer and Russian historian also "cannot be considered as impartial"). Such comments qualify his earlier reflections in his periodical essays about the value of private documents when writing history and document his evolving sense of historical method and analysis. While he acknowledged, in other words, that a "vast mass" of material about the French and the Portuguese was available, he also recognized that most of his historical evidence was subject to the scrutiny and "natural prejudices" of an enemy—in this case, England. Brown concludes in his note that "volumes might be filled with plausible inventions and gossiping surmises, but though more entertaining than the meagre narration we are obliged to give, they would contribute nothing to our instruction."[103] Such a statement suggests that while he acknowledged the relative value of less public sources of historical evidence, he nonetheless felt compelled to make distinctions about the reliability of such evidence for his narrative.

Nowhere, however, in Brown's "Annals of Europe" is his interest more evident in sorting out facts—and appropriating public or official documents to do so—than in his assessment of Napoleon's evacuation from Portugal in September 1808 and his conscious inclusion of and reference to primary sources. By specifically alluding to public documents he has published in the appendix to the magazine, Brown signals an important change in his narrative strategy and efforts to objectively re-present the past. After reconstructing how Arthur Wellesley and the English expelled the French from Lisbon in August, Brown relays the various stipulations that both sides agreed to in the treaty. "The British," he recounts, "were regarded by the people of Portugal as auxiliaries, who were bound merely to re-establish the native government."[104]

While communications errors were apparently committed during the armistice by the British, Brown immediately follows his historical narrative proper with material in the appendix titled "Official Papers Relative to the Evacuation of Portugal by the French Army."[105] Under this heading are documents such as "Letter from Sir H. Dalrymple to the Secretary of State—received September 16, 1808, containing the Armistice and Convention" and "Report of the Court of Enquiry, Appointed to

Examine the Conduct of British Commanders in Portugal, and Proceedings There-upon." These documents, in turn, are followed by American and foreign and state papers, including "An Account of Louisiana at the Time of Its Transfer to the United States" and an "Edict of the French Government at Lisbon."

Such documents, as they pertain to Brown's historical narrative for 1808 and specific events in his historical writing like the invasion and evacuation of Portu-gal, record his growing efforts to integrate, one might say, dialogically, support-ing primary sources and perspectives and represent the truth to the reader. They register, in other words, his emerging belief that the *American Register* itself might be considered valuable if it were "merely a general depository of papers of history and politics" available to readers for interpretation and historical analysis.[106] It is a heuristic in his annals that one finds more fully developed in his "Annals of America" and that further contributes to the reflexive, indeed "novel," means by which Brown sought to immerse his readers in the texture or heteroglossia of historical primary documents and events.

Although volume 4 of the "Annals of Europe" reflects increased editorial activity on Brown's part, especially with commentary in his footnotes, it continues to record Brown's developing awareness of the complexities of writing history. Specifically, one finds that Brown became acutely aware—as he was writing history—of the limitations and distortions of "conjecture" in historical writing, including his own, and of how the "language of diplomatic papers" as well as "private and anonymous information" is also tainted by personal or political bias, if not some sort of propa-gandistic intent. While this volume also documents Brown's ongoing efforts to rid history of many of the prevailing prejudices of his time, such as anti-Catholic senti-ments, it also yields important insights about the dynamics of "power" in an age of empire building and about how the premises and practices of imperialism and colonialism were intimately connected with assumptions of national "self-interest" and contemporary constructions of race and gender identities.

In sum, Brown's specifically American history of Napoleon's imperial march across Europe, the impact of the Napoleonic Wars on Turkey, Russia, and Prussia, British colonial efforts in South America and India, and the impact of aggression on Den-mark and Portugal not only illustrates his developing understanding of the period's various "instances of selfish and iniquitous policy" but also his ongoing reflections on the difficulties of being a historian. His text offers a rare contemporary critique of how European and non-European countries both exercised political "power" and the manner in which assumptions of racial or class superiority were complemented by equally patriarchal assumptions about gender and its strategies of submission and cultural control. While he continued to strive for historical "objectivity," he also became acutely aware in a practical sense of the ways his narrative text, and that those of his primary sources, communicate ideological biases. Moreover, Brown's double-voiced discourse about the "evils" of war—its carnage and the related "poverty, epidemical diseases, famine"—point not only to his Quaker upbringing and aversion to war but to his enduring political sympathies. Indeed, his willingness to ironically critique the racist dimensions of colonialism and his description of England's violation of Denmark in terms of female oppression, suggests that Brown continued in some respects to rely on Godwin's and Wollstonecraft's radical ideas as a measure of political and personal injustices.

What I have suggested thus far, then, about the secular nature of Brown's history writing and his increasingly sharp critique of European imperialism and colonialism raises questions about the underlying assumptions and aims in his "Annals of America." Does Brown, for example, merely extend his "impartiality" to the American scene because he aims to be consistent in his narrative? Or does he exclude such rhetoric because he desired not to associate American expansion with French imperialism? Can one infer that the omission of providential rhetoric from his narrative of domestic events is hard evidence that Brown could no longer sustain—if he ever really did—the assumption that America had been appointed by God to fulfill a special destiny?

Indeed, as Brown assessed Napoleon's imperial errand or the colonial ventures of other European countries and wrestled with expansion and race relations in the United States, it seems useful to consider how he responded to the Aaron Burr conspiracy, the embargo, or other events, and to reevaluate whether he critiqued American nationalism and imperialism in the same way he analyzed Napoleon's imperial errand. Such analysis provides important insights into the supposed conservatism of the later Brown but also his capacity, as an ironic historian, to engage the emergent ideology and rhetoric of American exceptionalism and manifest destiny.

Part 3

✳

The Politics of History

Chapter Six

American Exceptionalism and the

"Annals of America"

Europeans had started the "antiquating" of American history as early as the Renaissance, elaborating fantasies of Arcadia, Atlantis, and even Eden lying just over the geographical and temporal horizon. But while Europeans of the late eighteenth century put to rest their fantasies of locating in the American hemisphere a prior utopia that would serve as a mythic engine of empire, post-colonial Anglo-Americans found the very condition of post-coloniality a spur to theorizing American classical origins. In a flourish of Columbian thinking, they "newly" contemplated the precedents and possibilities of "American civilization," pre-discovery and post-colonial. A certain form of exceptionalism believed America was a nation without precedent; but there was a vital tradition that saw exemplars in the New World.
  —Eric Werthheimer, *Imagined Empires: Incas, Aztecs, and the*
  New World of American Literature, 1771–1876 (1999)

In his landmark study *The Radicalism of the American Revolution* (1993), historian Gordon S. Wood writes that Americans typically have thought of the American Revolution as a conservative, almost nonviolent affair that was concerned primarily, if not exclusively, with political inequities and constitutional rights; if the revolution is measured by the number of people killed and the level of misery and chaos that often accompanies such political and social upheaval, then the American Revolution was not as destructive or destabilizing as the French Revolution. However, he says, "If we measure the radicalism by the amount of social change that actually took place—by transformations in the relationships that bound people to each other—then the American Revolution was not conservative at all; on the contrary: it was as radical and as revolutionary as any in history." Simply put, from about 1776 until the early nineteenth century, American culture, politics, and geography had been "radically and thoroughly transformed," and America, amidst the turbulence of European empire building, became "the most liberal, democratic, and modern nation in the world"—the eye, in the context of colonialism and western history, of a revolutionary political hurricane.[1]

Similar to Woods's assessment of America's origins, Eric Wertheimer's remarks about American history generally speak to his interest in how South American cultures, especially the Incas and the Aztecs, contributed to America's perceptions of itself as an emerging political power and empire, but they also reference a basic set of assumptions or ideas about history, national identity, and American destiny that Brown and his contemporaries were wrestling with in various ways. That is, just as Europeans had gone back to the "annals of empire and civilization— Egyptian, Greek, Roman—trying to impart teleological, self-justifying stories of progress, renovation, and enlightenment," so members of the early Republic also sought to understand their classical origins, in addition to their Judeo-Christian ones. They inquired into and reflected upon, sometimes radically, the "precedents and possibilities" of American colonial culture and what that meant specifically for the course of American empire. The activation, observes Wertheimer, of a "national imaginary" or "exceptionalism" began to become apparent after the American Revolution and as the early Republic gained political and economic footing, with many, like Philip Freneau, Hugh Brackenridge, and Joel Barlow, articulating a vision for American empire that was both benevolent and powerful in purpose.[2]

More recently, Andy Doolen makes the case in *Fugitive Empire: Locating American Imperialism* (2005) that "the critical paradigm of *American exceptionalism,* which reaffirms the fundamental ideals of the age of revolution, has long denied the existence of imperial authority in America." "This critical perspective," he says, "proliferates the myth that the American Revolution extirpated the force and logic of empire with the irresistible and heroic dream of egalitarianism and freedom." He traces the beginnings of American imperial thought to the New York Conspiracy trials of 1741 and the ways slave insurrection, conspiracy theories, and Anglo solidarity coalesced. While I read Brown's role in the formation an imperial ethos differently than Doolen, I think he correctly identifies texts in Brown's *Monthly Magazine and American Review* as sites of patriotic belief and that a "hidden imperialism"—race issues, geography, and an "unstable mixture of idealism, force, and pragmatism"—arguably shaped American culture and politics from its earliest beginnings.[3]

In this chapter, then, I examine Brown's historical narrative in light of his evolving awareness of European imperialism and colonialism and his writing the "Annals of Europe." In tracing Brown's ongoing efforts at historical "impartiality" during a period of intensely radical change, I identify an ironic tone in his historical narrative that is critical of American ideas about empire and expansion. Brown's historical analysis and the developing nature of his interrogation or "judgment" can be seen in his view of the "progress of the American nation," especially in regard to the country's growth since the Louisiana Purchase; his assessment of the Aaron Burr conspiracy and New Orleans as a barometer of the American desire to extend its "empire"; the *Chesapeake* affair as measure of American nationalism and a catalyst for debate about political self-interest; and, last, Jefferson's embargo as evidence that American exceptionalism was a myth. Together, these lines of inquiry, along with how Brown continued to use historical footnotes, provide insight into his evolving historicism or consciousness—his ironic treatment of the potentially imperial aspects of American expansion and power—and a postcolonial ethos. Moreover, they revise the view that Brown's radical consciousness as a young man was extinguished by a latent cultural conservatism and, as Lawrence Buell has suggested, point to the existence of an ironic or satirical tradition of historians in American historiography.[4]

American Empire and the Louisiana Purchase

In his classic account of American exceptionalism and its role in the formation of American identity from the colonial period onward, Jack P. Greene makes distinctions about the United States as an "exceptional" nation, meaning "the absence of class conflict," and as "an '*exemplary* nation,'" meaning that providence or enlightened leadership had distinguished American destiny. He points out how scholarship has questioned the idea of "American exceptionalism" and found it "seriously deficient" in terms of its relationship to a European past. Greene writes that the "current effort to assimilate colonial America to early modern European history takes little account of an extraordinary large body of contemporary testimony from the sixteenth through the eighteenth centuries and beyond that did indeed see America as special, and in many ways even an exceptional, place."[5] Few "contemporary interpreters," he suggests, viewed America as a place without class conflict or social problems, yet on a comparative basis they did see America as a more promising environment for personal liberties. Ernest Tuveson, among others, concurs, noting how colonials and succeeding generations, including Brown's and Jefferson's, believed that "providence, or history, ha[d] put a special responsibility on the American people to spread the blessings of liberty, democracy, and equality to others throughout the earth, and to defeat, if necessary by force, the sinister powers of darkness."[6]

By contrast, David Lee Clark argues that Brown "early realized what it has taken many people long years to understand" about the relationship between Europe and the United States. Brown's cosmopolitanism and "reflection" on past and present events allowed him to see how the "destiny" of Europe and the United States were linked to one another, and how "trade" with the Continent was dependent upon the political and economic conditions of "European states" and their colonies. Like, in many ways, William Duane, he understood better than others the geopolitics of the day and how events and policies that occurred overseas had an influence on the United States. To be sure, Brown was "dizzied by the remarkable growth of the country" and at times "allowed his enthusiasm to exceed its usual bounds of moderation."[7] However, his embrace of the idea of expansion was eventually tempered by his wariness of American imperial ambitions in other parts of the Americas and the ways that democratic principles such as liberty could be compromised.

The treatment of these two phenomena—American exceptionalism and the ways America's imperial aspirations resembled Europe's—as separate, not as being mutually illuminating or as informing current conceptions of "republicanism" or "virtue," makes an examination of Brown's "Annals of America" especially valuable. For beyond providing a critical perspective of American nationalism and empire building, including Brown's own earlier enthusiasms, his history writing registers both a nationalist fervor and, later, a growing recognition of the imperial dimensions of American expansionism—a historiographical vantage point that seems to have been influenced by his resistance to a filiopietistic and teleological historical tradition as well as his analysis of French and English military aggression in his "Annals of Europe."

In his groundbreaking study *The Romance of Real Life*, Steven Watts has argued, minus consideration of Brown's historical writing, that Brown should be viewed as an "ardent expansionist in the early 1800s, promoting American growth into the 'property which God and Nature have made ours.'" Brown's "deep-dyed expansionism," suggests Watts, was anchored in a vision of "an American imperial republic," a vision rooted in an "ideology of geographic growth, commercial freedom, social coherence, and resolute, self-controlled character." Brown not only offered "stern bourgeois moralizing" but was "a persistent, articulate spokesman for social stability, cultural authority, and self-discipline." Thus, Brown's "instinct for social reform and cultural radicalism receded before a new respect for wealth and power" and subsequently extinguished the "cultural and ideological dissent of his earlier career."[8]

While I agree with Watts that Brown embodied changing attitudes toward authority and the idea of republican "virtue" and at times evinced nationalist sentiments, I disagree with his interpretation that Brown evolved from a "youthful utopian radical to stodgy middle-age conservative," a figure whose later role as a cultural critic was limited to toasting the blessings of American expansionism and, on occasion, sneering at events in Europe. Brown did not limit his later writing to articulating a "repressive bourgeois ethic of self-control" or reinforcing the status quo in a way that was consistent with genteel values. Rather, Brown's avoidance of a "redeemer nation" rationale in his annals and his emerging critique of Napoleonic imperialism and British colonialism point to the manner in which his narrative came to associate the "evil" of European imperialism and colonialism with American institutions and "self-interest." While Watts, therefore, accurately notes that Brown "disapproved of Americans' fervent cultural nationalism," his suggestion that Brown steadily embraced the "boisterous rhetoric of manifest destiny" fails to consider Brown's history writing and use of irony in the larger context of European colonialism and imperial expansion, nor does it distinguish Brown's views of American expansion—and "God and Nature"—as expressed around 1803 from those he expressed while writing his "Annals of Europe and America" several years later.[9] Brown's early enthusiasm, in other words, for western expansion was increasingly tempered by his understanding that racial inequities, displacement, and injustice were part of the equation for national progress.

Beginning with volume 1 of his "Annals of America," Brown conducts a general overview of the condition of the country since the Revolution. He offers a picture of the new Republic that is optimistic in tone and affirming of its unique situation, yet at the same time careful about describing cultural tensions:

> While Europe was thus laid waste by so many years of war, the United States of America remained in tranquility. For more than twenty-two years, their internal peace has been disturbed by no commotions of any importance. Scarcely a life had been lost, or a cottage been demolished, in any intestine feud or insurrection. Though divided by accidental circumstances, existing at their first settlement, into several independent states, unequal to each other in size, population, and riches, dissimilar in habits, manners, and interests, they had never quarrelled with each other; though obliged to undergo a thorough revolution in their government, this dangerous and critical experiment was conducted and completed without the drawing of a sword; though harbouring in their bosom a nation of slaves, whose bondage was exasperated by many extraordinary circumstances of hardship and cruelty, who were drawn into union with each other, and set in irreconcileable opposition to their masters, by the indelible tokens of feature and colour, and who were roused by the example of successful revolt in a neighbouring country, yet they have hitherto avoided the calamity of a servile war. The evils of internal dissention and rebellion, instead of approaching nearer, are every day removed to a greater distance; the gulf which divides the master and the slave is becoming gradually narrower, and the ties which bind together the various members of the nation multiply and strengthen by time.[10]

First, beyond contrasting European war and turmoil with American growth and assimilation, the passage avoids a "redeemer nation" rhetoric. Unlike that of his contemporaries, who treated such circumstances in light of the "providence" of God's will for the new nation, Brown's interpretation is enthusiastic but not in the traditional sense of fully appropriating the rhetoric of national redemption. Phrases such as "accidental circumstances" and "critical experiment" suggest— as they do in the "Annals of Europe"—that while Brown endorsed a program of national expansion, he was simultaneously reluctant to viewing the growth of the Republic as being shaped by the guiding hand of providence.[11]

At the same time, the passage points up Brown's nationalist interests. He optimistically asserts that "the ties which bind together the various members of the nation" are being multiplied and strengthened over time, and that despite dissimilar "habits, manners, and interests" the country has had an "internal peace" and prospered. He goes on to write about how the "increase in population, from three millions to six" corresponded with "an evident increase of individual opulence, refinement, and luxury."[12] While Watts says Brown had a "new respect for wealth and power, stability and responsibility," Brown more accurately registers the impact of increased population and prosperity as well as individual "opulence" and "luxury." He also expresses his "wonder" at the rapid expansion of population in the previous twenty years and how increased population in the future will necessitate additional "clothing, diet, and habitation." The increase, he calculates in a footnote, will be proportional: "While numbers are only doubled, the mass of general wealth will be more than doubled." Such speculation on Brown's part testifies not only to his awe of the remarkable growth of the country—its economic "improvements" and increased commercial and military strength—but to his recognition of the kinds of conditions that can lead to economic disparity.

His enthusiasm is measured though, for he also expresses his concern about the potential "evils of internal dissention and rebellion." In the case of the American Indian, for instance, Brown's analysis of European claims in America and of the early Republic's relations with the natives reveals ideological tensions. Only after the French and Indian War (1754–63), writes Brown, were boundaries clarified, and the Mississippi River, "which forms the western border of the American empire," fully appreciated. Brown recounts the commercial value of the Mississippi River, especially to settlers of the western region, and explains the significance of the French and Indian War. But, he says, "after the American states had finally subdued the aboriginal tribes, and recovered from the terrible shocks of the revolutionary war, their colonies crossed the mountains in vast numbers."[13] Then the true value of the Mississippi River, as an "outlet to the ocean," became clear.

France's eventual sale of her "claims in North America" precluded, of course, war between the two countries, allowing Brown to state: "That national zeal and unanimity which is awakened by a sense of justice, will be exerted much more warmly and completely in defending what a voluntary sale and full consideration have made our own, than in wresting from another what is merely convenient for us to obtain."[14] Such commentary, particularly about "wresting" claims of land from another entity, hints at his continued affinity for American expansionism. In fact, it opens the door for further investigation into how Brown's notions of American "empire" mirrored those of Europe, and how his narrative attempts to reconcile Native American rights and interests with an American policy of expansion.

Brown recounts the difficulties in establishing territorial limits, especially in regard to Spanish territory, or New Mexico, and the Louisiana Territory. Since "new colonies," he writes, "were every day advancing up the rivers, and penetrating further into the forests," it was difficult to ascertain hard-and-fast boundary lines. He remarks that "Spain has five or six millions of square miles of territory, in the western hemisphere, to which her right is wholly undisputed. About forty-nine fiftieths of this is unoccupied, except by savages, who are hastening to extinction, and whose claims are of no more regard than those of the stag or panther which roam in their company over the same wilderness." Whether or not, he says, New Mexico's "claim of sovereignty extend a few miles further into the bog or the forest or not, at this or that corner" is a matter for Spain to decide. Then, in commentary that aligns the rhetoric and rationale of Spanish colonialism more closely with the imperial designs of the United States, Brown writes:

> The same observations may be applied to the United States. A nation that has more than five hundred millions of acres unoccupied and even unsurveyed, and whose lawful limits on one side can only be reached by a journey of many weeks or months, through a vacant country, cannot feel deeply interested in debating, whether the frontier line on one part shall run forty miles further east or further west. Even if ten or twenty plantations, and some hundreds of subjects be lost to the empire by yielding to the adverse claim, a nation which has six million of subjects at present, and may count upon forty millions in the next generation, cannot be supposed to be very pertinacious in such a case.

Brown's description here of the United States in terms of "empire" and "subjects" corresponds with the prevailing ideology and discourse of imperialism and colonialism: the presumption that people or populations were resources, like minerals or crops, which could be manipulated or exploited at will for the benefit of the nation in power. Just as Spain will not trifle over a few miles of uncharted territory, so the United States, states Brown, is in a position in which it can afford to not be concerned about the exact location of a frontier line or a few "subjects." Moreover, while the ideas of "sovereignty" and "claims" come up in regard to both countries, Brown's reference to "savages, who are hastening to extinction" and whose "claims" to the land are no "more regarded than those of the stag or panther" raises an interesting question about Brown's later views of American expansion or imperialism and Native American land rights. Does he omit commentary on this aspect of American "claims" because he views displacement of Native

Americans as a necessary evil, the result of the course of empire, or because he became conscious of the inherent contradiction with such a position? Along with how he represented Indians in his novel *Edgar Huntly,* Brown's commentary in his pamphlets, particularly the ones he addressed to Congress in 1803 regarding the Louisiana Purchase, helps clarify this point and is worth digressing upon, especially in regard to his use of irony and the politics of the period concerning expansion and military ambition in the mode of Napoleon.

First, uncertain of whether he had the authority under the Constitution to acquire territory and grant U.S. citizenship, Jefferson considered a constitutional amendment but opted to ignore constitutional implications as long as Congress "overlooked the 'metaphysical subtleties' of the problem and ratified the treaty."[15] Several partisan Federalists attacked Jefferson's position, saying that he was compromising constitutional principles; however, other Federalists, among them Alexander Hamilton, John Adams, and John Marshall, eventually supported ratification of the treaty, despite reservations, for instance, about the size of the territory. The treaty was dated April 30, 1803, signed on May 2, and ratified on October 20 that year by the U.S. Senate with a vote of 24 to 7.

Brown's *Address to the Government of the United States, on the Cession of Louisiana to the French,* published in January 1803, opens with the reader eavesdropping on the author's use of a persona, a French counselor of state, supposedly advising Napoleon about the strategic importance of Louisiana and the advantages of acquiring it, rather than Santo Domingo. He says, "They call themselves *free,* yet a fifth of their numbers are slaves. . . . They call themselves *one,* yet all languages are native to their citizens." Although money and greed are problematic, the "great weakness," claims the counselor, "arises from their form of government and condition and habits of the people." Everyone's pursuit of their own individual interest is also indicative of the country's political chaos, making it a "hot-bed for faction and sedition." The Frenchman then underscores that the country is rife with internal dissension, as it concerns a slave population and disenfranchised Indians. "Devoted to the worst miseries," he says, "is the nation which harbors in its bosom a foreign race, brought by fraud and rapine from their native land, who are bereaved of all blessings of humanity." Likewise, he continues, the country is vulnerable because "INDIANS," in their "savage ignorance, their undisciplined passions, their restless and war-like habits, their notions of ancient right," are also ready to retaliate.[16]

After hearing the French counselor's argument, Brown, or more accurately, Brown's speaker, comments on his arguments, and on the "truth of the picture" in regard to the country's "unity of manners, laws, and government" and desire for "concord." He says that Americans should not "overrate" their own force or "underrate that of France." At the same time he argues for a "right to possession," he also protests the "stupid apathy" of the American government in regard to the Louisiana Territory, lamenting that "European powers toss about among themselves about the property which God and Nature have made *ours.*" "America is OURS," says Brown's speaker, "because the interests of that people [inhabitants of Louisiana] and of ourselves are common: not only because the peace and happiness of these States assign it to us, but because *their* welfare *claims* our alliance and protection."[17]

As Clark observes, the pamphlet had "considerable vogue," was reprinted in Martinsburg, Virginia, and was the focus of a forty-eight-page review (mostly excerpts) in the *New York Herald*.[18] Because of its favorable reception, Brown also published an abridged and slightly corrected version of the pamphlet.[19] However, in a subsequent companion pamphlet, *Monroe's Embassy, or the Conduct of the Government, in Relation to Our Claims to the Navigation of the Mississippi*, published in March 3, 1803, Brown offers a modified view of the situation. The speaker, "Poplicola," who Brown *now* claims also authored the previous pamphlet, openly cries for a more aggressive handling of the cession, that is, the physical appropriation of the Louisiana Territory and not just the action of sending an envoy to France to negotiate for the land. Frustrated, he remarks: "Heaven, indeed, has hitherto befriended us beyond our hopes or merits. We that have done nothing for ourselves, have had an auspicious providence busy in our preservation. . . . How long the invisible and unmerited protection, we have hitherto enjoyed, will continue, cannot be guessed." While Brown's speaker, who at times resembles Jonathan Swift's ironic persona in "A Modest Proposal," goes on to say that "fate has manifestly decreed, that America must belong to the English name and race," it is toward the end of the pamphlet that he laments in a heightened manner: "Our only refuge is in that SOVEREIGN PROVIDENCE, which has hitherto preserved us, in spite of ourselves. Under THAT protection, the folly of our rulers fights against us in vain."[20] It is difficult to determine if Brown meant what he said that about the role of providence in American history, or if his references to God and government are merely rhetorical gestures in an effort to prompt political action against France.

Regardless, the Louisiana political pamphlets reflect Brown's awareness of a providential rationale and his willingness in 1803 to employ such rhetoric on behalf of his views concerning the Louisiana Territory. One may argue, though, that while such sentiments are consistent with Brown's remarks about Christianity elsewhere, none of these statements necessarily suggests that Brown personally endorsed any sort of manifest destiny for the United States or, as I demonstrate later, a teleological view of history. That is, despite saying in a June 20, 1803, letter to Reverend Samuel Miller that "this age has likewise been eminently distinguished from all others by the progress the European or Christian nations have made towards that political ascendancy over the Earth to which they are destined to arrive" and despite writing in the "Editor's Address to the Public" of the October 1, 1803, issue of the *Literary Magazine and American Register* that in an age when the "foundations of religion and morality have been so boldly attacked," he would be, "without equivocation or reserve, the ardent friend and willing champion of the Christian religion," Brown does not always link God and nation.[21] The rhetoric of manifest destiny that appears in a political pamphlet like *An Address to the Government of the United States, on the Cession of Louisiana* gives voice to Federalist beliefs, especially if more partisan or conservative Federalists were actually against purchase of the territory.

As with the earlier pamphlet, then, it is difficult to say how much of these comments accurately reflect Brown's own true sentiments. Robert Levine argues that "rather than making a millennial appeal to divine right," Brown is actually underscoring "issues of national self-preservation." He is not suggesting that expansionism is "sanctioned by God," but rather he is illustrating how "power is at the center of the geopolitics of nationhood in the early nineteenth century." Further,

> In light of Brown's critique of French expansionist projects in Saint-Domingue and Louisiana, it would not be all that difficult, then, to argue that at the core of Brown's writings on Louisiana and imperialism during this time is a critique (or unmasking) of nationalist exceptionalism. Paradoxically, Brown pursues his nationalist ends in the Louisiana pamphlets through an anti-expansionist expansionism that aspires to bring about national unity, coherence, purpose, and self-defense. These are simultaneously anxious and reflective texts, texts that both critique and seek to sustain the nation. And they are hardly insistent on connections between whiteness and nation.

Levine's reading of the pamphlets, like my own, argues for understanding Brown's Louisiana materials as eschewing any boisterous rhetoric of American destiny, providential design, or exceptionalism. Indeed, as Levine suggests, in urging territorial expansion of this sort, Brown is not aligning himself with Federalist politics of the early 1800s or denigrating Indians and black slaves. Rather, just as Brown's writing and editing of antislavery and antiracist periodical materials in the *Literary Magazine and American Register* and elsewhere in the early 1800s show a Brown that "radically departs from the politics of fear and loathing of the Jeffersonians," so in 1803, on the subject of Louisiana, he may be seen as "dissenting somewhat from the northern Federalist position on Louisiana and taking a 'southern' position" on expansion that was even "more aggressive" than Jefferson's and Madison's.[22]

Despite, then, Brown's apparent sentiments, the fact that in his second pamphlet he ascribes the persona "Poplicola" to both his present and previous pamphlet is a revealing one—such a confession is an indicator that Brown was ready in some ways to distinguish, like Swift did, his views from those of his persona. Use of such a narrative or framing device helps establish, in other words, that although Brown was exposed early and often to a rhetoric of national redemption and even used it occasionally in some of his private and public writings, his publications from about 1804 until the end of his career in 1810 are largely devoid of such discourse.

That is, if, as Watts contends, "on or about April 1800 Charles Brockden Brown changed" and "pull[ed] back from radical social criticism," it seems plausible to say he apparently recanted in or around 1804, as he was composing the historical sketches and moving toward a more critical inquiry of domestic politics, and the role of religious and secular authority in the early Republic.[23]

To put it another way, Brown's marriage to Elizabeth Linn, daughter of a well-known Presbyterian minister and sister of the Reverend John Blair Linn, in 1804, does not seem to have affected his desire to avoid a rhetoric of exceptionalism. Neither Brown's translation, for instance, of C. F. Volney's *A View of the Soil of the United States of America* (1804), in which he dismantles Volney's stereotypes about Americans and interrogates policies of genocide toward the American Indian, nor his "Sketch of the Life and Character of John Blair Linn" (1805), which recalls his deceased in-law and late pastor of the First Presbyterian church of Philadelphia, contains a single reference to "Providence."[24] In addition, *An Address to the Congress of the United States, on the Utility and Justice of Restrictions upon Foreign Commerce* (1809) also ignores or plays down such discourse, as does his later personal correspondence.[25]

In contrast, then, to his contemporaries and claims by modern critics that Brown in his later years fully embraced the "boisterous rhetoric of manifest destiny," the omission, largely, in Brown's writing of a hardcore exceptionalism is significant and in keeping with a liberal tradition of American secular belief and radicalism.[26] The complete absence, as I suggest in later chapters, of a filiopietistic model of interpreting the past in Brown's "Annals of Europe and America," or a rhetoric of national redemption that resembled the discourse of Napoleonic Europe, is a central reason for revising the perception of Brown as "conservative" and the significance of his contributions to early national historiography. While one may read phrases like "particular care of Heaven" and "protection of providence" in the historical sketches as embellishing the imaginary histories of two families from the medieval ages to the present, Brown's historical sketches or fragments offer, like his novels and political pamphlets on Louisiana, their own brand of historical representation, ironic intervention, and performance.[27]

Just as Brown's commentary on God and nation in his Louisiana pamphlets can be difficult to parse, his narrative can, in the mode of the historical fiction or fragments he was composing at the time, also be read as embedding an awareness of wrongs committed against native peoples and statements about possessing the territory west of the Mississippi—what Brown's speaker refers to as the "American Nile." Brown's fictitious French counselor does not hesitate, for example, to tell Napoleon that "a savage and naked race, have mostly disappeared" and that other territories are also ripe for "colonization." Concerning the possibilities, for instance, of colonizing New Holland, the counselor remarks:

That it has hitherto been unpeopled, is that circumstance on which humanity must reflect with most delight, since all the miseries and all the vengeance of an oppressed or defrauded race will thus be avoided. The necessity of gin to disable, of fraud to betray, arms to destroy, and fortifications
to repel ferocious savages, will be saved. Expense, and calamities inflicted
and endured, the stain of injustice and of cruelty; . . . the evils of which the
Spaniards and the English have had their full share; . . . will be escaped by
the nation that shall colonize New Holland.

Because he favored western expansion and understood how past policies with
American Indian tribes made them "the fittest tools" for the French, Brown could
say in his 1803 Louisiana pamphlet that "Fate has manifestly decreed, that America
must belong to the English name and race."[28] And, as is evident in his translation of
C. F. Volney's *A View of the Soil and Climate of the United States of America* and his
*Address to the Congress of the United States on the Utility and Justice of Restrictions
upon Foreign Commerce,* he believed that the "savages may be profited by intercourse with civilized" whites and even each other. "One of the consequences," he
writes, "of extended empire is to pull down those barriers which separate mankind
from each other . . . to create one nation out of many."[29]

At the same time, however, one senses in this passage and in Brown's translation of C. F. Volney's writing that Brown was acutely aware of the price being paid
for such assimilation. Beyond Cecelia Tichi's view that Brown's commitment to
"continental expansion" obliged him to "counter Volney's indictments of America
as unhealthy territory riddled with incorrigible savages," Brown's narrative registers an element of cultural insight, even resistance, on the basis of moral principle.[30] For example, Brown repeatedly shows in his translation how Volney is an
"enthusiast against the savages, and is as zealous to depreciate, as Rousseau was
to exalt their character."[31] Responding to Volney's dialogue with Mr. Wells and
his assertion that "the Indians of the Wabash, the Miamis, Putewoatamies, &c.
are better than they were a few generations ago" and "they are as much improved
as the Creeks and Chactaws," Brown writes ironically in a footnote: "These hints
would lead us to suppose that the Indian tribes have really derived some benefit
from their vicinity to a civilised people. They very early learned the use of horses
and fire-arms, and thus acquired new means of killing game and defending themselves. They receive many useful, as well as some pernicious things, in the way of
trade, and have already probably taken several steps towards a total assimilation
to the customs of the whites, but they are hastening to extinction with a much
quicker pace than to civilisation." And in response to Volney's observation that the
"old men" of the tribes foolishly "exclaim against the degeneracy of modern times,"
especially when they tell younger tribe members to "throw away the hoe," Brown
writes: "Their condition would doubtless be improved, if they abjured *every thing*

new and European. They would profit, on the whole, if they got rid of spirits and the small-pox, together with every beneficial acquisition."[32]

On occasion, Brown articulates conventional views about the "savages" relative to western settlement. But similar to his earlier remarks in *An Address to the Government of the United States on the Cession of Louisiana* on the "necessity of gin to disable, of fraud to betray" an "oppressed" race, his ironic commentary on Volney's view of America and empire raises questions about his real view of the American Indian.[33] Does Brown minimize commentary in his annals on this aspect of American expansion because he views displacement of Native Americans as a necessary evil, the result of the course of empire? Or is his ambivalence evidence that he is somehow conscious of the moral contradiction such a position poses, and evidence that he understood American complicity in the process of colonial exploitation and cultural subversion? There is no easy answer, but it seems that Brown, who desired their assimilation into white civilization, also clearly understood the political injustice and evils of defrauding Native Americans of their land and exterminating them with rum and small pox. He regretted the fact that they were not able to fully assimilate with whites and saw their demise as part of the inevitable course of early republican western expansion.

As with settler-Indian relations, the situation with Santo Domingo and the slave uprising provides another instance of commentary on racial and ethnic differences. Acknowledging, for instance, the "extraordinary circumstances of hardship and cruelty" slavery has caused and the assumptions made by "masters" on the basis of "feature and colour," Brown observes the country has been fortunate to avoid the "example of successful revolt" in Santo Domingo—the "calamity of servile war." He also notes that such "evils" are every day "removed to a greater distance" and that tensions between the master and slave are lessening. Whether it was because he sought to be "impartial" or he had overtly opposed slavery in other writings, the commentary here is brief. Brown concerned himself with the United States as a "neutral nation" and its "commercial history," but he also was apprehensive about race relations in the United States as a result of the uprising in Santo Domingo. The "intercourse," writes Brown, "between American states and the maritime nations of Europe is intimately connected with the mutual relations subsisting between those nations."[34] While France's ongoing war with Britain allowed the United States to hold a neutral position in regard to shipping and exports, such a position was complicated by the rebellion of blacks at Santo Domingo—France's most lucrative colony. Brown's account of the role of the United States is limited, but it reveals both explicit and embedded colonial attitudes regarding race, slavery, and revolution in early nineteenth-century empires.

While Brown says little in the annals about controversial claims over West Florida, his comments on the significance of France obtaining the "Spanish empire" west of the Mississippi River reflect the prevailing "appetite for foreign possessions"—by both Europeans and Americans. Unlike in *An Address to the Government of the United States on the Cession of Louisiana to the French,* where Brown's speaker hotly urges war with France and force to ensure "the harmony and union of these States," in the annals Brown offers a toned-down assessment of the cession of Louisiana to the French—an assessment that nevertheless reveals his nationalist or expansionist interests:

> Great therefore was the anxiety occasioned by this transfer, in all who re-flected on the rapid progress of our population, and its speedy diffusion to the shores of the Pacific ocean, provided no untoward check or obstacle should rise up in its way. Those who had soothed their fancy by the images of glory and felicity, flowing from the occupation of one fifth of the fertile and habitable part of the globe, by a people of one blood, language, and policy, were dejected at the prospect of sudden and narrow bounds being put to their progress, by the intrusion of a race, whose habits, manners, and government were adverse and hostile, and whose vicinity would be an inexhaustible source of jealousy, dissention, and war. The supposed value of this territory to France made it hopeless that any pecuniary price would be thought equivalent to it, and that she would give up so splendid an in-heritance for a few million of dollars. Happily, however, the experiment was made, and she consented to sell us all her claims in North America, for a sum which it was easy and convenient for us to pay.[35]

Republican Samuel Harrison Smith, who edited the pro-Jefferson *National Intelligencer* and whose politics Brown's have been compared to, favored the purchase. By contrast, some Federalists supported the purchase of Louisiana, but others opposed it.[36] As John M. Murrin observes, "During the Louisiana crisis of 1802–03, the Jefferson administration and the Federalists both insisted on acquiring New Orleans from Napoleon, but the Federalists preferred to take it by conquest, the Republicans by purchase." Federalists like James Ross argued that Jefferson should use troops to acquire New Orleans but then, a few months later, opposed the Louisiana Purchase.[37] When Jefferson was offered Louisiana but not Florida, Federalists, says Murrin, were "appalled by the prospect of an agrarian empire." This event, he concludes, "exposed the limits to Federalist expansionist ambitions."[38]

While Brown goes on to articulate possible reasons for France's consenting to this "bargain" and to warn that France will respect the treaty only as long as it serves French interests, the above passage is important because of its nationalist tone and Brown's interest in seeing the land purchased. In writing, for example, that "a people of one blood, language, and policy, were dejected" because the French occupation of Louisiana would "check" western expansion, Brown expresses not uncommon nationalist feelings. And by saying that the "intrusion" of the French, a people whose "habits, manners, and government were adverse and hostile," would be a cause of "jealousy, dissention, and war," he also points up the manner in which American interests in the Continent were at odds with the colonial designs of France.

Brown, as I have suggested earlier, tried to put a positive spin on the internal state of the country and its race relations in regard to slavery. Despite "harbouring in their bosom a nation of slaves, whose bondage was exasperated by many extraordinary circumstances of hardship and cruelty" and despite being "roused by the examples of successful revolt in a neighboring country," the United States has "avoided the calamity of a servile war." The "gulf which divides the master and the slave is becoming gradually narrower, and the ties which bind together the various members of the nation multiply and strengthen by time." And after recalling French efforts to subdue rebellion in Santo Domingo, Brown writes:

This attempt was defeated chiefly by a renewal of the war, and it is now three or four years since the island has been in full possession of the negroes, and since they have maintained their claim to the dignity and privileges of an independent state. As they continue to cultivate, though to a less extent than formerly, the staple article, coffee, and to demand the manufactures of other countries, their trade is of very great value to a neutral nation. The French, however, were not only at war with the blacks of St. Domingo, and interested, therefore, merely as enemies in distressing and impoverishing them by cutting off their trade, but they likewise chose to consider the blacks as revolted subjects, whom to trade with was to assist, and required from their friends the discontinuance of all commercial intercourse with St. Domingo. Though it is obvious that a case of this kind is susceptible of much doubt and controversy, yet it was undoubtedly wise and politic in the United States to prohibit this trade, not only because the object was not of sufficient value to justify a war, even if justice were clear and prompt in her decision as to its propriety; but, because such are the shifts and artifices of traders, that the prohibition, though made with all the rigour that our equitable constitution allows, is easily evaded. The produce of St. Domingo is still brought into the American ports, and a part of it exported to Europe; but the trade is managed by adventurers, who, for this purpose, metamorphose themselves into Swedes or Danes, and who defend themselves, by force of arms, against assailants of equal or inferior force. How far the continuance of this trade depends upon remissness in the execution of the prohibitory law, or in the imperfect provisions of the law itself, or on the connivance of the French, whose subjects are enriched by the occasional forfeitures of the vessels engaged in it, is a matter of some doubt.[39]

While later nineteenth-century historians, such as Richard Hildreth and Henry Adams, commented generally on the point of Santo Domingo's newly acquired independence and the extreme nature of Napoleon's request for stopping of trade, Brown offers a bird's-eye-view of American interests and political motives.[40] Instead of remarking generally about the French claim that "blacks were revolted subjects" or the Haitian "claim to dignity and privileges of an independent state," he focuses more on why it was prudent for the United States to agree to France's request to "prohibit trade" with Santo Domingo.[41]

Brown recognized that trade with Santo Domingo was of value to the United States, but his legal training enabled him to question the efficacy of beginning a war with France, especially when the prohibition is "easily evaded" by "adventurers." Brown did not condone such action, but he saw the legal difficulties in enforcing a trade embargo and held this view as late as 1809 when in his address to Congress on "Foreign Restrictions" and the embargo he writes: "You were right in prohibiting the trade to St. Domingo, because you gratified a vain punctilio of France, and enjoyed the trade notwithstanding."[42]

This is not to say that Brown did not amplify or qualify these views elsewhere in his writing. He did, and that is why his views sometimes appear ambivalent—because of the tension between an emergent, enlightened understanding of colonial exploitation and lingering racial assumptions. For example, in his earlier pamphlet *An Address to the Government of the United States on the Cession of Louisiana*, his fictitious French counselor voices colonial sentiments about Santo Domingo and its riches: in "forbearing to molest this island, we gain every thing . . . their gratitude, their friendship, and every benefit which one nation can confer upon another." After commenting further about the valuable lessons of the English in managing their territorial possessions, the counselor admits: "Our islands prospered under that wretched policy, which converted men into cattle, and grasped at present benefits at the hazard of all the evils, by which it has since been overwhelmed." While the French counselor elaborates on his scheme for regaining control of the island and its riches, he (or Brown, rather) also reflects on the fact that Americans "call themselves *free,* yet a fifth of their number are slaves" and that "their characters and views are void of all stability." "Their prejudices," he continues, "are all discordant. . . . Their people are the slaves of hostile interests."[43]

Further complicating assumptions about the stability of the country and its racial disparities at the turn of the century, Brown's counselor then remarks:

> When *war* becomes the topic of discourse, this people will turn their eyes to the calamities of St. Domingo, and then to their own provinces, where the same intestine plague exists in a degree equally formidable, and where their utmost care is requisite to prevent the struggling mischief from bursting its bonds.

Devoted to the worst miseries, is the nation which harbours in its bosom a foreign race, brought, by fraud and rapine, from their native land; who are bereaved of all the blessings of humanity; whom a cruel servitude inspires with all the vices of brutes and all the passions of demons; whose injuries have been so great that the law of self-preservation obliges the State to deny to the citizen the power of making his slave free; whose indelible distinctions of form, colour, and perhaps of organization, will forever prevent them from blending with their tyrants, into one people; who foster an eternal resentment at oppression, and whose sweetest hour would be that which buried them and their lords in a common and immeasurable ruin.[44]

Just as the Jonathan Swift persona or speaker simultaneously uses overstatement and understatement to make ironic points about the abuses the Irish suffered at the hands of the English, so Brown's use of this device allows him to satirize French ambitions and American naïveté—to use speech that "serves two speakers at the same time and expresses simultaneously two different intentions: the direct intention of the character who is speaking, and the refracted intention of the author." This kind of "double-voiced" discourse is evident when the enthusiastic counselor (the character's voice) acknowledges the "calamities of St. Domingo" and how blacks have been oppressed under French rule (Brown's voice). In presenting a "concentrated dialogue of two voices, two world views, two languages," Brown critiques French colonial practices and, by implication, the form of "oppression" or enslavement practiced by their American counterparts.[45]

At the same time, he uses this critical alignment to alert the American public to the manner in which the French might exploit the "same intestine plague" in the United States. The French, writes Brown in his companion pamphlet *Monroe's Embassy,* were not daunted by the resistance of blacks in Santo Domingo. What should we "expect, when the prize in their view, is the wealth of the Mississippi, and when the opposition we can make must be infinitely less than that which they encountered in St. Domingo"?[46] Brown concludes this Louisiana pamphlet by having his "obscure citizen," whom he later names "Poplicola," remark that the French counselor has "given such a portrait of us as was most suitable to his views." "Our national pride," he says, "will induce us to deny, perhaps, the truth of the picture," yet the "paramount and present interest" of the country is the preservation of the union; therefore, we should secure the future by rising "as one man" and taking control of Louisiana.[47]

As discussed earlier, Brown's position on slavery can also be seen in his sketches of fictitious history, where he acknowledges the realities of slave ownership, particularly when he relates that "every master enjoyed, by law, unlimited power over his slave, and might even kill him with impunity" and that this "power, so liable to abuse, was generally abused. Chains, stripes, scanty fare, rags and excessive labour, was commonly the lot of this unhappy race."[48] Such commentary resonates very closely with the reality of slavery as Brown knew it. Robert Levine concurs, writing that "assertions of blacks' humanity" appear in Brown's *Monthly Magazine and American Review* (1799) and the *Literary Magazine and American Register* (1804). Brown, he argues, "aligns himself with the more humane and progressive politics of some northern Federalists."[49] While it must be observed that the race politics of some progressive northern Federalists were shared by Jeffersonian Republicans like Philip Freneau, Levine is nevertheless right to suggest that Brown largely endorsed an antislavery ethos and that his writings on Louisiana and imperialism at this time interrogate and unmask "nationalist exceptionalism."[50]

Finally, after commenting on French efforts to subdue the slave revolt at Santo Domingo, the prudence of not irritating the French, and the ease by which American traders could trade with Santo Domingo anyway, Brown remarks on the subject of emigrants and the British practice of impressing American sailors. While the latter in particular is seen as a source of discontent, Brown suggests relations with Great Britain and the war in Europe have had an impact on American commerce. Of the proper time to assess this situation, he writes that "historical perspicuity requires that we should take a clear view of the principles and facts relative to this important subject." "The actual consequences of the war in Europe to our national prosperity," he observes, is a complicated issue, and "we have not met with any plain, succinct, and historical view of these transactions." It is neither easy for him as a historian or for the average reader to form accurate conceptions of these events until either war or peace has developed. Likewise, alluding to the Aaron Burr conspiracy, he writes at the end of volume 1 that an "important event in the domestic history of the United States" remains to be examined; however, "a just regard to the truth, and to the reputation of an eminent person, will induce us for the present to be wholly silent on this subject."[51]

In these historical and discursive contexts, then, of Brown's historical sketches and political pamphlets, Brown's assertion in his "Annals of America" that "the evils of internal dissention and rebellion, instead of approaching nearer, are every day removed to a greater distance; the gulf which divides the master and the slave is becoming gradually narrower" can be seen as registering both the expectation that the state of slavery would improve as well as the knowledge that its oppressive features were a historical reality that deserved to be rectified. Brown's careful assessment of the politics surrounding the Louisiana Purchase and his lingering concern about the example of "successful revolt in a neighboring country" calls attention to what Dana Nelson terms the "inevitably political and economic motivation of any racial characterization in colonial America (in fact, in *any* colonial situation)."[52] Indeed, as Brown's representation in the "Annals of America" of the wildly mysterious Aaron Burr conspiracy further suggests, he continued to register concern about the role of ethnic others in the formation of the Republic.

The Aaron Burr Conspiracy and New Orleans

In *The Spanish Borderlands Frontier,* John Francis Bannon observes that after the Louisiana Purchase of 1803, Spain had allowed Americans to move into the area west of the lower Mississippi River. By 1804, some Americans lived in the Nacogdoches part of East Texas and along the Red and Ouachita rivers. Talk, he says, of "the good lands beyond the Red River, of well-watered river valleys and lush prairies, of wild cattle and wilder mustangs, fired American imaginations and built dreams, more often of settlement but not infrequently of possible conquest."[53] Men like Philip Nolan were seen as "adventurers" or "advance agents for American conquest" by the Spanish, suggesting that in such an atmosphere the Aaron Burr conspiracy had plenty of company. "There seems little doubt," writes Bannon, that "the conquest of Spain's northern provinces, at the very least, was one of the aims of Burr and his associates." Buckner F. Melton Jr. concurs, observing that while Jefferson may have been North America's "first great imperialist," Burr also had imperial ambitions, counting on war between Spain and the United States to provide him with the opportunity to "find recruits, equip a force, and march on Mexico with no opposition at home."[54] In historical hindsight, there has been debate about whether Burr intended to take New Orleans or simply a part of Mexico. Regardless, Brown, as a historian interested in impartiality, accuracy, and truth, had a difficult set of circumstances to figure out, especially given Jefferson's acts of retribution and Chief Justice Marshall's open "favoritism" toward Burr.[55]

According to most historians, Burr's launching in 1806 of a small force of men from Blennerhasset Island on the Ohio River was aimed at either the capture of New Orleans or territory in Mexico. Burr's exact objectives are unclear. But General James Wilkinson's betrayal of Burr led to his arrest on February 19, 1807, and his imprisonment in Richmond, Virginia. Although he was found not guilty of waging war or committing treason, Burr faced charges of murder or treason in other states and found himself in perpetual exile, except toward the end of his life, when he returned to New York. Newspaper and periodical publications of the day, from New York City to New Orleans, attempted to solve the mystery of Burr's actions. Publications and speculation about Burr's activities and guilt or innocence were published regularly through 1809, with Jefferson publishing *Message from the President of the United States, Transmitting Information Touching an Illegal Combination of Private Individuals against the Peace and Safety of the Union* in 1807.[56]

Brown, along with others, including the editors of Philadelphia's Federalist *Gazette of the United States* (August 2, 1805), was alert to American ambitions concerning the Spanish borderlands and Spanish America in general. As Nicholas Rombes has pointed out, Brown appropriates for his own use contemporary partisan accounts of Burr's actions that had been published after 1805 in newspapers such as the *Philadelphia Aurora, United States Gazette, New-York Commercial Advertiser,* and *Richmond Enquirer.*[57] While most of these accounts tried to "solve" the mystery of the case, Brown focuses on the difficulties of knowing the facts of the matter or truth. Brown's treatment of the Burr situation, says Rombes, recalls the method Brown employed in his novels—his use of "mysterious letters and voices, fragmentary explanations, and unknowable motivations."[58]

Brown's inquiry, though, into actions of Burr and Francisco de Miranda also reveals his ironic assessment of the manner in which the rhetoric of liberty, independence, and free trade betrayed more ambitious economic and political interests. His interrogation, I contend, of the imperialist interests of individuals like Burr prompted him to increasingly challenge the ethos of empire, especially as it sidelined democratic principles and contributed to class differences and the exploitation of racial and ethnic others. His efforts at historical impartiality, in other words, gave way now and then to the use of candor and irony.

To illustrate: Brown begins in volume 2 of his annals by recalling how the "peace and welfare of the United States seemed wholly to depend on the conduct and condition of the nations of Europe" and how trade with the latter affected the "wealth and employment" of the United States. He then comments on territorial borders within the United States and notes that while they are clear with respect to English territories, they are murkier in regard to Spanish claims to Mexico: "On the south-western border, the seeds of jealousy and dissention are more plentifully sown." Political negotiations between the United States and Spain had produced no resolutions. However, it is on the point of American progress relative to Spanish territories that Brown voices a patriotic nationalism. Remarking that Spain's distance from its colony makes the latter difficult to govern, Brown writes, almost sardonically, of America's "interests":

> The time is not yet come when numerous garrisons and fortresses will be necessary on the western banks of the Mississippi, and when, in order to divert or enfeeble a hostile purpose in its infancy, it will be prudent to maintain open and secret emissaries in the Mexican kingdom, to sow dissention between different classes of the people, to foment faction, or seduce remote or disconnected parts from its allegiance to the rest, or to alienate the whole from the parent state, by arguments or bribes. All these are expedients to which our national safety would not fail to reconcile our rulers, as they have always done the rulers of other nations. . . . As national interest is the sole foundation of our government, and as this interest, necessarily connected with local circumstances, necessarily varies in a nation which doubles its numbers and its peopled territory in a single generation, there are perpetual changes in the points from which we draw our political arguments. The constitution which is best adapted to our situation to-day becomes unsuited to our new situation to-morrow.[59]

Brown's apparent willingness here to use "open and secret emissaries" in the Span-ish/Mexican territories and to employ various methods of sowing "dissention be-tween different classes of people" recalls the political enthusiasm and rhetoric of his earlier political pamphlets—the kind of "deep-dyed nationalism" Watts refers to in his study. Brown, it seems, even goes so far as to suggest that while the "con-stitution" may be suited to "our situation today," it may not always accommodate the circumstances of tomorrow, and issues related to western expansion and ter-ritorial acquisition.

However, if Brown's narrative reflections here record a heightened national-ism, they also point to his sustained interest in race matters and domestic history. "Hitherto," observes Brown, "though much eloquence and technical erudition have been displayed in discussing those maxims of the law of nations which are thought to have some bearing on these subjects, we have not met with any plain, succinct, and historical view of these transactions." Further, he writes, "This undertaking is, indeed, a humble one, but it seems not deficient in utility, nor without it does it seem easy for common and unlearned readers to form accurate conceptions of a cause to which all of us are deeply interested."[60] While Brown later changes his target reader—or audience—from the "common and unlearned" to a more en-lightened or intellectual one, supporting perhaps claims about his later elitism, his narrative posture here nevertheless takes a "historical view" of recent events and analyzes American "national progress" in light of its imperial dimensions. That is, although such analysis in the early part of his annals reflects Brown's nationalistic tendencies, especially in regard to the "extension of our empire," an abrupt change in sensibility is registered in later volumes, where his analysis of Aaron Burr's pur-suit of a personal empire forces him to confront both Burr's and his own imperial-ist ambitions.

For instance, a year later, in volume 2, Brown states, "The extension of our empire to the mouths of the Mississippi was justly regarded as a grand step in our national progress, as a most important pledge of our safety, not only from foreign, but domestic enemies; and yet this possession was scarcely secured when the public tranquility appeared to be endangered from this quarter, and by per-sons whose ambition was least liable to be suspected."[61] Here, Brown begins to take a hard look at Burr's imperial designs and, in the process, not only points up contemporary "opinions" about the matter but begins to rethink the mind-set that undergirds American pretensions of empire building.

Brown initiates his analysis of the Burr conspiracy by reflecting on his own po-sition as an impartial historian. "In proportion," he writes, "as historical truth is connected with the reputation of living individuals ought an upright historian to scrutinize with accuracy, and decide with caution." Similar to the self-conscious posture he expressed in his *American Register* prefaces, and even his earlier periodi-cal reviews and essays, Brown is careful in his assessment of the Burr conspiracy to take a balanced, unbiased approach. He notes, for example, that no "eminent person in the United States was so generally known to be actuated by ambition, by the appetite for power and office, and to have this passion less tempered and modified by the kindred lust of wealth," but he also observes that few can compare with Burr in "courage, activity, and enterprise." Burr, he continues, has "great talents," yet his lust for pleasure and the consequences of his duel with Hamilton prompted him to capitalize on the "favourite pursuit of men of enterprize in America"—the "purchase and settlement of new lands."[62]

Burr's ambitions, like those of Napoleon, entailed the acquisition of land in the name of national interest, but, as Brown eventually realized, such aspirations were motivated more by a personal desire for wealth than any sort of desire to liberate a politically oppressed people. While Brown's criticisms of Burr might be read as eliding national imperialism by displacing it onto one ambitious individual, his reference to other "men of enterprize" and his later remarks about attitudes toward Mexico and American foreign policy suggest otherwise.

For instance, reflecting further on American pretensions toward territorial expansion and the desire to liberate Mexico from Spanish rule, Brown assesses the "circumstances of the time" and rumors concerning Burr:

> The wealth of Mexico had been, for some ages, almost proverbial, and the wary and timid policy of Spain, whose empire over its own colonies was more effectually promoted by peace than war, is vulgarly imputed to cowardice and imbecility. Men being always prone to impute their own feelings to others, we naturally cherish the notion that the colonists of Spain are as jealous of foreign controul, and as ambitious of political independence as we once were. A war with Spain, therefore, naturally fills the bold and adventurous mind with images of golden candlesticks and silver platters. Mexico is the native country of dollars, the treasures of which are only defended by unarmed monks or disaffected slaves. Its wealthy provinces are easily overrun by hardy soldiers, and the enemy is easily concealed under the mask of a deliverer. A rebellious temper will greedily listen to the promises of foreign succour, and blind them to the folly of confiding in the generosity of strangers and tyrants. Such were the images that naturally thronged the minds of many of the western people; and though enlightened minds entertained a juster and very different notion of the state of these provinces, of their wealth, their power, their attachment to Spain, and their credulity, these views were beyond the reach of ordinary minds.[63]

While Brown's comments concerning the "policy of Spain" might be construed as condoning imperialist principles and practices, particularly when he writes of how the Spanish use of "peace," not open war, "effectually" governed Mexico, they more accurately reflect his observations of popular attitudes toward Mexico. What Brown might have meant by the term "peace" is, of course, a valid question. But assuming that he saw Spanish strategies of cultural control and domination as less aggressive than Napoleonic rule, he nonetheless makes ironic and insightful observations about American pretensions of imperialism. That is, beyond making the aphoristic comment that humanity in general and Americans in particular ascribe their own feelings to others in regard to the issue of "political independence," Brown cites the more common "images" or assumptions held by Americans, westerners in particular. The notion that Mexico's wealth was only for the taking is made clear by his ironic references to images of "golden candlesticks," "unarmed monks," and rebellious "disaffected slaves," and the myth that Mexico was ripe for a political redeemer or "deliverer" from the north. As he notes in a strikingly critical tone, "enlightened minds" have a "juster and different notion" of circumstances in Mexico.

Brown's interrogation of the "adventurer" mind-set and the imperial ethos that fueled it continue in a footnote, where he remarks, ironically:

> The fate of the English expeditions to La Plata forms a salutary lesson on this head to us, and may tend, if any thing can tend, to reform the popular errors on this subject. The fate of Miranda, who proceeded with great pomp to *revolutionize* South America, at the head of a fleet of three small vessels, and an army (including major-generals and admirals) of three hundred men, will also instruct us in the chimerical nature of such projects, and, at the same time, in the abundance of that spirit which leads some of us to embark in them. It should seem as if we thought the times of Cortez and Pizarro were returned, and as if forty soldiers on horseback, equipped in our manner, were still equal to the conquest of an empire in South America. Wilkinson, with ten thousand troops, would make as little impression on Mexico, as Miranda, with his three hundred, did on Terra Firma.[64]

For Brown, both the failed English expeditions to the La Plata area in 1806 (and its invasion of Buenos Aires) and Francisco de Miranda's failed invasion and liberation of Venezuela represent a corrective to the assumption that a few good men or "adventurers," armed with bullets and a desire for bullion, could reenact the kind of colonial ventures Cortez and Pizarro practiced—or that elements of the American Revolution could be exported by ambitious individuals.[65] The "abundance of that spirit," says Brown, which motivated Burr to plan an invasion of Mexico is, or ought to be, tempered by the fact that even if General Wilkinson had had a large army, he would have made "little impression" on Mexico. Brown's assertions here regarding Wilkinson are, of course, hypothetical, but his account of how Jefferson and the country understood the mysterious events concerning the

Burr conspiracy is worth digressing on, especially as it pertains to Brown's efforts to impartially judge available historical evidence.

Brown's analysis of whether Burr intended to appropriate territory from the United States or from Spain begins with a consideration of a letter from Burr to General Wilkinson that outlines the former's desire to organize an army to seize New Orleans and establish in the western states an independent form of government. Jefferson, says Brown, received an "imperfect copy of this letter," but it is apparent from the content that a series of events was to take place, including some sort of "rendezvous on the Ohio" and a meeting with General Wilkinson concerning the fate of Baton Rouge. Other particulars suggest a "hostile expedition of some kind," but, writes Brown:

> The consideration of this letter must suggest to an impartial mind many different views, and all of them involved in obscurity and fettered with difficulties. How far these difficulties are to be imputed to the acknowledged imperfection of the transcript is an obvious inquiry. Any performance may be made to breathe any meaning, by omitting sentences and words at pleasure, by separating contiguous passages, or bringing together those whose genuine position was distant. This transcript, the original being written in cypher, is said by the general, upon oath, to be as faithful as he was able to make it; but as there are manifestly many chasms and broken sentences, the meaning of the original may widely differ from the transcript, without any imputation on the integrity of the interpreter.

Brown, in his effort to be "impartial," acknowledges the "difficulties" the historical evidence provides and goes on in his narrative—though not with complete accuracy because of later developments—to explain why Wilkinson probably had little direct connection with Burr's scheme, but he comments more insightfully on Burr's "double design of dividing the United States by the Allegheny mountain, and of making an inroad into Mexico," and on the political and social apprehension the Burr conspiracy generated across the country.[66]

After explaining Burr's inability to interest people in creating a separate set of western states, Brown proceeds to inquire into Burr's activities regarding New Orleans and its role in helping prepare for an invasion of Mexico. Brown goes so far as to incorporate in his footnotes an excerpt from Jefferson's January 22, 1807, message to Congress on the matter, but he even, more interestingly, appropriates Jefferson's own discourse when he remarks that after Burr's decision to forgo establishing a separate western empire, he "busily employed himself in collecting followers among the ardent, restless, desperate, and disaffected persons" who would be interested in an expedition to Mexico. By comparison, Jefferson notes that Burr "collected from all quarters where himself or his agents possessed influence, all the ardent, restless, desperate, and disaffected persons, who were ready for any enterprize analogous to their characters."[67] On this point, Jefferson and Brown were in complete agreement.

While it is difficult to determine the extent to which Brown in his historical narrative used sources without fully acknowledging them, it is probable that he did such a thing on occasion, which would not have been unusual for the time. More important, however, in the process of weighing arguments for and against Burr, Brown, to his credit, is able to separate his own personal biases from the evidence and to say self-consciously: "With regard to the general probability of these charges, the grounds of our judgment, in such cases, are too complex and various to allow of uniform or universal conclusions."[68]

Just as Brown records favorable and unfavorable opinions of Burr, then, so he documents the degree to which the Burr conspiracy affected people's notions of nation and focused attention on the imperial dimensions of American empire. In saying at the end of chapter 7 that the Burr situation had "occupied the minds of men, in all parts of the United States, during three months, with images of civil war and foreign expeditions of the most formidable and magnificent kind," Brown indicates the political impact of the incident and the level of social anxiety it generated. And in writing that "public apprehension arose to a high pitch" Brown also indicates how concerns about Burr's ambitions, the "turbulent spirit of the western country," the "disaffection of Louisiana," and the "political weakness of Mexico" all contributed to an atmosphere of national panic.

Of the secrecy and effect of "well-conducted plots," Brown writes: "The parties engaged in them are loudest in their profession of zeal for an opposite cause, or of ignorance or scorn of the rumoured project, and thus a popular panic seizes the coldest and most skeptical hearts, and the most tremendous exaggerations are propagated with rapidity and swallowed with eagerness." Further, "the maritime cities, during this period, were led to embrace the belief, at one time, that Burr was actually on his march, at the head of thousands, sometimes of ten thousands. At one time he was in full possession of New Orleans; at another he had commenced his reign in the new empire of the Mississippi; and, anon, he had reached, with a flourishing army, the borders of Mexico." In the end, says Brown, after Burr was finally apprehended on the Mississippi and rumors had settled, "apprehension gave place to shame, terror to ridicule, and credulity to wonder at the circumstances by which it was misled." The activities of a "rash and mysterious" Burr proved to be benign and a greater reflection perhaps of a collective ambition and anxiety over the preservation and progress of an American empire.[69]

While Brown's narrative about the general events surrounding the Burr incident highlights the manner in which individual and national identity was entangled in a discourse and ideology of empire, his analysis of its unfolding in New Orleans—as opposed to how the Burr episode played out in the "maritime states"—also yields insight into his evolving sense of historical process and narrative and his growing consciousness of the imperial dimensions of an expansionist ideology. To be sure, Brown envisioned, like many Jeffersonian Republicans and Federalists, the eventual settlement of the Louisiana Territory; however, as events unfolded concerning New Orleans and the purchase of French Louisiana, Brown continued to examine the expansionist ideology that fueled events like the Aaron Burr conspiracy and its regional and national impact.

For instance, although the Pinckney Treaty of 1795 with Spain gave Americans "the right of deposit" in New Orleans and facilitated commerce, the Spanish government's closure in 1802 of the Port of New Orleans and American shipping had multiple effects.[70] Jefferson's decision in 1803 to send James Monroe and Robert R. Livingston to France to obtain the port of New Orleans prompted Napoleon, surprisingly, to offer sale of all of Louisiana. Complicating the situation with New Orleans, numerous farmers between the Appalachian Mountains and the Mississippi River were increasingly using the port at New Orleans to export their produce. In addition to the debate about the territory's price ($15 million) and the location and process by which Jefferson negotiated its sale, conditions in the West were "ripe for revolt against the federal government" because of the way it failed to address ill treatment by the Spanish.[71] It is in this generally unstable situation that Brown continues trying to sort out fact from fiction in regard to Aaron Burr and the way his actions polarized the American populace and political system.

After suggesting that the effects of the Burr conspiracy had a more severe impact on the people of New Orleans than the rest of the country, especially in the manner in which civil and political power was abused, Brown observes:

> The history of transactions at New Orleans is chiefly supplied by letters of the commander in chief to the government, and by the legal depositions of a few officers and magistrates, in relation to particular events. Those who incurred suspicion and persecution, on account of their connection with Burr, have written copiously in their defense, and the truth, as usual among hostile and clashing statements, is not easily discovered. Amidst this labyrinth, it is incumbent on a pen studious of impartiality to proceed with caution; but the due caution, on occasions like the present, leads to no certainty, and is obliged to content itself with leaving the reader to decide on his own conclusions of the credibility of witnesses, and the probability of events.[72]

As in other places, Brown continues to strive for a measure of "impartiality" or objectivity in his rendering of historical events. However, he takes the unusual step of not only acknowledging the lack of "certainty" associated with such events but, crucially, of inviting "the reader to decide on his own conclusions." Such a remark is central to understanding Brown's historical self-consciousness and, more importantly, the evolving nature and radicalism of his historicism—his willing-ness, in the mode of Bakhtin's understanding of the novel, to admit voices other than his own into the process of constructing historical meaning. As I suggest later with Brown's historical representation of the controversial Republican nomi-nation caucus of 1808, he ultimately invites the reader to participate in the his-torical construction and meaning of history—a method he used for philosophical and political purposes in his novels. This type of intellectual self-consciousness and inquiry is a constant in his career as an author, editor, and historian.

Brown goes on in his narrative to bring his prior training in the legal profes-sion to bear on his analysis of the situation in New Orleans and comments on the conflict between the local judiciary and the military in regard to the arrests of Samuel Swartwout and Peter Ogden (suspected Burr accomplices). He also com-ments on the gap between the overzealous "suspicion and accusation" on the part of the governor and the general and the "legal evidence." But Brown articulates increasing criticism of colonial or imperialistic attitudes when he records in a footnote commentary published in New Orleans that sought to vindicate General Wilkinson:

> An eloquent narrative of these transactions, published at New Orleans by an adversary of Wilkinson, contains a curious account of the views and wishes of the American emigrants with respect to Mexican expeditions. Speaking of the inroads of the Spaniards in 1805, and their effect on popular feelings, he says: "Among the Americans, a spirit of enterprise and resentment uni-versally prevailed; *private* associations were formed, with objects *beyond* a mere *defensive* war; and signal retaliations on the Spanish possessions in that vicinity were every where spoken of with confidence and enthusiasm." Burr is merely charged with being the leader of *such* an association, and surely this confession reflects some little probability on this charge. A curi-ous account is afterwards given of an actual association of this kind, and of a trial at law, in which general had endeavoured to confound this fraternity with the Mexican part of Burr's conspiracy. This writer says, the expedi-tion planned by this association "had assumed a character eminently el-evated above all schemes of petty warfare and pillage. The object was not to steal upon and plunder the unarmed merchant. It was to raise the standard of natural rights, political liberty, and free trade, in the face of opposing armies; and deliver one of the fairest portions of the globe from a most odi-ous system of colonial bondage, conceived in tyranny, and nursed in fear, ignorance, and weakness. The project may have been visionary, or be con-sidered as impracticable. But it does credit at least to the hearts that warmed in the cause; and only required, like the American revolution, the sanction of success, to reflect immortal honour on all engaged in it."[73]

First, Brown's opinion that the account itself is "curious" alerts the reader to its claims regarding Burr and the motivations for any kind of military initiative. According to the speaker, Americans along the border felt both a sense of opportunity, as far as acquiring land, and an antagonism toward the Spanish and their "inroads." The formation of local "associations" was not uncommon, nor were their plans for retaliating against Spanish settlers and forcefully acquiring their land and other possessions. In this context, says the speaker, Burr and his men were only one such group with this type of interest.

Brown then mentions a "curious" account of such an association's plans to join Burr with the Mexican part of the "expedition" and its status within local courts, but he clearly is more interested in the speaker's claim that, "the object was not to steal upon and plunder the unarmed merchant. It was to raise the standard of natural rights, political liberty, and free trade, in the face of opposing armies; and deliver one of the fairest portions of the globe from a most odious system of colonial bondage, conceived in tyranny, and nursed in fear, ignorance, and weakness." For some, the speaker's rationale that motives for entering Mexico were purely patriotic and in line with improving "natural rights, political liberty, and free trade" is part of the era's colonial ethos and, as Woods might say, consistent with ideals behind the American Revolution. For many people, in other words, plans to liberate Mexico in this way were consistent with America's "special mission" in the world and its role as a redeemer nation. For others, like Brown, such plans were a political mirage intended to disguise or sanctify less patriotic or pure motives.

Brown's response, therefore, challenges this ideology, especially the alignment of ideals associated with the American Revolution and military aggression in Mexico, and he carefully examines the speaker's imperialist rhetoric and pretensions, using the remainder of the footnote to compare Burr to Francisco de Miranda and record a provocative assessment of the situation:

> This miserable cant must have been the favourite rhetoric of Miranda and Burr, and it is evident that such views must have been admirably calculated to give success to the intrigues of Burr at New Orleans. Burr's letter professes no intention of plundering banks and seizing ships, and his agents merely talk of the probable necessity of borrowing some specie and vessels. In another place he says, "the president's proclamation against Burr had reached New Orleans about the 6th of January, but produced no extraordinary sensation there. So far as Burr's designs were conceived against Mexico, *they excited no manner of uneasiness*. It indeed surprised the good people of Louisiana not a little to find the government so extremely solicitous about the territories of their neighbours, after having shown so much indifference as to the protection of their own." These passages, in a publication expressly designed to expose Wilkinson's conduct to contempt and abhorrence, on the principle that

the danger from Burr was imaginary, are very extraordinary. This pamphlet, indeed, though written with opposite intentions, reflects strong probability on the opinion that Burr had formed the plan of a Mexican expedition at least, and that New Orleans supplied him with many partizans. Burr's designs might naturally enough, in this state of things, excite no uneasiness among the American settlers at New Orleans, but the guardians of the nation were bound to be very uneasy on this account, because the most flagrant mischiefs could not fail to follow a war entered into thus unjustly and wantonly with France and Spain. And for what end? To gratify the lust of plunder and adventure, in a few unsettled individuals, who have the insolent folly of clothing their lawless views, under the stale, bald, flagitious pretences of giving liberty and independence to those whom they murder or despoil.[74]

As with earlier historical analysis on Burr and Miranda, Brown does not hold back in his criticism of the motives behind such language, saying, "This miserable cant must have been the favourite rhetoric of Miranda and Burr, and it is evident that such views must have been admirably calculated to give success, to the intrigues of Burr at New Orleans." He thus classifies both men as adventurers and as being motivated by expectations of personal gain, not political altruism. While such commentary points to Brown's continued effort at historical "impartiality" or judgment in his analysis, it also reveals his increasing interrogation of, and resistance to, nationalist or exceptionalist forms of American imperialism. In saying, for example, that the "miserable cant" of the Wilkinson advocate must have been the "favourite rhetoric of Miranda and Burr," Brown does more than just critique the messenger. Similar to his hard-hitting assessment of British imperialism in India, he offers a critical assessment of an "expansionist" ideology—of even American "exceptionalism"—by dismantling the claim that the Burr scheme was above carrying out "petty warfare and pillage" and that its object was solely to "raise the standard of natural rights, political liberty, and free trade . . . and deliver one of the fairest portions of the globe from a most odious system of colonial bondage."[75]

That is, in forcefully interrogating the speaker's claims for exposing Wilkinson's narrative, and suggesting that the political atmosphere around New Orleans and the pamphlet's rhetoric argue instead for the "strong probability" that Burr had at least "formed the plan of a Mexican expedition" and that in New Orleans many partisans were waiting, Brown explicitly challenges the expansionist, deliverer impulse of individuals. He radically articulates, in no uncertain terms, his aversion to the imperialist impulse to subject and exploit others, especially when conducted "under the stale, bald, flagitious pretences of giving liberty and independence to those whom they murder or despoil." While his critique is admittedly aimed at people who live on the western fringes of the Republic, he nonetheless deconstructs colonial precedent—as well as contemporary assumptions about empire building—and undermines notions of American exceptionalism.[76] He dismantles the belief, from the Revolutionary War onward, that the United States was destined to lead the world in exporting political liberties and that its culture and citizens were "inherently anti-imperialist."[77]

Brown's response, in other words, to the pamphlet and its "redeemer nation" rationale not only recalls Thomas Paine's critical assessment of General Miranda on April 3, 1806, in Duane's *Aurora General Advertiser* but surpasses it insofar as he critiques America's imperial ambitions—its own use of the politics of liberation and the assumption, as Said puts it, that "certain territories and peoples *require* and beseech domination."[78] In this way, Brown clearly enacts resistance to a colonial ethos that is every bit disruptive of the political hegemony as the repressed voices he seeks to represent. Brown's recognition, though, of the ethnocentric assumptions undergirding American imperialist or colonial ventures is not restricted to a few individuals or, in his annals, a couple of historical footnotes. As his later analysis of the Embargo Act shows, his early reluctance to identify the United States as having imperialist ambitions and policies similar to England or France gives way to an even more searing and insightful commentary on American exceptionalism and its claims of moral authority on the global stage.[79]

Brown, of course, was not the only intellectual to critique Americans' plans for amassing personal territory and wealth. Brown's contemporary, William Duane, close friend of Jefferson, editor of the *Aurora General Advertiser* of Philadelphia from 1798 until 1813, and author of numerous political treatises, aggressively advocated Republican positions on major issues and regularly exposed dubious Federalist schemes and tactics.[80] Like Paine, Duane was one of the foremost radicals committed to democratic republicanism, or what Michael Durey calls "the workingmen's political movement."[81] The similarity between Brown's denunciation of a deliverer nation rationale, as articulated by the likes of Burr and Miranda, and Duane's own examination of such plots can be seen most clearly in Duane's 1807 publication *Politics for American Farmers: Being a Series of Tracts, Exhibiting the Blessings of Free Government,* where he fleshes out Federalist interest in sanctioning military coups in Mexico and South America. Building on Camillus's argument in *The Mississippi Question Fairly Stated,* a pamphlet he published in 1803, about the "visions of false glory" the "massacre or the enslavement" of distant peoples engenders, Duane writes:

> Mr. *Rutgers* is "warmly federal"—what is meant by this? Why, the obvious meaning of this phrase, is that he is a *warm opposer of the measures and policy of the government of the United States.*
> Here you can perceive why *Miranda's* expedition was countenanced—it *was warmly federal*—and here too you may perceive why it is that there is

such a mixture of *triumph* and *apprehension* concerning Burr's expedition—triumph because it is *warmly federal* in opposition to the peace and liberties of his country; apprehension because it is *warmly federally* feared that it may be frustrated, and the *warmly federal faction* found at the *bottom of it*.[82]

Duane goes on to ask whether or not the *Aurora* is an enemy of the Federalist because it dares to tell "*too much truth*" and, at the same time, remarks that if mechanics and farmers are "classes" of people who are registered as "the *lowest grades of servants*" they must respond to the political machinations of the elite classes. "*Mechanics* and *farmers*," he calls out, "it rests with yourselves, if you are disposed to bend your necks to the *Burrs* or to the *British emissaries*—they are ready to set their *feet* upon you. If you are determined to be *freemen*—*only count your numbers*."

In short, Brown, who was conscious of class differences, especially domestically, may not, like Duane, have overtly linked republican reading habits with class consciousness and resistance to the plots of Miranda and Burr, but, like him, he clearly abhors the "deliverer" or "redeemer nation" rationale endorsed by Federalists and increasingly associated with the idea of American exceptionalism. Unlike Paine and Duane, however, Brown seems to have understood the proto-imperial dimensions of American foreign policy, the ability of the early Republic, like imperial powers in Europe, to enact its own brand of cultural ethnocentrism and subordination. Therefore, just as Brown's earlier commentary in the annals participates in the expression of cultural nationalism, particularly when he suggests methods for sowing "dissention between different classes of people" in the Spanish or Mexican territories, so his assessment of the Aaron Burr conspiracy marks his increasing consciousness of divergent attitudes toward the idea of an American "empire" and participates in what Edward Watts calls the "process of decolonization"—an effort to address post-1776 manifestations of American imperialism, in print or the public sphere, and enable readers "to resist republican recolonization" of others.[83]

In particular, Brown begins to make a distinction between popular views of Mexico's riches—and how to acquire them—and how "enlightened minds" such as his own viewed the provinces. Beyond calling attention to the varying degrees of "public apprehension" concerning the Burr scheme, Brown begins to more explicitly challenge the "miserable cant" that excused cultural subversion as part of the American "enterprize" of empire building and—by implication—ideology of American "exceptionalism." Brown did not at this point overtly critique American imperialism, but his willingness to challenge such constructions does not end with his analysis of American "progress" out on the frontier or the Burr conspiracy. Rather, Brown increasingly reflected, especially in light of the *Chesapeake* affair, on institutional expressions of national self-interest or imperialism, not just the patriotic fervor of a few individuals.

The Chesapeake *Affair*

By 1805, as the American reexport trade increased tremendously, the Jefferson administration conceded the right of the English to impress British subjects from American merchant ships, and between 1803 and 1812 some five thousand sailors, mostly Americans, were taken from American ships so they could forcibly serve in the British Royal Navy. While many were eventually released, the practice continued, with minimal intervention by Jefferson, until the June 22, 1807, incident of the forty-six-gun frigate *Chesapeake,* off the coast of Norfolk, Virginia. Up to that point, Napoleon had seized some two hundred ships, and England some five hundred, and when approached by the British *Leopard,* Captain James Barron had allowed the British to board ship but refused the demand that four "deserters" be handed over.[84] The *Leopard* opened fire on the American ship, killing three American sailors and forcing the *Chesapeake* to surrender, yield the four sailors, and crawl back to port.[85]

The attack, as modern historians have observed, was a violation of international law, since no country could impress sailors from warships. And although the American press was outraged, Jefferson's options for recourse were, as he saw it, largely limited to ordering English warships to leave American waters, keeping American merchant boats off the seas and out of foreign ports, and denying European countries American goods through the use of a boycott, a tactic that worked prior to the Revolution. As Henry Adams observes in his *History of the United States:* "While Jefferson at Washington was fuming over Chief-justice Marshall's subpoena, and while the grand jury at Richmond were on the point of finding their indictment against Burr, an event occurred at sea, off the entrance to Chesapeake Bay, which threw the county into violent excitement, distracting attention from Burr, and putting to a supreme test the theories of Jefferson's statesmanship." "For the first time in their history," he continues, "the people of the United States learned, in June, 1807, the feeling of a true national emotion."[86] As in Adams's history, the *Chesapeake* affair is the subject of significant analysis in Brown's "Annals of Europe and America." In volume 3 of the "Annals of America," Brown spends no less than ten chapters assessing the *Chesapeake* affair, paying specific attention to aspects of British conduct and its impact on American identity and American political parties. His analysis highlights in distinct detail how different parts of the populace responded differently at different times to the incident, relative to political, commercial, or ideological interests.[87]

Although less ironic and more direct rhetorically, Brown's history begins by analyzing the British habit of placing squadrons and single frigates alongside coastlines and at the mouths of rivers to stop American ships and "obstruct the commerce of the United States." The practice, he says, was hard to stop because British ship captains were inclined to ignore the rights of neutral countries and not fear reprisal. This lack of regulation eventually led to repeated "injustice and oppression," especially in regard to the abduction of seamen from their vessels, and bred "indignation and resentment" in Americans. Such was the severity of the situation that

> An impartial observer would, indeed, be astonished to find that these insults and injuries were borne for so many years, without any hostile effort to resist or prevent them. If mankind were governed by a due regard to consequences; if a state forebore to go to war with its neighbours, whenever its real and solid interests would be more impaired by war than by peace, the forbearance of America towards Great Britain and France, under so many provocations, would not be wonderful, since war with either of these powers would be infinitely more pernicious than the repetition of any injury hitherto inflicted by them; but as men, collectively, are even more under the influence of their passions than individuals, it is truly wonderful that hostilities had not long ago commenced.

In pointing to the abuses American shipping and commerce endured, Brown continues his efforts at historical impartiality and highlights an era in American foreign policy toward England and France that perhaps lacked a firm sense of the consequences of allowing England a free hand in regard to American ships and their cargo. His surprise that hostility between the two countries had not occurred sooner is underscored by comments that address the "rights of a warring nation over neutrals" and their "unjust" nature as well as the fact that the only recourse for such "indignity and injury" was "patience." Observing that the United States was more irritated by the English than the French, Brown relates how in 1804 British ships entered the New York harbor and impressed sailors within American territory, an act he characterizes as "altogether lawless and hostile."[88]

He expressed similar views of the incident concerning the *Leander* a short time later, when an American sailor was killed outside the mouth of the New York harbor and his "mangled and lifeless body" was publicly displayed, enraging New Yorkers. Even though brought to court in England, such incidents, writes Brown, testify to the ineptness of judicial processes. In the case of the sailor who was shot near the harbor mouth, the acquittal of Captain Whitby was a "gross outrage" and only further evidence that the "injured party" was merely "a foreign state in relation to Great Britain" and to be ignored.[89] Although, he continues, a French ship was destroyed off the coast of North Carolina in 1806 by a British squadron, and promoted little more than a diplomatic complaint by France, even from Americans, the case of the *Chesapeake* had a completely different effect.

Brown begins his analysis of the subject in chapter 2 by reflecting on the difficulty of sorting through competing claims and unreliable sources of historical information. He remarks, for instance, on how seldom one can identify the first offender or offense in a disagreement: "As long as mankind are endowed with the same passions, there will never occur a quarrel between individuals or nations, in which either party is wholly blameless." Because there are usually so many "particulars" spread over a "wide surface," the "first injury" is "seldom possible to trace." The British and the Americans, according to Brown, are in a similar situation, with English ships forcibly taking property and stirring up resentment by Americans. American resistance to British claims that they can physically take English subjects off American ships is, says Brown, a source of injury to Great Britain, one that has sparked "resentment in the other party" and led to "insults and aggravations." This, in turn, has engendered conflict, of which it is nearly impossible to "ascertain the exact degree of injustice or of cruelty in the injurer, or of innocence or merit in the injured." Of these circumstances, Brown concludes, "It is evident that no full assent can be given by an impartial observer to an account of any particular transaction of this nature, not accompanied with written and official proofs." "The prevalence," he says, "of mutual complaint sufficiently proves the existence and the nature of evil; but to repeat anonymous tales, or record oral rumours, would be unworthy of historical veracity or dignity."[90]

Brown, as is evidenced here, was relentless in his efforts to analyze the historical moment fully and impartially. And in recounting how outside the Chesapeake Bay area five British sailors—William Ware, Daniel Martin, John Strachan, John Little, and Ambrose Watts—deserted the English ship *Melampus* and rowed to "liberty" on American soil, he carefully lays out the circumstances under which Ware, Martin, and Strachan enlisted for service onboard the *Chesapeake,* the officers involved, and the differences among the three men in terms of ethnicity and prior impressments, as Americans, aboard a British ship. Both Ware and Martin, observes Brown, had "*protections,* or notarial certificates of their being American citizens." "Strachan's history," he asserts, "was by no means equally satisfactory" because he had shipped out on an English ship at Liverpool earlier and consented to be on the *Melamphus.* Recalling arguments for and against their escape, and conceding that the certificates of American identity themselves were a subject of debate because they were so easily forged or obtained for almost anyone, Brown astutely writes, "An impartial observer cannot but perceive the weakness of the evidence given by these men of their American nativity, and of their compulsive service."[91]

The remainder of the chapter examines British conduct in regard to these three sailors aboard the *Chesapeake* and the manner in which the conflict erupted into gunfire by the British *Leopard,* killing three Americans and wounding sixteen others. Strachan, Martin, and Ware were removed as deserters, as was John Wilson, a supposed runaway from another English ship. "The circumstances of this contest," writes Brown, "were extremely humiliating to America" and had no small effect on the American public or its political leaders. Further, because not a single shot was fired in defense, the event was "highly discreditable" to the American navy and its requirement that American ships be prepared for military aggression at sea.[92]

Brown's examination of the impact of this event on the American public is revealing, and it insightfully draws attention to differences in geographical and class response: "Intelligence of this event flew, with wonderful rapidity, from one end of the United States to the other." Everywhere, it produced "a loud and unanimous burst of indignation." The American reaction resulted in "hastily assembled" meetings, declarations of revenge, and a general concurrence with whatever military response the U.S. government would undertake. The Federalist party, he observes, which had been seen as partial toward Britain, was "loudest and most vehement." The "language of every meeting" was one of rage and deemed the attack to be "unprovoked, piratical, assassin-like, murderous, cowardly, inhuman, savage; a breach of the faith of nations and the laws of war." Nor was there "any dissenting voice among their members. No one was heard to palliate, to suggest doubts, to recommend inquiry, or encourage delay. A more entire unanimity, and absolute extinction, or, at least, suspension of feuds and faction, was probably never witnessed. This flame of zeal burnt as vehemently in the remote, rural, and inland districts, on the shores of the Allegheny and Ohio, as in the maritime stations, the great cities, and even the towns upon the Chesapeake, the immediate scene of this transaction." Sparking a reaction of the most patriotic kind, the incident left few options for recourse—either "ample and immediate reparation on the one hand, or open war on the other." Those, he says, who reflected on relations with other nations and how the security of the United States was tied to the "jealousy and contentions" of countries like England and France were concerned about the outcome of events.[93]

This reaction abated a little, says Brown, when some reflected on what motivated the British admiral to act violently, and "the wiser part of the people found considerable difficulty in restraining the fury of the populace." He then applauds the people of Hampton for taking immediate measures to protect their port and recommends similar resolutions in maritime areas of the United States.[94] Such observations on his part, especially in regard to how a particular "class" of people responded to the incident, further historicizes the social dynamics of the period and the ways public anger and political policy intersected.

Brown, as always, attempts to take an even hand in his assessment of the incident, and his analysis of the controversial conditions under which the *Chesapeake* surrendered is both factual and accurate. Here, he acknowledges, for instance, the investigating committee's line of inquiry and Commodore Barron's claim that the *Leopard*'s movements at sea did not warrant undue concern. Saying later, however, that all the ship's "principal officers, except the captain," petitioned the secretary of the navy to investigate the circumstances of the incident, Brown relates the findings of the inquiry, in which officers determined that Commodore Barron failed to observe the *Leopard*'s hostile ship maneuvers and prepare his ship for possible battle and that his conduct indicated "great indecision, and a disposition to negotiate, rather than bravely to defend his ship." The apparent breaches of protocol, says Brown, caused a court martial where Barron was determined innocent or guilty of specific charges. Although found innocent of many of them, including the manner in which he ordered his men to quarters, his being judged guilty of neglecting to clear the *Chesapeake* for action and suspended from all naval command for five years without pay causes Brown to remark that the sentence is not only "very severe" but that "an error of such a kind, and in such circumstances, is not only the most venial in itself, but the most harmless in its consequences, that can be easily imagined."[95]

While Brown indicates that he is unclear about evidence used to prove the commander's knowledge that hostilities were being planned by the *Leopard,* in chapter 4 he continues to analyze responses of the American government to the incident, stating that besides appealing to the British government, complaining of the abuse, and demanding reparations, what "measures could be safely and properly adopted by the executive government, was a topic of much doubt and controversy." He specifically examines the case for reparations, arguing that the British government's "pride and arrogance" have as much to do with events as does the military man's appetite for war. Saying that war is a universal calamity and license for "abuse," Brown relays his pacific Quaker views in this area, seeking some sort of self-control on England's part concerning America's commercial and "unarmed" status: "To avoid, therefore, with utmost care, every act of immediate vengeance, and thereby deprive the British government of every pretext for refusing justice, was deemed the wisest policy by those who were anxious for a pacific termination to the present scene."[96]

At this point, Brown more openly questions how the U.S. government would resolve the situation in light of "popular feelings," saying that retaliation "was wished for by many and expected by all" and that the masses waited with "painful impatience" to hear from its government. His subsequent remarks, for instance, on Jefferson's July 2, 1807, proclamation is a careful analysis of how Jefferson presents the problem and its solution of protecting American waters from armed British ships, both the ones already in American harbor waters and those arriving from England. Agreeing with Jefferson, Brown observes that the "universal approbation" and applauses of the people as well as both political parties seemed to confirm the soundness of the decision. The government's "ministers," he writes, "are beings of the same passions and views as the governed, and, if they disagree in opinion, can seldom, with safety, deviate in practice from the unanimous or general resolutions of the people." And although, suggests Brown, people were united in their disdain for Great Britain, such "unanimity was momentary." In time, party differences would emerge again and "the domestic causes of dissention" would gradually return, regardless of foreign troubles and transactions.[97]

Brown's continued efforts at historical impartiality are also evident in the manner in which he relates how the British minister George Canning communicated news of the event to James Monroe (the U.S. minister to Britain), the way in which he imagines the English people responded to the incident, and the official response of the British government in regard to Jefferson's proclamation and measures such as the "embargo on American vessels." While Brown describes the impact of these communications on the public, American shipmasters, merchants, American residents in England, and others, what is particularly interesting here is the way he applies the concept of historical evidence to articulate the process by which the American government sought to uncover the truth. Saying that the American government was "obliged to collect and sift evidence, to take counsel, and to draw up and revise its dispatches with the utmost caution and deliberation," Brown candidly adds: "The conduct of the British government, on receiving this intelligence, was such as seemed to argue their total previous ignorance of the measures of their admiral: but national affairs are, in general, conducted with so much fraud and stratagem; ends so distant and obscure are generally meditated and effected by means so circuitous and complex, that the common laws of evidence are seldom of any avail in enabling us to lift the curtain." Brown's reluctance here to accept British "ignorance" of the situation as an excuse is tempered by his willingness to wait until more evidence becomes available, and to let time "fully confute or vindicate" suspicions.[98]

Brown's inquiry into interactions between Monroe and Canning further demonstrates his willingness to closely examine the "truth" concerning American and British communications, the behavior of the *Leander,* the practice of impressment, and the issue of British compensation. However, as with his assessment of American imperial designs in Mexico and South America, he also resorts here to irony. For instance, in asking how the "controversy" of British impressment is to be resolved, he examines how both England and the United States lay claim to the "practice of foregoing times," appeal to prior international case law, and rely on principles of independence and the idea that each country's "subjects" or sailors cannot be detained for military or commercial purposes. The appeal, asserts Brown ironically, "to past times, to musty volumes, to diplomatic rolls, to definitions of national equality or political independence, is a futile and nugatory parade. . . .Usage and justice are in the mouths of both, but in the hearts of neither."[99]

More to the point, though, and in a manner that recalls his earlier remarks about American interests in border territories and American claims of exceptionalism, he comments on the controversy in a way that is critical of American political assumptions and foreign policy practices. He uses a series of rhetorical questions and assertions:

The principle which actuates their conduct, and inspires their eloquence, and inflames their zeal, is their own interest. In judging of their interest they may be erring or infallible. No matter; their opinion governs them, and governs them alone. Does any nation renounce a claim? The victory has not been gained in argument. The concession is not made to justice. It is made to necessity; it is enjoined by interest. The claim cannot be effectually maintained by arms: to assert it, would be attended with more injury and inconvenience than the renunciation.

Does any nation insist upon a claim? Not because it is just and equitable: they consider nothing but its benefits. Equity and justice may be pleaded, but such is the peculiar quality of national interest in its influence on human minds, that what is beneficial will always appear to be just; to claim it will always appear to be duty; to die for it will always appear to be virtue; but still the two views are eternally separate in the mind of the king or the statesman. Though his claims will always appear just in his own eyes, their justice is no motive of his conduct. The impulse to his actions is derived from the perception of national benefit alone.

Although Brown proposed later that the only solution to the impressment issue is to "prohibit naval commanders from taking away seamen from neutral ships, on any pretence whatever," his remarks here underscore his perceptive analysis of national self-interest and the motivations for political conduct. They speak directly to his intense engagement with assumptions about American greatness or exceptionalism and his evolving critical sensibility on that point. No nation, he asserts, concedes a claim or admits wrong for fear it will damage their national image. "Equity and justice" rarely are motivations for action; instead, what is "beneficial" to a country's interests, including the United States, is what drives policy and behavior. Unlike earlier parts of the annals, in other words, where Brown is critical only of the motives and actions of other countries, here one senses that he is willing to examine the behavior of both England and the United States in the same light and to suggest that justice may be in the "mouths" of both countries but "in the hearts of neither." For that reason, he concludes, to urge the "justice" of American claims against England would be "arrogant and useless." "The arguments," he says, "of the writer, and the convictions of the reader, are settled by some arbitrary, capricious, or personal motive; or by the nation to which he belongs."[100]

Of relevance here again is Edward Watts's study, in which he observes how American literary culture struggled to become postcolonial and how in a novel like *Arthur Mervyn* Brown "rehearses and indicts colonial modes of reading . . . thrusting the act of interpretation upon the reader" and compelling readers to "explore the ramifications of their own interpretive authority." Brown, he asserts, "asks the reader to reject that subject position and authorize themselves to think independently, to decolonize themselves."[101] While Brown increasingly sees a role for the reader when it comes to the construction of historical meaning, his "thrusting" of the interpretive process upon the reader becomes more overt in this part of the annals—and is essential for understanding the "novel" or dialogical character of his historicism. His handling of constitutional issues and of the *Chesapeake* affair, in particular, signals his efforts to critically examine or interrogate an inherited model of republican colonialism—to self-reflexively examine assumptions about political might and right, especially as they pertain to the special inheritance and responsibilities of the early Republic. It documents his continuing attention to how readers regard historical narrative and interpret the past.

Brown's representation of this debate and the political and moral intervention he articulates are postcolonial to the extent that his comments and use of irony disrupt historical assumptions about American destiny and purpose under God. Instead of reinforcing the dominant ideology that American might makes right and that enlightened nations are benevolent, Brown's depiction of this historical moment offers a site of resistance, of oppositional discourse. In articulating how nations, including the United States, act out of self-interest, Brown exposes the myth of American exceptionalism and the manner in which "national benefit" trumps equity and justice in political and economic matters. He writes history that radically challenges the historical status quo.

In the remaining chapters of his annals, Brown bores in to congressional reports and debates on the *Chesapeake* affair, the implications of an embargo against England, and the American response to Britain's October 16, 1807, proclamation.[102] While it may have been easier to cloak his analysis in the rhetoric of national redemption or providential destiny, he does neither, instead steering a middle path and allowing himself to question assumptions about America's exceptional historical status. For instance, although he proceeds to recount committee reports on American jurisdiction, the protection of American waterways and ports, and the impact of the embargo's nonimportation measures, he concludes this volume of the annals with analysis of why the British government sent George Rose to America and Madison's negotiations with him.

Brown details how in response to American demands for reparation, the British government's own proclamation asserted the right to continue impressing "natural-born subjects" of England. With no renunciation forthcoming and Rose restricted by his government from resolving as long as Jefferson's proclamation was in effect, relations, observes Brown, were strained: Rose wanted to confine negotiations to the affair between the *Leopard* and the *Chesapeake;* Madison wanted not only "redress and reparation" but a complete stop to the practice of impressing American sailors. On this point of disagreement, Brown writes, "When, therefore, a special minister was sent to America, directed not only to exclude the subject of impressment from merchant ships, but even every injury but that commited on the Chesapeake, they either meant a mere pageantry, intended and expected to end in nothing, or they expected that America would retract her most vehement assertions, and renounce her most solemn claims."[103] Brown's remarks here are critical, almost sarcastic, and highlight what he sees as disingenuous motives on behalf of the British or reasons for meeting with American representatives.

While Madison would offer to revoke the American proclamation on the same day England acceded to reparations and promised not to conduct future impressments, Rose spurned such a proposal for several reasons, including that he was not authorized by the British government to accept such terms and that the recall of Jefferson's proclamation was a condition that had to be met before resolving the situation. Ignoring Madison's claim about prior offences, Rose continued to emphasize "the impropriety of mingling any other matter with that of the Chesapeake." The controversy eventually ended, says Brown, with neither side conceding, the British demanding the withdrawal of Jefferson's proclamation, and the Americans refusing to do such until reparation was offered. While Brown remarks, ironically, on how the "medium of self-love" provides perspective on Britain's behavior, his most astute commentary focuses on the role of bias and subjectivity in regard to the event: "Different judgments were formed of this catastrophe, as men were influenced by factious or by national biases, and even appeared in very different lights to different men, whose integrity was unimpeachable." "It is," he continues, "easily perceived, by the most impartial, that the whole was matter of punctilio."[104] Brown, as has been argued throughout this study, was highly self-conscious, and as his last words here about "factious" and "national biases" documents, his historical inquiry was almost always accompanied by this kind of modern self-reflexive historical subjectivity.

In retrospect, Brown's historical treatment of the *Chesapeake* affair provides historians of the early Republic with penetrating analysis of the controversial conditions under which the *Chesapeake* surrendered and the manner in which different elements of the American public responded to the event. It also accounts for varying political interests, both on behalf of the British and among American political parties. In addition, Brown's assessment of political motivation, self-interest, and "national benefit" in regard to events surrounding the *Chesapeake* affair provides provocative analysis of American assumptions about destiny and commercial and political exceptionalism, topics Brown delves into more fully in regard to the period's other major event—Jefferson's controversial embargo policy.

Jefferson's Embargo

Just as the *Chesapeake* affair thrust the United States into a quandary with England and immersed the country in debate, so Jefferson's 1807 embargo also became a major subject of heated dispute. The embargo, observes Clark, "brought squarely

before the country for the first time since the days of the great debate over the formation and adoption of the Constitution the all-important question of whether
our government was to be a democracy, or an oligarchy ruled by wealth and privilege."[105] As historians have noted, Jefferson's decision caused a Federalist uproar and
a rift in Jefferson's own party. It also caused major strife in states such as New York
and Pennsylvania, especially as the effects of the embargo began to be felt by individuals connected with exports. Protests became so violent that the Embargo Act
was repealed on March 1, 1809, some two months after Brown penned his address
to Congress on the subject. While in retrospect the embargo crippled American
merchants and failed to affect the course of events with England and France, during
Brown's day it was an intense political moment with an uncertain outcome.[106]

To be sure, Brown covers the embargo more thoroughly in a political pamphlet
titled *An Address to the Congress of the United States, on the Utility and Justice
of Restrictions upon Foreign Commerce,* in which he protests it. He nevertheless
develops his position on the embargo in his "Annals of America." Thus, while he
may have been reluctant at first to be overtly critical of Jefferson's policy, over
time, as he came to understand its full impact on the nation's economy, he took a
more critical or radical stance, arguing that the economic motivation behind the
embargo and its impact on the innocent, both abroad and domestically, contra-
dicted the claim that the United States was an exceptional nation and stated that
the country's "interests" and pretensions of "political justice" were no different
from those of its European counterparts.

To illustrate: as with the *Chesapeake* affair, Brown first takes up the embargo
issue in volume 3 of the annals, noting that on November 23, 1807, a committee report addressed the *Chesapeake* situation and British aggression in general
against Americans. While the committee's powers were themselves the subject of
controversy, it nevertheless recommended "protecting the ports and harbours by
an adequate force" and stated that the ports in need of immediate attention were
"New Orleans, Savannah, Charleston, Wilmington, Norfolk, Baltimore, Philadelphia, New York, [and] New London" among others. After recounting how nearly
260 gunboats, each costing about $5,000, would be necessary, Brown writes:

> The scene of political contest began more distinctly to unfold itself on the
> 27th of November, when a petition of some of the merchants and traders of
> Philadelphia was presented. In this memorial they request that the commer-
> cial interests of the United States may not be endangered by insisting, in our
> negotiations with Great Britain, on claims dubious or unimportant; that the
> non-importation act of the 18th of April, 1806, might be repealed, because
> the execution of it would not be favourable to a friendly settlement of the
> present controversies with Great Britain, since, while it injured and embar-
> rassed ourselves, it tended to disgust and irritate that nation; and because

this repeal would evince a magnanimous and conciliating spirit on our part, and tend to reconcile the nation more unanimously to the evils of war, if war, not withstanding, should ensue.

Nearly five months had passed since the *Chesapeake* affair, and the public was still relatively "unacquainted with the state of the controversy between America and Great Britain, and with the terms offered by Mr. Monroe, or by the British ministry." Nevertheless, Clay, J. Randolph, Milnor, and Basset all urged that the "non-importation act was essentially defective, full of contradictions and absurdities; incapable of being, in many cases, carried into execution, and injurious to the very purpose for which it was made."[107]

The motion, observes Brown, was opposed by Rowan, Crowninshield, Smilie, Rhea, Nelson, and others.[108] And while some argued for supporting the law and others acknowledged its defects, in the debates, says Brown, "all the usual spirit of party began to display itself." The memorialists and their advocates were viewed as traitors loyal to Britain, and the government was "accused of aiming at an unnecessary war, and the representatives of submitting with servility to the mandates, and trusting with mischievous devotion to the wisdom of the government." Ultimately, the motion was rejected, and Brown recounts the process by which the Senate and House of Representatives debated and then authorized the defense of ports and harbors with gunboats. Party interests played a role in the law's final resolution; during this process, he observed that the public had more questions than answers and was generally concerned about whether or not the nation's own ships would be restricted to ports by a general embargo. Jefferson, writes Brown, asserted that American commerce was in danger because of the French and English actions and subsequently "recommended a law prohibiting the departure of all American vessels from the ports of the United States." Despite opposition to the recommendation, Jefferson's embargo was made law on December 22, 1807, and "the wheels of foreign commerce," says Brown, came to a halt, the "chief or only source of subsistence of millions was sealed up by this decree; and yet it was submissively received and patiently obeyed by the people."[109]

Continuing his historical analysis and probing, Brown remarks that such "conclusions," were, however, more "specious than solid," as the suspension of shipping and commerce is affected by the time of the year and the actual length of the embargo itself. The prohibition, he contends, must operate by "slow degrees," and the flow of trade may not necessarily be interrupted by an embargo lasting a week or month. In addition, he asserts that "laws are not omnipotent" and are successful only to the degree in which they coincide with the "usual occupations and darling interests of a great number of the people." People who rely on trade for their livelihood would, in his mind, seek ways to avoid it. And while many imagined that the impact of the embargo would be immediate, the fact was that the "motives" for initiating the embargo were hidden for a time and "people were thrown into a kind of astonishment and terror" once the law was enacted. More specifically, "The embargo was never represented as a measure connected necessarily with the attack upon the Chesapeake, or with those injuries of a similar nature, lately in discussion between the ministers of the two nations in London. Its advocates pleaded only the encroachments made by France and Great Britain on the liberties of neutral commerce, flowing from their arbitrary detentions and confiscations, their orders and decrees."[110]

Brown's observation here is an important one because it not only attends more closely to perceptions of the "the people"—an aspect of his historicism—but offers a ringside assessment of competing claims concerning the motivations for and effects of the embargo, including, for instance, the question of whether or not it was largely a direct response to the *Chesapeake* affair itself or a conservative approach to a long history of assaults on neutral trade. He asserts, for instance, that advocates argued that France and Great Britain encroached on "the liberties of neutral commerce" and that the embargo was needed to protect property. Advocates, he remarks, also argued that an embargo would preserve ships and sailors from the enemy and help protect America from future provocations. Further, proponents of the embargo believed that restricting trade would not only "impair the manufactures of Great Britain" but cut off France, and to some degree Spain, from supplies and luxuries as well.[111]

By contrast, says Brown, opponents "insisted on the inefficacy of the measure," and its injurious effects on American commercial interests. "No pillage," said some, "to which it can now be exposed, is equal, to the injury of keeping it at home to mould and perish." Stores of "fish and flesh, bread and timber" would be wasted, and inactive ships and unemployed sailors undermine profit. Further, if the only way to justify an embargo is by "the interests of the people," then the proposed restrictions on commerce fail to meet that test. Opponents, says Brown, argued that Great Britain could easily obtain supplies for manufactures from other countries in the east, Canada, and Portugal and that an embargo could also benefit England by allowing the British to usurp American shipping contracts.[112]

Although relatively neutral in his analysis to this point, Brown comments forcefully on the embargo's limited or neutral effects. He recalls how the "impartial effects of the embargo are boasted" and how both England and France would be affected: "Here lies the irreparable evil, the invincible objection: the benefit of one is the evil of the other; the injury to France is the strongest reason why Britain should promote it; the injury to Britain is a powerful inducement for France to submit to it, to exert herself for its continuance." Further, he asserts, "But how small is the injury to France! How little is that potent state influenced by such effeminate, such remote considerations!"[113]

Brown analyzes France's insulation from harm and general preoccupation with its own interests, but he goes on to note more ironically the manner Napoleon's councils might have to accommodate "the passion of one in ten thousand of his subjects for sugar and coffee." These comments are followed by a series of rhetorical questions about the impact of the embargo relative to war with England and the efficacy of using commercial sanctions to extract political concessions. Brown concludes his assessment in volume 3: "Such were some of the arguments by which the embargo was attacked and vindicated. To enter more minutely into its history would be unsuitable to this occasion, as it must be considered as chiefly suggested by attacks and restrictions upon neutral commerce, disconnected with the conduct of the British commanders, in relation to the Chesapeake."[114] As he had done throughout most of his annals, Brown consciously restrained himself from further analysis in the name of historical objectivity or impartiality.[115]

Considering, though, the effects of the embargo, its cutting off of American exports to foreign markets in response to violations of American neutrality, Brown writes in the last volume of his annals in 1809 that the American government was "obliged to pause in its hostile career"—that as an "engine of public vengeance" the embargo had a negative impact, both economically and morally, on the American people.[116] Brown does not go into great detail here on what he means by "hostile career," but the comment clearly qualifies the harmony depicted in his early annals and amplifies previous criticisms of American innocence and cultural redemption—its pretensions of being an "exemplary" or "redeemer nation."

Although Brown's "Annals of America" say little more that is directly related to the embargo, it is worth examining *An Address to the Congress of the United States, on the Utility and Justice of Restrictions Upon Foreign Commerce*—his political pamphlet on this topic, and the ways it relates to Brown's analysis in the annals. For, if Paine, in a July 8, 1808, letter to Thomas Jefferson, merely identified the British Orders of Council and the Milan decree as "the cause of the Embargo" and proposed that Jefferson negotiate with France and England to end the stalemate, Brown, for his time, had a different, more radical response—one more critical of the political and economic motivations underlying American foreign policy.[117] Published on January 3, 1809, some six months after Paine's letter, it is Brown's strongest negation not only of the embargo but also of American exceptionalism.

Addressing Congress, Brown writes in the pamphlet's advertisement that he has tried to "trace the present differences between Europe and America to their true source, and to place the controversy between them on its true basis." Alert, as always, to his own limitations, he goes on to not only acknowledge that he was "greatly mistaken" in his earlier understanding of the embargo and its end of restoring the "blessings of a free trade," but he articulates the "motives and ends" of the embargo. He passionately relates the "sufferings" to different elements of the American population and raises important questions about foreign trade, commercial produce, and manufacturing as they pertain to the American economy.

Drilling down into the underlying motives of the embargo and the similarities between American foreign policy and those of imperial powers, Brown mounts, I contend, *the* most provocative criticism of American exceptionalism for his time and years to come. Surpassing Jefferson, Paine, and Duane in his dissent, he jettisons lingering assumptions of American uniqueness and republican progress and writes in a defiant, distinctly Godwinian tone:

> All this is very true. Europe, Britain has done this: and alas! those who fancied that the spirit of Europe was regenerated or improved by crossing the Atlantic, are woefully mistaken. It was indeed quite ridiculous to think that *this* branch of the European body was exempted from any of the vices of *those.* How should it happen? What is there in our intellectual constitution that should make us wiser or better than our kinsmen beyond sea? If any proof were wanting that our system of *political* justice is as narrow, selfish, depraved, unfeeling, as that of European states, we have only to consider the *purpose* of the embargo, the *intention* of imposing it: the *effects* on foreign nations which some of us rejoiced that it *would,* and which the rest of us lamented that it would *not* produce.[118]

Of this passage, Alan Axelrod observes that there is "evidence of a final disappointment with the American experiment" and "something of the same subversive spirit that animated *Arthur Mervyn.*"[119] Although, a final disappointment would come later in the annals in regard to the Constitution, Axelrod is dead on concerning the relationship between Brown's earlier radicalism and the contestatory spirit in the annals. Brown, as is evident from his earlier resistance to British colonialism and the imperialist pretensions of American adventurers in Mexico, extends his critique here of colonial ambition and exploitation to the United States—to the economic motivation behind American foreign policy.

By using rhetorical questions and emphasizing points of contrast and comparison, such as "*this*" and "*that*" part of Europe, openly rejecting the "redeemer nation" rhetoric *and* rationale as it applies to the United States, and saying that the "glorious end" of the embargo was anchored in a desire for personal "profit and aggrandisement," Brown puts American "interests" and "political justice" on the same table as its European counterparts. He refuses to separate New World ambitions and interests from "Old World wickedness"—that is, to see the United States as morally superior or exceptional in its political means or ends.[120] He has determined, reluctantly, that the United States is, ironically, no more protected, blessed, or "exemplary" than its imperialist peers. It is not unique or exceptional—it too is motivated by economic self-interest and political expediency, even if harmful to others. Thus, if, according to Jefferson historians Robert Tucker and David Hendrickson, Henry Adams believed "the failure of the embargo meant the repudiation not merely of Jefferson's theory of foreign relations but of the whole notion of American exceptionalism," the same may be said about Brown's historical assessment of the situation several decades earlier.[121] Even if sometimes located in his footnotes, Brown's deconstruction of such an American mythology so early in the history of the early Republic is one of the most radical political statements of the period and clearly distinguishes him from his peers, including Jefferson and Paine, each of whom either closed an eye to American imperial ambitions or could not see how American self-interest and policies resembled those of Europe.

In sum, Brown's assessment of the embargo was dead on—and his analysis of the "exceptionalist" rationale that Jefferson and others assumed was also on point in ways that historians and early Americanists only now can fully appreciate. According to Tucker and Hendrickson, "both in the incorporation of Louisiana and in the prosecution of the embargo" Jefferson "abandoned constitutional principle, and thus provided a critical precedent for the consolidation of national power." He "detested his own creation and refused to the end to acknowledge that the government of extended powers that arose from the Republican ascendancy was in anyway his own offspring." Constitutional historian Leonard Levy concurs, saying of the fifth Embargo Act, signed on January 9, 1809, that under its terms "the privilege against self-incrimination was rendered meaningless; the right to trial by jury made a farce; the protection against property being taken without due process of law ignored; and the freedom from unreasonable searches and seizures abolished." To this day, argues Levy, the fifth Embargo Act was "the most repressive and unconstitutional legislation ever enacted by Congress in time of peace."[122]

While Levy's observation may be quite accurate, the consolidation of power and error in political judgment Brown and others witnessed in their day is, as I suggest later, historically relevant to our own. As the absence of a "redeemer nation" rhetoric in his annals shows, Brown increasingly understood and distanced himself from the emerging discourse of manifest destiny and an ideology of unlimited institutional power. In this respect, his efforts at historical impartiality with Napoleonic rule and British colonialism in India and Egypt enabled him to employ a stinging indictment of imperialist attitudes associated with American exceptionalism—a hard-hitting and ironic reevaluation of America's prophetic promise. In this light, Brown's "old instinct" for "cultural radicalism" did *not* completely succumb to an "imperialist vision of America's expansionist future."[123] Rather, it regenerates itself in the form of a postcolonial sensibility and an enlightened way of understanding the past—and future—course of the early Republic. This ethos, manifests itself in one other distinctive way when Brown focuses more directly on alerting readers to congressional debates related to the Constitution and eroding democratic processes—and the necessity of "the people" to also judge the present against the past.

Chapter Seven

Constitutional Limits—and "Liberalism"

We have now finished our contemplated review of the American Register, and we confess, we entertain some prejudice against the affected sensibility and croaking of our author, and indeed against many of his peculiarities of style; but we are much pleased with the publication on the whole. We consider it highly useful in its nature; it seems unexampled in this country, for industry and general accuracy of information, and though we recommend to our author not to show so evidently the democratic impulses of his feelings, in the historical narrative; yet we cannot but consider that his book may be rendered an important acquisition to the literature as well as politics of the country.

—From the *Boston Ordeal*, April 29, 1809

Daniel Edwards Kennedy observes that Benjamin Pollard's review in the *Boston Ordeal*, was a "puzzling mixture of censure and praise probably due to the political rancour" of the day.[1] The review was of a Federalist or conservative orientation and "praised the intentions of Brown but found that when he departed from being a chronicler he drew conclusions that were not only dangerous but 'lapses of correctness and deviations from authority,' especially in the study of the affair of the ship Chesapeake that embroiled the United States with Great Britain."[2] Kennedy goes on to remark that the review was typical of its day in terms of "political bias" and that despite the presence of editorial shortcomings in Brown's project, such as "clumsy" pagination, Brown's publication found a favorable reception in other quarters.[3] Complaints in the *Federal Gazette* and elsewhere about "the affected impartiality of democratic scribblers" in regard to foreign affairs were indeed not uncommon—and readily speak to Brown's "democratic," not Federalist, sympathies, his willingness to question, both privately and publicly, the political motivations of individuals as well as official accounts of events.

Brown, as I have argued thus far, tried to be historically self-conscious, resist a filiopietistic tradition of history writing, avoid participation in partisan party politics, and, increasingly, distance himself from a nationalist rhetoric of manifest destiny. In doing so, he also gravitated toward the use of ironic discourse in his history writing, offering a critique not only of European imperialism and its related "evils" but also of the imperialist dimensions of American exceptionalism. His historical thinking and practice, in other words, testify to an evolution of sorts, where his periodical essays and reviews, novels, political pamphlets, historical sketches, and annals all enabled him to develop increasingly sophisticated ideas about historical impartiality and subjectivity as well as the degree and ways he was willing to employ history for the national good. While I have suggested ways Brown's historical writing in the *American Register* is original—or, as the *Boston Ordeal* asserted in 1809, "unexampled"—and influenced by his earlier novelistic techniques, I have not said as much about how Brown's historicism is "novel" in a Bakhtinian sense or, as a consequence, uniquely relates to more modern, and even postmodern, historiographical principles and practices.

In this chapter, I examine how in the last volume of the annals Brown's historicism moves beyond an ironic tradition of historiography, and even documentary editing, departing significantly not only in content but also in form from traditional hierarchical or monological models of history. Contrary to Pamela Clemit's claim that Brown's history writing was a "conservative defence of perceivable reality," I argue that his historicism continues to move beyond a teleological tradition toward a mode of representation that is more accurately described as imaginative or dialogical in form and, importantly, "democratic" or liberal in principle.[4] More specifically, Brown's refusal to embrace traditional historical and teleological assumptions, and part of what makes his historical writing "novel," is not only the degree of his historical self-consciousness but also his willingness to integrate other discourses as part of his own historical narrative and alert readers to the lessons of history.

For these reasons, I argue it is no coincidence that Brown's prefaces to the *American Register* are methodologically self-conscious and also relate why he increasingly used primary or public documents in lieu of traditional historical narrative as part of his inquiry into, and representation of, historical events. In his last volume of the annals, Brown analyzed congressional proposals to amend the Constitution, the debate over relocating the nation's capital to Philadelphia, and, finally, Stephen Bradley's controversial 1808 Republican caucus memo as compromising constitutional liberties and democratic processes. Brown's decision to focus on these events not only recalls anti-Federalist concerns in the 1780s but points to his increasingly active engagement with constitutional issues and the consolidation of political power. His individualistic resistance to party politics and concerns about the consolidation of political power at the expense of individual rights and liberties not only recall his affinities with 1790s British radicalism but place him within an eighteenth-century tradition of "liberalism" or liberal thought. It explains what compelled him, as he grew ill, to represent the immediate past to the people in an impartial yet imaginative and instructive way—a manner that recalls the enlightened inquiry and intellectual radicalism of his novels.[5]

Republicanism, the American Register, *and History*

Although not usually read as a composite text, Brown's five prefaces to the *American Register* (1807–09) and "Annals of Europe and America" are remarkably revealing and record his increasingly imaginative approach to historical representation. They chart his recognition of the limits of a monological view of the past, and his understanding that the boundaries between form and content in historiography, especially in regard to the carnivalesque potential of primary documents, could be fluid. As I have been arguing, Brown's historicism was never static but instead "evolutionary"—even, perhaps, dialectical insofar as his novels, periodical writing, historical fiction, and annals themselves informed one another. The composition of these various texts contributed collectively, over time, to his self-conscious understanding of history and truth and how the motives, interests, and contradictions embodied by individuals also found expression in the actions and policies of countries on both sides of the Atlantic.

Since the 1980s, both Joyce Appleby and Cathy Davidson have made important observations about the historical imagination in the early Republic and the ways it served a nation uncertain about the limits or potential of human freedom and other ideals in an emerging democracy. In *Liberalism and Republicanism in the Historical Imagination,* for instance, Appleby writes that "liberalism entered the history of America as a set of powerful ideas" and that while these assumptions were often hard to articulate they more or less centered on the ideas of freedom and equality. It was increasingly believed, she says, that nature endowed human beings with the capacity for self-thought and self-governance and that "free choice in matters of religion, marriage, intellectual pursuits, and electoral politics is the right of every individual." Further, if "free inquiry discloses the nature of reality," a reality "whose laws are accessible to reason," then the "rule of law is binding on all citizens as long as its positive statutes conform to the natural law protection of life, liberty, and property."[6]

Elizabeth Dillon concurs, stating that the "innovation of liberal political theory lies in the claim that individuals have the right to exercise political choice or consent (as well as dissent) with respect to governing authority"—that "liberalism also, by implication, constructs and relies upon a strong definition of the modern subject as one who is free, autonomous, and capable of self-government and rational behavior." Although long associated, in other words, with the growth of a market economy and the politics of participation, the "original passion of liberal reformers was outrage: outrage at institutions that interfered with free inquiry; outrage about the tyranny that groups exercised over individuals; outrage with the human debasement in the aristocratic assumption of innate superiority." It was a concept, in the aftermath of 1776, affiliated with "both liberation and liberality" and premised on the idea that the affirmation of inalienable natural rights, such as the pursuit of truth and happiness, would help stem the tide of injustice.[7] In historiography, as in politics, the pursuit of truth, therefore, was driven by a passion for free, rational inquiry and understanding.

If, as Appleby argues, memory and the imagination can return us to the liberal origins of our founding ideals and facilitate the moral and political direction of the future, Cathy N. Davidson makes similar observations insofar as she posits a metahistorical understanding of the past and of the role of oppositional discourse in literary history. In her still highly regarded study *Revolution and the Word,* she states that "oppositional or dialogical history challenges conventional literary history by questioning both the relative value of what is examined and the implicit values of the examiner." Such history "sees the very processes and ambitions of historiography as products of much larger forces and it seeks to understand the relationships between those present forces and the hierarchical imperatives of the past." According to Mikhail Bakhtin, she says, "The dialogical text is particularly subversive since it challenges complacency, forces the reader's active participation in the text, and resolutely refuses to assuage uncertainty with comforting, final solutions."[8]

Bakhtin himself makes distinctions between "epic" literature and the "novel"; for him the "epic past" is both "monochronic" and "hierarchical" and represents the past in an absolutist way. He asserts that while it "lacks any relativity" or "any gradual, purely temporal progressions that might connect it with the present," the novel, by contrast, "can be defined as a diversity of social speech types (sometimes even diversity of languages) and a diversity of individual voices, artistically organized. . . . Authorial speech, the speeches of narrators, inserted genres, the speech of characters are merely those fundamental compositional unities with whose help heteroglossia . . . can enter the novel; each of them permits a multiplicity of social voices and wise variety of their links and interrelationships (always more or less dialogized)." In contrast to traditional epic discourse, which is monological, "completed, conclusive, and immutable, as a fact, an idea and a value," the language of the novel is "ever questing, ever examining itself and subjecting its established forms to review." Unlike the "distance" and immutability one associates with epic discourse and time, the novel encourages "contact with the developing, incomplete and therefore re-thinking and re-evaluating present."[9]

While Brown's reflections on history and history writing do not, of course, perfectly parallel Bakhtin's theory of the novel, his theory and practice of history writing, especially as articulated in the series of prefaces to the *American Register,*

unmistakably record his emerging dialogical perspective on the carnivalesque nature of historical representation and his concern with how readers understood the
past relative to the present. They chart his increasing recognition of the limits of a
monological view of the past and his understanding that the boundaries between
form and content in historiography, especially in regard to the use of primary documents, could be fluid. That is, if over the duration of his career Brown reflected self-
consciously on issues of historical truth, representation, and uncertainty, and his
"Annals of Europe and America" increasingly integrated the heteroglossia of external primary documents, his historical writing is the product of late Enlightenment
rational inquiry, insofar as it departs from and disrupts the historiographical status
quo. It embraces "heteroglossia" and the multiple voices and ideologies of speech
and writing and questions the existence of a single authoritative discourse.[10]

To illustrate: in the first preface to the *American Register,* dated, November 1,
1807, Brown articulates the difficulties in both launching the project and the manner in which he hoped to be a "faithful historian." It records, among other things,
his consciousness of his own "incapacity or ignorance" and the manner in which
the "progress of the press" and his readership affected the production and even the
content of the magazine. If his rendering of history is not sufficient, he hopes that
the "Abstract of Laws and Public Acts of the United States" that follows the annals
will be of "some value to the lawyer and political enquirer." By contrast, in his second preface, after noting the difficulty of retaining "impartiality" in his historical
narrative amid political factions, he suggests that appended historical documents
could be conveniently read by "the enlightened part of the community."[11] Not only
does he seem to have reflected on or redefined his notions of audience from one
preface to another (becoming more inclusive), but he also becomes more explicit
about his own political agenda and about those principles or biases that guide his
editorial decisions. He articulates a more inclusive sense of audience and how the
democratic reader might benefit from historical materials in his periodical.

The third preface (published in 1808) continues to comment on "deviations"
from the original plan for the magazine and also records Brown's developing awareness of his own limitations as a historian and his ability to construct a singular, authoritative point of view. His remarks, for instance, on historical materials and how
the particular "selection and arrangement have been made as was best calculated to
display them" indicate the degree to which he consciously sought to impart an accurate sense of the historical past to his readers.[12] In the same preface, however, Brown
also admits that he is facing an editorial problem—excessive amounts of public and
political materials—and mentions the fact that the public papers presented to Congress in the most recent session took up more than "*six octavo volumes.*"

What is noteworthy here in terms of understanding Brown's increasingly dialogical view of historical evidence is that he takes the unusual step at the end
of the preface to insert an editorial annotation in the form of a letter by Condy

Raguet (claiming he is the author of a work Brown identified as being anonymous). Brown, as I have already shown, had been integrating primary materials, ironic commentary, or other voices all along in his footnotes, especially after the first two volumes of the annals. But his inclusion of the letter in his preface marks a conceptual shift in his thinking about history and his role as a historian or, to use more modern phrasing, "one who knows." It marks Brown's willingness to include voices other than his own as a vehicle of historical authority or analysis.

The letter concerns a private document Brown included in the previous volume. That document, remarks Raguet, was titled "Account of the Massacre in St. Domingo, in May, 1806." Of it, he says: "The above narrative is an anonymous performance, originally published in the American newspapers. Its only claim to credit must arise from the probable nature of the incidents contained in it. Imperfect as this kind of testimony is, it is, in general, the only kind accessible to a minute historian of contemporary events, where official intelligence is wanting."[13] Raguet identifies himself in the letter to Brown as the author of the anonymous piece, saying that even though the account of the massacre did not appear in an "official form," it still was of value not only as a source of information for future generations but because it was doubtful that "any other gentleman who was present at the time of that distressing event will ever take the pains to commit it to print." Although not in his historical narrative proper, Brown's inclusion of this material in his preface marks his willingness to depart from the historiographical status quo and to consider alternative sources of historical evidence, especially in regard to "official intelligence" of government officials or other entities.

In his fourth preface of the *American Register* (published in 1809), Brown indulges in the hope that the present volume of his magazine "will be found to contain materials of more value and variety than any former volume." This preface, unlike the previous prefaces, is considerably shorter than the previous ones. Domestic events, he observes, are in a "state of extreme uncertainty"; he felt it would also be more appropriate to consider them in the next volume. While Brown notes that laws enacted by Congress are too numerous—even in abstract form—for him to include more than once a year, he does bring in commentary concerning the narrative proceedings of the Quakers "in relation to the Indians" and geographical sketches concerning Louisiana, and he ends the preface with remarks on the state of American literature and the "falacy [sic] and misrepresentation of reviews."[14] However, in contrast to Brown's emphasis in the third volume on the "selection and arrangement" of historical texts and on the "curious details" of select papers, the fourth preface demonstrates his increased willingness to use various historical discourses as a means of shoring up accounts of history. It indicates his ongoing recognition of how multiple documents and discourses—not a monological narrative—more accurately reflect history.

That is, if Brown hoped the fourth volume would "contain materials of more value and variety than any former volume," he makes two revealing comments concerning his expanded use and arrangement of documents. First, of his decision to republish certain documents regarding the decrees of France and Britain, he says: "The repetition was admitted by the editor, from the persuasion that it was best to preserve the series entire, especially as these copies are completely authentic." Second, and more explicitly testifying to his rethinking of the relationship between historical narrative and evidence, he writes: "The intrinsic value of the narrative of the proceedings of the friends in relation to the Indians, and of the geographical sketches respecting Louisiana, will, the editor believes, be evident to every judicious reader," not just lawyers, the social elite, or those interested in politics. This "work . . . would be entitled to no small share of public regard, if it were merely a general depository of papers so valuable as these."[15]

Both of these comments suggest a heightened appreciation of how texts can be used as intertexts: what Louis Montrose calls "a reciprocal conditioning by the discourses of the past and our discourses about the past."[16] Brown's use of "repetition" and willingness to accord other texts the same value as his own collapses the hierarchy of traditional historical narrative and its use of primary documents or "other" texts for making historical meaning. In the mode of Bakhtin and, even Robert Berkhofer's ideas about historical authority, multivocality, and poststructuralism, Brown became more willing to include multiple voices in the text—to essentially include other discourses as narrative vehicles—and implicitly challenged the assumption that a single master historical narrative can adequately represent the past. Thus, while as early as volume 3 Brown's prefatory material records his growing recognition of how multiple documents and discourses, not a monolithic narrative, might more accurately reflect history, he continues to raise the issue, if recent reception theory is a guide, of the role the "judicious reader" plays in the construction of historical meaning.[17]

Brown's fifth and final preface, published late in 1809, just a few months before his death, offers further evidence of his dialogical understanding of historical representation and contains his most provocative statements regarding history and the use of public documents. He begins by reminding readers that two years have passed since the first publication of the *American Register*, a work "previously unattempted in America," and that experience has "instructed him in the best form for such publication, and enabled him gradually to mould the plan of it, in conformity to the judgement of the public." The "experiment" has been successful, and as evidence he outlines the changes in the magazine:

This work is particularly designed to be a repository of American history and politics. These topics are, in themselves, so copious, that the extent of this publication, amounting to 1000 closely printed octavo pages, in a year, is scarcely sufficient for a comprehensive view of them. Public and official papers, both foreign and domestic, relative to American affairs, are found, upon experiment, to be very voluminous, and a selection of them to be absolutely necessary, in order to bring them within reasonable limits. We have hitherto contracted these limits beyond what was expedient, for the sake of matters of less intrinsic consequence. Hereafter, we shall consider public and official papers connected with American affairs as of the first importance.

An impartial and well-digested history of American affairs, and of foreign transactions, so far as they illustrate and are connected with those of our native country, will be given in this work. Public documents are the only legitimate bases of history. These, in our times, are so copious, so circumstantial, and so authentic, that they almost supersede the business of the historian, and will ever obtain, with all judicious inquirers into history, their principal attention. In this work the original materials are inserted, and the facts, authenticated by them, methodized and illustrated in a regular narration.

And of the significance of various types of "Public documents":

The Register includes a comprehensive abstract of all the laws passed by the general government. This is not introduced for the benefit of the lawyer, to whom the originals only are of any service, but as the most important historical documents. The laws of the United States, from the nature of the government, relate almost wholly to the levying and collection of a revenue; to the formation, distribution, and maintenance of a military force by land and by sea; to the modelling and government of frontier territories; to the public intercourse with the Indian tribes; and to modes of conduct with regard to foreign nations. Regulations on these points are closely connected with the current history of the nation, and are absolutely necessary to be known by those who would be acquainted, not with the municipal law, but the political condition of their own country.[18]

Although Brown also suggests that a "list of the deaths of eminent or remarkable persons of our own country, with all the information concerning them, is a necessary branch of our domestic history," he is clear about the larger plan for the *American Register.* Unlike in his first preface, in which he planned a "summary narrative of the affairs of Europe" and to "view" those of America, the emphasis here is on "American affairs" as they are illuminated by foreign and domestic documents. Also, in contrast to an earlier preface, where he found congressional records "uninteresting," he now classifies public and official papers as being of "first importance"—as being the "only legitimate bases of history." In particular, "laws" reflect the historical and cultural core of a country better than other texts. They may be considered a culture's "most important historical documents." In addition, Brown is careful to appeal to "all judicious inquirers into history" and even goes so far as to say that the abstract of laws is "not" only for "the benefit of the lawyer." While such reflections record his continued efforts to produce a marketable literary product, they also bear directly on his theory of historical narrative, and his selection of documents in volume 5, in two important ways.

First, it must be acknowledged that Brown still aspired toward historical "objectivity." Evidence of this is the fact that he inserted original materials or documents into the fifth volume of the "Annals of America," in lieu of a traditional historical narrative. To be sure, Brown had been incorporating primary documents into the footnotes of his annals as early as volume 2; and in the fourth volume of the *American Register* he commented on the "intrinsic value" of particular texts. One can argue—by modernist standards at least—that in this kind of reconstruction of the past Brown attempted some measure of "impartiality" or historical objectivity and that he was making an attempt to rid himself of personal bias and let the documents or facts speak for themselves in a manner that went beyond mere compilation.[19]

At the same time, Brown's claim of impartiality and increasing willingness to integrate multiple documents and voices into his historical narrative is qualified by other comments in the passage and the larger context of the prefaces themselves. That is, if Brown admitted to moments where he was frustrated by the "difficulty of managing . . . topics with impartiality" and later observed that "public documents . . . almost supersede the business of the historian," such self-conscious responses not only question the "epic" or "hierarchical" relationship between historical fact and interpretive or authoritative text but hint at his questions about how reliance on master historical narrative, his own included, could adequately reconstruct the past.[20] In this light, Brown's untraditional use of historical documents to record history implicitly questions turn-of-the-century assumptions about historical continuity and progress, the idea—whether in the histories of Hume, Robertson, or Trumbull—that a linear narrative should be superimposed on events to give them unity, coherence, and causality.[21]

Second, if, like modern metahistorians, Brown eventually came to understand that history is essentially an imaginative "assemblage of texts," the appropriation and intersection of various texts by different historians, the "dialogical" character of Brown's use of public documents in volume 5 recalls what Bakhtin calls the "distinguishing feature of the novel as a genre."[22] Just as the prose writer makes use of words that are "already populated with social intentions of others and compels them to serve his own new intentions," so Brown's imaginative refraction of "heteroglot" language or discourse invites the reader of his historical narrative to understand his "parodic" or ironic intentions.[23] His willingness, in other words, to integrate other voices in his historical narrative—whether they are "dispersed in public offices," buried in congressional records, or printed in the form of obituaries—shows a willingness to validate other texts as vehicles of both historical truth and representation for a broader reading public.

Implicit here, therefore, is the suggestion that the construction of history is not an insulated, monological exercise but rather the dialectical integration of multiple voices, ideologies, and details.[24] By extension, as the remainder of the chapter illustrates, Brown's analysis of public documents concerning the Constitution and Congress—and his decision to strategically integrate select primary documents in lieu of a historical narrative proper—may be understood as a democratic and "liberal" form of historical representation. His last volume of the annals interrogates the status quo, offering insight into his understanding of the meaning and function of a representative form of government in the early Republic.

Constitutional Debates and Amending the Federal Constitution

Brown's "Annals of America," it may be argued, appeared precisely when older "republican" values of civic virtue and the "common good" gave way to a politics of "private interest."[25] Echoing John Adams's 1807 observation that "there is not a more unintelligible word in the English language than republicanism," Daniel Rodgers observed that the key terms of republicanism—*virtue,* the *republic,* the *commonweal*"—were hotly contested and in permanent "conflict."[26] Drew McCoy agrees, saying that the "intellectual dilemma" of the time was "inescapable" and that "the problem of finding a way to permit liberty, commerce, and prosperity and, at the same time, to deny their potentially corrupting effects was neither new in American history nor unusual in the context of the eighteenth century's poignant endeavor to bridge the growing gap between antiquity and modernity."[27] The country was increasingly attuned to the potential for republican values to be compromised or corrupted by self-interest.[28]

On this point, historian Steven Watts concurs, saying that the economic dimension of "republicanism" or the "massive multifaceted transformation away from republican traditions and toward modern capitalism in America" helps explain the events to which Brown was reacting. Watts argues that while the republican values of "virtue," "civic humanism," and "independence" had become the dominant ideology in the United States by the early to mid-1800s, they were also being eclipsed by a movement toward "liberal capitalism." The established values of self-sacrifice and civic community were eroded by a growing appetite for personal advancement and an increasingly commercial set of values that endorsed a growing "program of geographic expansion, limited commercial agriculture, household manufactures, and international free trade for the export of surplus commodities." According to Watts, the ideological crisis at the beginning of the nineteenth century led by 1810, after eroding foreign relations with Britain and France, to a "fear about the vitality and durability of American republicanism itself."[29]

Brown's historicism and annals are, on the one hand, enmeshed in republican ideals such as liberty and political freedom; however, on the other, they also participate in a highly self-conscious interrogation of historical representation itself and the ways democratic principles and processes may be compromised by individuals and institutions. It seems fair, therefore, to say, especially in light of modern revisionist interpretations of "republicanism," that from 1787, when the Constitution was ratified, to 1807, when Jefferson's presidency was nearing an end, Brown was an eyewitness to various efforts at republican synthesis—and constructing a government for the people—as well as to points of ideological or political inconsistency, elision, and resistance that he was able to identify.

Although, then, not everyone may be in agreement about the level of "fear" or anxiety in America by 1810 or even the War of 1812, historically Jeffersonian assumptions about the Constitution were being tested during and after his presidency. To be sure, dissenting anti-Federalist concerns about "consolidated government," the lack of elections and adequate rotations, the separation of powers, the absence of a bill of rights, and the "extensive powers given to the president" date back to 1787 and its ratification. If the 1790s brought about a plethora of constitutional challenges, none was more significant than the "crisis of the Alien and Sedition Acts." The Sedition law of 1798, remarks Saul Cornell, "prompted the most serious examination of the tenets of oppositional constitutional theory since ratification."[30] The attempt by John Adams and others to restrain the press was seen as a violation of the First Amendment and as undermining individual liberty and the public sphere.

Aside from the capture, in 1803, of the frigate *Philadelphia* by Tripolitanian pirates, Jefferson's first term as president (1800–04) was one of successes, capped off by the Louisiana Purchase. Under Jefferson, the economy expanded and people prospered. During Jefferson's second term, however, factionalism among his Republican party emerged, led in part by John Randolph of Roanoke and his concerns about preserving states' rights. The Aaron Burr Conspiracy in 1806, the Impressment Controversy with the British, and the 1807 attack on the American frigate *Chesapeake* all caused considerable problems for Jefferson, with the latter leading to Jefferson's failed embargo policy, which crippled the American economy between 1807 and 1808.[31]

However, even as foreign and domestic events unfolded, and factionalism was brewing within Jefferson's party, there were Federalist efforts to respond to Jefferson's presidency, the most significant of which was Senator James Hillhouse's 1808 Senate bill, which proposed seven amendments to the Constitution. It became the most important proposal for altering the structure of the Constitution since 1789. Strikingly similar to anti-Federalist concerns two decades earlier, Hillhouse called for changes in reduced terms for senators, limitations on presidential terms, and confirmation by the House and the Senate of appointments made by the president. While these proposed changes were not approved by Congress, they were arguably the basis for establishing a separate confederacy of New England states and have been proposed in various forms since as part of constitutional reform efforts.

James Hillhouse, a Federalist lawyer who served as a U.S. senator from 1796 to 1810, was concerned about the use and abuse of power in the Federal government, especially in the office of the president.[32] After reading Hillhouse's proposal to amend the Constitution, Brown did more than urge "restraint and taste" in response to economic and political crisis. He addresses in his last chapter of the "Annals of America" the roles of the Constitution and Congress in maintaining a stable government. His appropriation of congressional speeches such as Hillhouse's in regard to proposed amendments to the Constitution indicate the degree to which he thought historical writing such as his could enlighten the reading public about debates contesting Congress's authority relative to the Constitution. His insertion and editing of such materials offer evidence of the urgency in which Brown felt compelled to alter his historical narrative in the service of alerting readers more immediately to ways democratic processes related to the Constitution were being compromised.

Brown begins by observing in the annals that the Constitution authorized Congress to provide a "defensive force" and to maintain healthy foreign relations. "To regulate the conduct of the nation towards others," he writes, "in peace and war, must form its principal occupation."[33] Yet for Brown this straightforward mandate became—at least initially—the source of several "schemes" that occupied the legislative body and raised questions about the role of Congress in regard to the Constitution and attempts to revise it relative to a range of motives.

The "first and most important of these," he writes, which has caused considerable interest, is the "project for changing many parts of the federal constitution."[34] While the proposal of an investigation into the conduct of James Wilkinson and his involvement in the Aaron Burr conspiracy and "a scheme for transferring the seat of government from Washington to Philadelphia" are also topics Brown says he intends to address, he changes his focus on these in his narrative and omits the Wilkinson material, making Senator James Hillhouse's 1808 proposal to amend the Constitution the first major document he incorporates into his narrative proper. This editorial change is one of several ways Brown departs from tradition so that his annals are more responsive to the immediate historical moment.

Before reproducing debates associated with the Hillhouse amendment, Brown comments on the Constitution's capacity to adapt amendments and on what he thinks are "reasonable sources of change" and how certain clauses or provisions in the document allow it to regenerate itself from one era to the next. He remarks:

The federal constitution resembled the human in this: that provision was made only for maintaining the body in health and existence for a limited time, and since the individual must perish, a peculiar organization was annexed to it, by which it is enabled to produce a creature like itself, in an endless succession. In plain terms, certain clauses in the frame of national government, provided the means of making any alteration in its form and texture, without anarchy or violence, or without endangering the ruin of the whole at once. Amendments, proposed with certain forms, and adopted with the concurrence of certain members, both of the Union and of the general Congress, might be engrafted on the constitution.

Alterations in the frame of any government may be suggested by many circumstances. The usefulness of its rules can be verified by experience, and experience will frequently inculcate the necessity of changing rules, which had appeared free from all objection to the purest theoretical wisdom. All rules must be adapted to the actual state of a nation, and laws, therefore, which both theory and experience recommended at the time they were adopted, an important change in the condition of the people may make it expedient to annul or modify anew.

These are the reasonable sources of change, but these are much less abundant and urgent than the spirit of faction.

Amendments, for Brown, are appropriate under certain conditions, provided "experience" is relied on as a guide. But, he says, such "reasonable sources of change" are overshadowed by "the spirit of faction." That "spirit," he continues, makes "miserable havock" of government by the way it promotes only a "partial or temporary end" to matters. In such an atmosphere, even honourable individuals always "connect the ruin or salvation of the whole state with the failure or success of the smallest of their own schemes."[35]

Brown accepted that the Constitution would necessarily change over time and that it was possible the impact of such changes would appear minimal over the long run. Yet he was also concerned about changes that could cause irrevocable damage to the Republic, and hoped the tumultuous changes he witnessed in the short period may be sufficient: "Portions will be cut out, and replaced patch after patch, till no remnant of the original cloth shall remain." "Perhaps like the human body," he continues, "it may harden and grow permanent as time advances, and become, every year, less and less ductile and tractable to the rude and presumptuous hand of innovation."[36]

While Brown assumed that the "history of the changes" in the Constitution would be a useful study, he suggests that the difficulties of such a task would require one to "mingle in the tumults and intrigues of parties as to be intimately acquainted with their plans and movements, and yet be perfectly exempt from all their sinister biasses and blinding passions." He offers, in other words, his own take on how to objectively or impartially examine such historical circumstances but then says, "We shall not enter into such a path, but content ourselves with stating the nature of the present proposal, and the arguments by which it was commended." "This project," he continues, "originated in Mr. Hillhouse, a member of the senate from Connecticut, and was laid before that body on the twelfth of April. . . . As we have the very terms, which he employed on that occasion, we are not authorised to deviate from them. Mr. Hillhouse introduced the subject in the following manner."[37] Up to this point, Brown has given no clear signals about his position regarding the Hillhouse proposal to amend the Constitution. However, against the larger context or background of the annals, Hillhouse's document creates a "dialogic tension" between the discourse in Brown's historical narrative and Hillhouse's proposal. That is, just as the genres or languages introduced into the novel more often than not "refract, to one degree or another, authorial intentions," so Brown's integration of the Hillhouse document into his historical narrative expresses authorial biases, but in "a refracted way."[38] He appropriates and reproduces the Hillhouse narrative to let it speak to constitutional issues he is also concerned about.

Deeply concerned about the use and abuse of power in the federal government, especially in the office of the president, Hillhouse's submission to the Senate in 1808 of *Propositions for Amending the Constitution of the United States* ranged from suggesting annual elections for representatives and term limits of three years for senators to doing away with the office of vice president and having the president chosen by lot for a one-year term. Brown does not mention the title of Hillhouse's proposal in his annals, but the document is identified by its date, April 12, 1808, and contents.

The most conspicuous ideological similarity between Brown's brief narrative and Hillhouse's centers on the shared concern with the many attempts to alter the Constitution. Similar to Brown's commentary on "schemes" to modify it, Hillhouse begins by remarking on the recent changes: "It has been with anxious concern that I have seen a disposition, and various attempts, to make *partial* amendments to the constitution, which have, in some instances, prevailed. Others are in progress; all are aimed at *particular detached parts*, which, without examining or regarding their bearing on *other parts*, like partial alterations in a curious, complicated machine, may, instead of benefitting, destroy its utility."[39] As suggested earlier, editors of periodical publications before and after the American Revolution frequently borrowed content from other sources and frequently altered punctuation for editorial or political purposes. But even though Brown removes Hillhouse's italics for such words as "partial" and "particular detached parts" and changes capitalization, thereby introducing a more moderate tone, Hillhouse and Brown both demonstrate a "concern" or "just apprehension" about the types of "partial alterations" being made to the Constitution. Brown believes that such changes may "deform" it, while Hillhouse believes that numerous "partial amendments" may "destroy its utility" and expose the nation to "incalculable evils."[40]

Although the phrasing is slightly different between the two texts and their political sympathies even more different in other respects, there is a dialogical or ideological echo in Hillhouse's text. Similar to how Jefferson "detected a design to subvert the Constitution" at the beginning of the Washington administration (when Hamilton agreed with measures to enhance state powers), here Hillhouse and Brown are concerned about the impact of submitting the Constitution to multiple amendments.[41] Of course, Brown's comment that such amendments are made out of an "eagerness for reformation" raises questions about the motives behind Hillhouse's own "radical cure" or proposed amendments, but later rhetorical parallels between Brown and Hillhouse suggest a certain amount of ideological agreement.[42]

Hillhouse, for example, is quite open about how in proposing his amendments he is appealing to no one particular party but that, like Brown, he is seeking to avoid party faction and obtain bipartisan consensus in regard to his proposed amendments. Similar to Brown's own efforts to be fair and impartial, he says: "Before I proceed with explanatory remarks, I must take the liberty of stating, that in using the terms, monarchy, aristocracy, or democracy, I do not use them as cant words of party: I use them in their fair, genuine sense"; further, "the terms federalists and republicans, I do not use by way of *commendation* or *reproach;* but merely by way of description, as the first name of individuals to distinguish them from others of the same family name."[43] Although Brown removes italics in his reprinting of the original—and Hillhouse goes on to give a brief history of the parties and their differing views, remarking that in proposing his amendments he does not wish to make any "personal or party allusion"—the texts in this case essentially communicate the same meaning.[44] And while Hillhouse later comments in more depth on the divisiveness of parties, it is in his remarks on how the "scourge of party rage" exposes the country to "that worst of all calamities, *civil war*" that he offers a revealing view not only of the times but also, to the extent that Brown retains Hillhouse's use of italics and emphasis on "*civil war,*" of Brown's own growing concerns about contemporary democratic processes and threats to the national polity.[45]

First, in reprinting Hillhouse's comments that in the United States the "PEOPLE are the source of *all power*" and that the "evils" of "*ambition* and *favouritism*" must be guarded against because "unprincipled men" readily "assume the garb of *patriotism*" as part of quest for "POWER," Brown seems to implicitly agree with the basic premise for Hillhouse's amendments—that individual and party appetite for the elective office of president should be held in check. Unlike other documents concerning removal of the capital to Philadelphia and where Brown removes italics or makes other editorial alterations, here Brown's retention of capitalization and italics suggests, at least in part, that he did not disagree with Hillhouse's concern with the "power" of the "PEOPLE." In fact, one might argue, Brown's exact transcription suggests an implicit agreement. As part of his proposal to counter the "sudden impulse of passion" or the "intrigues of artful, designing men," he suggests frequent elections and term limits for the office of president and for seats in the Senate and House of Representatives.[46]

Like Brown, Hillhouse believes that government affairs are most effectively regulated in light of "fact and experience." For this reason, he argues that when shorter terms of service have been in effect in state legislatures, "the more uniformly and steadily have the same members been returned."[47] Further, he states: "It is an axiom not to be questioned, that the people left to a *free, unbiassed* exercise of the right of suffrage, will, in most instances make a judicious and wise choice."[48] Here, Brown's decision to not use italics with the words "free" and "unbiased" indicates perhaps a reluctance to fully endorse Hillhouse's belief in purely objective reasoning. Likewise, when Hillhouse says "they have no interest or inducement to do otherwise: when they have found a good man, *capable* and *faithful,* they will, if left to themselves, be inclined to continue him in the public service, so long as he shall continue to be capable and faithful," Brown's removal of italics from "*capable*" and "*faithful*" again suggests a reluctance to fully endorse his rhetorical emphasis.[49]

Brown may or may not have agreed with the unquestioned "axiom," but it is probable, given his reflections on history writing and his handling of the Burr conspiracy, that he agreed with Hillhouse's comments on the role of "bias" in political processes and its potential for compromising the "judicious" selection of a president. Hillhouse's claim that the people would have no gratuitous "interest" at stake when voting for officials recalls Brown's own usage of the term in the annals, particularly his enduring concern with the "motivation" behind people's actions. Rhetorically, therefore, and possibly even ideologically, there is some consistency between Brown's thinking and writing about history and Hillhouse's reflections on political processes. However, in Hillhouse's proposal that Congress pursue a "radical cure" or alternative of choosing the president "by lot from the senate" in order to minimize party spirit and to maximize the use of the "best talents" one can more clearly identify grounds for seeing Brown's own approach to historical representation as equally "radical."[50]

Hillhouse begins by saying that he would not have proposed such an approach for electing the president "if any other could have been devised, which would not . . . bring upon the nation incalculable evils—evils already felt, and growing more and more serious." He then explains why the appointment of the president by lot is free of "all the evils of a contested election" and why a system by lot will tone down the current "influence of a presidential electioneering fever," ensure a higher degree of "impartiality" when selecting a candidate, and contribute to a greater continuity in terms of candidate talent and integrity. However, after downplaying the "novelty" of his proposal by comparing it to the way officials are replaced in the "republics of Switzerland," Hillhouse articulates more specifically why he believes "popular election and the exercise of such powers and prerogatives as are by the constitution vested in the President, are incompatible."[51]

Saying that "party spirit is the demon which has engendered the factions that have destroyed most free governments," Hillhouse observes about the office of president:

> There is but a single point in the constitution, which can be made to bear upon all the states, at one and the same time; and produce an *unity* of *interest* and *action;* and so serve as the *rallying* point of party, and that is the presidential election. This most dignified and important office of president, made more desirable by having attached to it a high salary, great power, and extensive patronage, cannot fail to bring forth and array all the electioneering artillery of the country; and it furnishes the most formidable means of *organizing, concentrating,* and *cementing* parties. And when a president shall be elected by means of *party influence,* thus powerfully exerted, he could not avoid *party bias;* and thence become the CHIEF of a PARTY, instead of taking the dignified attitude of a PRESIDENT OF THE UNITED STATES. . . . Indeed, this presidential election does more than any thing else towards making parties in states—parties dangerous to their *ancient institutions,* and producing an injurious effect upon their most important concerns. In a word, it is now manifest that the present mode of electing a president is producing and will produce many and great evils to the *union,* and to the *individual states.*[52]

In his reprinting of this part of the speech, Brown removes all italics and capitalization, thereby toning down some of Hillhouse's concern with party interest and "*party bias*" in political processes, especially relative to the presidential election processes. Hillhouse reiterates here his general concern about the Constitution and the influence and impact of party differences on the Republic. But he also takes more direct aim at what he believes contributes to party faction—the "interest" in presidential prestige and power. Brown may not have been in complete agreement with Hillhouse on this point when he decided to include this document as part of his historical narrative, but he did understand to a great extent the role of "interest" in political matters—whether they be foreign or domestic. Also, since Brown knew full well the influences and effects of "party bias," it is more than likely that he would have been sympathetic to Hillhouse's view of the issue, including his concern that party faction could "produce many and great evils to the union."

Brown seems to have been in general agreement with Hillhouse concerning the Constitution, the prevalence of "party faction," and the larger "evils" associated with a "sudden impulse of passion," but he did not fully align himself with

Hillhouse's views, at least initially, of how "power" could compromise the integrity of the election process. Reflecting on the intentions of those who framed the Constitution and on the current atmosphere, Hillhouse asks if it is "not to be feared that the time will come . . . when the country shall be so divided into parties, that a small number of persons, and those exclusively members of Congress (who are intended by the constitution to be excluded from all intermeddling in presidential elections) and that too in the very focus of presidential and official influence (which the constitution meant carefully to guard against,) shall nominate a president?" Further, he writes, "And to secure his election, it will be required that every person, before he shall receive a vote or an appointment as an elector, shall pledge himself to support such nomination, and thus the *president* will in *fact* be made to *choose* the *electors*, instead of the *electors choosing* the *president*."[53] As he had with prior passages, Brown does not include italics in his reproduction of the text, thereby altering the tone of the material in his annals.

Brown was familiar enough with events in Europe, particularly Napoleon's rise to power, and he was concerned about party factions and what he perceived to be the growing imperial dimensions of American foreign and domestic policy—that is, the measures that were taken to investigate the Burr conspiracy and enforce the embargo, some of which, in Brown's mind, were inappropriate, if not illegal. But because of the way Brown sets up the emphasis of the chapter and then later suddenly shifts gears and deviates from it in his selection and arrangement of primary documents, one can infer that Hillhouse's warning about the potential subversion of the electoral process was one that was not necessarily popular or that members of Congress wanted to hear. However, Brown clearly understood the potential for Hillhouse's scenario to play itself out and for political processes to be compromised by individual and even institutional self-interest.

While Hillhouse provides further proof of the "impropriety and impolicy of the present mode of electing a president" and goes on to argue for an amendment that requires the consent of both houses for "appointments to office" and "removals from office," it is toward the end of his proposal that he sums up the checks and balances he has put forth. After making a few general observations about "different kinds of governments," particularly the "evils" that can attend a democracy, Hillhouse states:

> Ours is a *free representative republic*, deriving all power from the people, and when amended, as I propose for the purpose of checking *party spirit*, *executive influence* and *favouritism*, will correctly express the *public opinion*, and declare the *public will*. . . . The only effectual way of remedying these evils, is to remove the causes. This may be done by returning the representatives by frequent elections to the people: by shortening the term of service of the president and senate; by reducing the salary of the president; by

avoiding as mxch [*sic*] as possible the accumulation of power in the hands of an individual, or a small body of men; and above all by constituting such a mode of obtaining a chief magistrate, that it shall not be made the instrument of arraying the people, from one end to the other of this empire, into parties under different chiefs, the candidates for the presidential chair.[54]

Although Brown does not include Hillhouse's italics or emphasis on a *"free representative republic," "party spirit," "influence," "favouritism,"* and other aspects of the *"public,"* Hillhouse's focus on the "excess" of liberty and its role in promoting a "torrent of party spirit and violence" had no doubt an influence on Brown's own thinking. Brown too was increasingly aware of the "evils" that could result in a republican form of government as a result of "party spirit" and the authoritarian wielding of power. It is, of course, difficult to state the exact degree to which Brown concurred with Hillhouse, but it is plausible to suggest from Brown's own comments at the beginning of the chapter, from earlier chapters in the "Annals of America," and from the attitudes or values echoed in the Hillhouse document, that Brown continued to come to a clearer understanding of the imperial dimensions of American foreign and domestic policy. He understood how political "experience" necessitated a revision of "theory," or constitutional amendments, in order for the Republic to survive. Indeed, beyond the manner in which Brown's inclusion of the Hillhouse document dialogically illuminates Brown's own beliefs, there is evidence that in his capacity as historian—and editor—he also registered resistance to what he perceived to be less-than-democratic practices of government.[55]

Thus, while Brown states that he is not "authorized" to "deviate" from Hillhouse's narrative, he in fact does when he selectively removes and, some cases, retains Hillhouse's italics and emphasis, thereby producing an eclectic text or separate rhetorical context in which to understand Hillhouse's proposal to amend the Constitution. Just as Brown's editing of the documents is, on the one hand, part of standard editorial practice, so on the other hand, it may also be construed as a politically active historical or editorial gesture. In this light, Brown's inclusion, and editing, of the Hillhouse speech, a singular voice like his own, is part of a larger historical, ideological, and rhetorical framework from which to understand debates about the meaning and function of the Constitution. Brown's integration of congressional debates—or primary documents—into his own historical narrative may be considered as evidence of his desire to achieve historical objectivity or impartiality in his narrative and to eliminate political bias from democratic processes.[56] This motivation on Brown's part, as a historian, becomes, I contend, clearest with his analysis—and dialogical representation of—the Republican caucus proceedings of 1808 and concerns by members of Jefferson's own party about secretive or biased nomination procedures.

The Republican Caucus of 1808

The year 1808 was one of political intrigue, and Brown's decision as a historian to suddenly remove from his "Annals of America" inquiry into General Wilkinson and to replace it with a focus on the congressional debates over the removal of the capital from Washington to Philadelphia must have proven interesting to anyone who was anticipating further coverage of the Aaron Burr incident. This abrupt change of intention—along with his introduction of new historical documents in the last chapter of the annals—testifies to Brown's continuing inquiry into congressional proceedings and argues for his idiosyncratic participation in the public sphere. Brown remarks that the idea of removing the capital to Philadelphia is a subject that has captured the "attention of the public and of the national legislature."[57] A pamphlet, he says, appeared in the autumn of 1807 and after that a motion was made by Representative James Sloan (Republican) of New Jersey. Sloan, he writes, addresses the "evils" of having the capital in Washington, elaborating on its "remoteness" from ports and its inconvenience and expense.[58] He also counters objections regarding the healthiness of Philadelphia and concerns about violating the Constitution.

Before reprinting documents associated with the debates, Brown pauses to comment on why "people" were at odds over the proposition, especially as it concerned declining property values and the difficulty of getting impartial information through the media. To stop the proposal, he says, "the people resorted as usual to threats, importunities, and intreaties" but with no real organized resistances. Further, he remarks:

> This is a plain state of controversy. The motives of human conduct are so gross and selfish, that there is no merit in discovering, nor scandal in disclosing them. There would be much amusement and instruction in surveying the real course of this debate, and in detailing the arguments actually employed. We shall therefore after this hasty sketch proceed to recount the particulars of this discussion. While we admit the frequent misconstructions of the reporters, we must satisfy ourselves with doing the best that they will enable us to do. Their party prejudices, their unskillfulness in their own art, the miserable defects in the hall as a place of audience, and the clumsy and feeble articulation of many of the members, deprive us all of hope of an accurate account of any debate, unless the orator's vanity prompts him first to write, an afterwards to publish.

Brown, as historian, acknowledged the difficult circumstances under which the debate was conducted, citing "party prejudice" among reporters and poor speaking skills and acoustics as being factors that could alter the veracity of positions.

And, as in his novels, he also raises questions about human "motives" as related to personal conduct, suggesting that self-interest was somehow attached to proposals to move the capital. Brown's reproduction of these debates resembles the tone of a reporter at times, but also contains the high drama of Benjamin Tallmadge reviewing what powers the Constitution grants to Congress and asserting his belief that "the removal of the session of Congress to any other place in the United States cannot be made a constitutional question."[59]

Although the debates themselves are lengthy and highlight the extent to which members of Congress disagreed about whether or not removal of the capital was a constitutional issue, Brown's substantial coverage of the capital controversy arguably provides evidence that he was attuned to the proposed resolution, the nature of discussion and objections to it, and concerns about resolution and committee procedures. The debates clearly take up questions about the extent to which members of Congress were erecting themselves as a "tribunal to construe their constitution" and indulging in an "assumption of power dangerous to the liberties of the people." Aside from concerns by certain members about being "imperiously called on" to make a decision, Brown's annals document, then, the remaining discussion and the manner in which a committee to investigate the proposal and bring the bill forward was voted on and, ultimately, defeated.[60]

However, Senator Stephen Bradley's controversial announcement on January 19, 1808, of a private Republican caucus and the response of some Republican members of Congress concerned Brown and prompted him to alter the last section of his historical narrative in a surprising and provocative way. That is, if Brown's selection and arrangement of material reflects his struggle to identify or, to borrow from Michael Warner, to "disclose" the darker aspects of American democracy, his historical narrative takes on a distinctly dialogical quality, particularly in the way his inclusion of select primary documents in lieu of traditional historical narration enables his readers to come into contact with the facts or primary documents themselves, thereby allowing a range of voices to "illuminate each other" more objectively and making his historical writing radical in both content and form.[61]

Similar, in other words, to Paine's, Jefferson's, and Franklin's resistance to political tyranny before the American Revolution and, later, anti-Federalist concerns about centralized authority and the Constitution, Brown's attention to how democratic principles could be compromised by ambition and men of power in Congress becomes most evident in his last chapter of the "Annals of America." Here he takes the bold step of inserting into his narrative primary documents concerning Senator Bradley's controversial 1808 memo requesting a Republican caucus and the response of some Republican members of Congress. Brown's representation, I argue, of this political moment and its relation to a tradition of political dissent with the status quo, especially as it pertains to his readers, raises questions not only about the nature and use of private and public documents but about their role in constructing historical meaning. It also clarifies Brown's anxiety about those who sought to alter existing Constitution principles for personal or political reasons and his efforts, as a historian, to preserve them in a way consistent with the founding principles of democracy, a representative form of government, and the rights of the people.

Historically, although in 1800 Jefferson's Republican party gained political control and dominated early nineteenth-century politics, with the Federalist party disappearing after 1816, there was growing concern by 1808 about the means—usually a caucus—by which the Republican party chose its presidential and vice presidential nominees. Of party processes, "Discontented Federalists," observes Winifred Bernhard, "were convinced that a highly disciplined Republican Party in Congress controlled its members through the dictatorship of its caucus." Even for the supporters of Monroe, Madison, and George Clinton, all members of the Republican party, the caucus of 1808 produced much infighting—and criticism. The caucus system had the effect of "subordinating the President to members of Congress, and in a self-consciously democratic era it smacked too much of political intrigue."[62]

Contemporary responses on this point are quite revealing. John Quincy Adams, for instance, attended the caucus and writes in his diary on January 23, 1808, that "there has been much question as to Mr. Bradley's authority to call this convention." Bradley "had issued his circulars to every republican member of both Houses; indeed, to every member, excepting five of the Senate and twenty-two of the House of Representatives. Nor should I have omitted them, said he, but they have never been in the habit of acting with us."[63] Representative Edwin Gray of Virginia responded in a letter to Bradley, dated January 21, 1808, that he was offended by the "usurpation of power" Bradley assumed as well as the "mandatory style" and the "object contemplated therein." He declined to attend the caucus on the grounds that he would participate in a process whereby a small body of men would "arrogate to themselves the right, which belongs alone to the people, of selecting proper persons to fill the important offices of President and Vice President."[64]

While caucus members adopted and published a resolution explaining their actions in the *Washington National Intelligencer,* January 25, 1808, and others defended it in venues like the *Richmond Enquirer* (February 2, 1808) or pamphlets like an *Address to the General Committee of Republican Young Men, of the City and County of New York,* change was needed.[65] A second-party system eventually emerged in which presidential electors were chosen by the people and conventions replaced caucuses, and as Everett Ladd notes of the caucus system: "popular participation was on the rise and the caucus, never a popular instrument, more and more seemed anti-democratic, a small group of closed party leaders selecting the president. Inevitably in this situation, ambitious men would not passively acquiesce to a caucus defeat."[66]

Similar therefore to the ways Brown had earlier highlighted the Constitution's resilience to various personal and political "schemes," his analysis now focused on Bradley's memo to select members of Congress and the anger it aroused in fellow Republicans. Brown, like his anti-Federalist predecessors, feared the consolidation of political power in the hands of a few, and writes:

> One of the most singular transactions which happened during this session, was a formal and public convention of a certain party in the legislature, to influence the impending election of a president. The genius of the constitution displayed itself on this occasion in a remarkable manner. It afforded a curious example of the subtlety and power of party in moulding every thing to its own purpose and advantage. Several private meetings of the republican party had been held previous to the twenty first of January for that end, but on that day Stephen Rowe Bradley, a representative from Vermont, transmitted to the democratic members a circular letter concluding in the following terms [quoting Bradley]:
>
> "In pursuance of the power invested in me, as president of the late convention of the republican members of both houses of Congress, I deem it expedient, for the purpose of nominating suitable characters for the president and vice president of the United States, for the next presidential election, to call a convention of the said republican members, to meet at the senate chamber, on Saturday, the 23d instant, at 6 o'clock P.M. at which time and place your personal attendance is requested, to aid the meeting with your influence, information and talents. Dated at Washington, this 19th day of January, 1808."
>
> "Stephen R. Bradley."

Brown's inquiry into, and dismay with, Bradley's memo is apparent in his comments about the "genius of the constitution" and its ability to check the "subtlety and power of party." While the meeting itself was public, "this summons could not but disgust and anger all those who had not the same political views with the projectors of this meeting, and was certainly couched in a style too dictatorial and official."[67] It smacked, in other words, of political party control at the expense of the people and democratic processes for nominating a presidential candidate. Representative Gray was among the first to respond to the "circular letter." While Gray was a known supporter of Monroe (who was not expected to receive the nomination), his letter nevertheless agrees in content and tone with Brown's remarks and reflects Brown's concern with legislative practices that could compromise democratic process and the representative rights of the people.[68]

The following letter from Gray, says Brown, illustrates the "indignant zeal" with which some members of Congress responded to Bradley:

Your proclamation dated the 19th inst. and addressed to me I have just received, and I take the earliest moment to declare my abhorrence of the usurpation of power declared to be vested in you—of your mandatory style, and
the object contemplated. I deny that you possess any right to call upon the
republican members of Congress or other persons at this time and place to
attend a caucus for the presidential election. You must permit me to remind
you that it was a far different purpose for which my constituents reposed
their confidence in me. I cannot consent either in an individual or representative capacity to countenance by my presence the midnight intrigues
of any set of men who may arrogate to themselves the right (which belongs
only to the people) of selecting proper persons to fill the important offices
of president and vice president, nor do I suppose that the honest people of
these United States can much longer suffer in silence so direct and palpable
an invasion upon the most important and sacred right belong exclusively
to them.[69]

Gray's first objection regards Bradley's use of power and his pretentious or "mandatory style" of calling together a meeting to select nominees. Bradley's titling it
a "proclamation" also fleshes out the "power" implications of the letter. Second,
Gray's objection to the purpose of the meeting—selecting a nominee for president and vice president—recalls discourse in the Hillhouse document about the
reins of power being in the hands of a few men. It raises questions about the rights
of "the people" to select leaders and the role of representatives in the electoral process, and the manner in which a democratic republic chooses its officials. Brown
goes on to describe the actual assembly and what transpired, but his publication
of a "manifesto," which he says was "drawn up by certain leading members of
Congress of the democratic or republican party," articulates most fully the concerns expressed in the earlier parts of Brown's narrative.

Saying that it is addressed to "the people of the United States" and that he
will publish it "without alteration or abridgment" (another significant statement
about his efforts at historical impartiality, especially in light of how he handled
or edited earlier documents), Brown inserts into his own historical narrative a
protest drawn up by John Randolph and seventeen members of Congress that
was published on March 7, 1808, in Jefferson's Washington-based *National Intelligencer*. Because of its considerable length, I quote the document in parts and then
offer analysis; I then comment on the document's significance in light of Brown's
theory about history and its importance as one of the last primary documents
Brown published in the annals.

This segment addresses the "distinctions between public and private expression" and Brown's ongoing concern with the threat of factionalism to democratic
processes.[70] The Randolph letter opens:

In the course of the events which have marked the conduct and characters of those, to whom you have, at different periods intrusted by your suffrages, the power of making laws for your government, few measures have occurred since the adoption of the present constitution, more extraordinary, than the meeting lately held for the purpose of nominating a president and vice-president of the United States.

Our alarm is equally excited, whether we advert to the mode in which the meeting was summoned, or to the proceedings after it was convened. The senator who assumed the power of calling together the members of Congress, did it under the pretext of that power being invested in him, by a former convention; this pretext, whether it be true or not, implies an assertion of a right in the Congress of 1804, to direct their successors in the mode of choosing the chief magistrate; an assertion which no man has ever before had the hardihood to advance. The notices were private; not general to all the members of the two houses; nor confined to the republican party; a delegate from one of the territories was invited and attended; a man who in elections has no suffrage, and in legislation no vote. The persons, who met in pursuance of this unprecedented summons, proceeded without discussion or debate, to determine by ballot the candidates for the highest offices in the union. The characters of different men, and their pretensions to the public favour, were not suffered to be canvassed, and all responsibility was avoided by the mode of selection. The determination of this conclave has been published as the act of the republican party; and with as much exultation as the result of a solemn election by the nation. Attempts are making to impress upon the public mind, that these proceedings ought to be binding upon all republicans, and those who refuse to attend, or disapproved of the meeting, are denounced as enemies of liberty, and as apostates from the cause of the people. In this state of things, we think it our duty to address you, and we deem ourselves called upon to enter our most solemn protest against these proceedings.[71]

First, the letter calls attention to the manner in which notices to nominate a president and vice president were sent out by Bradley and how those actions could compromise democratic processes as Randolph and other republicans knew them. The notices, he says, were "private; not general to all the members of the two houses," meaning that a select group of politicians would be involved in selecting nominees. In addition, an outside delegate was also apparently summoned. Despite the fact that those who signed the protest were in favor of either Monroe or Clinton and clearly thought Madison was unfit for office, the formal caucus protest recalls Brown's earlier concerns about political self-interest and faction.

Second, and in line with Brown's editorial handling of previous documents, the caucus protest highlights his attention to how "proceedings or nominations" were being conducted behind "closed doors." Similar to Representative Gardenier's earlier concern about voting down the resolution to remove the capital "without debate," so the opposition in the caucus protest to nominating candidates for the presidency and vice presidency "without discussion or debate" arguably references Brown's own concern on this point with democratic processes. Brown may have been reluctant initially to "mingle in the tumults and intrigues of parties as to be intimately acquainted with their plans and movements" and to distance himself from their "sinister biasses and blinding passions"; yet he became acutely aware of how democratic processes could be compromised by exclusionary legislative procedures. Although he did not alter phrases like "without debate" by adding italics, the decision to include the text as part of his historical narrative documents, dialogically, his interest in democratic processes and specifically compromised nomination procedures.[72]

And, last, what also seems to offend Randolph and his colleagues is the manner in which it was communicated that proceedings "ought to be binding upon all republicans" and that those who might disagree with nomination results were somehow represented as "enemies of liberty" or threats to the "cause of the people." This kind of political branding in regard to complaints about the lack of public scrutiny and the selection of candidates is for Randolph and other republicans a breach in the public trust, especially as it regards democratic processes associated with nomination procedures. It recalls Brown's earlier writing in his historical sketches about authority and control as well as about one party's efforts to "influence the impending election." It also correlates with his belief in the "genius of the constitution" and the ways democratic procedures might be compromised by imperious designs or the "subtlety and power of party." Brown, in other words, clearly understood Hillhouse's concerns, and his question about intense party faction, specifically if it were possible for "a small number of persons, and those exclusively members of Congress (who are intended by the constitution to be excluded from all intermeddling in presidential elections) . . . [to] nominate a president?"[73]

But if the middle section of the letter distinguishes former election procedures from earlier ones, it also calls attention to the people's "right of election without any undue bias," asking, "Is it not the evident intention of such consultations to produce a bias?" and focuses on why the caucus is "exceptionable." By comparison, the last section of the letter emphasizes how its "undue bias" amounts to a "dictatorial" style, and recalls Brown's previous efforts to adhere to historical impartiality and avoid personal and political bias. Continuing with reasons for being alarmed at the caucus, the letter distinguishes between previous elections and the present one and clarifies why there is sufficient reason to protest the caucus:

> So conscious were the members who attended the late meeting, of the weight of objections which might be urged against their proceedings, that

they thought it proper to publish an exculpatory resolution, proposed by Mr. Giles of Virginia, and unanimously adopted. They have declared, that in "making their nominations, they have acted only in their individual characters as citizens;" this is very true, because they could act in no other, without a breach of their oaths, and a direct violation of the letter of the constitution. But it was not intended that those nominations should be enforced by the sanction of Congressional names?—They proceed to assert "that they have been introduced to adopt this measure from the necessity of the case, from a deep conviction of the importance of union to the republicans throughout all parts of the United States, in the present crisis of both our external and internal affairs." We trust we have shewn that no such necessity exists, and that a union among the republicans, in favour of an individual, is not important.— We acknowledge that the aspect of our foreign affairs is unpromising. We are perhaps on the eve of a war with one of the great powers of Europe; we are therefore strongly impressed with the difficulties of our situation. In such a crisis, if unanimity in the choice of president is necessary, that choice should be directed to a man, eminently calculated by his tried energy and talents, to conduct the nation with firmness and wisdom, through the perils which surround it: to a man who had not in the hour of terror and persecution, deserted his post, and sought in obscurity and retirement, a shelter from the political tempest; to a man not suspected of undue partiality or enmity to either of the present belligerent powers; to a man who had not forfeited his claim to public confidence, by recommending a shameful bargain with the unprincipled speculators of the Yazoo companies, a dishonourable compact with fraud and corruption. Is James Madison such a man? We ask for energy, and we are told of his moderation; we ask what were his services in the cause of public liberty, and we are directed to the pages of the Federalist, written in conjunction with Alexander Hamilton and John Jay, in which the most extravagant of their doctrines are maintained and propagated. We ask for consistency as a republican, standing forth to stem the torrent of oppression which once threatened to overwhelm the liberties of the country; we ask for that high and honourable sense of duty which would at all times turn with loathing and abhorrence from any compromise with fraud and speculation; we ask in vain.

But further. One of the reasons, assigned by Mr. Jefferson for declining to stand again as a candidate for the chair of the chief magistrate, is the propriety of a rotation in that office. The great advantage of this principle of rotation is, that appointing as a successor to the present office, a man not immediately connected with him, the acts of the administration may be impartially reviewed; those measures which tend to promote the public good will be adopted, and those of a contrary tendency, which from the fallibility of human nature may have been pursued, will be abandoned, and if necessary exposed. All other rotation is a mockery.

We do therefore in the most solemn manner protest against the proceedings of the meeting held in the senate chamber on the twenty-third day of January last, because we consider them—

As being in direct hostility to the principles of the constitution:

As a gross assumption of power not delegated by the people, and not justified or extenuated by any actual necessity:

As an attempt to produce an undue bias in the ensuing election of president and vice president, and virtually to transfer the appointment of those officers from the people, to a majority of the two houses of Congress.

And we do in the same manner protest against the nomination of James Madison, as we believe him to be unfit to fill the office of president in the present juncture of our affairs.

JOSEPH CLAY,
ABRAHAM TRIGG,
JOHN RUSSELL,
JOSIAH MASTERS,
GEORGE CLINTON, jun.
GURDON S. MUMFORD,
JOHN THOMPSON,
PETER SWART,
EDWIN GRAY,
W. HOGE,
SAMUEL SMITH,
DANIEL MONTGOMERY,
JOHN HARRIS,
SAMUEL MACLAY,
DAVID R. WILLIAMS,
JAMES M. GARNETT,
JOHN RANDOLPH.

City of Washington, Feb. 27, 1808.[74]

Just as Montesquieu was concerned in *The Spirit of the Laws* (1748) with the dangerousness of secret meetings in a senate and how such intrigues led to the demise of the republic in Rome, so the closing section of this letter suggests concerns about the usurpation of political power and the threat to democratic processes in the early Republic. In fact, in calling attention to the way meeting members quickly published an "exculpatory resolution" and claimed to have "acted only" as "citizens," the letter claims that nominating caucus committee members came to understand how their actions concerning republican candidates' nominations jeopardized their public trust as representatives. Of particular interest is the manner in which the "propriety of a rotation" in office is compromised by "appointing as a successor to the present office" James Madison, Jefferson's preferred candidate. Such an appointment, maintains the signers of Randolph's letter, does not allow administrative policies to be "impartially reviewed."

Moreover, and closely tied to Brown's understanding of the Constitution as a document that ensures basic rights or principles of the people, the letter identifies the Constitution as ensuring fundamental rights to the citizens of the Republic. Similar to Hillhouse's belief that the "PEOPLE are the source of *all power*" and that the "evils" of "*ambition* and *favouritism*" must be guarded against because "unprincipled men" readily "assume the garb of *patriotism*" as part of quest for "POWER," the letter protesting the caucus identifies the meeting as "being in direct hostility to the principles of the constitution" and a "gross assumption of power not delegated by the people." In suggesting that the attempt to "produce an undue bias" virtually transfers "the appointment of those officers from the people" to a select group of men, the letter appealed, no doubt, to Brown's intuitive sense of historical impartiality and objectivity, prompting him to be concerned about the limitations and liabilities of a republican form of government that is not subject to "impartial" processes.

On this point, and with the issue of his supposed conservatism, Brown's concerns with the caucus proceedings can usefully be juxtaposed with those of the English political émigré James Cheetham (1772–1810), who, along with William Duane, John Binns, and other radicals, used local newspapers, says Michael Durey, to advance their often militant democratic views and promote constitutional reform. When the January 1808 Republican caucus nominated Madison, Cheetham opposed the selection, arguing instead for George Clinton. A caucus, he lamented, "is an assemblage on intriguers, privately convened to plot their own elevation, upon the ruin, not unfrequently, of better men." For Cheetham, says Durey, "the caucus violated the separation of powers by giving one branch of government an undue influence over the affairs of another, at the expense of the rights of people. By resorting to strict construction principles, Cheetham was following the practice common among radical exiles when Federalists had dominated government." Just as radicals like Cheetham were concerned with the oligarchic nature of the caucus process and the potential abuse of presidential power, so Brown, then, exhibits a similar concern with the democratic party's nomination process.[75]

To be sure, Brown had been incorporating primary documents into the footnotes of his "Annals of Europe and America" as early as volume 2; and in later volumes of the *American Register* he commented on the "intrinsic value" of particular texts. But in the last volume, he essentially replaced his narrative with primary

documents themselves—a move consistent with historiographic insights he outlines in his various prefaces to the *American Register* about the "intrinsic value"
of such materials to the country's history. Such narrative illustrates his continued
effort at "impartiality"—his attempt to let the documents, facts, or events speak
for themselves. However, in light of recent discourse, reader response, and performance theories and Brown's own theory of reading, such use of documentary
evidence argues for a radical historiography on Brown's part.[76] It collapses what
Michael Warner calls differences between "history" as chronological narrative
and as a "narrative device of disclosure" in the "public sphere."[77]

In other words, just as Brown admitted to moments where he was "conscious
. . . of his own ignorance" or frustrated by the "difficulty of managing . . . topics with impartiality," so his later remark in his preface to volume 5 that "Public
documents" "almost supersede the business of the historian" not only questions
the traditional dichotomy between historical fact and interpretive text but hints at
his continued self-consciousness. Such statements suggest Brown's growing consciousness of how conventional historical narrative, including his own, was subject
to personal and political bias and how multiple documents and discourses might
more accurately comprise the history of a nation. Brown's historicism takes on a
dialogical dimension; it demonstrates a willingness to include other discourses as
part of his historical or heteroglossic narrative.[78] Interpreted this way, his historicism boldly challenges turn-of-the-century assumptions about historical representation, American destiny, and progress with the idea that the construction of
history is not an insulated, monological, or even romantic enterprise.[79]

The introduction, therefore, of such "discontinuity" or disruption into his narrative not only recalls Brown's "novelistic" technique for representing his eleventh-
hour awareness of the procedures of nominating caucuses and the potential for
abusing political power but is an extension of his earlier inquiry into European
imperial and colonial practices and his refusal to wrap the rhetoric of national
redemption around recent American events from the Embargo Act to the Aaron
Burr situation.[80] Brown's arrangement and editing of debates and documents are
not only consistent with his efforts at historical impartiality, search for truth, and
his reader-oriented literary theory but chart his own radical or novel response to
a moment of political crisis by pointing to antidemocratic tendencies in the policies and practices of a new republican government. His orchestrated use and appropriation of discourse concerning the Congress's view of the Constitution, the
debates concerning the removal of the capital, and, finally, issues of representation
and authority associated with the Republican caucus of 1808 all illuminate each
other mutually in dialogically political and critical ways—ways that run counter to
a filiopietistic interpretation of the past or Francis Parkman's romantic history of
American greatness.

"Liberalism"—and "Radical History"

Unlike those of his peers, and the patriotic histories of Jeremy Belknap, Benjamin Trumbull, and William Gordon in the eighteenth century and Mercy Otis Warren, George Bancroft, and Francis Parkman in the nineteenth, Brown's historical narrative interrogates the idea of American history as progressive or destined and counters the broader assumption that the United States was an "*exemplary nation*' that either 'by Providence' or by the wisdom of its founders had been exempted 'from the laws of decadence or the laws of history.'"[81] If, as Joyce Appleby, Lynn Hunt, and Margaret Jacob observe, "these original efforts served as a template for successive reworkings of the story of American nation-building" and "its fundamental assumptions were not challenged for over a century," Brown's historicism clearly suggests otherwise.[82] His annals not only point to an ironic tradition of historical writing but also record self-conscious efforts to transcend party bias and difference in an effort to represent historical truth. They register a radical response to the political status quo and, I want to argue, reenact what Bernard Bailyn says is one of the "major themes of eighteenth-century radical libertarianism": "The first is the belief that power is evil, a necessity perhaps but an evil necessity; that it is infinitely corrupting; and that it must be controlled, limited, restricted in every way compatible with a minimum of civil order. Written constitutions, the separation of powers; bills of rights; limitations on executives, on legislatures, and courts; restrictions on the right to coerce and wage war—all express the profound distrust of power that lies at the ideological heart of the American Revolution and that has remained with us as a permanent legacy ever after."[83] If liberty, natural rights, resistance to aristocratic authority structures, and belief in a free market economy are hallmarks of "libertarian" thought in the eighteenth and, later, nineteenth century, Brown's brand of dissent is in line with a political tradition, as Bailyn points out, that dates back to the Revolutionary War and supersedes political party. Libertarian political beliefs in the twentieth century, of course, about free-market individualism have evolved and correspond to Brown's in anachronistic ways.[84] But if Brown is drawing from French philosophers like Voltaire, British radical democratic thinkers like Godwin and Wollstonecraft, and the economic theories of Adam Smith, then it seems plausible that his interrogation of individual and institutional oppression is also in line with those of Thomas Paine, William Duane, Thomas Jefferson, and others.[85]

That is, if one traces "liberalism" back to its early eighteenth-century roots of John Locke, David Hume, and Adam Smith and looks at how the pursuit self-interest in a free market can contribute to individual and collective human happiness, then one might argue that ideas about free will or individual rights, as articulated by Jefferson, Paine, and others, can be seen as inextricably linked to the American

Revolution. This clash between the pursuit of liberty and a tradition of institutional and absolutist authority produced an ethos of independence that cherished a representative form of government and the principle of property rights. On the specific point of how late Enlightenment economic shifts informed political ones, David Boaz observes that during the eighteenth century French physiocrats articulated the idea that the "best way to increase the supply of real goods was to allow free commerce, unhindered by monopolies, guild restrictions, and high taxes." It is from this era, he argues, that "the famous libertarian rallying cry 'laissez faire' comes. . . . Individualism, natural rights, and free markets led logically to agitation for the extension of civil and political rights to those who had been excluded from liberty, as they were from power—notably slaves, serfs, and women."[86]

In further clarifying, then, the unprecedented nature of Brown's historicism as it relates to eighteenth-century forms of liberalism, I want to make what may be considered a radical claim as well—that Brown's response to the late Enlightenment debate about historical representation, despite concerns about the anachronistic use of concepts like "liberal" or "libertarian," anticipates what Robert Berkhofer calls in *Beyond the Great Story* the "postmodernist challenge to traditional history." If, as Berkhofer argues, the "crisis in the historical profession today is both conceptual and political, both methodological and practical," and a solution to that crisis involves a "revision of the normal history paradigm and a new vision of historical authority," I want to return to the argument that Brown's mode of historical inquiry and insights about the "uncertainty" of history are useful and cast doubt on claims about the flat rationality of Enlightenment historians and that "romance" and the grand narratives of nineteenth-century historians prompted modern historiographical debates.[87] Brown and his late Enlightenment predecessors and peers anticipate much of the debate today surrounding the "objectivity question" and the subjective nature of historical representation.

Additionally, if, as Berkhofer asserts, "true experiments in multivocality are rare because they challenge the normal historical paradigm of an ultimately single authorial viewpoint," nowhere is he clearer about what constitutes the role of the radical historian than in his analysis of arguments in Howard Zinn's essay "What Is Radical History?" Berkhofer comments on Zinn's goals for "raising the political consciousness of the readers of history":

> First, radical history ought to "intensify, expand, sharpen our perception of how bad things are, for the victims of the world." As part of this goal a history should dissolve the separation between the "us" of the historian's and reader's world and the "them" in the victims' worlds. Second, such a history must "expose the pretensions of governments to either neutrality or beneficence." The reader must be convinced that the government will not right many of the wrongs exposed in the first goal, and may even cause or

exacerbate the plight of the victims. Third, radical history should "expose the ideology that pervades our culture" so that the reader doubts the "rationale for the going order." Fourth, a history with these aims can "recapture those few moments in the past which show the possibility of a better way of life than that which has dominated the earth so far."

Berkhofer goes on to cite Alan Trachtenberg's and Lawrence Goodwyn's historical writing as examples of radical history, to qualify Zinn's representation of "victims," and to warn of the "new Great Story" or "metanarrative of past power relationships" and intolerance. However, Brown's sympathetic rendering of oppressed Others in British India, his ironic representations of American exceptionalism in regard to the embargo, his interrogation of political forces that would undermine constitutional principles and democratic election processes, and his efforts to imaginatively engage readers all clearly speak to the novel and democratic elements of his historicism—and how, according to Berkhofer, "radical history seeks to demystify the politics of domination through the self-representation of experience of the powerless and the oppressed." "The historian," he continues, "has a moral and political obligation to introduce more voices (and presumably more viewpoints) as implicit or explicit criticism of the existing order." In this way, the "active reader and critical reviewer make a historical text a collaborative effort through their reading and reviewing, even to the extent of creating a counter text."[88] Brown, the novelist turned historian, seems to have understood this in ways his peers and even many modern historians could not.[89]

Moreover, in this light and in the larger context of Brown's five prefaces and narrative, it seems fair to say that his methodological self-consciousness and his interest in "the textuality of history" have a clear evolution. When we reflect on Brown's evolving historical sensibility and his efforts to recover and edit various historical documents, it becomes evident that he indeed made imaginative or "radical attempts to reappropriate the past." Similar to how the "novelist does not acknowledge any unitary, singular, naively (or conditionally) indisputable or sacrosanct language," so Brown the historian not only consciously reflected on the "impartiality" of his narrative, but he reconsidered the use of a monological narrative discourse as a means of representing the past.[90] His willingness to accord "other" discourses or texts the same value as his own introduces "centrifugal" or "dialogical" forces into the process of historical interpretation and understanding.

In bridging the "gap," then, between what James Machor calls the "historically specific conditions" that shape a text and the historical "role of the reader" within that context, Brown's willingness to include other voices in his history and to eventually juxtapose such sources in politically provocative ways constitutes a radical, imaginative form of historical liberalism and representation consistent with Bakhtin's "discourse theory of democracy" in the public sphere.[91] His dialogical use of public documents alerts the reader points of potential political crisis concerning the Constitution and the consolidation of power within the hands of a few. As in his novels, Brown's historical writing invites reflection, meditation on the manner in which the integrity of democratic processes in a fledgling government could be compromised. Regardless of whether it is Brown's historical representation of Senator James Hillhouse's proposal to change the Constitution, or the controversial Republican caucus of 1808, his imaginative rendering of the past challenges assumptions about historical representation and progress.

Brown's historical narrative charts anything, then, but a "boisterous rhetoric of manifest destiny" and instead reveals uncertainty—concern about how "personal interest" and "the usurpation of power" in the pursuit of an "American imperial republic" can compromise the Constitution and its democratic principles. In the way it juxtaposes the tensions and discourses of a particular time and place and invites readers into the "process of contextual examination and judgment that constitutes historical understanding," Brown's narrative eschews what Foucault calls a "millennial ending" or an "ideal continuity" of events and aims to "illuminate the imagination" of a range of readers, not just literary elites.[92] To the extent that the idiosyncratic or novel form of Brown's historical narrative forgoes an authoritative point of view, it also positions readers to draw their "own conclusions" about the immediate past—and impending future.

Thus, similar to his fiction, which dialogically engages a host of historical, cultural, and philosophical issues for the purposes of moral reflection and understanding one's motives for actions, Brown's use of primary materials in his historical narrative is no mere compilation of historical documents or conservative defense of the status quo. Rather, it is part of a novelistic method that seeks to engage readers. His historical narrative aims to preserve democratic processes by integrating other voices and speech in an effort to make more transparent events pertaining to the Constitution and political governance. In the process of creating a history that demystifies the status quo, empowers the people with knowledge and political agency, Brown writes "radical history." Brown is, of course, not Michel Foucault or a philosophical contemporary, nor is he fully "postmodern" in his thinking. But similar to how Howard Zinn sees such history as "raising the political consciousness" of the people, so Brown's historicism denaturalizes historiographical conventions in an attempt get at the truth about the past and enlighten those living in the present.

Epilogue

To contemplate war is to think about the most horrible of human experiences. On this February day, as this nation stands at the brink of battle, every American on some level must be contemplating the horrors of war.

Yet this Chamber is, for the most part, silent—ominously, dreadfully silent. There is no debate, no discussion, no attempt to lay out for the nation the pros and cons of this particular war. There is nothing.

We stand passively mute in the United States Senate, paralyzed by our own uncertainty, seemingly stunned by the sheer turmoil of events. Only on the editorial pages of our newspapers is there much substantive discussion of the prudence or imprudence of engaging in this particular war.

And this is no small conflagration we contemplate. There is no simple attempt to defang a villain. No. This coming battle, if it materializes, represents a turning point in U.S. foreign policy and possibly a turning point in the recent history of the world.

—From "The Reckless Bush Administration War Path May
Prove Disastrous," a speech on the Senate floor by
Senator Robert Byrd, February 12, 2003

On January 9, 2006, the cover of *Newsweek* read, "How Much Power Should They Have?" and made allusion to the "imperial presidency" of George W. Bush and Dick Cheney and their consolidation of military, economic, and political resources after September 11, 2001, when the World Trade Center was destroyed by Islamic militants headed by Osama bin Laden. The resultant debates over the second Iraq war have focused on the second Bush administration's use—or misuse—of intelligence concerning weapons of mass destruction in Iraq and representation of a terrorist threat, the limits of the Constitution in regard to civil liberties and national security, the measure of success in building a democratic Iraqi Republic, and the urgency of an exit strategy that leaves that country in a stable economic and politic condition. The foregoing chapters of this book have—in the mode of New Historicist inquiry and intertextuality—sought to objectively yet self-consciously account for Brown's early interest in history and, during his later years, historiography. In asking what could reasonably link a scholarly study on Brown's historicism, a Senate speech by Robert Byrd, and the presidency of George Bush, I want to suggest, along the lines of Brown's own meditations on the past, but also more provocatively, that "political transactions" are indeed "connected together in so long and various a chain," and an "active imagination" is necessary not only to look back and write history but to look forward and fully understand and apply it. Unless, in other words, the past is contemplated relative to the present, it seems that memory is apt to fail us, motives for events and actions become misunderstood, and history, as this study implies, repeats itself endlessly on the point of American historiography and American efforts to spread democracy around the world without appearing imperial or arrogant.[1]

To illustrate: Bob Woodward in his best-selling account of the Iraq war, *State of Denial*, has concluded that the Bush administration misrepresented events to the public and Congress—that the president chose "to make repeated declarations of optimism and avoid adding to any doubts" as part of a larger "strategy of denial."[2] While the Bush administration and its supporters disagreed, in retrospect Byrd's 2003 warning about the lack of debate in Congress and the consequences of unilateral military action appears to have resonated with the American public. As measured by the 2008 presidential debates, Barack Obama's success relied in part on his promise to withdraw American troops from Iraq responsibly.

Writing history, especially recent history, impartially and in a nonpresentist way, is no easy task, especially if one aims to do it in a historically self-conscious manner, with minimal intrusion of bias and in a way that imparts historical judgment, not circular or empty relativism. Likewise, epilogues of this sort rarely read well in the long run for any number of reasons. Whatever one thinks, though, of writing "recent history" in Brown's day or our own, Brown's thinking about history and his historical writing offer a perspective on historical and political events that speak to American culture today as well as contemporary assumptions about history and truth. Like Brown, Byrd spoke to the lack of debate or discussion among those in power and the effort to manipulate constitutional processes for personal or political ends. He addressed the Senate's paralysis and inability to candidly and critically analyze the case for preemptive war. In his speech of dissent, he engaged what Clyde Prestowitz calls the "radicalism, egotism, and adventurism" evident in the Bush administration and "articulated in the stirring rhetoric of traditional patriotism."[3] Conversely, like Byrd, Brown in his history writing reflects on the cruelties of war and addresses the motives for human conduct and the role of "self-interest" in political and military events. He is deeply concerned with the influence of power and absence of debate or discussion in a democracy, and he is alert to the ways America perceives itself as a "redeemer nation" in spreading democratic principles throughout the world.

Unlike Byrd though, Brown lived during the Jefferson administration, almost two hundred years before, and was among a generation of intellects, both radical and conservative, still learning how to challenge the political status quo in the public sphere. Also, Brown's relationship to a then filiopietistic or teleological view of American politics and history meant that he had to wrestle with the limitations of late Enlightenment historiography and a readership enthusiastic about western expansion but not necessarily ready for Godwinian or dissenting thoughts on the course of American domestic and foreign policy. For this reason, Brown's historiography, like his Louisiana and embargo pamphlets, raises provocative questions about "political injustice" at home and around the world, earning him a reputation for candid and liberal thought as well as philosophical and political radicalism in the mode of William Duane and Thomas Paine.

In the end, not everyone will fully agree that the historical meditations and writing of Charles Brockden Brown are either "novel" or significant. But a question lingers: how was Brown—a Quaker child of the Enlightenment, not poststructuralism—able to formulate views of historical methodology, genre, representation, and truth so similar to those of historians and literary and cultural critics today? In situating his historiographical inquiries, insights, and ironic observations into our own debates, one inevitably encounters differences in terminology and meaning. But the issues of historical representation and objectivity Brown explores at the end of the eighteenth century seem to parallel our own, asking us to not only reassess traditional disciplinary and theoretical boundaries but also to reevaluate "postmodern" views of historical narrative and objectivity themselves. In this regard, Brown's historiographical inquiry complicates our understanding of early national history writing and the postmodern moment—the idea of history as textual construction—in three important ways.

First, if, as H. Aram Veeser observed, "New Historicists threaten all defenders of linear chronology and progressive history," Brown's self-conscious reflections on history, the dialogical nature of his historical discourse, and his willingness to question the political status quo sound strangely familiar.[4] But beyond pointing to the need to reassess neglected or marginalized historians like Hannah Adams, Brown, and others in the colonial and early national periods, Brown's negotiation of rational and romantic principles of history writing is instructive on the point of historical subjects and objectivity. In addition to highlighting the importance of the imagination as a subject of cultural debate and formation, Brown's interest in the "little particulars" and the lives of common people not only charts romantic era interest in "the individual," but it historicizes or anticipates our own multicultural concerns and interest in neglected histories or pasts. It speaks to the issue of historical representation and who is in the position to do it.

At the same time, however, Brown's willingness amid an emerging market economy to interrogate commercial interests and effects associated with the construction of history raises provocative questions about the motivations, methods, and circulation of contemporary histories. To what extent, we might ask, for example, do identity politics—whatever their location—influence historical inquiry or enable us to more accurately historicize the past? Do particular ideological investments enable us to meet private interests or professional needs? How do we separate, if we can, personal interest in a particular facet of history from any sort of past historical reality? In other words, to what degree, if any, do personal philosophical or political biases, material circumstances or book publishers' interests about what pushes the historiographical envelope, or what satisfies an ideological appetite or best meets a particular profit margin, compromise or influence historiographical principles and historical accuracy (however such terms are defined)? Whatever we may conclude about Brown's own biases and philosophical investments, his inquiry into the motivations behind and reception of history writing in his time raises useful but thorny questions about the impetus for—and impact of—our own inquiry into the past.

Second, in contrast to the investigations into historiography and postmodernism of Perez Zagorin, Frank Ankersmit, and arguments by Dorothy Ross and others about the rise of romantic historical writing and uncertainty, Brown's historiography points to a neglected tradition of linguistic self-consciousness and historiographical inquiry—and a major misconception among modern historians about historical subjectivity and the rise of the self-conscious, linguistically informed historian. That is, beyond further historicizing debates about the relationship between "history" and "romance," Brown's radical reflections on narrative meaning and truth ask us to reconsider stereotypes about the Enlightenment as flatly and completely rational, empirical, or objective—and to revise existing assessments of nineteenth-, twentieth-, and twenty-first-century American historiography because of their significant inaccuracy. No longer should historians think that historical self-consciousness and uncertainty were born sometime in the second half of the twentieth century when we can trace such ideas and debates, and even historiographical discourse itself, back at least to the eighteenth century.

In fact, Brown's—and Bolingbroke's and Bayle's—observations in the seventeenth century about the constructed nature of history writing qualify images of the Enlightenment as giving monolithic birth to historical objectivity, notions of social improvement and progress, and national history. Their self-conscious thinking about historical narrative and representation arguably anticipate Nietzsche's and Heidegger's critique of historicism and even postmodern considerations of historical representation. Their writings, as well as the thoughts of less well-known thinkers and writers, argue, like Berkhofer's for the existence of a metacritical historical tradition beginning, at least, in the late Enlightenment. Brown's historical writing, in turn, raises questions about the existence, and almost complete neglect, of an ironic tradition of American history writing and its relationship to political journalism at the beginning of the nineteenth century and an ongoing construction of American exceptionalism.

Third, while Brown may or may not have spearheaded inquiry into historicist issues in his time, Berkhofer's provocative question, "As literary theorists turn to history in their criticism and explication of texts, should historians turn to literary theory in their description and explanation of contexts?" is answered, I believe, in at least one way.[5] His call for greater "dialogic and reflexive contextualization" and "new forms of historical representation" is being met by alternative histories such as Jill Lepore's *The Name of War: King Philip's War and the Origins of American Identity* but also by the recent interest in interdisciplinary scholarship and the ways, for example, literary scholars and historians have begun to have dialogue—at conferences, in journals, online, and elsewhere—about topics and approaches of mutual interest.[6] Contrary to claims by some historians that the influence of postmodernist doctrines is "not only fading but increasingly destined to fade," the writings of Brown and others suggest that postmodernist philosophy, especially as it is articulated in the margins of nontraditional thinkers and historians, *is* capable of enhancing our understanding of historiography as a form of thought engaged in the attainment of knowledge and understanding of the human past.

It seems, then, that one of the ironic implications of historicizing history writing and its relationship to the "postmodern moment" is to consider the extent to which poststructuralist claims of originality concerning language and representation—that is, the work of Lyotard, Barthes, Derrida, and others—are themselves insulated theoretical assertions. To be sure, such work, along with the emergence of feminist, Marxist, postcolonial, and other theories, has broadened our scope of understanding. To what degree, though, we may ask, are poststructural assumptions and arguments grounded in a limited understanding of historiography, semiotics, and seventeenth- and eighteenth-century philosophical inquiry—or a less than adequate knowledge of the deep structure of historical and linguistic representation. Thus, implicit, I believe, in Berkhofer's call over the years for historiographical self-consciousness or "reflexivity" in regard to the "great story" is a reevaluation of not only traditional models of historical interpretation but of nontraditional modes of historical narrative as well. We might find that just as "history" may "repeat itself," so principles of historiography—postmodern or otherwise—also circulate in nonlinear or recurring patterns of development.

In closing, democracy may indeed take stronger root in Iraq, Iran, and other parts of the world as a result of the U.S. invasion, election of President Barack Obama, and other factors.[7] But Andy Doolen's remarks in *Fugitive Empire: Locating American Imperialism* seem apropos. He observes that "the patriotic belief that republicanism always trumps imperialism in U.S. political development, except in irregular moments, is hegemonic, determining the production of knowledge across the disciplines."[8] Moreover, in a review of studies by Robert Ferguson, Andrew Trees, and Ed White, he notes that "the historical study of early America has immediate urgency in a world where the U.S. depends upon republican rhetoric and ideology to advance its imperial ambitions in the Middle East. In the days following the invasion of Iraq, having discovered no weapons of mass destruction and having lost their justification for preemptive war, U.S. officials embraced the patriotic doctrine that a constitutional republic could be planted in Iraq and a new civil society be made to flower, inevitably tracing their reasons back to the American Revolution."[9] Doolen makes an important point about early American republicanism and the rhetoric of freedom, liberty, and rights employed today on behalf of American interests. Also, unlike in college classrooms after September 11—where, often with the American flag next to the whiteboard, the specter of being "unpatriotic" loomed if one questioned American foreign policy or those of Homeland Security—American studies provides, as Doolen points out, perhaps one of the few places where academics can openly engage issues of historical and political importance, without fear of reprisal.[10]

In this light, if, according to his contemporaries, Brown's "ardent curiosity," "philosophic candour," "habits of analysis," and "search of the truth" are part of his legacy as a late Enlightenment intellectual and historian, it seems useful to ask what Brown himself would make of contemporary events, especially as they concern academic constructions of history, narrative, and "objectivity." What kind of response would he, as an enlightened Quaker, offer concerning the status and rights of women around the world today, the spread of AIDS, genocide in Darfur and other parts of Africa, the war in Afghanistan, NAFTA and other trade agreements, or global warming? Or should such speculation not even be contemplated or imagined? Should the spheres of scholarship and political commentary, or ideology, remain separate? Or, more to the point, can they?

In assessing Brown's accomplishments as a novelist, Emory Elliott once remarked that Brown was "far ahead of any other American writer of his time in his themes and in his literary experimentation."[11] Elliott and others of his generation, a generation that witnessed the ideological and rhetorical maelstrom of the Vietnam War, would agree, I think, with the observation that just as Brown's understanding of historical circumstances may be said to influence his novels, so his understanding of fiction may be said to inform his historical writing. Likewise, there would likely be consensus that Brown's historicism serves as a useful site for historiographical and cultural inquiry—for understanding not only political and historicist issues of his day but, importantly, the assumptions and conceptual paradigms that inform our own.[12]

Notes

1. "Annals of America," *American Register; or, General Repository of History, Politics, and Science* (1809): 5:35.

2. William Dunlap, *The Life of Charles Brockden Brown: Together with Selections from the Rarest of His Printed Works, from His Original Letters, and from His Manuscripts before Unpublished*, 2 vols. (Philadelphia: James P. Parke, 1815), 2:88.

3. David Lee Clark, *Charles Brockden Brown: Pioneer Voice of America* (1952; repr., New York: AMS Press, 1966), 292.

4. Brown's father, Elijah, copied this obituary into his journal: ms. Am 03399, number 10, Historical Society of Pennsylvania, Philadelphia. He notes incorrectly at the bottom of the page: "The above is from the pen of one of his particular literary friends in New York, A. Mecker," [1]. Daniel Edwards Kennedy writes in his unpublished biography that "the name is doubtless an error for Anthony L. Bleecker." Kennedy, "Charles Brockden Brown: His Life and Works," ms., Charles Brockden Brown Collection, Kent State Univ., folder 49, 1989.

5. Kennedy notes that this obituary is possibly by Anthony Bleecker or "elaborated by the new editor from the shorter one by him" in the preface to the *American Register* (1991), and Clark reproduces the obituary in *Charles Brockden Brown* (292–94). An earlier handwritten draft version, which also gives the year of Brown's death as 1809, exists in the Charles Brockden Brown Papers, 1742–1810, at the Harry Ransom Center at the Univ. of Texas–Austin. The obituary is cataloged as "[Obituary of Charles Brockden Brown]" and listed as being written by an "unidentified author." If Bleecker did not compose it, the incorrect date of Brown's death was, as Kennedy suggests, most likely corrected by the editor of the *American Register*.

6. Clark, *Charles Brockden Brown*, 293.

7. The terms "annalist," "chronicler," and "historian" have different meanings historically. Annals such as that written by St. Gall during the medieval period are simply a list of events recorded by a contemporary, for example. "709. Hard winter. Duke Gottfried died." A chronicle, however, tended to summarize events on the basis of several annals and could take the form of a personal narrative. History, of course, uses the same materials but is distinguished by its literary style and qualities of analysis and judgment. See Harry Elmer Barnes, *A History of Historical Writing*, 2d ed. (New York: Dover, 1962), 65–67. Since by Brown's day the term "annals" generally referred to a descriptive account or history of successive years, I use the terms "annalist" and "historian" interchangeably. Brown's narrative is at once contemporary and of the past, and it is both narrative and the artful selection of historical events and documents.

8. In the nineteenth century, says David S. Reynolds, George Lippard (1822–54) was a cultural, political, and literary "radical" who admired Brown's work (introduction, 2). Like Brown, he was a Philadelphian and chose novel writing over the law. He dedicated *The Monks of Monk Hall* to Brown and wrote a eulogy seeking to rescue Brown from an obscure burial place and move his body to Laurel Hill Cemetery (268). Lippard wrote that Brown's novels were read by "tens of thousands" in England and that "men like Godwin or Bulwer, or even the crabbed Editor of a Scotch Review, hold this Philadelphia Novelist in high estimation, as a man of remarkable and original genius" (271). Reynolds, *George Lippard, Prophet of Protest: Writings of an American Radical, 1822–1854* (New York: Peter Lang, 1986).

9. Representative cold war literary or New Critical statements situating Brown as a moderately interesting but aesthetically suspect writer appear in Alexander Cowie, *The Rise of the American Novel* (New York: American Book Company, 1951) and Richard Chase, *The American Novel and Its Tradition* (New York: Doubleday, 1957). Perhaps the most prescient cold war commentary is that of Leslie Fiedler, who situates Brown as an "anti-bourgeois" writer whose discursive strategies are subordinated to cultural work concerning emerging categories of gender and selfhood. Fiedler, *Love and Death in the American Novel*, rev. ed. (New York: Stein and Day, 1966), 98–104, 145–61.

10. William Charvat and Frank Luther Mott can be said to have been least impressed with Brown's history writing. Charvat, in his well-known study, *The Profession of Authorship in America, 1800-1870*, ed. by Matthew J. Bruccoli (Columbus: Ohio State Univ. Press, 1968), remarks that Brown's lack of success as a novelist left him no other choice but to spend "the rest of his life storekeeping and doing hack work for Philadelphia publishers" (28). Concurring on this point, Mott writes, "There is something very pathetic in the thought of Brockden Brown reduced to the slavery of almanac-making. Failure in his most ambitious literary attempts, the unfaith of his promising friends, the responsibilities of marriage, the lectures of his conventional brother, and—finally—physical illness, tamed his high spirit and made him a hack. Undoubtedly the confinement of hackwork—the labor of getting out a thousand encyclopedic pages a year—had much to do with Brown's early death in 1810" (Frank Luther Mott, *A History of American Magazines, 1741–1850* [Cambridge, Mass.: Belknap Press of Harvard Univ. Press, 1966], 222). Standard historical studies such as Michael Kraus's *A History of American History* (New York: Farrar & Rinehart, 1937), Harvey Wish's *The American Historian: A Social-Intellectual History of the Writing of the American Past* (New York: Oxford Univ. Press, 1960), George Callcott's *History in the United States, 1800–1860: Its Practices and Purposes* (Baltimore: Johns Hopkins Univ. Press, 1970), and John Higham's revised edition of *History: Professional Scholarship in America* (Baltimore: Johns Hopkins Univ. Press, 1983) also neglect Brown, as does historian Steven Watts's revisionist cultural biography on Brown: *The Romance of Real Life: Charles Brockden Brown and the Origins of American Culture* (Baltimore: Johns Hopkins Univ. Press, 1994).

11. Some early critics who have recognized the historiographical value of Brown's annals and the historical importance of his novels include William Prescott, Fred L. Pattee, David Lee Clark, and Warner Berthoff. In Jared Sparks's Library of American Biography series (New York: Harper and Bros., 1860), Prescott wrote about Brown's *American Register*: "The historical portion of 'The Register,' in particular, comprehending, in addition to the political annals of the principal states of Europe and of our own country, an elaborate inquiry into the origin and organization of our domestic institutions, displays a discrimination in the selection of incidents, and a good faith and candor in the mode of discussing them, that entitle it to great authority as a record of contemporary transactions" (160). Fred L. Pattee made a similar observation in his introduction to *Wieland* (New York: Harcourt, 1926) when he remarked that Brown's "thoroughness and accuracy and literary skill" make him "unquestionably the pioneer American historian in the modern manner" (xxiv).

By comparison, David Lee Clark makes two important points about Brown in *Charles Brockden Brown: Pioneer Voice of America*. First, he notes that the "treatment of Brown as a political pamphleteer and historian calls for frequent quotation" of Brown's pamphlets and that Brown's "cool discriminating reasoning—largely an analysis of the principles of commerce and benefits derived therefrom—against the Embargo Act . . . marks a milepost in early American historical writing" (261). While he specifically praises Brown's "moderation and impartiality" and his "choice of significant current events" in the annals, he also acknowledges that "Brown at times allowed his enthusiasm to exceed its usual bounds of moderation" (284–85).

Second, in addition to observing that Brown's pamphlets are inextricably tied to his historical annals, Clark says about the annals and their historical value:

> Brown early realized what it has taken many people long years to understand: that America's welfare is closely bound up with European affairs and that whatever disturbs the peace of Europe will affect the peace of America. . . . "The Annals of America," occupying increasingly more space in each succeeding number of the *Register*, is particularly interesting to the student of American history. The aftermath of the Louisiana Purchase, the trouble with Spain, the Aaron Burr Conspiracy—all come to life and gain new significance in these vivid contemporary accounts. (283–85)

Finally, Warner B. Berthoff, in his groundbreaking dissertation, "The Literary Career of Charles Brockden Brown" (Ph.D. diss., Harvard Univ., 1954), makes astute commentary about Brown and later nineteenth-century historians when he writes that Brown "did not make an art of narrative in the manner of Prescott or Parkman and the historians of that later generation." Rather, he says, Brown's skill was with "analysis." His "best historical writing has the penetration into causes and probabilities which he attributed to the 'romancer' and bespeaks a mind trained to the practice of philosophic generalization. In the degree to which his record of current history is directed by a speculative concern for the idea embodied in the event, in the degree narrative passages are dialectically organized, Brown's work stands closer to that of Richard Hildreth and Henry Adams" (333–34).

12. Mary Chapman, introduction to *Ormond; or, the Secret Witness* (Peterborough, Ontario: Broadview, 1999), 11.

13. Philip Barnard, Mark L. Kamrath, and Stephen Shapiro, introduction to *Revising Charles Brockden Brown* (Knoxville: Univ. of Tennessee Press, 2004), x.

14. Most recently, several essays by Bryan Waterman and others have appeared in *Early American Literature* under the title "New Scholarship on Charles Brockden Brown." Waterman, for instance, offers several explanations for the "upsurge of scholarly interest in Brown" in his essay "Reading Early America with Charles Brockden Brown" (235). See *Early American Literature* 44, no. 2 (2009).

15. "Historicism" generally means the theory and practice of history writing that attempts to be impartial or factual and avoid biased judgments of the past. It also can mean that events are determined or influenced by conditions or processes beyond human control. Brook Thomas's definition of the term "historicism," as set forth in his *The New Historicism and Other Old-Fashioned Topics* (Princeton, N.J.: Princeton Univ. Press, 1991), is useful. It can "refer generally to any sort of historical method. But it can also refer to a specific brand of historiography that flourished in the nineteenth century, especially in Germany, where it was known as *Historismus*"; that is, an approach that viewed the present as the result of past developments (4). The term, he says, was never used widely, but its general meaning (for purposes of defining "new historicism") has been best summed up by Fredric Jameson when he defined historicism as referring to "our relationship to the past,

and of our possibility of understanding the latter's monuments, artifacts, and traces" (4). By "historicism," I mean a theory and method of history writing that concerned itself with the quest for historical understanding and factual truth.

16. By New Historicist assumptions about history, textuality, representation, discourse, and the cultural relevance of historical or rhetorical particulars, I mean those principles that H. Aram Veeser's *The New Historicism* (New York: Routledge, 1989), Catherine Gallagher and Stephen Greenblatt's *Practicing New Historicism* (Chicago: Univ. of Chicago Press, 2000), and others have argued for in regard to the need for greater historical self-consciousness, especially as it concerns the limits of narrative meaning and access to absolute truth. For additional explanation of how New Historicist concerns inform this study, see "Charles Brockden Brown and the 'Art of the Historian': An Essay Concerning (Post)modern Historical Understanding" in *Journal of the Early Republic* 21, no. 2 (Summer 2001), 231–33, 256–60.

17. Robert F. Berkhofer Jr., *Beyond the Great Story: History as Text and Discourse* (Cambridge, Mass.: Belknap Press of Harvard Univ. Press, 1995), 284.

18. Amy Kaplan, "'Left Alone with America': The Absence of Empire in the Study of American Culture," in *Cultures of United States Imperialism,* ed. by Amy Kaplan and Donald E. Pease (Durham, N.C.: Duke Univ. Press, 1993), 17.

19. Watts, *Romance of Real Life,* 164–66.

20. Dingquan Zhang, "The Ideological Polyphony in the Fictional World of Charles Brockden Brown" (Ph.D. diss., Indiana Univ. of Pennsylvania, 1995), 199.

1. European and Colonial Traditions

1. The obituary was possibly written by Bleecker or, says Kennedy, the new editor of the *American Register.* See the Elijah Brown journal in Charles Brockden Brown Manuscripts at the Historical Society of Pennsylvania, and Kennedy, "Charles Brockden Brown," folder 49, 1991. In Greek, ἰστορία, or "history," means "a learning or knowing by inquiry, an account of one's inquiries, narrative, history." *The Oxford English Dictionary,* ed. by J. A. Simpson and E. S. C. Weiner, 2d ed. (New York: Oxford Univ. Press, 1989), 261.

2. Cheng challenges the ahistorical assumption that early historians were merely patriotic romantics influenced by blind idealism. She also examines how Revolutionary historians sought to "differentiate between history and the novel" (64). See *The Plain and Noble Garb of Truth: Nationalism and Impartiality in American Writing, 1784–1860* (Athens: Univ. of Georgia Press, 2008), 12.

3. Barnes, *History of Historical Writing,* 26.

4. Ibid., 27.

5. J. B. Bury, *The History of the Freedom of Thought* (New York: Holt, 1913), 22–23.

6. Barnes, *History of Historical Writing,* 28–34. Francis R. B. Godolphin, in his introduction to *The Greek Historians: The Complete and Unabridged Historical Works of Herodotus, Thucydides, Xenophon, Arrian,* 2 vols. (New York, Random House, 1942), notes that "for Thucydides, above all, causes exist inside the human sphere, and it is the historian's business to find them and relate them to events" (1:xxiii). Thucydides, he observes, rejected the "external causation of Herodotus" and instead saw "a plurality of causes related to problems of economic wants and political power" (xxiii–xxiv).

7. Maurice Croiset, *Hellenic Civilization,* trans. by Paul B. Thomas (New York: Alfred A. Knopf, 1935), 143–44, quoted in Barnes, *History of Historical Writing,* 28.

8. Barnes, *History of Historical Writing,* 29.

9. Donald Lateiner, *The Historical Method of Herodotus* (Toronto: Univ. of Toronto Press, 1989), 7, 32, 33, 227.

10. Barnes, *History of Historical Writing*, 31–33.

11. Ibid., 28–35.

12. George H. Callcott, *History in the United States*, 1, 2–4, 5.

13. Hayden White, *Metahistory: The Historical Imagination in Nineteenth-Century Europe* (Baltimore: Johns Hopkins Univ. Press, 1993), 39, 38, 69.

14. Callcott, *History in the United States*, 8.

15. Sherman B. Barnes, "The Age of Enlightenment," in *The Development of Historiography*, ed. by Matthew A. Fitzsimmons et al. (Port Washington, N.Y.: Kennikat, 1954), 160, 167.

16. Callcott, *History in the United States*, 9.

17. Alfred G. Pundt, "The Age of Enlightenment," in Simmons et al., *Development of Historiography*, 170.

18. Ibid., 176.

19. For example, see John Whitaker's *History of Manchester* (London, 1771) and *Mary Queen of Scots Vindicated* (London: Murray, 1787), John Pinkerton's *Dissertation on the Origin and Progress of the Scythians or Goths* (London: Printed by John Nichols, for George Nicol, Pall-Mall, 1789) and *The History of Scotland from the Accession of the House of Stuart to that of Mary* (London: Printed for C. Dilly, 1797), and Turner's *The History of the Anglo-Saxons* (London: Printed for T. Cadell, Jun., and W. Davies, 1799–1805).

20. Peter Novick, *That Noble Dream: The "Objectivity Question" and the American Historical Profession* (New York: Cambridge Univ. Press, 1988), 2, 8.

21. Michael Kraus, *The Writing of American History* (Norman: Univ. of Oklahoma Press, 1953), 59.

22. Jack P. Greene, *The Intellectual Construction of America: Exceptionalism and Identity from 1492 to 1800* (Chapel Hill: Univ. of North Carolina Press, 1993), 5.

23. Although I examine them more fully later, historians, besides Increase and Cotton Mather, whose works typically rely on a providential paradigm include William Bradford's *History of Plymouth Plantation* (1630), William Hubbard's *A General History of New England from Discovery to MLDCLXXX [1630]* (unpublished until 1815), Thomas Prince's *Chronological History of New-England in the Form of Annals Being a Summary and Exact Account of the Most Material Transactions and Occurrences Relating to the Country, in the Order of Time Wherein They Happened, from the Discovery by Capt. Gosnold in 1602 to the Arrival of Governor Belcher, in 1730* (Boston: S. Gerrish, 1736), Jeremy Belknap's *History of New-Hampshire* (Philadelphia: Printed for the author by Robert Aitkin, in Market Street, near the Coffee-House, 1784), David Ramsay's *The History of the American Revolution* (Philadelphia: Printed and Sold by R. Aitken & Son, 1789), and Mercy Otis Warren's *History of the Rise, Progress, and Termination of the American Revolution* (Boston: Printed by Manning and Loring, for E. Larkin, 1805).

24. In 1553, Richard Eden published *Treatise of the New India*—a translation, observes Michael Kraus, of material from Sebastian Muenster's *Cosmography* (*Writing of American History*, 16). Thomas Hariot, an adviser and companion of Sir Walter Raleigh, wrote *A briefe and true report of the New found land of Virginia* in 1588. Yet Norse sagas and Spanish chronicles of travel in the New World constitute, of course, the earliest historical narratives of American history (10).

25. Ibid., 22.

26. William Bradford, *Bradford's History of Plymouth Plantation, 1606–1646*, ed. by William T. Davis (New York: Barnes and Noble, 1908), 33, 92, 100, 103.

27. Wish, *American Historian*, 3, 4.

28. Cotton Mather, *The Wonders of the Invisible World* (Boston: N.p., 1693), 27, 11, 57.

29. For a recent study of how seventeenth-century Puritan historians such as John Winthrop, Edward Johnson, Increase Mather, and Cotton Mather "self-consciously" struggled in their narratives to attend to the "socio-cultural crisis" of the present by rewriting the past (vii, 189), see Stephen Carl Arch's *Authorizing the Past: The Rhetoric of History in Seventeenth-Century New England* (Dekalb: Northern Illinois Univ. Press, 1994).

30. Kraus, *Writing of American History,* 38, 39.

31. Ibid., 49, 87, 48.

32. In the preface to his *Chronological History of New England in the Form of Annals,* Prince observes, "Next to the sacred History, and that of the Reformation, I was from my early Youth instructed in the History of this Country." He also remarks that in his foreign travels he "found the want of a regular History of this country every where complained of," and that "Providence" eventually enabled him to do so ([i]–[ii]).

33. Kraus, *Writing of American History,* 56, 55.

34. Frank Luther Mott, *Golden Multitudes: The Story of the Best Sellers in the United States* (New York: Macmillan, 1947), 59, 60, 88. By 1830, Mott observes, "Miss Porter's *Scottish Chiefs,* Irving's *History of New York,* Cooper's *The Spy* and *The Pilot,* Scott's Waverly series, Shakespeare's histories, and other best sellers dealing less prominently with the past, were showing the pleasures of history, or antiquarianism, or what have you, to the great popular audience" (88).

35. Lester H. Cohen, introduction to *The Revolutionary Histories: Contemporary Narratives of the American Revolution* (Ithaca, N.Y.: Cornell Univ. Press, 1980), 15, 21.

36. Robert Allen Skotheim, *American Intellectual Histories and Historians* (Princeton, N.J.: Princeton Univ. Press, 1966), 9.

37. Kraus, *Writing of American History,* 57.

38. Jeremy Belknap, *The History of New-Hampshire,* 3 vols. (1792; repr., New York: Arno, 1972), 3:332.

39. Philip Gould makes this observation of Edward Johnson's work in his review of Arch's *Authorizing the Past.* See Gould's review in *Early American Literature* 30, no. 3 (1995): 286–88.

40. Belknap, *History of New-Hampshire,* 1:v–vi, 91.

41. Kraus, *Writing of American History,* 136.

42. Mott, *History of American Magazines,* 3.

43. Mott notes that A. H. Shearer, in his article "American Historical Periodicals," *Mississippi Valley Historical Review* 4 (Mar. 1918), analyzes the range of periodicals "devoted to history exclusively" and what constitutes history writing as opposed to "well-written trash, or popular articles, or even misinformation" (484-91).

44. Kraus, *Writing of American History,* 58–59.

45. Callcott, *History in the United States,* 13, 20, 122.

46. See Benjamin Trumbull, *A Century Sermon; or, Sketches of the History of the Eighteenth Century* (New Haven, Conn.: Reed and Morse, 1801), 4.

47. Benjamin Trumbull, *A General History of the United States of America; from the Discovery in 1492, to 1792: or, Sketches of the Divine Agency, in Their Settlement, Growth, and Protection; and Especially in the Late Memorable Revolution,* 3 vols. (New York: Williams & Whiting, 1810), 1:2.

48. Callcott, *History in the United States,* 16.

49. Steven Blakemore remarks of the era and Barlow that if Timothy Dwight's *Conquest of Canaan* (1785) is the first American epic but one that contains an "Old Testament form and typology," Barlow's "creation of a teleological, New World republican epic" signals a "radical break from the ancient literary regime and that a thematic binary between the old and new histories and literatures would be a primary concern of the poem." Blakemore, *Joel Barlow's Columbiad: A Bicentennial Reading* (Knoxville: Univ. of Tennessee Press, 2007), 30–31.

50. Anthony Molho and Gordon S. Wood, introduction to *Imagined Histories: American Historians Interpret the Past*, ed. by Anthony Molho and Gordon S. Wood (Princeton, N.J.: Princeton Univ. Press, 1998), 4.

51. Daniel T. Rodgers, "Exceptionalism," in Molho and Wood, *Imagined Histories*, 22.

52. Gordon S. Wood, "The Relevance and Irrelevance of American Colonial History," in Molho and Wood, *Imagined Histories*, 145.

53. The belief in a providential history and millennial future is still quite alive in the United States, especially among religious conservatives. See, for instance, Mark A. Beliles and Stephen K. McDowell's *America's Providential History* (Providence Foundation, 1989) and its championing of nineteenth-century historian George Bancroft's assertion that "Providence is the light of history and the soul of the world. God is in history and all history has a unity because God is in it."

54. Wood, "The Relevance and Irrelevance of American Colonial History," in Molho and Wood, *Imagined Histories*, 22.

55. Kraus, *Writing of American History*, 144, 128–29; Callcott, *History in the United States*, 21.

56. Jeffrey Richards, *Mercy Otis Warren* (New York: Twayne, 1995), 128, 142, 143.

57. Jeffrey Richards, "Mercy Otis Warren," in *Dictionary of Literary Biography*, vol. 200: *American Women Prose Writers to 1820*, ed. by Carla Mulford, with Angela Vietto and Amy E. Winans (Detroit: Bruccoli Clark, 1999), 396–97.

58. Sharon M. Harris, introduction to *Women's Early American Historical Narratives*, ed. by Sharon M. Harris (New York: Penguin, 2003), ix, x–xii.

59. Skotheim, *American Intellectual Histories*, 14–15.

60. Kraus, *Writing of American History*, 59, 58.

61. Abiel Holmes, *American Annals; or, A Chronological History of America*, 2 vols. (Cambridge, Mass.: W. Hillard, 1805), 2:503.

62. Kraus, *Writing of American History*, 59.

63. Callcott, *History in the United States*, 31–32, 34–35.

64. Washington Irving, [Diedrich Knickerbocker's] *A History of New York* (New York: A. L. Burt, 1880), xxvii–xxviii, 100.

65. William L. Hedges, *Washington Irving: An American Study, 1802–1832* (Baltimore: Johns Hopkins Univ. Press, 1965), 72.

66. Irving, *A History of New York*, xiii, 133, 304, 28.

67. Ellen Fitzpatrick, *History's Memory: Writing America's Past, 1880–1980* (Cambridge, Mass.: Harvard Univ. Press, 2002), 3–4, 6.

68. Joyce Appleby, *A Restless Past: History and the American Public,* (Lanham, Md.: Rowman & Littlefield, 2005), 1–2, 3.

69. Callcott, *History in the United States*, 122.

70. J. William Frost, *The Quaker Family in Colonial America: A Portrait of the Society of Friends* (New York: St. Martin's, 1973), 110.

71. Clark, *Charles Brockden Brown*, 18.

72. Peter Kafer, *Charles Brockden Brown's Revolution and the Birth of American Gothic* (Philadelphia: Univ. of Pennsylvania Press, 2004), 46–47.

73. Jean S. Straub, "Teaching in the Friends' Latin School of Philadelphia in the Eighteenth Century," *Pennsylvania Magazine of History and Biography* 91, no. 4 (1967): 453.

74. Kafer, *Charles Brockden Brown's Revolution*, 21.

75. Howard Brinton, *Friends for 300 Years; The History and Beliefs of the Society of Friends Since George Fox Started the Quaker Movement* (New York: Harper, 1952), 35.

76. See Appendix B in David Lee Clark's *Charles Brockden Brown: Pioneer Historian* (1952; repr., New York: AMS Press, 1966), and Kennedy, "Charles Brockden Brown," ser. 8, box 13, folder 66, "Books Owned by Brown," 1712A, 1715.

77. Kafer, *Charles Brockden Brown's Revolution*, 69, 70.

78. Clark, *Charles Brockden Brown,* 131, 4-5.

79. Bryan Waterman, *Republic of Intellect: The Friendly Club of New York City and the Making of American Literature* (Baltimore: Johns Hopkins Univ. Press, 2007), 77.

80. Charles Brockden Brown to Joseph Bringhurst, Oct. 24, 1795, Charles Brockden Brown Papers, 1792-1821, n.d., Hawthorne-Longfellow Library, Bowdoin College, Brunswick, Me.

81. Letter 8 to Henrietta in Clark, *Charles Brockden Brown,* 71, 72.

82. Brown's evolving and somewhat ambivalent understanding of classical knowledge also answers, in part, John Shields's provocative questions about how early Americans absorbed classical knowledge and why the Greco-Roman part of our cultural heritage has been ignored in favor of an Adamic or biblical explanation of how American history and culture emerged. If, as Shields asserts, America developed out of an "interaction" or "dialectic" between Adamic and Aenean ideologies, Brown's absorption of classical materials and simultaneous desire to distance himself from classical languages speaks to the larger ambivalence Americans had about the role and function of classical knowledge in the formation of a new republic. See John Shields, *The American Aeneas* (Knoxville: Univ. of Tennessee Press, 2001).

83. Charles Brockden Brown to Rev. Samuel Miller, Mar. 16, 1803, Samuel Miller Papers, 1754-1898 (bulk 1800-1849), Firestone Library, Princeton Univ., Princeton, N.J.

84. Karl H. Dannenfeldt, "The Heritage of Antiquity," in Fitzsimmons et al., *Development of Historiography,* 3-4. Dannenfeldt also notes that Herodotus collected his material from numerous sources and that he "did not credulously record, without criticism or evaluation, the vast amount of material told him by his informants. . . . [He] was a religious man and believed in a divine providence, yet he was cautious in relating tales of the intervention of the gods in the affairs of men (VII.129)" (4). His "'researches,' his criticism, his naiveté and charming style," says Dannenfeldt, make his *History* a classic.

85. Holmes, *American Annals,* 1:iv.

86. Lawrence Buell, *New England Literary Culture: From Revolution Through Renaissance* (New York: Cambridge Univ. Press, 1986), 214–15.

87. Ibid., 215, 228, 230, 232. Although Hildreth's history writing reflects elements of rationalist and utilitarian traditions, critical historians, writes Harvey Wish, "have found Hildreth's explanation of parties to be downright partisan. He pictured the Federalists under Washington and Hamilton as representing 'the experience, the prudence, the practical wisdom, the discipline, the conservative reason and instincts of the country.'" This, says Wish, "left Jefferson's party with a monopoly of quixotic ideas and undisciplined individualism" (*American Historian,* 66).

88. For yet another perspective on the development of "historical objectivity" in American historiography, see G. P. Gooch's study *History and Historians in the Nineteenth Century* (London: Longmans, 1913). In contrast to Callcott and Buell, he writes:

The most important study of recent events is the "History of the United States from the Compromise of 1850," by James Ford Rhodes, who narrates the critical years of the slavery struggle with a detachment and impartiality which no other American has approached. . . . He is naturally severe on Andrew Johnson and Blaine, emphasizes Grant's ignorance of statesmanship, and describes his rule as the high-water mark of corruption. The work marks the immense distance which American scholarship had travelled since Bancroft.

The crude elation and national arrogance are dead and buried, and a younger generation has learned to respect the motives of men whose actions the world has agreed to condemn. (409–10)

If Callcott identifies Vico as promoting a "self-conscious" historical method and Buell identifies Belknap as being ahead of his time in terms of historical "objectivity," Gooch points to Rhodes, as the first American historian to write with "detachment and impartiality." Rhodes, suggests Gooch, brings balance and insight to his history about the slavery era, and he largely avoids the rancor of party biases. Unlike his nineteenth-century contemporaries, Bancroft in particular, he avoids "crude elation and national arrogance." He rises above providential or partisan interpretations of historical events and, claims Gooch, is able when necessary to be severe in his judgment and to be sympathetic toward those "men whose actions the world has agreed to condemn." Brown anticipated all of these historians in his impartiality but could also be ironic when dispensing historical judgment.

89. In contrast, Novick claims that von Ranke was the first to "apply to modern history those documentary and philological methods which had been developed for the study of antiquity" (*That Noble Dream,* 26). Chief among these were his wide use of primary sources, his "impartiality" or relative "abstention from moral judgement," his reluctance to give a nationalist spin to his narration of events, and his use of seminar methods to promote the study of history (26–30). Von Ranke, says Novick, continued the German idealist position and rejected a historiography "based on a priori philosophy" and instead worked from the assumption that "the course of history revealed God's work" (27). Phrases such as "The hand of God" and "God's gift" repeatedly occur in his work. So, while German historians saw von Ranke as "the antithesis of a non-philosophical empiricism," Americans saw him as an empiricist—a nonpartisan practitioner of factual presentation.

90. Callcott, *History in the United States,* 208.

91. Kraus, *Writing of American History,* 236–38.

92. Skotheim, *American Intellectual Histories,* 15–16.

93. See my own essay "Charles Brockden Brown and the 'Art of the Historian': An Essay Concerning (Post)Modern Historical Understanding," *Journal of the Early Republic* 21.2 (Summer 2001): 258, and Ross's "Grand Narrative in American Historical Writing: From Romance to Uncertainty," *American Historical Review* 100, no. 3 (June 1995): 673.

94. Callcott, *History in the United States,* 22.

2. *"Domestic History" and the Republican Novel*

1. "Sample of Liberty to Conscience 1783," ms., Papers of Charles Brockden Brown, Accession 6349, Special Collections, Univ. of Virginia Library, Charlottesville.

2. See autograph manuscripts (glossy photograph only) n.d., two pages of a notebook beginning, "With great courage and elevation of sentiment he told the Court that the pretended crime," Accession 6349a-70 ms. Papers of Charles Brockden Brown, Special Collections, Univ. of Virginia Library.

3. "Aretas," 1787, Brown Family Papers, 1715-1837 (collection 84), Historical Society of Pennsylvania.

4. Benjamin Rush, quoted in Kraus, *Writing of American History,* 59.

5. Poem, 1787, "By Charles Brockden Brown—aged 16 years." The Verses of Charles Brockden Brown Studied in Metre," transcription by Daniel Edwards Kennedy, 1922, folder 1, box 2, Charles Brockden Brown Papers, Special Collections, Univ. of Virginia Library.

6. For scholarship that details the relationships among Brown, sentiment, nation, and the novel, see Julia A. Stern, *The Plight of Feeling: Sympathy and Dissent in the Early American Novel* (Chicago: Univ. of Chicago Press, 1997), Bruce Burgett, *Sentimental Bodies: Sex, Gender, and Citizenship in the Early Republic* (Princeton, N.J.: Princeton Univ. Press, 1998), and Mary Chapman and Glenn Hendler's *Sentimental Men: Masculinity and the Politics*

274   NOTES TO PAGES 31–32

of Affect in American Culture (Berkeley: Univ. of California Press, 1999). For the extent to which Brown's sympathy intersects with male friendship and the homoerotic, see Caleb Crain's *American Sympathy: Men, Friendship, and Literature in the New Nation* (New Haven: Yale Univ. Press, 2001) and Stephen Shapiro's "'Man to Man I Needed Not to Dread His Encounter': *Edgar Huntly's* End of Erotic Pessimism," in Barnard, Kamrath, and Shapiro, *Revising Charles Brockden Brown*, 216–51. More recently, Elizabeth Dillon has argued that a novel like *Edgar Huntly* is less concerned about women and property rights than it is about the main character's "*heteropathic* narrative," resistance to a heterosexual or republican marriage paradigm, and search for "liberal" sociality or a "*republican embodiment*" or validation among men. See *The Gender of Freedom: Fictions of Liberalism and the Literary Public Sphere* (Stanford, Calif.: Stanford Univ. Press, 2004), 161, 166, 177.

     7. Karen A. Weyler, *Intricate Relations: Sexual and Economic Desire in American Fiction* (Iowa City: Univ. of Iowa Press, 2004), 9–10.

     8. Susanna Haswell Rowson, preface to *Charlotte Temple: A Tale of Truth,* 2d ed. (1791; repr., Philadelphia: D. Humphreys, 1794), v.

     9. Shirley Samuels, *Romances of the Republic: Women, the Family, and Violence in the Literature of the Early American Nation* (New York: Oxford Univ. Press, 1996), 19.

     10. In his preface to *The Emigrants* (London: A Hamilton, 1793), Gilbert Imlay writes, more self-consciously than most novelists, "In this history I have scrupulously attended to natural circumstances, and the manners of the day; and in every particular I have had a real character for my model. The principal part of the story is founded upon facts, and I was only induced to give the work in the style of a novel, from believing it would prove more acceptable to the generality of readers." As W. M. Verhoeven and Amanda Gilroy note in the introduction to *The Emigrants* (New York: Penguin, 1998), this Anglo-Jacobin novel envisions "the 'true' trans-Alleghenian America in the West, which was radically discontinuous with the earlier European colonization of North America," at the same time it engages the "language and rhetoric" of "ongoing cultural debates" and adopts, for instance, the "language of political libertarianism for a feminist position" (xxiii, xxxii–xxxiii).

     11. *Memoirs of Stephen Calvert* mingles Calvert's personal history with the "violent world of European history and political intrigue." See Robert D. Arner, "Historical Essay," in *Alcuin: A Dialogue with Memoirs of Stephen Calvert,* bicentennial ed., ed. by Sydney J. Krause, S. W. Reid, and Robert D. Arner (Kent, Ohio: Kent State Univ. Press, 1987), 310.

     12. Fritz Fleischmann, *A Right View of the Subject: Feminism in the Works of Charles Brockden Brown and John Neal* (Erlangen, Germany: Palm & Enke, 1983), 25.

     13. For a detailed examination of exactly how a women's rights discourse developed in American culture, see Rosemarie Zagarri's "Morals, Manners, and the Republican Mother," *American Quarterly* 44, no. 2 (June 1992): 192–215, where she traces its transatlantic germination and how Scottish theorists like Hume, Millar, and Kames had "argued that women should be educated primarily so they could better amuse men in their leisure." While Americans, she says, "perceived the profoundly political dimensions of women's role," especially in regard to raising future male patriots, most "justified female education primarily in terms of women's relationship to men" (205–6). In a later article, she establishes the impact of Wollstonecraft's *A Vindication of the Rights of Women* in American culture, arguing that while American periodicals facilitated the spread of a women's rights discourse, publications like Judith Sargent Murray's "On the Equality of Sexes" were rare because "many Americans anticipated the radical consequences of natural rights talk and rejected its implications for women" (209, 228). See "The Rights of Man and Woman in Post-Revolutionary America," *William and Mary Quarterly,* 3d ser. 55.2 (Apr. 1998): 203–30. In publishing *Alcuin: A Dialogue,* Charles Brockden Brown, like Murray, apparently did not fear such consequences.

14. Elizabeth Jane Wall Hinds writes of *Alcuin* and women:

Taking up both the moderate and radical ends of the debate, Brown's *Alcuin,* then, was a timely synopsis of the woman question rather than, as several critics have assumed, a forward-looking and, therefore, radical tract by America's first professional novelist. *Alcuin* does offer, in the manner of Godwin, the specter of an extreme, radical version of the debate, illustrating as it does the possibility of absolute equality, offering up a vision of coeducation, equal property rights, political representation for women, and—most radical of all—the abolition of marriage as an institution. But this utopianism represents only one side of Brown's presentation; the debate itself turns up an alternative position, once as conservative and as viable for Brown as Godwinian radicalism.

See *Private Property: Charles Brockden Brown's Gendered Economics of Virtue* (Newark: Univ. of Delaware Press, 1997), 35.

15. Fleischmann, *Right View of the Subject,* 30, 40.

16. Bruce Burgett, "Malthus's Essay on the Principle of Population and Charles Brockden Brown's *Alcuin,*" in Barnard, Kamrath, and Shapiro, *Revising Charles Brockden Brown,* 130.

For other recent essays on Brown's provocative inquiry into women's issues, see Fredrika J. Teute, "A 'Republic of Intellect': Conversation and Criticism among the Sexes in 1790s New York," and Julia Stern, "The State of 'Women' in *Ormond;* or, Patricide in the New Nation," both in Barnard, Kamrath, and Shapiro, *Revising Charles Brockden Brown,* 149–81, 182–215; Sydney J. Kraus, "Brockden Brown's Feminism in Fact and Fiction," in *Early America Re-Explored: New Readings in Colonial, Early National, and Antebellum Culture,* ed. by Klaus H. Schmidt and Fritz Fleischmann (New York: Peter Lang, 2000); Dietmar Schloss, "Intellectuals and Women: Social Rivalry in Charles Brockden Brown's *Alcuin,*" in *The Construction and Contestation of American Cultures and Identities in the Early National Period,* ed. by Udo J. Hebel (Heidelberg, Germany: Carl Winter Universitätsverlag, 1999), 355–69; and Mary Chapman, introduction to *Ormond,* 22; Paul Lewis, "Attaining Masculinity: Charles Brockden Brown and Woman Warriors of the 1790s," *Early American Literature* 40 (2005): 37–55; Kristin M. Comment, "Charles Brockden Brown's *Ormond* and Lesbian Possibility in the Early Republic," *Early American Literature* 40 (2005): 57–78.

17. Sydney J. Krause, S. W. Reid, and Robert D. Arner, "Historical Essay," in *Alcuin; A Dialogue; with Memoirs of Stephen Calvert,* bicentennial ed. (Kent, Ohio: Kent State Univ. Press, 1987), 275.

18. *Wieland,* perhaps more than any other Brown novel, has been written about extensively by scholars. Pamela Clemit, *The Godwinian Novel: The Rational Fictions of Godwin, Brockden Brown, Mary Shelley* (Oxford: Clarendon, 1993) and Christopher Looby, *Voicing America: Language, Literary Form, and the Origins of the United States* (Chicago: Univ. of Chicago Press, 1996) are but two studies that dissect the intentions of Brown's first novel. Clemit, for instance, contends that as Brown "rewrites that fate of Godwin's impartial enquirer to point up the dangers of extreme individualism" and "invites the reader to piece together contradictory bits of information, he turns the provisional quality of the narrative to a radically different end, aiming to shock the reader by successive revelations of the limits of rational knowledge" (112–13). Looby regards the novel as a "measure also of Brown's doubts regarding the efficacy of legal institutions for preserving social order" and his interest in questioning the "foundational epistemological assumptions of his society" (186). In that respect and relative to the novel's concerns about "political order," Brown is a "complex counter-revolutionary writer" (193, 202).

19. Donald A. Ringe, *Charles Brockden Brown,* rev. ed. (Boston: Twayne, 1991), 13.

20. Charles Brockden Brown, *Wieland; or, The Transformation: An American Tale;* with *Memoirs of Carwin: The Biloquist,* bicentennial ed., ed. by Sydney J. Krause, S. W. Reid, and Alexander Cowie (Kent, Ohio: Kent State Univ. Press, 1977), 3, 6, 193, 235.

21. In "Ventriloquizing Nation: Voice, Identity, and Radical Democracy in Charles Brockden Brown's *Wieland,*" *American Literature* 78, no. 3 (2006), Eric A. Wolfe draws on the work of Jacques Lacan, radical democratic theorists Ernesto Laclau and Chantal Moufee, Christopher Looby, and others to argue that in light of the XYZ Affair, Alien and Sedition Acts, and Federalist efforts to achieve national unity, *Wieland* is "an oblique commentary on the crisis that occupied the forefront of American politics and the front of many a newspaper as Brown was writing" and that "Brown critiques the Federalist fantasy of vocal unity through the figure of ventriloquism" (434).

22. Brown, *Wieland,* bicentennial ed., 6–9, 14, 18.

23. Ibid., 18, 19.

24. Ibid., 23, 67–68.

25. Ibid., 147.

26. Samuels, *Romances of the Republic,* 46.

27. Brown, *Wieland,* bicentennial ed., 234–35, 237.

28. Ibid., 3, 240, 243, 244.

29. Ringe, *Charles Brockden Brown,* 34.

30. Chapman, introduction, 22.

31. Charles Brockden Brown, *Ormond; or, The Secret Witness,* bicentennial ed., ed. by Sydney J. Krause, S. W. Reid, and Russel B. Nye (Kent, Ohio: Kent State Univ. Press, 1982), 3.

32. Ibid., 3, 16, 27, 34, 35, 43.

33. Ibid., 47, 52, 48, 53–54, 58.

34. Ibid., 80, 84.

35. Ibid., 85, 94, 329.

36. Ibid., 160, 127, 128, 119, 120, 141, 142.

37. Ibid., 190–91, 191–92, 201, 206.

38. Lewis, "Attaining Masculinity," 50–51.

39. Comment, "Charles Brockden Brown's *Ormond,*" 57, 59–60.

40. Chapman, introduction, 27–28, 31.

41. Waterman, *Republic of Intellect,* 98, 129.

42. Brown, *Ormond,* bicentennial ed., 224.

43. For examples of Brown's use of "staging," see, for instance, Sydney J. Krause's "Historical Essay" in *Edgar Huntly; or, Memoirs of a Sleep-walker,* bicentennial ed., ed. by Sydney J. Krause and S. W. Reid (Kent, Ohio: Kent State Univ. Press, 1984), 365; and Jared Gardner's "Alien Nation: Edgar Huntly's Savage Awakening," *American Literature* 66, no. 3 (1994): 430. This facet of Brown's novel writing, now commonly accepted, is underscored in Philip Barnard, Mark L. Kamrath, and Stephen Shapiro's introduction to *Revising Charles Brockden Brown,* xix.

44. Brown, *Ormond,* bicentennial ed., 224, 225–27, 228, 230, 244, 251.

45. Ibid., 111, 157, 262.

46. Philip Barnard and Stephen Shapiro, introduction to *Edgar Huntly; or, Memoirs of a Sleep-Walker with Related Texts* (Indianapolis: Hackett, 2006), xiv–xvi. For an alternative reading of Brown's "Godwinian radicalism" and the ways Brown went beyond Godwin in engaging, and responding to, the philosophical and political status quo and its more conservative elements, see W. M. Verhoeven's "'This blissful period of intellectual liberty': Transatlantic Radicalism and Enlightened Conservatism in Brown's Early Writings," in Barnard, Kamrath, and Shapiro, *Revising Charles Brockden Brown,* 7–40.

47. Brown, *Edgar Huntly,* bicentennial ed., 3, 290.

48. Ibid., 3, 5–6.

49. First, as Norman S. Grabo observed about the novel, in his introduction to *Edgar Huntly: Memoirs of a Sleep-walker* (New York, Penguin, 1988), during the summer of 1787, when Edgar and Clithero had indulged their irrational sensibilities, the nation itself was debating the limits of personal liberty and what constraints, if any, the federal government might levy in a newly formed democracy that embraced republican virtue. Grabo remarks of this period: "Representatives from all the colonies were gathered in Philadelphia in an attempt to address for the nation the very questions Edgar and Clithero represent: how to harness the passionate and irrational aspects of human nature without destroying human nature itself; how to check and balance their destructive anti-social impulses and convert them to sociable and cultivated virtue without simply expunging them" (xviii). James Madison tackled this issue in *Federalist 10*, where he argued that the impulses and passions of individuals can be restrained but that such control comes at "the tyrannous expense of liberty" (xvii). The impassioned illusions, for instance, of Clithero concerning Mrs. Lorimer and, by contrast, Sarsefield's authoritarian efforts to regulate those impulses illustrate the philosophical and moral extremes Edgar must negotiate if he, like his countrymen, is to survive. While Brown appears to offer no explicit solution to these issues in the novel, he seems to suggest that reflection on and honesty about one's motives in regard to others can perhaps help mitigate, benevolent or not, misguided actions.

50. Likewise, as Sydney Krause argues in "Penn's Elm and Edgar Huntly: Dark 'Instruction to the Heart,'" *American Literature: A Journal of Literary History, Criticism, and Bibliography* 66 (1994), part of the ignored context for reading Brown's novel was the story of a treaty William Penn made with the Delaware by an elm tree in the autumn of 1682. "In the case of *Huntly,* an awareness of meanings available to Brown's readers regarding the Penn connections," particularly as it is contextualized by Brown's "Memorandums" in his *Literary Magazine,* point to Brown's "emotional indictment of the white man's victimization of the Indian" (464). While, as Krause notes, these sentiments clearly suggest how Brown could be of "two minds about the Indian," his essay identifies Brown's willingness to symbolically deconstruct imperial discourses in the context of the novel, thus enabling us to see Brown's sympathetic view of subject peoples not only as mere sentiment about the vanishing Indian but as an early expression of a postcolonial ethos (474).

51. Brown, *Edgar Huntly,* bicentennial ed., 89.

52. Ibid., 207, 173, 281, 193, 201, 60–61.

53. Norman S. Grabo, introduction to *Edgar Huntly: Memoirs of a Sleep-walker* (New York: Penguin, 1988), xii–xiii.

54. Krause, "Penn's Elm and Edgar Huntly," 473.

55. For an alternative view of Brown's representation of Indians, race, and history, see Gardner, "Alien Nation." Similar to Edward Watts in *Writing and Postcolonialism in the Early Republic* (Charlottesville: Univ. of Virginia Press, 1998) about Arthur Mervyn and decolonization, Elizabeth Jane Wall Hinds in "Deb's Dogs: Animals, Indians, and Postcolonial Desire in Charles Brockden Brown's *Edgar Huntly,*" *Early American Literature* 39 (2004) uses postcolonial and Second World theory to read Deb as "a colonized indigenous figure caught in a discursive matrix of colonial and postcolonial desire" (325). She suggests that Deb's story of resistance, within "Edgar's 'official' history," arguably "bespeaks her own and possibly Brown's postcolonial desire, a desire to disrupt 'the dominant language by interpolating it'" (342).

For an emerging consensus of how Brown's novel both stages and interrogates "the impulses that animate colonialism and imperialism," see Barnard and Shapiro's introduction to the Hackett edition of *Edgar Huntly* (ix–xlii) and its collection of contemporary documents.

56. Brown, *Edgar Huntly*, bicentennial ed., 46–47, 56.

57. In a letter to Joseph Bringhurst on July 29, 1793, Brown Papers, Hawthorne-Long-fellow Library, Bowdoin College, Brown remarks that he is "convinced that truth has never yet been exceed by imagination" and claims that a story of drunkenness and domestic abuse he is about to relate is "strictly true." In telling the story, he says to Bringhurst, "Only imagine that instead of happening Seven years ago, it happened yesterday." The fictional letter begins by explaining that in relating "the gloomy tale," the writer, Brown, offers a story that provides an "infinite subject of reflexion." Saying that "the fear of exposing her husband was a sufficient motive with her to abstain from all public complaints," her "do-mestic wretchedness" was finally discovered one evening when Mr. Waring heard screams and the cry of "murder and help" from "*Cooke's* house" next door.

Hearing the "sound of the lash" and the supplication "Oh Jackey, don't expose your-self," Mr. Waring entered the house and "beheld Mrs. Cooke kneeling before her husband, intreating his forebearance, while seizing ber [*sic*] by the hair with one hand [lacuna] with a horsewhip in the other inflicted the most dreadful severities on her back and shoulders from which he had torn away almost all covering." Mr. W. physically intervenes, and the scene repeats itself a few weeks later when the drunken husband again attempts to batter his wife. Having already "received a fatal blow" and rejected offers to send for a physician, the ashamed wife later dies and the children are removed from the home's "horrid tyr-anny." While Brown then states that he is not sure if he should read this "imaginary letter" to the society, he remarks to Bringhurst on August 16, 1793, Brown Papers, Hawthorne-Longfellow Library, Bowdoin College, that such stories, while true, are tales about "classes of the vulgar," which their peers are "inclined to believe have no existence, or at least none in the degree which dealers of fiction are accustomed to describe them."

Brown's remarks to Bringhurst about the story suggest that their contemporaries may not have been ready for the kind of "domestic history" or literary realism about the urban poor that would appear later in the violence of urban gothic writers such as George Thompson and George Lippard as well as later nineteenth-century naturalists such as Ste-phen Crane and Theodore Dreiser. For an examination of poverty and the urban poor in nineteenth-century America, and the way it influenced Protestant morality, see Keith Gandal, *The Virtues of the Vicious: Jacob Riis, Stephen Crane, and the Spectacle of the Slum* (New York: Oxford Univ. Press, 1997).

58. Elizabeth Jane Wall Hinds writes, "At the same time, this place of security, the home, so defined by propertied, aristocratic virtues, is proven over and over to be insecure, to be *not* private, to be in fact part of the public workings of an increasingly economic system" (*Private Property*, 40).

59. Brown, *Edgar Huntly*, bicentennial ed., 226, 228–29.

60. Ibid., 112, 288.

61. Ibid., 62.

62. Ibid., 89, 90–91.

63. Charles E. Bennett, "The Charles Brockden Brown Canon" (Ph.D. diss., Univ. of North Carolina, 1974), 227.

64. Charles Brockden Brown, *Arthur Mervyn; or, Memoirs of the Year 1793*, bicenten-nial ed., ed. by Sydney J. Krause, S. W. Reid, Norman S. Grabo, and Marvin L. Williams Jr. (Kent, Ohio: Kent State Univ. Press, 1980), 3.

65. Norman S. Grabo, "Historical Essay," *Arthur Mervyn*, bicentennial ed., 464. Louis Kirk McAuley argues in "'Periodical Visitations': Yellow Fever as Yellow Journalism in Charles Brockden Brown's *Arthur Mervyn*," *Eighteenth-Century Fiction* 19, no. 3 (2007) that Brown is not concerned about the impact of disease on America but rather the "radi-cal exchange of ideas: he fears the gradual infiltration of radical exiles into Philadelphia,

America's cultural, economic, and political capital and the command centre of public opinion." While McAuley's evidence on the point of Brown's supposed "xenophobia" fails to account for Brown's interest in Godwin, other British radicals, or Brown's socially progressive "Original Communications: Portrait of an Emigrant. Extracted from a Letter" (*Monthly Magazine and American Review* 1 [June 1799]: 161–64), he accurately details Jefferson's relationship to newspapers of the day and Brown's concerns about the truthfulness of information in periodical media (317).

For scholarship on *Arthur Mervyn* that is rich in historical documentation and sees Brown as using a "core set of Woldwinite beliefs to craft a programmatic story of property and sex about how individuals might overcome class, gender, and racial prejudice and communicate their changing consciousness to others" and how a poor farm boy "can teach urban elites something about the concrete enactment of political liberty," see Philip Barnard and Stephen Shapiro's introduction and commentary to *Arthur Mervyn; or, Memoirs of the Year 1793 with Related Texts* (Indianapolis: Hackett, 2008), xliv.

66. For more on how Brown's novels employ "*wrested authority*" to engender a critical sensibility in the reader and a counterinstitutional ethos in the mode of Bage, Godwin, Holcroft, and Wollstonecraft, see Stephen Shapiro's Atlantic studies approach in *The Culture and Commerce of the Early American Novel: Reading the Atlantic World-System* (University Park: Pennsylvania State Univ. Press, 2008), 257, 260.

67. "Memoirs of Stephen Calvert" (eight installments, from June 1799 through June 1800) continues Brown's interest in domestic history, paternal authority, and appearances versus reality. Although incomplete, the story focuses on Stephen's familial history in Europe, the family's participation in religious disputes between Protestants and Catholics, and Stephen's attempts to harness his passions in order to succeed socially. As in *Edgar Huntly,* history becomes synonymous with one's personal past, and the story's plot is regulated by the degree to which a character's "memory" is forthcoming. Incidents of doubling and female domestic abuse—"of depravity and tyranny"—are accompanied by moments of self-delusion and self-realization. The novel, writes Robert Arner, may be seen as a continuation of "Brown's interest in William Godwin, an extension into fiction of his continuing inquiry, articulated in *Alcuin* and elsewhere, into the questions of marriage, property, and sex—into, in other words, the rights reserved to, as well as the wrongs done unto, women in the name of, and under the often deceitful banner of, love" (Krause, Reid, and Arner, "Historical Essay," 303).

68. Grabo, "Historical Essay," 456–57.

69. Brown, *Arthur Mervyn,* bicentennial ed., 6, 19.

70. Ibid., 50, 61, 67, 75, 107.

71. Ibid., 121.

72. Frank Shuffelton, "Juries of the Common Reader: Crime and Judgment in the Novels of Charles Brockden Brown," in Barnard, Kamrath, and Shapiro, *Revising Charles Brockden Brown,* 92.

73. Brown, *Arthur Mervyn,* bicentennial ed., 120.

74. Bennett, "Charles Brockden Brown Canon," 227–28.

75. Brown, *Arthur Mervyn,* bicentennial ed., 286, 3, 461.

76. Ibid., 219, 229, 232, 221, 222.

77. Ibid., 379.

78. Weyler, *Intricate Relations,* 2–3.

79. Brown, *Arthur Mervyn,* bicentennial ed., 315.

80. Ibid., 316, 318, 318, 320, 321, 321.

81. Ibid., 321.

82. Weyler, *Intricate Relations,* 3.

83. Brown, *Arthur Mervyn*, bicentennial ed., 322, 321.

84. Ibid., 232, 385, 220, 229, 231, 343, 344.

85. Ibid., 286, 295, 305, 302, 303, 308, 309.

86. Ibid., 286, 397, 412, 414.

87. Ibid., 416, 417, 419, 445.

88. Ibid., 385.

89. Ibid., 250–51, 446.

90. Watts, *Romance of Real Life*, 112–13.

91. Bennett, "Charles Brockden Brown Canon," 232.

92. Michelle Burnham, "Epistolarity, Anticipation, and Revolution in *Clara Howard*," in Barnard, Kamrath, and Shapiro, *Revising Charles Brockden Brown*, 271, 263, 267, 277.

93. Charles Brockden Brown, *Clara Howard in a Series of Letters* and *Jane Talbot: A Novel*, bicentennial ed., ed. by Sydney J. Krause, S. W. Reid, and Donald A. Ringe (Kent, Ohio: Kent State Univ. Press, 1986), 5, 9, 10, 11.

94. Ibid., 13, 15, 16, 17.

95. Donald A. Ringe, *Charles Brockden Brown*, 94.

96. Brown, *Clara Howard*, bicentennial ed., 23.

97. Jane Tompkins, *Sensational Designs: The Cultural Work of American Fiction, 1790–1860* (New York: Oxford Univ. Press, 1985), xvi–xvii.

98. Brown, *Clara Howard*, bicentennial ed., 91, 88, 90, 92.

99. Ibid., 93, 94.

100. Ibid., 94, 95, 96, 104.

101. Ibid., 106–7, 142, 144, 147.

102. Martin Brückner, "Sense, Census, and the 'Statistical View' in the Literary Magazine and Jane Talbot," in Barnard, Kamrath, and Shapiro, *Revising Charles Brockden Brown*, 305.

103. Charles Brockden Brown, *Jane Talbot, A Novel*, bicentennial ed., ed. by Sydney J. Krause, S. W. Reid, and Donald A. Ringe (Kent, Ohio: Kent State Univ. Press, 1986), 227.

104. Ibid., 154, 155, 156.

105. Ibid., 287, 330, 348.

106. Ibid., 348.

107. Ibid., 409, 412.

108. Ibid., 423, 424.

109. Ibid., 427, 428, 430, 431.

110. Watts, *Romance of Real Life*, 54, 58.

3. Historical Representation in the Monthly Magazine and American Review *and the* Literary Magazine and American Register

1. Suzanne Gearhart, *The Open Boundary of History and Fiction: A Critical Approach to the French Enlightenment* (Princeton, N.J.: Princeton Univ. Press, 1984), 13, 10, 58.

2. Everett Zimmerman, *The Boundaries of Fiction: History and the Eighteenth-Century British Novel* (Ithaca, N.Y.: Cornell Univ. Press, 1996), 4.

3. Ibid., 22. While Godwin later concedes that the romance writer is "continually straining at a foresight to which his faculties are incompetent, and continually fails," the essay nevertheless is historically and culturally important to the extent that it engages debates at the end of the eighteenth century about the meaning and function of historical representation relative to the historian and the writer of "romance" or realistic fiction. Despite how Godwin's views were qualified by his European contemporaries, his essay further

documents the eighteenth century's awareness of the fictive nature of history writing and, importantly, helps contextualize attitudes American novelists and historians held in the early national period.

4. Scott Slawinski, *Validating Bachelorhood: Audience, Patriarchy, and Charles Brockden Brown's Editorship of the* Monthly Magazine and American Review (New York: Routledge, 2005), 15, 18, 25.

5. Few reviews of Trumbull's *History of Connecticut* exist, which makes Brown's valuable. The *Hartford Connecticut Courant* for November 23, 1801, vol. 36, no. 1922, contained a "Review of Dr. Trumbull's History of Connecticut," which stated, "In the Supplement to the *(British)* Monthly Magazine, published July 1801, under the head of Retrospect of American Literature, are to be found the following observations." The review sums up how chapters are organized and remarks, "As a complete history of America is only to be collected from the local history of its several states, contributions like the present towards such a general history are particularly valuable." While, says the reviewer, Trumbull gives a "cursory but interesting account of the aborigines of the country," other chapters detail settler purchases, wars, and the growth of Connecticut and New Haven from 1630 to 1635. The reviewer states that from that time forward "is given the civil and political history of the State, to the year 1713," with emphasis on the "ecclesiastical history of Connecticut and New Haven both antecedent and subsequent to the union very properly occupying distinct chapters of the book." The review also appeared in the November 27, 1801, *Boston Mercury and New-England Palladium*, vol. 18, no. 43; the November 30, 1810, *Jenks's Portland (Maine) Gazette* vol. 4, no. 188; and the December 4, 1801, *New-York Commercial Advertiser,* vol. 5, no. 1292.

6. Charles Brockden Brown, "Art. I. [Review of] A Complete History of Connecticut, Civil and Ecclesiastical, from the Emigration of its first Planters from England in 1630, to 1713. By Benjamin Trumbull," *Monthly Magazine and American Review* 1, no. 1 (April 1799): 45.

7. Ibid., 45, 46.

8. Brown's review of Abiel Holmes's *The Life of Ezra Stiles* analyzes a different kind of history—the increasingly popular "great man" biography. Saying that Holmes employs "the chronological method" of historical narrative and that he was probably aware of its shortcomings, Brown suggests improvements to Holmes's history. He remarks, for instance, that it is difficult to write about a complex subject "without systematic division, without throwing the component parts into distinct groups." If the annals had been "more contracted, and afterward a more distinct and systematic sketch" given to various facets of Stiles's life, then the work would have been more pleasing to the eye and effective. However, after stating that Holmes's choice of approach is adequate, Brown goes on to say that one commonly perceived weakness of the history is actually a strength.

Of the criticism that extracts from Ezra Stiles's letters are "too numerous, and unnecessarily burden the pages," Brown remarks: "We think otherwise. We believe that such extracts, if judiciously made, (which in this case we have no reason to doubt), present a more faithful picture of their author's mind, and furnish materials for a more just estimate of his character, than can be readily given by another." Such relics, says Brown, best illuminate the development of Stiles's mind and thus become valuable documents. Importantly, in terms of Brown's later historiographical theory and writing, this remark seems to indicate early on his willingness to depart from conventional wisdom. That is, while such comments resemble Boswell's defense for using extracts from Johnson's letters in his *Life of Johnson* (1791), from Brown's point of view, primary documents such as private letters complement historical narrative. If judiciously chosen, they represent a better evaluation of Stiles's character. It is a view that is consistent with Brown's later attitudes toward historical materials and which Brown would propound more forcefully and creatively in his essays and—after he had had experience writing history—in the prefaces to his historical annals. See his review in the *Monthly Magazine and American Review* 1, no. 1 (Apr. 1799): 47–48.

9. Charles Brockden Brown, "Parallel between Hume, Robertson and Gibbon," *Monthly Magazine and American Review* 1, no. 2 (May 1799): 90, 92.

10. Ibid., 91.

11. Ibid.

12. Ibid., 91, 94.

13. While popular, Robertson's *History of America* seems to have received few reviews in America, aside from Brown's. See *Russell's Gazette* 4, no. 35, July 5, 1798, and the *Porcupine's Gazette* 3, no. 582, Jan. 17, 1799, both of which reprinted a March 17, 1798, Parisian review that remarked, "The history of America was the master-piece of one of the two ablest, or rather one of the two *only* modern historians. . . . To ensure this last volume circulation, 'tis necessary only to name its author, and to remark it possesses all the acuteness of observation that perspicuity of exposition, the art of referring effect to causes, and of mingling with the account of events, the wholesomest and most approved principles of morals and politics, for which this writer was so eminently conspicuous—in short, that it exhibits the talents of Robertson." In an article titled "An Author's Evenings" in the *Port Folio* 1, no. 43 (Oct. 24, 1801), the author remarks of Robertson, "It is very fashionable, among young, students, to read the histories of Dr. Robertson," and his style, "always stately and magnificent . . . is a model of purity. . . . The histories of Charles V. and of America, are constantly read and praised" (338).

14. Charles Brockden Brown, "Art. IV. [Review of] The History of America, Books IX. and X. Containing the History of Virginia to the Year 1688, and of Connecticut to the Year 1652. By William Robertson." *Monthly Magazine and American Review* 1, no. 2 (May 1799): 130.

15. Ibid., 131.

16. Ibid., 132.

17. Samuel Miller, *A Brief Retrospect of the Eighteenth Century*, 2 vols. (New-York: T. and J. Swords, 1803), 1:397.

18. Proud's history was advertised, but not apparently reviewed, in Philadelphia newspapers like the *Gazette of the United States* 13, no. 1680, Jan. 27, 1798. The *Aurora General Advertiser*, no. 2563, May 25, 1799, remarked, however, that Proud's history was "A Work entirely New, Original, and highly Interesting."

19. "Art XII. [Review of] The History of Pennsylvania, in North-America, from the Original Institution and Settlement of that Province, &c. in 1681, till after the year 1742; with an Introduction, respecting the Life of William Penn, and the Society of Quakers; with the Rise of the Neighboring Colonies, &c. &c. &c. By Robert Proud." *Monthly Magazine and American Review* 1, no. 3 (June 1799): 216.

20. Ibid.

21. Kraus, *History of American History*, 121; "Art XII. [Review of] The History of Pennsylvania," 216.

22. "Art XII. [Review of] The History of Pennsylvania," 216–17.

23. Ibid.

24. Wolfgang Schäfer, *Charles Brockden Brown als Literaturkritiker*, Studien und text zur Amerikanstik, Studien Bd. 12 (Frankfurt am Main: Peter Lang, 1991), 136–37.

25. Charles Brockden Brown, "Walstein's School of History. From the German of Krants of Gotha," *Monthly Magazine and American Review* 1, no. 5 (Aug. 1799): 337.

26. Watts, *Romance of Real Life*, 75.

27. Brown, "Walstein's School of History," (Aug. 1799): 336–37.

28. Scott Slawinski, *Validating Bachelorhood*, 14, 18, 59.

29. Brown, "Walstein's School of History," (Aug. 1799): 337, 338.

30. Charles Brockden Brown, "Walstein's School of History," *Monthly Magazine and American Review* 1, no. 6 (Sept.–Dec. 1799): 407–8.

31. Ibid., 409, 410, 411.

32. Brown, "Walstein's School of History," (Aug. 1799): 337, (Sept.–Dec. 1799): 410–411.

33. Slawinski, *Validating Bachelorhood*, 18, 59.

34. Supporting a reading of Brown and women quite different from that in *Validating Bachelorhood* is Brown's publishing, for instance, in June 1799, a letter to the editor titled "Female Society *for the Relief of Widows with Small Children*." Written by "Egeria," the letter addressed "*To the Editor of the Monthly Magazine*" calls Brown a "philanthropist" who is interested in benevolent undertakings and helping the "indigent and the helpless" and goes on to announce the formation and successes of the society by the "ladies of New-York," stating that in the winter of 1798–99 some 250 widows and 643 small children were saved by the society and by "the supply of provisions, cloathing, and needle-work" (173–74). Brown decided to publish a poem "On Miss Linwood's Admirable Pictures in Needle-Work," "By a Lady" (June 1800), and he also printed a dialogue titled "Remarks on Female Politicians" (Dec. 1800), in which a "sprightly and sensible girl" openly questions the domestic politics of "Miss M" and an older gentleman who "is censor of the republic of females" with his "inquisitorial tribunal." Although the essay begins and ends with the "censure of several females . . . for their love of politics," it takes up with gusto the issue of whether "women had not an equal right with men to be politicians" (416–17).

Likewise, Brown is sympathetic to the plight of women in "Selections; Condition of the Female Sex at Constantinople" (Aug. 1799). Observing how James Dalloway described the treatment of "virgin slaves" at the "Avrèt Bazar" or "woman market" in Constantinople, Brown writes in an editorial footnote how women were sold for domestic servitude or on account of their beauty. Commenting on how sexual relations with the "female slaves" are "concealed by the application of poisonous drugs, which often occasion death, and upon detection of pregnancy they are instantly drowned," Brown remarks sympathetically, "One shudders to relate how many of these victims are taken out into the sea at the dead of night, and committed to the deep" (381–82).

For further assessment of Brown and women in the *Monthly Magazine and American Review,* see my review of Slawinski's *Validating Bachelorhood* in *Early American Literature* 41, no. 3 (2006): 577–83.

35. As with the works of other historians during Brown's time, few reviews are available. This is the case for Adams's *Summary History of New-England* as well, where in addition to Brown's review only one other seems to have been published. As the review praises Adams for her "candid and honest elucidation" of events associated with the American Revolution and her ability to avoid being "inflammatory," it also commends her for her efforts to avoid recent "corrupt innovation upon the English language." See "The Literary Review, No. III. A Summary History of New-England," *Columbian Phoenix and Boston Review* 1 (Mar. 1800): 129–31.

Brown, arguably, references Hannah Adams's historical writing as late as 1805, in "A Literary Lady," *Literary Magazine and American Register* 3, no. 20 (May 1805), when "O" remarks on the state of female education, especially relative to female historians, and favorably compares Adams to Mrs. M'Cauley: "It is a little remarkable, and not a little honourable to our native country, that America has produced a woman, who makes no contemptible figure in the historical field. I allude to Hannah Adams, whose personal character is as much superior, in propriety and dignity, to that of Mrs. M'Cauley, as her productions are superior in solidity and usefulness" (360).

36. On the status of women as historians, Nina Baym, in *American Women Writers and the Work of History, 1790–1860* (New Brunswick, N.J.: Rutgers Univ. Press, 1995), writes that

"the amalgam of Protestant Christianity, historicism, and national patriotism in women's historical writing is commonplace for the age, shared by men and women, visible in popular and scholarly texts alike" (47). Christian republican women did not always conform to any "paradigm of sequestered, submissive, passive domesticity," but they largely saw themselves "at work for women, for the nation, for God" (239). While Baym uses Adams's *View of Religion* (1801) as evidence of this, she refers minimally to Adams's *Summary History of New-England,* which, in Brown's judgment, deserved recognition for its strong rationalist impulses. Such a judgment on Brown's part admittedly suggests a bias against didactic histories such as Mercy Otis Warren's, which was immersed in a providential or millennial apparatus.

37. Charles Brockden Brown "Art XXVIII. [Review of] A Summary History of New-England, from the first Settlement at Plymouth, to the Acceptance of the Federal Constitution. By Hannah Adams." *Monthly Magazine and American Review* 1, no. 6 (Sept.–Dec. 1799): 445.

38. Ibid.

39. Callcott, *History in the United States,* 20.

40. "[Review of] A Summary History of New-England," 445.

41. Ibid., 446.

42. Ibid., 447.

43. Chapman, "Notes on the Appendices," 277.

44. "[Review of] A Summary History of New-England," 446.

45. Mary Wollstonecraft, *A Vindication of the Rights of Woman with Strictures on Political and Moral Subjects,* ed. by Katha Pollitt (1792; repr., New York: Modern Library, 2001), 4, 10, 171; Baym, *American Women Writers,* 66–67.

46. Michael W. Vella, "Theology, Genre, and Gender: The Precarious Place of Hannah Adams in American Literary History," *Early American Literature* 28 (1993): 31. Vella also notes that in 1805 William Emerson, Ralph Waldo Emerson's father, reviewed in the *Monthly Anthology* the abridged—school use—versions of Adams's history and Jedidiah Morse and Elijah Parish's *A Compendious History of New England Designed for Schools and Private Families* (Charlestown, Mass.: Samuel Ethridge, 1804). Emerson, says Vella, thought the Morse-Parish history was "peculiar" and "smelled strongly of sect" while Adams's text was "correct, comprehensive, popular" and displayed Adams's sound "judgment, and fidelity as an historian" (28–30).

47. Ibid., 28.

48. Buell, *New England Literary Culture,* 230.

49. Alfred Weber and Wolfgang Schäfer, in collaboration with John R. Holmes, *Charles Brockden Brown: Literary Essays and Reviews* (Frankfurt am Main: Peter Lang, 1992), 229.

50. Charles Brockden Brown, "The Difference between History and Romance," *Monthly Magazine and American Review* 2, no. 4 (Apr. 1800): 251–52, 253.

51. Ibid., 251.

52. Ibid., 252, 253.

53. Michael Cody, *Charles Brockden Brown and the Literary Magazine: Cultural Journalism in the Early American Republic* (Jefferson, N.C.: McFarland, 2004), 9–10, 15, 23, 27.

54. Weber, Schäfer, and J. Holmes identify these essays as Brown's in *Charles Brockden Brown: Literary Essays and Reviews.* While they elaborate on ideas presented in Brown's "Walstein's School of History," they more properly may be identified, says Philip Barnard, as the work of Isaac D'Israeli in *Miscellanies; or, Literary Recreations* (London: Cadell and Davies, 1796) or, in the case of "Modes of Historical Writing," a reviewer from the *Edinburgh Review* (April 1805): 210–12. Brown, observes Barnard, has edited the passage to remove the reviewer's references to "Dr. Ranken." Conversation with Barnard, June 2009.

55. White, *Metahistory,* 40.

56. Brown, "Editor's Address to the Public," 2.

57. James Pettit Andrews, "The Women of the Romans," *Literary Magazine and American Register* 3, no. 20 (May 1805): 331, 332. A report from Andrews's *Anecdotes, &c. antient and modern* (1790).

58. See Brown's "The Romance of Real Life," *Literary Magazine and American Register* 4, no. 26 (Nov. 1805): 396; and his "Remarks on the Russian Empire," *Literary Magazine and American Register* 6, no. 39 (Dec. 1806): 445. In comparing Russia's "national power" to France's, for example, Brown finds that the combination of sheer geographical expanse with people who are "poor, ignorant, disunited, and imperfectly subjected" contributes to Russia's domestic stagnation and makes it a "perfect specimen of political debility" ("Remarks on the Russian Empire," 448). His analysis here, especially in regard to how Russian peasants might be more effectively controlled, can be read one of two ways. Either Brown saw the natural aristocracy of France as unifying the nation is productive, or he was suggesting, ironically, that the Russian people be exploited on top of their present misery, a remark that seems to anticipate similar comments in his "Annals of Europe and America" about subject races and peoples under colonial power. Another political essay, "On the Merits of the Founders of the French Revolution," *Literary Magazine and American Register* 6, no. 38 (Nov. 1806), which is not Brown's, examines "the injury" the French Revolution "has done to the cause of rational freedom, and the discredit in which it has involved the principles of political philosophy" (351).

59. "Observations on Military History," *Literary Magazine and American Register* 7 no. 41 (Feb. 1807): 90. Some of Brown's own publications in the *Literary Magazine and American Register* fall, no doubt, between essays on "domestic manners" and essays on historiography. "Romances" (Jan. 1805) appears to be Brown's; its assertion that "A TALE, agreeable to truth and nature, or, more properly speaking, agreeable to *our own* conceptions of truth and nature, may be long, but cannot be tedious" speaks indirectly to historical concerns and resonates with a modern self-consciousness about time, narrative, and subjectivity (6). Likewise, its remarks about being rooted in the "manners and habits of the age in which they were written" and having, at the same time, a degree of "historical veracity and probability" recall "Walstein's School of History"—and even, in retrospect, some of the fundamental assumptions now associated with modern cultural studies (6). As in our time, Brown's identification of change in "taste and manners" over time and subsequent neglect of certain types of literature in his own is anchored by an understanding of cultural taste, criticism, and literary subjectivity. See "Romances," *Literary Magazine and American Register* 3, no. 16 (Jan. 1805): 6–7.

60. Also, Brown authors the first two paragraphs and the final one, but the four central paragraphs are reprinted, as Michael Cody notes, from the *Critical Review; or, Annals of Literature* (Sept. 1796): 13–14. Note to author, July 2, 2009.

61. "The Law of Nations," *Literary Magazine and American Register* 3, no. 20 (May 1805): 347.

62. Review of John Burk's "The History of Virginia, from its first settlement to the present day," *Literary Magazine and American Register* 3, no. 20 (May 1805): 389, 391.

63. Isaac D'Israeli, "On 'the Enlightened Public,' and 'the Age of Reason,'" *Literary Magazine and American Register* 4, no. 23 (Aug. 1805): 111, 112, 113–14. A reprint from *Miscellanies* (1796).

64. Frank Luther Mott, in his *History of American Magazines* (260–61) states that Stephen C. Foster founded the *Monthly Register and Review* in Charleston in 1805 and then late in 1806 moved to New York. It seems more accurate to say that Foster published the *Monthly Review and Literary Miscellany of the United States* in Charleston from Jan. 1, 1805, through the July 1806 issue and that the *Monthly Register, Magazine, and Review* carried the same material from January 1805 through July 1806. Beginning with the December 1, 1806, issue, Carpenter exclusively edited the *Monthly Register, Magazine, and Review.* Mott correctly

notes that the Charleston magazine contained a "Retrospective History" of the American Revolution and a "History of the Passing Times" and that Carpenter's associate, John Bristed, took over the New York periodical in June 1807, before it stopped in December 1807.

65. "History," *Monthly Review and Literary Miscellany of the United States* 1 (Jan. 1805): 1, 2, 4-5, 8. This same essay, along with other magazine content, appeared in the January 1805 issue of the *Monthly Register, Magazine, and Review* in New York.

66. Ibid., 9, 1-4, 17, 15. American periodicals dating back to the *American Magazine and Monthly Chronicle* (1745) have acknowledged the difficulties of writing history; however, as Carpenter's and Brown's publications reveal, around 1805-07 a series of essays appeared, perhaps influenced in part by publication of Joseph Priestley's *Lectures on History, and General Policy* (Philadelphia: Printed for P. Byrne, 1803). See, for example, "On History," *Evening Fireside; or, Literary Miscellany* 2, no. 16 (Apr. 19, 1805): 124-25; "On History," *Weekly Visitant* 1, no. 9 (Mar. 1, 1806): 65-66. John Bigland's *Letters on the Study and Use of Ancient and Modern History* (Whitehall, Penn.: Printed for W. W. Woodward . . . , 1806) also documents Americans' heightened interest in historical matters. By comparison, British periodicals, also dating back to the mid-eighteenth century, record a similar, though less prolific, interest in historical matters. The *Edinburgh Magazine and Literary Miscellany*, for example, printed various articles in 1802, 1805, and 1806 on the uses of history, and an essay in the *British Critic* 25 (Apr. 1805) went so far as to say, "It is now universally admitted that history and romance have a much more intimate connection than was suspected by the antiquaries of the last century" ("Art. II. Sir Tristrem, a Metrical Romance of the Thirteenth Century, by Thomas of Erceldoune, called The Rhymer," 361). But overall, British magazines do not appear to record the kind of debate one finds in American periodicals or in Brown's various essays.

67. Stephen Carpenter, "History," *Monthly Review and Literary Miscellany of the United States* 1 (Charleston, Jan., 1805): 1-3, 8.

68. Stephen Carpenter, "Prospectus of the *Monthly Register, and Review of the United States*," *Monthly Review and Literary Miscellany of the United States* 1, (Charleston, Jan. 1805): 3A-B, 3C-D.

69. Stephen Carpenter, Preface to *Monthly Review and Literary Miscellany of the United States* 1, (New York, Jan. 1805): AI.

70. Stephen Carpenter, "Address to the Public," *Monthly Register, Magazine, and Review of the United States* 1 (Jan. 1806): 2.

71. Stephen Carpenter, "Sixth Section. Retrospective History of America," *Monthly Register, Magazine, and Review of the United States* 1 (Dec. 1806): 45-46; vol. 2 (Mar. 1807): 262.

72. Stephen Carpenter, "Seventh Section. History of the Passing Times," *Monthly Register, Magazine, and Review of the United States* 2 (Apr. 1807): 335.

73. Holmes, *American Annals*, 2:508.

74. Philip Barnard observes that "On Anecdotes" is edited together from disparate passages in D'Israeli's *A Dissertation on Anecdotes* (London: C. and G. Kearsley, 1793). Note to author, July 5, 2009.

75. D'Israeli, "On Anecdotes," *Literary Magazine and American Register* 5, no. 28 (Jan. 1806), 37.

76. Ibid., 37.

77. Ibid., 38.

78. The text, says Philip Barnard, is originally from Isaac D'Israeli's *Miscellanies*. D'Israeli (1766-1848) was a British writer of Jewish-Italian heritage whose literary works on the lives of various personages earned him significant fame. His *Curiosities of Literature* (1791) included various anecdotes about historical events and people.

79. D'Israeli, "Comparison of Memoirs and History," *Literary Magazine, and American Register* 5, no. 28 (Jan. 1806), 40.

80. Ibid., 40.

81. Philip Barnard, note to author, June 2009.

82. Isaac D'Israeli, "On Literary Biography," *Literary Magazine and American Register* 5, no. 28 (Jan. 1806): 46, 48, 49.

83. Ibid., 51.

84. Weber and Schäfer, with Holmes, *Charles Brockden Brown*, 255.

85. Philip Barnard, note to author, June 2009. .

86. Isaac D'Israeli, "Historical Characters are False Representations of Nature," *Literary Magazine and American Register* 5, no. 29 (Feb. 1806), 117.

87. Ibid., 113.

88. Ibid., 113, 114.

89. Ibid., 116

90. See Judith Sargent Murray's "On the Equality of the Sexes," *Massachusetts Magazine* 2, no. 3 (Mar. 1790): 132–35, no. 4 (Apr. 1790): 223–26. Although Brown, in other words, did not author material such as "Sketches in America, in the Year 1740," which takes a retrospective look at colonial America along the Atlantic, plantation life, slave practices, and female manners, or, probably, "On the Influence of Women," which offers a provocative historical retrospective on why "in religion and politics, female influence has been infinitely greater than appears in historical records," such material is provocative (403). Seeking the "truth of history," the latter essay suggests, in a voice evocative of Brown's own, that "if we throw a philosophic glance on its instructive records, and have the discernment to read what often is not in history, we shall observe that the female character has ever had a singular influence on most of the great characters and great events of human life" (405). See "Sketches in America, in the Year 1740," *Literary Magazine and American Register* 4, no. 27 (Dec. 1805): 403–12; and "On the Influence of Women," *Literary Magazine and American Register* 5, no. 33 (June 1806): 403–5.

91. D'Israeli, "Historical Characters Are False Representations of Nature," *Literary Magazine and American Register* 5, no. 29 (Feb. 1806): 116, 117.

92. Weber and Schäfer, with Holmes, *Charles Brockden Brown*, 259. Weber, Schäfer, and Holmes identify the essay as Brown's. It is, as noted earlier, a reprint from the *Edinburgh Review* (Apr. 1805), 210–12.

93. "Modes of Historical Writing," *Literary Magazine and American Register* 6, no. 39 (Dec. 1806): 431, 432.

94. Ibid., 433, 432.

95. Ibid., 432, 433.

96. Weber and Schäfer, with Holmes, *Charles Brockden Brown*, xvi–xvii.

97. I am grateful for Philip Gould's astute remarks on the importance of and the relationship between sentiment and eighteenth-century faculty psychology. Also extremely useful were the comments on late Enlightenment views of language and its arbitrary nature he included as part of a response to papers delivered at the 1998 Organization of American Historians meeting.

98. The Federalist papers originally appeared in several newspapers, including the *Independent Journal or the General Advertiser* (Oct. 27, 1787–Apr. 2, 1788, and June 14–Aug. 16, 1788) and the *New York Journal and Daily Patriotic Register* (Dec. 18, 1787–Jan. 13, 1788). See Roy P. Fairfield's edition of *The Federalist Papers: A Collection of Essays Written in Support of the Constitution from the Original Text of Alexander Hamilton, James Madison, John Jay*, 2d ed. (Baltimore: Johns Hopkins Univ. Press, 1981), 101.

99. *Autobiography of Thomas Jefferson*, ed. by Dumas Malone (New York: Capricorn, 1959), 35–36.

100. Echoing Godwin and others, Bolingbroke writes in his *Letters on the Study and Use*

of History, A new edition, corrected.(London: Printed for A. Millar, 1752): "But now, as men are apt to carry their judgments into extremes, there are some that will be ready to insist that all history is fabulous, and that the very best is nothing better than a probable tale artfully contrived and plausibly told, wherein truth and falsehood are indistinguishably blended together. All the instances, and all the common-place argument, that BAYLE and others have employed to establish this sort of Pyrrhonism, will be quoted" (98–99).

101. John Locke, *An Essay Concerning Human Understanding,* ed. by Peter H. Nidditch (Oxford, Clarendon, 1975), 405.

102. Pierre Bayle, *A General Dictionary, Historical and Critical: In which a new and accurate translation of that of the celebrated Mr. Bayle, with the corrections and observations printed in the late edition at Paris, is included; and interspersed with several thousand lives never before published. The whole containing the history of the most illustrious persona of all ages and nations particularly those of Great Britain and Ireland, distinguished by their rank, actions, learning and other accomplishments. With reflections on such passages of Bayle, as seem to favor skepticism and the Manichee System,* 10 vols. (1695 and 1697; repr., London: Bettenham, 1734–41), 4:109, 125, 6.

103. White, *Metahistory,* 69.

104. David Levin, *History as Romantic Art* (Stanford, Calif.: Stanford Univ. Press, 1959), 230.

105. Joyce Appleby, Lynn Hunt, and Margaret Jacob, *Telling the Truth about History* (New York: Norton, 1994), 3–4, 7, 10. Historians are constantly reinterpreting historiography, especially relative to postmodern principles. Since Hayden White's 1973 *Metahistory,* Peter Novick's *That Noble Dream* (1988), and H. Aram Veeser's *The New Historicism* (New York: Routledge, 1989) reassessed the issue of history and representation. In addition to Appleby, Hunt, and Jacob's *Telling the Truth about History,* Alun Munslow, in *The New History* (Harlow, England: Pearson, 2003), points to Berkhofer's *Beyond the Great Story* and remarks that "it is clear that the most significant contributions to the narrative-linguistic understanding of history as a form of representation have been made by a group of philosophers and historians that include Hayden White, Frank Ankersmit, Paul Ricoeur, Roland Barthes, Michel Foucault, Artho Danto, Louis Mink and David Carr" (203).

In the last several years, F. R. Ankersmit, *Historical Representation* (Stanford, Calif.: Stanford Univ. Press, 2001), Ernst Breisach, *On the Future of History: The Postmodernist Challenge and Its Aftermath* (Chicago: Univ. of Chicago Press, 2003), J. C. D. Clark, *Our Shadowed Present: Modernism, Postmodernism, and History* (Stanford, Calif.: Stanford Univ. Press, 2004), C. Behan McCullagh, *The Logic of History: Putting Postmodernism in Perspective* (New York: Routledge, 2004), Willie Thompson, *Postmodernism and History* (New York: Palgrave Macmillan, 2004), Joyce Appleby, *A Restless Past* (2005), and Alun Munslow, *Deconstructing History,* 2d ed. (New York: Routledge, 2006) and *Narrative and History* (New York: Palgrave, Macmillan, 2007) examine the intersections of historiography and postmodern or poststructural thought. Thompson, for instance, classifies studies that are defenses of postmodernist historiography, such as F. R. Ankersmit and Hans Kellner's *A New Philosophy of History* (Chicago: Univ. of Chicago Press, 1995) and those that are more critical or suspect of its methods and assumptions.

106. Appleby, Hunt, and Jacob, *Telling the Truth about History,* 61, 67, 102–3. For more on the concepts of nation and national imagination, see Benedict Anderson's *Imagined Communities: Reflections on the Origin and Spread of Nationalism* (London: Verso, 1983).

107. Berkhofer, *Beyond the Great Story,* 16, 76.

108. Ross, "Grand Narrative in American Historical Writing," 673. Like Ross's study, others continue to embrace the idea that historical self-consciousness and uncertainty is a relatively recent phenomenon associated with the "linguist turn" generated by poststruc-

turalists and postmodernists. Beverley Southgates asserts, for instance, that only in recent years "foundational concepts as 'truth,' 'fact,' and 'objectivity' have been exposed as at worst meaningless, and at best in need of radical redefinition," *Postmodernism in History: Fear or Freedom?* (New York: Routledge, 2003), 29.

Likewise, Alexander Lyon Macfie contends that "the origins of the postmodern critique of history advanced by Jenkins and Munslow (and, of course, by many other contemporary philosophers of history) lie, as both Jenkins and Munslow make clear, in the works of a number of mainly French and American philosophers of history, writing over the last hundred years or so, from Saussure to Derrida, Foucault, Lyotard, Barthes, Rorty, Hayden White, and Baudrillard. What most of these authors had in common is an unwillingness to accept the idea that language can be used to describe reality, truthfully and accurately." See Macfie's introduction to *The Philosophy of History: Talks Given at the Institute of Historical Research, London, 2000–2006*, ed. by Alexander Lyon Macfie (New York: Palgrave Macmillan, 2006), 3.

4. The Historical Sketches—and "A Government, Ecclesiastical and Civil"

1. Bennett, "Charles Brockden Brown Canon," 233.

2. Samuels, *Romances of the Republic*, 14–15, 47.

3. Steven Mintz, "Regulating the American Family," in *Family and Society in American History*, ed. by Joseph M. Hawes and Elizabeth I. Nybakken (Urbana: Univ. of Illinois Press, 2001), 17, 37–38, 39.

4. "On the Church," *Churchman's Monthly Magazine* 1, no. 1 (Jan. 1804): 2.

5. Ibid., 4–5.

6. Mintz, "Regulating the American Family," 18.

7. Susan Jacoby, *Freethinkers: A History of American Secularism* (New York: Henry Holt, 2004), 5.

8. Ibid., 29, 43.

9. "An Act of the Legislature of Virginia, passed December 16th, 1785, for establishing 'religious freedom,'" *National Magazine; or, A Political, Historical, Biographical, and Literary Repository* 1, no. 4 (Dec. 1, 1799): 305, 306.

10. "An Act, for Establishing RELIGIOUS FREEDOM, passed in the Assembly of Virginia, in the beginning of the Year 1786," *National Magazine; or, A Political, Historical, Biographical, and Literary Repository* 2, no. 6 (May 1800): 181–82. Publications like "Memorial and Remonstrance of the Citizens of the Commonwealth of Virginia, to the General Assembly of that Commonwealth, against a Bill 'establishing a provision for teachers of the Christian religion'" protested that the special treatment of teachers of religion would be a "dangerous abuse of power" and openly appropriated Madison's language about "ecclesiastical establishments" in civil matters and "spiritual tyranny" as part of its argument. *The American Museum, or Universal Magazine, Containing, Essays on Agriculture* 6, no. 2 (Aug. 1789): 120, 122.

11. "To the PEOPLE of the UNITED STATES," *National Magazine; or, A Political, Historical, Biographical, and Literary Repository* 2, no. 7 (Sept. 1, 1800): 224.

12. Jacoby, *Freethinkers*, 31.

13. Thompson, for instance, argues that those who "wish to perpetuate the happiness of our favoured land, or who wish to perpetuate the blessings of *Liberty*, ought to come forward, at this period of degeneracy, and strenuously to oppose an idea, so absurd, so fatal, as that a republican government can be maintained without the aid and supportive energy of Religion" (3–4). His oration was delivered in the Baptist meetinghouse in Providence, Rhode

Island, at the commencement of Rhode Island College on September 5, 1798 (Providence, R.I.: Printed by Carter and Wilkinson, 1798).

14. Jacoby, *Freethinkers*, 60.

15. G. Adolph Koch, *Religion of the American Enlightenment*, (New York: Thomas Y. Crowell, 1968) 33, 59, 65–66, 73, 90–91, 106, 169–170.

16. Herbert M. Morais, *Deism in Eighteenth Century America* (New York: Columbia Univ. Press, 1934), 120, 141–42, 174.

17. Koch, *Religion of the American Enlightenment*, 262.

18. "Review of Literature," ["A Sketch of American Literature for 1807"], *American Register; or, General Repository of History, Politics and Science*, vol. 2 (Philadelphia: C. & A. Conrad, 1807), 149.

19. Ibid., 151. William Paley (1743–1805) was a utilitarian philosopher and Archdeacon of Carlisle who published *The Principles of Moral and Political Philosophy* in 1785, where he articulated the God as "watchmaker" analogy, along with works on the nature Christianity. His *Natural Theology; or, Evidences of the Existence and Attributes of the Deity* was published in 1802.

20. "Review of Literature," 151.

21. Watts, *Romance of Real Life*, 55–56.

22. Charles Brockden Brown, "Sketches of a History of Carsol" in Dunlap *Life of Charles Brockden Brown*, 1:257.

23. Charles Brockden Brown, "Sketches of a History of the Carrils and Ormes," in Dunlap, *Life of Charles Brockden Brown*, 1:242, 277–78, 287, 394.

24. Dunlap, *Life of Charles Brockden Brown*, 1:258.

25. Clark, *Charles Brockden Brown*, 41. Warner B. Berthoff refutes Dunlap's claim that the project was linked to Brown's interest in a "Utopian system of manners and government" (1:258) by remarking at length:

> No guiding philosophic ideal is presented, no standard of justice is raised. Instead there is a bewildering profusion of administrative designs and historical settlements drawn from a two-thousand-year past: some are frankly unjust, some deliberately oppressive; some lead to revolution and war; some end in equalitarian division of wealth and some in a feudal division of labor; and most depend for coherence and effectiveness not on the triumph of rational principle, but on the imposition of ecclesiastical discipline. In so far as there is a common theme, it is the constant practical problem of organizing and re-organizing institutional society, whether the island-nation of Carsol or the county-size holdings of the Carril-Orme families. The approach, however, is not prescriptive or even ideological, and it is certainly not Utopian, as Allen and Dunlap assumed. Rather it is descriptive and historical, and the product is a narrative catalogue of the varieties of social organization. (151)

He goes on to say that Brown was concerned here with "history as morphology," not as organic development in the sense of Herder and Humboldt. Brown, asserts Berthoff, is interested in "the total movement of history, the sequence and the differences between era," and his "practice is still in the encyclopedic stage of historiography" (152). He says that "It is as though Brown, whose earlier interest in the radical ideology of William Godwin's *Political Justice* is well known, had decided that the problems of political association, and collaterally of historical judgment, involve not simply the constitution of model governments but consideration of the entire active culture" (153). See Berthoff, "Charles Brockden Brown's Historical 'Sketches': A Consideration" in *American Literature* 28, no. 2 (May 1956): 147–54.

Inez A. Martinez, however, observes that while the Crusades the Carrils and Ormes participate in are factual or not original with Brown that his "attempt to write fictional history in which the history of a people rather than of a single protagonist was the focus of interest and the thread of continuity is unique." (186). She argues that Brown saw ficti- tious history—or "benevolent leadership" and "moral utilitarianism"—as a means of of- fering moral inspiration and effecting social cohesion (213). Building on Berthoff's sense that Brown was exploring a "conservative" approach to the problem of "cultural unity" ("Sketches," 154), she views elements of Brown's sketches—for example, his reference to a "Convicata" (196) to police religious heresy or diversity—as suggesting that the "tendency" in Brown's thinking was not only toward "cultural homogeneity" but "unmistakably to- ward totalitarianism" (212). See Martinez, "Charles Brockden Brown: Fictitious Historian" (Ph.D. diss., Univ. of Wisconsin–Madison, 1979).

26. Clark, *Charles Brockden Brown*, 41, 42.

27. Ringe, *Charles Brockden Brown*, 107, 108.

28. Watts, *Romance of Real Life*, 170, 175–76, 172. Just as Watts acknowledges that Brown "consistently denounced the corruption and superstition, the cupidity and oppression of traditional European society," including the Roman Catholic Church, he also admits that the project allowed Brown to "define and promote a particular vision of civilized progress" and that it was "highly ambivalent in its overt reformist simplicity" (171, 175).

29. Philip Barnard, "Culture and Authority in Brown's Historical Sketches," in Barnard, Kamrath, and Shapiro, *Revising Charles Brockden Brown*, 313, 318, 316, 327, 328.

30. Kennedy, "Charles Brockden Brown," folder 9, 687, folder 38, 1695.

31. Bennett, "Charles Brockden Brown Canon," 227.

32. Brown, "Walstein's School of History," (Aug. 1799): 338.

33. In Latin, Bede is *Beda*. The Venerable Bede is known as "the father of English his- tory." Completed around 731, the *Historia Ecclesiastica* is rich in documentary sources and charts the ecclesiastical and political history of England from about the time of Caesar to the time the book was completed. While its central focus is the tension between Roman and Celtic Christianity, Bede commingles historical fact with fictional quotations along with critical assessment of particular rulers. See Kennedy, "Charles Brockden Brown," folder 38, 1689.

34. Brown, "Sketches of a History of the Carrils and Ormes," 1:271.

35. According to *A Catalogue of the Books, Belonging to The Library Company of Phila- delphia: To Which Is Prefixed, A Short Account of the Institution, with the Charter, Laws, and Regulations* (Philadelphia: Bartram & Reynolds, 1807), Brown would have had access to John Oldmixon's *The Critical History of England; Ecclesiastical and Civil*, 3d ed., 2 vols, (London: J. Pemberton, 1728).

Kennedy is also not confident that Brown consulted sources listed in Max Fricke's study *Brown's Leben und Werke*, such as S. Whatley's *A Short Account of a Late Journey to Tuscany, Rome and other Parts of Italy* (London: R. Hett, 1741), J. Hildyard's *An Accu- rate Description and History of the Metropolitan and Cathedral Churches of Canterbury and York, from the First Foundation to the Present Year* (London: Printed for W. Sandby, 1755), and J. Duncombe's *An Historical Description of the Cathedral and Metropolitan Church of Christ, Canterbury, Its Antiquities, etc* (Canterbury: N.p., 1772). Although Brown read Latin, Kennedy is less certain about his use of texts like Muratori's *Rerum Italicarum Scrip- tores* (Modena: N.p., 1723–51). The "Carlovingian authorities," he observes, that Henry C. Lea used in his *Studies of Church History* (Philadelphia: Henry C. Lea's Sons, 1883) are more promising sources for the ecclesiastical elements of Brown's sketches.

With the exception of Bede's *Historia Ecclesiastica*, few to none of the sources Ken- nedy mentions appear to have been available in the Library Company of Philadelphia in the early 1800s. For further discussion of Max Fricke's thesis *Charles Brockden Brown's Leben und Werke* (Hamburg, 1911), see Kennedy, "Charles Brockden Brown," folder 38, 1690.

36. Berthoff, "Charles Brockden Brown's Historical 'Sketches,'" 149.

37. Brown, "Sketches of a History of Carsol"; Dunlap, *Life of Charles Brockden Brown*, 1:171.

38. Kennedy, "Charles Brockden Brown," folder 38, 1679.

39. Brown, "Sketches of a History of Carsol"; Dunlap, *Life of Charles Brockden Brown*, 1:183–84, 181.

40. Brown, "Sketches of a History of the Carrils and Ormes," 1:302, 307, 309, 317.

41. Ibid., 317, 319, 321, 322.

42. Brown, "Sketches of a History of Carsol," 1:242, 249–50, 252.

43. Historically, Christian jubilees are associated with Pope Boniface VIII in 1300, Pope Clement VI in 1350, Pope Urban VI in 1390, and Pope Martin in 1423. Brown, "Sketches of a History of the Carrils and Ormes," 1:262, 327, 387.

44. Ibid., 340, 341, 342, 343.

45. In a letter to the author May 2007, Ed White probes the types of worship that Brown represents in the sketches, raising questions about the extent to which Brown endorsed or believed in "natural religion" of the day.

46. Individual histories also appear in the "Sketches of a History of Carsol." The life of Charles Martel, for instance, receives some attention as it pertains to his capture by the Saracens, purchase, and, later, release by Degarba, and the island's history and governance, specifically the impact of the "evils of war and misgovernment." The life of Michael Praya, a man "profoundly versed in the history and ordinances of the Christian church," and his role as a head tribunal of justice, is relayed, as is the rise and demise of Achmet Pruli, a Syrian slave who plots with Mahomet to conquer Carsol through "foreign invasion" and the "domestic insurrection" of slaves. In addition to Timon, a Roman citizen, according to the annals of Carsol—who met St. Paul, became a "convert and companion" of his, and contributed to the formation of a sect that believed passionately in Christ—the life of Alexandra receives considerable detail, especially as it pertains to her successful rule over Carsol and the manner in which she compares to her "two illustrious contemporaries," Mary of Scotland and Elizabeth of England. Brown, "Sketches of a History of Carsol," 1:182, 193, 203, 224–25, 242.

47. Paul Allen, *The Life of Charles Brockden Brown* (Delmar, N.Y.: Scholars' Facsimiles & Reprints, 1975), 243, 271.

48. Brown, "Sketches of a History of the Carrils and Ormes," 1:271, 299.

49. Ibid., 345, 346, 348.

50. Ibid., 364, 365; Jacoby, *Freethinkers*, 27.

51. Brown, "Sketches of a History of the Carrils and Ormes," 1:365, 381, 387.

52. Ibid., 388, 391, 393.

53. Ibid., 394, 395, 396.

54. Ibid., 395–96.

55. Brown, "Sketches of a History of Carsol," 1:173, 174.

56. Ibid., 176.

57. Ibid., 186, 187–88.

58. Ibid., 188–89.

59. Brown to Joseph Bringhurst, Oct. 24, 1795. Brown writes in *Edgar Huntly*, "All the members of this convent, but he who had been my first benefactor, and whose name was Chaledro, were bigoted and sordid. Their chief motive for treating me with kindness, was the hope of obtaining a convert from heresy. They spared no pains to subdue my errors, and were willing to prolong my imprisonment, in the hope of finally gaining their end. Had my fate been governed by those, I should have been immured in this convent, and compelled, either to adopt their fanatical creed or to put an end to my own life, in order to escape their well meant persecutions." See *Edgar Huntly*, bicentennial ed., 146; Charles Brockden Brown, "Sketches of a History of Carsol," 191.

60. Dunlap, *Life of Charles Brockden Brown,* 1:192–93.

61. Ibid., 194, 195, 208.

62. Ed White to author, May 2007. White concurs with this analysis of the Convicata and its abuses of power but is interested in the extent Brown's speaker, or the narration, "also seems attuned to the unintended but nonetheless positive consequences of the Convicata in purifying the population," of criminal behavior, and "specifically in (indirectly) ending slavery." Dunlap, *Life of Charles Brockden Brown,* 1:196–97.

63. Ibid., 198–200.

64. Ibid., 202, 205.

65. For further analysis of Brown's political thinking about slavery and U.S. nationalism, see Robert Levine's "Race and Nation in Brown's Louisiana Writings" (in Barnard, Kamrath, and Shapiro, *Revising Charles Brockden Brown,* 332–53), especially the way he argues that "Brown's writings on Louisiana and imperialism during this time are a critique (or unmasking) of nationalist exceptionalism" (349–50).

66. Thomas Jefferson to John Adams, May 5, 1817, in *The Adams-Jefferson Letters: The Complete Correspondence between Thomas Jefferson and Abigail and John Adams,* ed. by Lester J. Cappon, vol. 2, *1812–1826,* 2 vols. (Chapel Hill: Published for the Institute of Early American History and Culture, Williamsburg, Va., by the Univ. of North Carolina Press, 1959), 512 (my emphasis).

67. For Melville's use of irony, especially with religious topics, see "Benito Cereno" (1855) and its closing line, "Benito Cereno, borne on the bier, did, indeed, follow his leader." The story was serialized in the October, November, and December issues of *Putnam's Monthly.*

68. John Adams to Thomas Jefferson, Quincy, May 18, 1817, in Capon, *Adams-Jefferson Letters,* 2:515.

69. Barnard, "Culture and Authority in Brown's Historical Sketches," 330.

70. Brown, "Sketches of a History of Carsol," 1:196, 242, 243, 253–54.

71. Callcott, *History in the United States,* 9.

5. Empire and the "Annals of Europe"

1. The "Annals of Europe and America," which Brown was responsible for, are contained in the first five volumes of the *American Register.* The "Annals of Europe" are found in volumes 1, 2, and 4, and the "Annals of America," or a narrative about American events, are in volumes 1, 2, 3, and 5. After Brown's death in 1810, the annals were edited by Robert Walsh (1784–1859). The preface to volume 6 maintains that the "original matter" was not supplied by Brown due to his death and references "a mysterious and inscrutable Providence." Although not a focus in this study, Brown may have initiated some of the volume's material before his death in February 1810. Preface to *American Register; or, General Repository of History, Politics, and Science,* vol. 6 (Philadelphia: C. & A. Conrad, 1806), iii.

2. European countries did not always align such rhetoric with the historical patterns of ancient Israel or the "language of biblical revelation and eschatology," as the New England Puritans did, but such prophetic language nevertheless reflected a symbolic means of interpreting national and international events. See Mason I. Lowance Jr., *The Language of Canaan: Metaphor and Symbol in New England from the Puritans to the Transcendentalists* (Cambridge, Mass.: Harvard Univ. Press, 1980), vii–viii.

3. In the *American Citizen* of New York on May 3, 1804, one of several newspapers most likely, William Duane advertised a proposal for publishing by subscription the *American Annual Register; or, Repository of History, Politics, Literature, Science, and Commerce.* Similar to Brown's *American Register* a few years later, it was to contain "a digested and impartial history of the public transactions of the United States; and a comprehensive review of foreign

history," "State papers, domestic and foreign," and, among other elements, a "Literary Review of American productions." Ambitious as it was in scope, the publication never materialized. Brown's publication focused more on historical and political events.

4. Review of Brown's *American Register, Port Folio* 4 (Oct. 31, 1807): 279.

5. Review of Brown's *American Register, Port Folio* 5 (Feb. 27, 1808): 140–41.

6. See Barnard and Shapiro's introduction to *Edgar Huntly,* where they contend that Brown enthusiastically read radical-democratic materials, specifically the writings of "Mary Wollstonecraft, William Godwin, Thomas Holcraft, Robert Bage, Helen Maria Williams, and Thomas Paine." Brown, they argue, integrated ideas about social order, rational thought, and progressive cultural and political change into his novels, developing an "antistatism" and "distrust of institutions" that would influence his later historical writings as well (xiv–xv).

7. The *American Register; or, General Repository of History, Politics, and Science* itself also included a rich cache of primary documents pertaining to both European and American events that Brown hoped his readers would read for further context. It included "Declaration of Great Britain, on the Failure of the Negotiation with France," "Statistical View of the Prussian Monarchy in 1806," Napoleon's "Letter from the Emperor to the Archbishops and Bishops of France," "State of the Income, Stock, Expenditure and Debt of the British East-India Company for 1803–4–5–6," "Official Papers Relative to the Evacuation of Portugal by the French Army," "Abstract of the Constitution Designed for Spain, by the Emperor Napoleon," and "Proclamation by the Superior Junta of the Government," to name but a few. Publication of such documents authenticated, in Brown's mind, his historical narrative and, in some cases, provided even better perspective on historical events.

The *Philadelphia Gazette* of January 2, 1808, published an advertisement that said the periodical was "modeled on the plan of the British Annual Registers" and that it would "be continued semi-annually, and contain an accurate and impartial history of all national and political events of the passing time."

8. Charles Brockden Brown, "Annals of Europe and America," *American Register; or General Repository of History, Politics, and Science,* vol. 1 (Philadelphia: C. & A. Conrad, 1807), iii.

9. Charles Brockden Brown, "Annals of Europe and America," *American Register; or General Repository of History, Politics, and Science,* vol. 2 (Philadelphia: C. & A. Conrad, 1808), iii–iv.

10. Of the actual history at this time concerning Europe, Patrice Higgonet observes in *Sister Republics: The Origins of French and American Republicanism* (Cambridge, Mass.: Harvard Univ. Press, 1988) that both the American and French Revolutions "stood for popular sovereignty, nationalism, the rights of man, no taxation without representation, Republicanism, and suspicion of established religion" but had vastly different outcomes in regard to political and governmental structures (1). By the late 1790s, American republicanism had taken on an "individualist and pluralist form, and the French Revolution, which forced absolutism to bow to republicanism, and class hierarchies to give way to the ideology of social equality, served to bring Napoleon to power and to make France the premier military and political force in Europe—a position undone by, among other things, the nationalist resistance of surrounding countries. But because Napoleon and France were the dominant political and military force during this period, the effect of his various military campaigns was to further export the revolutionary or Enlightenment ideas of "liberty, equality, and fraternity." For example, as Napoleon challenged the Holy Roman Empire (1806), he abolished feudalism and serfdom, acknowledged within gender limitations the equality of all people, and instituted the Napoleonic Code—a series of legal reforms having to do with commercial and economic law. The code, writes Pieter Geyl, was drawn up with "an eye to the interest of the bourgeoisie" and aimed before everything at "consecrating and sanctifying the rights of property." It saw the right to own property as a natural right—one which was "anterior to

society, absolute, and belonging to the individual." Pieter Geyl, *Napoleon: For and Against*, trans. by Olive Renier (New Haven, Conn.: Yale Univ. Press, 1949), 432.

11. Georges Lefebvre, *Napoleon: From Tilsit to Waterloo 1807–1815*, trans. by J. E. Anderson (New York: Columbia Univ. Press, 1969), 368, 369.

12. Stuart Woolf, *Napoleon's Integration of Europe* (New York: Routledge, 1991), 243.

13. Stuart Semmel, *Napoleon and the British* (New Haven, Conn.: Yale Univ. Press, 2004), 14, 175, 189, 193, 175–76.

14. Ian Copeland, in *The Burden of Empire: Perspectives on Imperialism and Colonialism* (Melbourne: Oxford Univ. Press, 1990), assesses the terms "imperialism" and "colonialism": "Imperialism is about the *acquisition* of power and influence, colonialism is about *what happens* to native societies which come under European rule. Thus, colonialism is a possible *outcome*—the next stage—of imperialism" (2).

15. Edward Said, *Culture and Imperialism* (New York: Vintage, 1993), 9.

16. George Bourne, preface to *The History of Napoleon Bonaparte; Emperor of the French, and King of Italy* (Baltimore: Warner & Ahnna, 1806), v–vi. Also see Hume Robertson's *An Impartial History of the Life of Napoleon Bonaparte, Emperor of France and King of Italy, from His Youth to 1808* (Philadelphia: Mithra Jones, 1808).

17. Articles such as "Political Remarks upon the Present Situation of the United States, with Regard to France and Great Britain" (1807) also provide a glimpse of the era's concerns about European instability, especially as it pertains to American efforts at political neutrality. The author remarks,

France and Great Britain now exhibit the most astonishing spectacle of hatred and animosity which mankind has ever witnessed. On the one hand France has subjugated all Europe, carried terror into Africa, and is about to draw all Asia into the impetuous course of her exterminating legions; the regular and armed force of the whole ancient continent is, as it were, at her command; and Great Britain alone struggles with the intrepidity of despair against oceans of soldiers and bayonets which menace her. On the other hand (thanks however to the protection of a narrow arm of the sea) by the force, wondrous, and yet new in the annals of history, which England possesses in her armies and floating citadels, this haughty nation of Islanders may at any moment be in a condition to carry fire and sword to the remotest regions of the globe!" *Observer* 2, no. 16 (Dec. 26, 1807): 400

18. See, for instance, William Duane's *Aurora* for 1806—which regularly published "Latest Foreign Intelligence" from London newspapers, French war bulletins, and German letters—and "Latest from Europe. Translated for the New York Mercantile Advertiser. Thirtieth Bulletin of the Grand Army. Austerlitz," *Poulson's American Daily Advertiser*, Mar. 13, 1806.

Duane's January 13, 1806, "Political Views of Europe" links Napoleonic aggression with that of Russian "plunder of Poland," and English policy in the Far East that sought to "prohibit the native powers of the country from obtaining aid or advice for their own defence from any nation of Europe!" Although it most likely arrived after Brown's publication of a particular volume of the annals, publications such as the *Monthly Magazine; or, British Register* 22, no. 150 (Dec. 1, 1806) regularly featured "State of Public Affairs in November, Containing Official Papers and Authentic Documents" related to the Grand Army's advancements, battles, and peace treaties. Brown likely appropriated content from sources such as these, but I have not been able to locate evidence that he simply copied source material verbatim into his historical narrative.

19. While periodicals in Brown's day did not, generally, attempt to write contemporary history of events in Europe, histories were published in Brown's time and later in the nineteenth century that document Napoleon's imperial expansion in Europe, Great Britain's

colonial ambitions, and other events. Histories to which Brown's own writing might be compared include James Thomson Callender's *The Political Progress of Britain; or, An Impartial History of Abuses in the Government of the British Empire, in Europe, Asia, and America: From the Revolution, in 1688, to the Present Time* (Philadelphia: Wrigley & Berriman, for W. Young; New York: T. Allen; Baltimore, A. Keddie, 1794), Francois Poultier's *A Sketch of the History of the War in Europe, from Its Commencement to the Treaty of Peace between France and Austria* (New York: Printed by T. Kirk, 1798), Charles Coote's *The History of Modern Europe: Comprising the Progress and Establishment of the British Power in India, the American War, and the Revolution in France: To the Treaty of Amiens in 1802* (Philadelphia: Printed for Birch and Small, 1812), Edward Baines's *History of the Wars of the French Revolution: From the Breaking Out of the War, in 1792, to the Restoration of a General Peace, in 1815* (Philadelphia: M. Carey, 1819), and Sir Alison Archibald's *History of Europe from the Commencement of the French Revolution in 1789, to the Restoration of the Bourbons in 1815* (New York: Harper & Bros., 1842–43).

20. Brown, "Annals of Europe and America," 1:iii.

21. Ibid., 3, 4.

22. Ibid., 6–7, 10, 11.

23. Ibid., 10.

24. Ibid., 15, 17.

25. Ibid., 21, 34, 36.

26. Ibid., 34.

27. Ibid., 37.

28. Ibid., 54, 44.

29. Ibid., 51. The specific context for Brown's referring to himself as an "impartial observer" is his explanation of why the Prussian officers and soldiers could not be blamed for having yielded to Napoleon when under siege at Magdeburg, Erfurth, Spandau, and other fortresses. Napoleon's successes with garrisons of similar strength, says Brown, was ample reason to speedily submit and avoid their "own destruction and that of the towns they defended" (54).

30. Ibid., 51, 40, 57.

31. Ibid., 52, 53.

32. Ibid., 54, 58, 2:31, 34–35.

33. Ibid., 61.

34. Charles Brockden Brown, "Annals of Europe and America," *American Register; or General Repository of History, Politics, and Science* (Philadelphia: C. & A. Conrad, 1809), 4:iii, iv.

35. Ibid., 12, 13.

36. Ibid., 16, 19, 12, 22.

37. Anthony Grafton, *The Footnote: A Curious History* (Cambridge, Mass.: Harvard Univ. Press, 1997), 1, 195, 200.

38. Siraj Ahmed, in "The Theater of the Civilized Self: Edmund Burke and the East India Trials," *Representations* 78 (Spring 2002), examines Burke's understanding of imperialism relative to the "degenerative influence of empire upon the civilized self." He recounts Burke's effort to impeach Warren Hastings, "the Company's former Governor-General (1773–85), for the crimes that his administration had committed in India, which Burke alleged included the violation of property, the destruction of native customs and institutions, and the dishonoring of native women." Burke remarked in February 18, 1788, testimony before the House of Lords that "the Heads of villages . . . were . . . tied together by the feet, . . . thrown over a bar, and there beaten with bamboo canes upon the soles of their feet until their nails started from their toes" and that in addition to publicly violating wives

and daughters the East India Company "put the nipples of the women into the sharp edges of split bamboos and tore them from their bodies." "My Lords," remarked Burke, "I am ashamed to go further"; "those infernal fiends, in defiance of everything divine and human, planted death in the source of life" (28–29). See also Richard Koebner and Helmut Dan Schmidt, *Imperialism: The Story and Significance of a Political Word, 1840–1960* (London: Cambridge Univ. Press, 1965), 1.

39. Wellesley quoted in Brian Gardner, *The East India Company: A History* (New York: McCall, 1971), 154.

40. Allen Edwards, *The Rape of India: A Biography of Robert Clive and a Sexual History of the Conquest of Hindustan* (New York: Julian, 1966), 311.

41. For analysis of how East India Company activities and Indian resistance by figures such as Hyder Ali and Tipu Sultan were represented in the British media at different times, see Amal Chatterjee, *Representations of India, 1740–1840: The Creation of India in the Colonial Imagination* (New York: St Martin's, 1998). More recent studies of British colonial efforts in India include Randolf G. S. Cooper, *The Angle-Maratha Campaigns and the Contest for India: The Struggle of Control and the South Asian Military Economy* (Cambridge: Cambridge Univ. Press, 2003); Nicholas B. Dirks, *The Scandal of Empire: India and the Creation of Imperial Britain* (Cambridge, Mass.: Harvard Univ. Press, 2006); and Robert Traver, *Ideology and Empire in Eighteenth-Century India: The British in Bengal* (Cambridge: Cambridge Univ. Press, 2007).

42. In his fifth *American Crisis* pamphlet (1778), Paine writes that England's "late reduction of India, under Clive and his successors, was not so properly a conquest as an extermination of mankind. She is the only power who could practise the prodigal barbarity of tying men to mouths of loaded cannon and blowing them away. It happens that General Burgoyne, who made the report of that horrid transaction, in the House of Commons, is now a prisoner among us, and though an enemy, I can appeal to him for the truth of it, being confident that he neither can nor will deny it. Yet Clive received the approbation of the last Parliament." *The Complete Writings of Thomas Paine*, ed. by Philip S. Foner, 2 vols. (New York: Citadel Press, 1945), 1:118–19.

William Duane also remarks in *Politics for American Farmers, Being a Series of Tracts Exhibiting the Blessings of Free Government . . . Compared with the Boasted Stupendous Fabric of British Monarchy* (Washington City: Printed by R. C. Weightman, 1807), "When Cobbett was here, the subject of the cruelties committed by the British government in India on the editor of the Aurora, was a constant treat from his pen to the depraved appetite of *federalism*" (33).

43. For a more in-depth study of British colonialism in India and debates as they relate to Brown's historical writing, see Mark L. Kamrath, "American Exceptionalism and Radicalism in the 'Annals of Europe and America,'" in Barnard, Kamrath, and Shapiro, *Revising Charles Brockden Brown*, 354–66.

44. Brown, "Annals of Europe and America," 1:6, 7.

45. Ibid., 17.

46. Ibid., 18, 19.

47. Ibid., 21, 24.

48. Ibid., 24.

49. Edward W. Said, *Orientalism* (New York: Pantheon, 1978), 40, 105, 188; Said, *Culture and Imperialism*, 10.

50. Vron Ware, "Moments of Danger: Race, Gender, and Memories of Empire," in *Feminists Revision History*, ed. by Anne-Louise Shapiro (New Brunswick, N.J.: Rutgers Univ. Press, 1994), 224; Said, *Orientalism*, 63.

51. Brown, "Annals of Europe and America," 1:25.

52. Ibid., 27.

53. Daniel E. Ritchie, "From Babel to Pentecost: Burke's India, Ideological Multicultural-ism, and a Christian Poetics," *Christianity and Literature* 43 (Spring–Summer 1994): 400.

54. Brown, "Annals of Europe and America," 1:33, 10; 2:10, 11, 13–14.

55. Ibid., 2:28.

56. Ibid., 29.

57. Ibid., 29, 30.

58. Ibid., 20.

59. Ibid., 28–29.

60. Ibid., 67. Brown includes two footnotes at this point. The first, which corresponds with "Italy*," reads: "The conduct of France towards Hamburg, Lubeck, Bremen: towards Geueva, Genoa, and the Valais (not to mention Egypt, Holland, Savoy, and the papal terri-tory) was simply the result of power and convenience, without even the plea or pretext of right or justice. To complete the resemblance between these cases and the British invasion of Denmark, i[t] is necessary that this latter should have taken absolute possession of Zea-land, and *not* to have pleaded, as their motive, an impending alliance between Denmark and France." The second footnote, marked "success†," reads: "The English, in demanding of Turkey what was virtually the military possession of the seat of empire, pleaded merely an offensive alliance with Russia, by which they were bound to go to war with those whom Russia thought proper, right or wrong, to go to war with. They likewise complained of the influence obtained by the French in the sultan's councils; but this influence they themselves described as appearing only in the sultan's opposition to the Russian claims."

61. Edmund Burke, "Speech on Mr. Fox's East India Bill," Dec. 1, 1783, *The Writings and Speeches of Edmund Burke*, gen. ed. Paul Langford, vol. 5, ed. by P. J. Marshall and William B. Todd (Oxford: Clarendon, 1981), 383.

62. Brown, "Annals of Europe and America," 2:68, 69.

63. Ibid., 19–20.

64. Mikhail Mikhailovich Bakhtin, *The Dialogic Imagination*, ed. by Michael Holquist, trans. by Caryl Emerson and Michael Holquist (Austin: Univ. of Texas Press, 1981), 324.

65. Uzoma Esonwanne, "Feminist Theory and the Discourse of Colonialism," *Reimag-ining Women: Representations of Women in Culture*, ed. by Shirley Neuman and Glennis Stephenson (Toronto: Univ. of Toronto Press, 1993), 249.

66. Burke, "Speech on Mr. Fox's East-India Bill," 381, 386, 383, 390.

67. White, *Metahistory*, 29, 30–31.

68. Brown, "Annals of Europe and America," 1:10, 11.

69. Ibid., 14, 15, 34, 40.

70. Ibid., 42, 44, 45.

71. Ibid., 47–48, 50.

72. Ibid., 54, 58, 60–61, 63, 64.

73. Ibid., 2:3, 4.

74. Ibid., 4, 5, 9.

75. Ibid., 19, 20.

76. Ibid., 21.

77. Ibid., 35.

78. Levin, *History as Romantic Art*, 229, 182–83.

79. If, in his depiction of Edgar Huntly's fighting with Indians, Brown included the "doleful shrieks" and "contorsions which bespeak the keenest agonies to which ill-fated man is subject" and the "spectacle" of using a "bayonet" to put a wounded Indian out of his misery, he also included philosophical reflection on war, in general, with Edgar telling: "I dropped the weapon and threw myself to the ground, overpowered by the horrors of this

scene. Such are the deeds which perverse nature compels thousands of rational beings to perform and to witness! Such is the spectacle, endlessly prolonged and diversified, which is exhibited in every field of battle; of which, habit and example, the temptation of gain, and the illusions of honour, will make us, not reluctant or indifferent, but zealous and delighted actors and beholders" (*Edgar Huntly*, 201–2).

80. Berthoff, "Literary Career of Charles Brockden Brown," 317, 312, 324.

81. For further background on Brown's Quakerism, see Harry R. Warfel, *Charles Brockden Brown: American Gothic Novelist* (Gainesville: Univ. of Florida Press, 1949), Clark, *Charles Brockden Brown* and Kafer, *Charles Brockden Brown's Revolution*. Additional studies of the influence of Brown's Quakerism on his novels include dissertations by John Ullmer, "The Quaker influence in the Novels of Charles Brockden Brown" (Saint Louis Univ., 1968) and Kenneth J. Kinslow, "Quaker Doctrines and Ideas in the Novels of Charles Brockden Brown" (Univ. of Notre Dame, 1978). These studies illustrate Brown's embrace of Quaker beliefs and practices such as pacifism, equality, and simplicity.

82. Brown, "Annals of Europe and America," 2:38, 39.

83. Ibid., 37, 40.

84. Ibid., 40. One might expect that unlike his novels, where Brown tended to explore Godwinian values of reason and truth in explicit terms, his historical writing, following conventions, would retain a more objective tone. This is true to a large degree, but just as he aimed to be objective in his historical narrative, so he continued to make use of philosophical generalizations or maxims, as when he observes: "Those who are accustomed to examine and compare different accounts of the same military transactions, perceive the insuperable difficulty of gaining exact information on the subject. To comprehend the clearest narrative, a topographical acquaintance with the theatre of war is absolutely necessary" (40). It is important to note here that Brown's use of the phrase "theatre of war" was a rhetorical device commonly found in post-Revolutionary writings, such as the letters of John Adams (circa 1776–78).

85. Ibid., 45, 48–49, 52, 53, 59.

86. Ibid., 59.

87. Ibid., 61, 62, 63, 64. On the topic of a trade embargo against England, Brown writes in a footnote:

This must be understood with some qualification and exception. All commercial restrictions are adverse to the interest of individuals. The very nature of commerce affords endless opportunities of eluding these restrictions. The utmost energies of government cannot avail to their perfect execution. But Prussia obeys the French in imposing these restrictions, and the interest and inclinations of the people and the prince are equally adverse to them. How imperfectly then are they likely to be executed! The utmost connivance and remissness will take place, and in these we may see a fruitful cause of jealousy and complain on the side of France, and convenient pretexts for neglecting or breaking the late treaty. That part of it which relates to the British trade can be executed only be a French army and French agents. (62)

88. Ibid., 4:6.

89. The original newspaper appears to be the *Federal Gazette and Baltimore Daily Advertiser*, which was published three times a week by J. Hewes.

90. "Democratic Impartiality," *Balance and State Journal*, May 26, 1809, 2.

91. In the September 1, 1809, issue of the *Balance and State Journal*, news about Copenhagen was published, reprinted from the *Baltimore North American*. Complaining that democrats are blind to historical inconsistencies, the editorial asks:

Was the attack upon Copenhagen in any respect as deceitful or cruel as that by the French upon Lisbon or Madrid? How many Spaniards were slaughtered in the massacre of Madrid, instigated last year by the bloodhound Murat? How many men, women and children were butchered and ravished by the "Lamb-like" Junot in Portugal? . . . But you do not hear a syllable of complaint from the French faction respecting the injustice of these acts. Their feelings of humanity are not attuned to such sufferings. . . . If we may credit the British, the cause of seizing the Danish fleet was a well grounded apprehension, that it would fall into the hands of the French— Since therefore nature herself consecrates the right of self-defence, the appropriation of an instrument of destructive use to prevent your enemy from anticipating you, is, upon abstract principles, justifiable. (2)

92. Brown, "Annals of Europe and America," 4:iii–iv.

93. Christer Jorgensen, *The Anglo-Swedish Alliance against Napoleonic France* (New York: Palgrave Macmillan, 2004), 90.

94. Ibid., 99, 100, 101.

95. Brown, "Annals of Europe and America," 2:64; Bakhtin, *Dialogic Imagination,* 354.

96. Brown, "Annals of Europe and America," 2:75–76.

97. Kamrath, "American Exceptionalism and Radicalism," 363.

98. Brown, "Annals of Europe and America," 2:78.

99. Ibid., 4:11, 9.

100. Josephine Donovan, *Feminist Theory: The Intellectual Traditions of American Feminism* (New York: Frederick Ungar, 1985), 3, 4.

101. Brown, "Annals of Europe and America," 4:11.

102. Ibid., 14, 15, 18, 29.

103. Ibid., 21, 23, 24.

104. Ibid., 30.

105. Ibid., 31.

106. Ibid., 2:iv.

6. "American Exceptionalism and the "Annals of America"

1. Gordon S. Wood, *The Radicalism of the American Revolution* (New York: Knopf: 1992), 5, 6–7.

2. Eric Werthheimer, *Imagined Empires: Incas, Aztecs, and the New World of American Literature, 1771–1876* (Cambridge: Cambridge Univ. Press, 1999), 2, 11.

3. Andy Doolen, *Fugitive Empire: Locating Early American Imperialism* (Minneapolis: Univ. of Minnesota Press, 2005), xiii, xiv. In contrast to Doolen's understanding of Fourth of July orations, sermons, and other texts in Brown's *Monthly Magazine and American Review* (1799–1800), I do not read Brown as patriotically embracing a Federalist agenda concerned with "imperial warfare and expansionism," or eschewing democratic sympathies (42, 47). "C B" (Brown), for instance, does not hesitate to praise Benjamin Smith Barton's *New Views of the Origin of Tribes and Nations of America* (Philadelphia: John Bioren, 1799), and he flattens the self-authored *Memoirs of Major-Gen Heath* (Boston: I Thomas and E. T. Andrews, 1798) as "delusive" and a "meager journal, a dry gazette account of facts, often trivial and unimportant" (124). It is likely the May 1799 review of "A Sermon, Delivered May 9, 1798, Being the Day of National Fast" is Brown's, but a close reading suggests that his reference to the "zeal" of the John Thornton of Boston, the minister who delivered the sermon, is slightly ironic. Further evidence of Brown's critical stance is his remark that "the

objection which has been made by some against mingling religion and politics, if it be a just objection at all, will lie with full as much, if not greater force against this sermon" (130). Also, just as "B"'s May 1799, review of William Robertson's *The History of America* takes into account the "avarice and cruelty" associated with the settlement of North America and how the "founders of Virginia" searched for "gold, quarrelled and tormented each other, massacred the natives" (131), so his willingness to help Samuel Miller (July 1799) collect historical information for his history of New York is quite open to preserving information about how tribes were eradicated and slaves were introduced into the colony.

Additionally, I believe that the various orations Brown prints and reviews should be read as factual correctives or ironic commentaries on religious exuberance and the political status quo. Brown, for instance, does *not* in his August 1799 issue endorse John Lowell Jr.'s twenty-seven-page "Oration, pronounced July 4th, 1799, at the request of the Inhabitants of the Town of Boston." Rather, he deconstructs its emotional claims and exhortations about the American and French revolutions, saying that beliefs that the French have infected American sects in a way that will "overwhelm all religion, law, and liberty" are simply wrong-headed: "That sentiment of gratitude, so natural and so powerful, after the termination of our revolution, towards our then ally, has been artfully wrought upon, to lead the people to regard with equal sensibility and approbation, the conduct of the successive ruling parties in France. The absurdity of this claim of gratitude, and its abuse, are, indeed, palpable; but the charm is now dissolved, and we are no longer to apprehend being the dupes of such dangerous hallucinations" (374).

Likewise, Brown's review of Jedidiah Morse's and Josiah Bartlett's "A Prayer and Sermon, delivered at Charleston, Dec. 31, 1799, on the death of George Washington" (Feb. 1800) is not an endorsement of Federalist or orthodox religious belief. Rather, in accounting for the "numberless discourses, orations, eulogies, poems, & c.," Brown praises the lack of "pomp and extravagance of diction" in Morse and Bartlett's eighty-two-page pamphlet. Yet toward the end of his review he remarks, with an irony that would appear later in his Volney translation and annals in the *American Register*, "But upon recollecting how deeply Dr. M. has lately embarked in the business of detecting conspiracies, publishing intercepted dispatches, and exposing French villainy, we concluded, at length, that he was unwilling to let an opportunity escape of adding another exertion to the very zealous and laudable services which he has already, in his way, rendered his countrymen" (127).

In this spirit, Brown also interrogates, it seems, an imperial ethos in his novels, especially with his representation of Indian displacement and the "encroachments" by English colonists in *Edgar Huntly*. For additional information on Brown and the late Enlightenment, particularly Voltaire, see my earlier study "Brown and the Enlightenment: A Study of the Influence of Voltaire's *Candide* in *Edgar Huntly*," *American Transcendental Quarterly*, new ser. 5, no. 1 (Mar. 1991): 5–14.

4. Lawrence Buell to author, Mar. 1, 1996. Buell suggests that Brown seems to be part of a larger tradition of ironic or dissenting American historians who date back to Samuel Peters and Isaac Backus in the eighteenth century. See his *New England Literary Culture*, where he discusses Hildreth's "sardonic astringency" and ability to expose "self-interested" behavior in Hildreth's six-volume *History of the United States* (1849–51). He astutely remarks that Hildreth's "*History* was by no means a throwback to the annalism of Thomas Prince and Abiel Holmes. It was informed throughout by a consistent though complex point of view, namely that of a hardheaded social critic with a keen sense of social justice." Disposed toward critiquing "political and religious establishments," Hildreth sharply contrasted the romantic historiography of Bancroft (231). Committed to writing history on the basis of facts, he asserts that "Hildreth's Olympian 'objectivity' of perspective served, in his historical circumstances, as an instrument for satirical corrective" (463).

5. Greene, *Intellectual Construction of America*, 5, 6.

6. Ernest Lee Tuveson, *Redeemer Nation: The Idea of America's Millennial Role* (Chicago: Univ. of Chicago Press, 1968), viii. In addition to Greene's and Tuveson's remarks on the history of American exceptionalism, see John M. Murrin, "The Jeffersonian Triumph and American Exceptionalism" *Journal of the Early Republic* 20 (Spring 2000): 1–25. So embedded was this belief in American history and culture, says Amy Kaplan, that "the absence of the United States in the postcolonial study of culture and imperialism curiously reproduces American exceptionalism from without." "The United States," she writes, "either is absorbed into a general notion of 'the West,' represented by Europe, or it stands for a monolithic West. United States continental expansion is often treated as an entirely separate phenomenon from European colonialism of the nineteenth century, rather than as an interrelated form of imperial expansion. The divorce between these two histories mirrors the American historiographical tradition of viewing empire as a twentieth-century aberration, rather than as part of an expansionist continuum" ("Left Alone with America," 17). The history and mythos of American exceptionalism, in other words, are still with us but also have deep roots in early colonial history and historiography. Historian William Earl Weeks concurs: "While no one ever has denied the existence of an American nationalism, until quite recently there has been widespread reluctance even to acknowledge the existence of an American imperialism or an American empire." This has changed in recent years, but the perception that post-Revolutionary America had imperial ambitions along the lines of the French or the English is still one that is reluctantly embraced. "American Nationalism, American Imperialism: An Interpretation of United States Political Economy, 1789–1861," *Journal of the Early Republic* 14, no. 4 (Winter 1994): 486.

7. Clark, *Charles Brockden Brown*, 284–85. Born to Catholic parents, William Duane (1760–1835) was trained as a printer in Ireland, worked as a reporter in London, and went to Calcutta, India, in 1787 to edit a number of newspapers, including *Indian World*. Because of criticisms against the East India Company and his opposition to the local government, he was jailed and then deported back to England in 1795. He later moved to New York and then Philadelphia, where he and Benjamin Franklin Bache edited the *Aurora*, which became a leading radical newspaper that consistently, but not always, supported Jefferson's policies. Duane also sought to reform the Pennsylvania constitution. He retired from the *Aurora* in 1822.

8. Watts, *Romance of Real Life*, 177, 180, 160, 161, 164–65.

9. Ibid., 25, 168, 177.

10. Brown, "Annals of Europe and America," 1:66.

11. John B. Colvin's *Republican Policy; or, The Superiority of the Principles of the Present Administration over Those of Its Enemies, Who Call Themselves Federalists* (Frederick, Md.: N.p., 1802) and Allan Bowie Magruder's *Political, Commercial, and Moral Reflections on the Late Cession of Louisiana to the United States* (Lexington [, Ky.]: Printed by D. Bradford, 1803) are typical of the period's conflicting views over Louisiana. Colvin remarks, "The federalists may now continue to rave and to rant; to call names and to prostitute the small understandings which God has given them. They may roar their lungs into pieces about Jefferson and Gallatin, and Louisiana, and the Bank Stock" (23). Magruder, however, writes, "When I contemplate the train of incident that occasioned the late purchase of Louisiana, I perceive the same benevolent hand of Providence, that originally led to the discovery of this country" (137).

Even one year after the acquisition of Louisiana, on May 11, 1804, Abraham Bishop observed that "to federalists this territory, for which they would have shed blood, now seems a barren waste, where no verdure quickens; but to us it appears fruitful, abounding in broad rivers and streams, producing whatever is necessary to our commerce with foreign nations" (6). And on May 12, 1804, historian David Ramsay passionately asserted,

"Louisiana is ours! If we rightly improve the heaven sent boon, we may be as great and as happy a nation as any on which the sun has ever shone, . . . but with two exceptions, the acquisition of Louisiana is the greatest political blessing ever conferred on these States" (6). See Abraham Bishop, *Oration, in Honor of the Election of President Jefferson, and the Peaceable Acquisition of Louisiana, Delivered at the National Festival, in Hartford, on the 11th of May, 1804* ([New Haven, Conn.]: Printed for the General Committee of Republicans. From Sidney's Press, 1804) and David Ramsay, *An Oration on the Cession of Louisiana to the United States delivered on the 12th of May, 1804 at Charleston, South-Carolina,* (Newport [, R.I.]: Reprinted and sold wholesale and retail, by Oliver Farnsworth, 1804).

12. Brown, "Annals of Europe and America," 1:67.

13. Ibid., 67, 68, 69.

14. Ibid., 70, 72–73.

15. John A. Garraty and Robert A. McCaughey, *The American Nation: A History of the United States,* 6th ed. (New York: Harper & Row, 1987), 188.

16. Charles Brockden Brown, *An Address to the Government of the United States, on the Cession of Louisiana to the French; and on the Late Breach of Treaty by the Spaniards: Including the Translation of a Memorial, on the War of St. Domingo, and Cession of the Mississippi to France, Drawn Up by a French Counsellor of State* (Philadelphia: John Conrad, 1803), 62, 70, 73, 74. Brown's critique of the inhumanity of slavery continues and is most penetrating when he remarks: "Whom a cruel servitude inspires with all the vices of brutes and all the passions of demons; whose injuries have been so great that the law of self-preservation obliges the State to deny to the citizen the power of making his slave free; whose indelible distinctions of form, colour, and perhaps of organization, will forever prevent them from blending with their tyrants, into one people; who foster an eternal resentment at oppression, and whose sweetest hour would be that which buried them and their lords in a common and immeasurable ruin" (73). Recently, Brown scholars have identified "A Negro's Lamentation. Written at Charleston" as Brown's. See the *Monthly Magazine* 3, no. 5 (Nov. 1800): 398.

17. Ibid., 77, 80, 79, 86.

18. Clark, *Charles Brockden Brown,* 268.

19. Daniel Edwards Kennedy writes in his unpublished biography that "the Philadelphia *Gazette* for 18 February 1803 notices the forthcoming second edition, and (quoting the *Gazette*) that it "appears that the rapid sale of the first edition of this work, and the acknowledged importance of its contents to the interests of America, have induced the publishers to begin a larger impression, on a more convenient and cheap scale" (folder 33, 1584). See Brown, *An Address to the Government of the United States, on the Cession of Louisiana to the French* A New Edition, Revised, Corrected and Improved. Published by John Conrad & Co. (Philadelphia and Baltimore) and Rapin, Conrad & Co. (Washington City); H. Maxwell, Printer. [Feb. 18] 1803.

20. Charles Brockden Brown, *Monroe's Embassy, or the Conduct of the Government, in Relation to Our Claims to the Navigation of Mississippi, Considered* (Philadelphia: John Conrad, 1803), 52–53, 54, 57.

21. Registering colonialist attitudes of the day, Brown also remarks in his June 20, 1803, letter to Samuel Miller: "The eighteenth century will likewise be ever memorable for the colonization of New Holland. This is the only considerable portion of the globe that remained until lately unexplored & unclaimed by European nations. . . . On an impartial survey of the globe we inhabit every dispassionate observer must perceive that the last age has forwarded in a wonderful [degree] & unexampled degree the progress of mankind to that state in which the most distant parts will become members of the same vast community." Charles Brockden Brown, "Editor's Address to the Public," *Literary Magazine and American Register* 1, no. 1 (Oct. 1, 1803): 5.

22. Levine, "Race and Nation," 349–50, 347.

23. Watts, *Romance of Real Life,* 131–32.

24. Evidence perhaps of Brown's moderating position on America as a "redeemer nation" is his response to Volney: "These will doubtless be thought very daring assertions, after all the eulogies lavished on this people by their own writers, and by those of Europe, and after the motion in congress, to decree that *their nation is the wisest and most enlightened upon earth** (xv–xvi). Brown writes in a footnote: "* Where is the record of this motion to be found?—TRANS." See C. F. Volney, *A View of the Soil and Climate of the United States,* trans. by Charles Brockden Brown (Philadelphia: J. Conrad, 1804), xv–xvi.

25. Brown's embrace of a secular sensibility can also be found in his last published work, his "Sketch of the Life of General Horatio Gates" (1809–10). Published serially in three issues of Dennie's *Port Folio* (the last published days after Brown's death), Brown's biography of the former Loyalist turned Revolutionary War hero is completely lacking in the rhetoric of national redemption. Instead, Brown writes of Gates's accomplishments relative to the defeat of Burgoyne: "How far the misfortunes of Burgoyne were owing to accidents beyond human control, and how far they are to be ascribed to individual conduct and courage of the American commander, would be a useless and invidious inquiry. Reasoning on the ordinary ground, his merits were exceedingly great, and this event entitled him to a high rank among the deliverers of his country" (481). Words such as "misfortunes" and "accidents" suggest a secular sensibility much in line with that expressed in his private life. In short, while it is not easy to trace Brown's later orthodoxy, especially as it mingled with notions of national destiny, it seems more accurate to say that Brown did *not* sustain the "boisterous rhetoric of manifest destiny" he expressed in his 1803 Louisiana pamphlets—that, instead, his later thinking and writing reflect a drifting away from the orthodoxy of his peers.

An influence perhaps of Brown's interest in keeping history and providential design separate may be the essay "On Literary Biography," which he selected and edited: "Burnet, in the 'History of his own Times,' is continually appealing to God and his conscience for the veracity of his work. . . . Our bishop had warm prejudices, and a lively imagination; indulging these to an excess, he left far behind him the sober truth of 'a faithful chronicler'" (48), in the *Literary Magazine and American Register* 5, no. 28 (Jan. 1806): 45–51. Regarding his personal correspondence, for instance, in an October 16, 1807, letter to W. Keese, Brown congratulates Keese on his newborn son, telling him that he hopes the "powers" above will be good to his son (120). As for his own children, however, Brown confesses that when he reflects on the "innumerable chances" against his living to see the "fate" of his children he "give[s] all wishes to the air" (119). Likewise, in his last known private letter (dated 1809), he relates to his wife, Elizabeth, the nature of his travels near Hoboken and his general lack of health. And in telling her about his passing through the village of Passaick, he writes, "Chance gave me, for a companion, a well disposed, well informed Virginian" (87). See Dunlap *Life of Charles Brockden Brown,* vol. 2.

26. Watts, *Romance of Real Life,* 177.

27. Brown, "Sketches of a History of Carsol," 1:243; Brown, "Sketches of a History of the Carrils and Ormes"; Dunlap, *Life of Charles Brockden Brown,* 1:387.

28. Charles Brockden Brown, *Address to the Government,* 40, 15, 21, 22, 74; Brown, *Monroe's Embassy,* 54.

29. Charles Brockden Brown, *An Address to the Congress of the United States, on the Utility and Justice of Restrictions Upon Foreign Commerce. With Reflections on Foreign Trade in General, and the Future Prospects of America* (Philadelphia: C. & A. Conrad, 1809), 86–87.

30. Cecelia Tichi, "Charles Brockden Brown, Translator," *American Literature* 44 (1972): 5–6.

31. Volney, *View of the Soil and Climate,* 399. For example, in his "Sketch of the Life of General Horatio Gates," *Port Folio,* 3d ser., 2 (Nov. 1809): 383–90, Brown comments on Native American complicity with the British: "The Indians who composed a large part of St. Leger's army, began to display their usual fickleness and treachery, and after many efforts made by the British general to detain them, finally resolved to withdraw" (388). Brown refrains from using a derogatory term like "savages," yet points to native "fickleness and treachery."

32. Volney, *View of the Soil and Climate,* 381, 385.

33. Charles Brockden Brown, *Address to the Government,* 22.

34. Brown, "Annals of Europe and America," 1:74, 73.

35. Charles Brockden Brown, *Address to the Government,* 92. Brown, "Annals of Europe and America," 1:70.

36. In the July 8, 1803, issue of the *National Intelligencer,* a pro-Jefferson newspaper, Smith wrote: "By the cession of Louisiana, we shall preserve peace, and acquire a territory of great extent, fertility and local importance." After the purchase, he wrote in a January 30, 1804, editorial, "Never have mankind contemplated so vast and important an accession of empire by means so pacific and just, and never, perhaps, has there been a change of government so agreeable to the subjects of it. May the example go forth to the world, and teach rulers the superiority of right to violence." By contrast, the *Boston Columbian Centinel,* July 13, 1803, and the *Boston Mercury and New-England Palladium,* Aug. 16, 1803, were among those against the purchase because of the secrecy with which it was conducted, the large amount of money needed to make the purchase, and the ability to actually settle on land that was generally unseen.

37. Patricia L. Dooley, *The Early Republic: Primary Documents on Events from 1799 to 1820* (Westport, Conn.: Greenwood, 2004), 150.

38. Murrin, "Jeffersonian Triumph," 12–13. For more on the Louisiana Purchase, Federalism, and Brown's political pamphlets, see Robert S. Levine's study. He posits that Brown, from a more liberal northern Federalist perspective, attempted to use his Louisiana pamphlets not only to "bring the Louisiana Territory under the control of the United States but also to prompt U.S. citizens toward respect for peoples of color, particularly the black rebels of Saint-Domingue, while raising questions about U.S. exceptionalism." "Race and Nation," 335. Despite his shared perspective with some northern Federalists on the Louisiana Territory, Brown's contemporaries, as shown elsewhere in my study, saw Brown as anything but a Federalist on constitutional and other matters. In William Duane's *Aurora General Advertiser,* a contributor to the November 23, 1803, issue writes, "The federalists seize on every trifling circumstance to throw doubts in the way of our taking possession of Louisiana and New Orleans; they now tell us that we cannot take possession of Louisiana because Spanish officers yet exercise authority over it."

39. Brown, "Annals of Europe and America," 1:75–76.

40. Hildreth, for example, states:

The compliant Jefferson, dreading the interference of France in the dispute with Spain, had pointedly called the attention of Congress to this trade, "as an attempt to force a commerce into certain ports and countries in defiance of the laws of those countries, tending to produce aggression on the laws and rights of other nations, and to endanger the peace of our own." Upon this hint, Logan brought a bill into the Senate to prohibit altogether the trade with the new empire of Hayti. But as the blacks, beyond all question, were de facto an independent nation, this was thought to be carrying complaisance toward France a little too far. The most that could be obtained, and that not without a great deal of opposition, was an act requiring armed vessels to give bonds not to use their armaments for any unlawful purpose, but only for resistance and defense in case of involuntary hostilities; and to bring them back to the United States. Richard Hildreth, *The History of the United States of America*, 6 vols. (New York: Harper & Bros, 1856), 5:547.

Adams, however, in his *History of the United States of America*, vol. 1: *The First Administration of Thomas Jefferson* (New York: Charles Scribner's Sons, 1910) says that the "story of Toussaint Louverture has been told almost as often as that of Napoleon, but not in connection with the history of the United States" (378). He goes on to write of the racial and political composition of Haiti, the subsequent conflict of power between different racial populations, and Congress's Act of June 13, 1798, "suspending commercial relations with France and her dependencies" (383). He also recounts the treaty negotiated by Edward Stevens to resume trading between the two nations and the first "overt act of independence" taken by Toussaint (384–85, 387). Yet of the Jefferson administration's policy toward Toussaint, there is limited discussion. As a result of the treaty of Morfontaine, the United States began treating Santo Domingo as a "French colony" while Napoleon schemed to overthrow the black leader and to take him prisoner (389). While Adams does not tell the story of General Leclerc's expedition to Haiti, he does tell of the successful efforts of Leclerc and the eventual imprisonment of the black leader (397–98).

41. It is important to note that Brown had reason to play down the aspirations of rebels on Santo Domingo. His family was involved in the mercantile business, and, as he relates to his wife, Elizabeth Linn, on March 25, 1804, the rebellion cost him personally and financially: "What sad news has this day brought! Some three months ago we sent a vessel to St. Domingo with a valuable cargo; a young man, our particular friend and kinsman, the hope and joy of a numerous and worthy family, went as supercargo. This day tells us that he and the captain are dead, and by their death the vessel and cargo, worth $15,000, are probably lost and certainly exposed to great delay and imminent risk." Despite this connection to Santo Domingo, in a later political pamphlet Brown articulates ideas sympathetic to colonized populations in this part of the world. This letter and others to Elizabeth Linn are available at the Harry Ransom Center, Univ. of Texas at Austin. See also Clark, *Charles Brockden Brown*, 212.

42. Brown, *Address to the Congress*, 72.

43. Brown, *Address to the Government*, 5, 12, 31, 62–63.

44. Ibid., 72–73.

45. Bakhtin, *Dialogic Imagination*, 324–25.

46. Brown, *Monroe's Embassy*, 39.

47. Brown, *Address to the Government of the United States*, 77, 86, 92.

48. Charles Brockden Brown, "Sketches of a History of Carsol," 200. Brown also shows his awareness of how sex and power worked in master-slave relationships. He writes:

> The morality current in Carsol, allowed the master to exact what services he pleased from his slave. The latter lived for no end but the gratification of the former, and provided no cruelty was wantonly employed, there was no bounds to the reasonable demands of the lord, but such as mere physical capacities established. The female slave was considered as performing her mere duty, in gratifying her master's appetites, and in bringing forth and nourishing those who will belong to him by the double title of father and master. Intercourse with the slave, was not considered as interfering with the rights of matrimony. No moral, nor ecclesiastical, nor legal cognizance was taken of such transactions. (202)

See Brown's "Sketches of a History of Carsol" and "Sketches of a History of the Carrils and Ormes" in William Dunlap's *Life of Brown*, 1:170–258, 262–396 and Paul Allen's *Life of*

Brown, 170–222, 242–358. Other fragments appear in three issues of the *Literary Magazine,* which are discussed by Charles Bennett.

49. Levine, "Race and Nation," 338, 339. Brown also arguably registers antislavery sentiments by publishing an obituary on the death of James Pemberton on February 9, 1809, presumably written by him, in his *American Register.* The author writes that Pemberton was a Quaker "merchant of unimpeached integrity" who managed the Pennsylvania hospital from "motives of pure benevolence." In addition to being a "religious man" who was "untainted with bigotry and unsullied with hypocrisy," he "evinced the strongest partiality for the rights, liberties, and prosperity of Pennsylvania." "Nor were his exertions as president of the Abolition society, in obtaining the freedom of the *much injured black people,* less conspicuous than in his other diversified services to mankind in general." Brown's use of italics (and other punctuation) for emphasis dialogically underscores how blacks in Philadelphia and the early Republic had been abused and disenfranchised under the system of slavery and the ways Pemberton, who emulated "Christ," was an "example of true charity to his own society," an individual "always in the practice of compassionate assistance to suffering humanity!" Brown, obituary, *American Register* 5 (1809): 268.

50. Levine, "Race and Nation," 349–50. Also see Philip N. Edmundson's intriguing dissertation, "The St. Domingue Legacy in Black Activist and Antislavery Writings in the United States, 1791–1862," in which Brown, along with Leonora Sansay, is understood as using the Santo Domingo slave rebellion to interrogate the limited mentalities of Atlantic male national characters relative to a larger antislavery effort (Ph.D. diss., Univ. of Maryland, 2003).

51. Brown, "Annals of Europe and America," 1:76–77, 78–79.

52. Dana D. Nelson, "Economies of Morality and Power: Reading 'Race' in Two Colonial Texts," *A Mixed Race: Ethnicity in Early America,* ed. by Frank Shuffelton (New York: Oxford Univ. Press, 1993), 28.

53. John Francis Bannon, *The Spanish Borderlands Frontier 1513–1821* (1970; repr., Albuquerque: Univ. of New Mexico Press, 1974), 209.

54. Buckner F. Melton Jr., *Aaron Burr: Conspiracy to Treason* (New York: Wiley, 2002), 83.

55. Garraty and McCaughey, *American Nation,* 204.

56. Newspapers that covered the trial and related events include the *New York American Citizen, Charleston (S.C.) Courier, Lexington Kentucky Gazette,* and the *Raleigh (N.C.) Minerva.* Other publications include *A Plain Tale Supported by Authentic Documents Justifying the Character of General Wilkinson* (New York: N.p., 1807); John Wood, *A Full Statement of the Trial and Acquittal of Aaron Burr, Esq.* (Alexandria, Va.: Printed by Cottom and Stewart, 1807); J. H. Daveiss, *A View of the President's Conduct Concerning the Conspiracy of 1806* (Frankfurt, Ky.: from the Press of Joseph M. Street, 1807); and Daniel Clark, *Proofs of the Corruption of Gen. James Wilkinson, and of his Connexion with Aaron Burr with a Full Refutation of his Slanderous Allegations in Relation to the Character of the Principal Witness Against Him by Daniel Clark* (Philadelphia: William Hall, Jun. & George W. Pierie, Printers, 1809). See Thomas Perkins Abernethy, *The Burr Conspiracy* (New York: Oxford Univ. Press, 1954), for a complete list of primary sources.

57. In addition to an account of "The Conspiracy" in the December 4, 1806, issue of the *Aurora General Advertiser,* Brown would have had access to materials published in the January 28, 1807, *United States Gazette,* such as a reprinting of the *Richmond Inquirer's* publication of "Burr's Conspiracy," in which the author claims that Burr's "scheme was viewed with the greatest satisfaction by the executive government of the United States, because it resembled their favourite plan of creating a military force upon the south western frontier." Likewise, Brown would have had access to *Poulson's American Daily Advertiser,* Feb. 2, 1807, and its coverage of William Eaton's January 26, 1807, deposition in Washington.

58. Nicholas Rombes, "Mutilated Interpretations: The Dialogic Poetics of Brown's Late Historical Writings," paper delivered Oct. 24, 1998, at the Revising Charles Brockden Brown Conference, hosted by the University of Pennsylvania, the McNeil Center for Early American Studies, and the Library Company of Philadelphia. Rombes also insightfully remarks that Brown's analysis of the Burr conspiracy casts doubt on claims that Brown's career began in radicalism but ended on a conservative note. Instead, he suggests, Brown's interpretive stance with Burr provides a glimpse into Brown's fascination with the "ideological play between order and anarchy, control and freedom, sincerity and duplicity"— elements that characterize Brown's most engaging fiction.

59. Brown, "Annals of Europe and America," 2:79, 80–81.

60. Ibid., 1:78.

61. Ibid., 2:83.

62. Ibid., 84, 86.

63. Ibid., 87.

64. Ibid., 87–88.

65. The history of Spanish American wars of independence from about 1763 to 1825 is a complicated one. And while there were many early heroes who set the stage for the liberation of countries such as Argentina, Brazil, and Chile, Francisco de Miranda is certainly one of the more colorful and controversial figures. Mario Rodríguez, for example, suggests Miranda can be called the "first 'liberator' of Spanish America" because of his efforts to liberate Venezuela from Spain (*"William Burke" and Francisco de Miranda: The Word and Deed in Spanish America's Emancipation* [Lanham, Md.: Univ. Press of America, 1994], 506). William Spence Robertson also recognizes Miranda's virtues as a "patriot"; however, he also acknowledges that Miranda may be seen as "mercenary soldier," an opportunist who loved Venezuela but also enjoyed a bountiful pension from England (*Rise of the Spanish-American Republics* [1918; repr., New York: Free Press, 1965], 80). "Incidents," he writes, "in the career of this chronic revolutionist . . . raise the query whether or not he was engaged in the attempt to liberate Spanish America for selfish gain." Brown clearly saw Burr and Miranda as being the same "type" (81).

Contemporary reactions to Francisco de Miranda's attempted invasions of Venezuela are plentiful in newspaper and periodical publications. Articles in the March 26, 1806, *Aurora General Advertiser* and the August 14, 1806, *United States Gazette*, both of Philadelphia, referred to Miranda as an "adventurer." Over two hundred reports or editorials were published in Pennsylvania publications alone between 1805 and 1809, when attempts subsided. See also *Poulson's American Daily Advertiser* and the *Democratic Press*, newspapers Brown could have easily read.

James Biggs's pamphlet *The History of Don Francisco de Miranda's Attempt to Effect a Revolution in South America* (Boston: Oliver and Munroe, 1808) is also typical, remarking in his preface that he aimed to "give account of the commencement, progress and termination of Miranda's attempt to effect a revolution in South America" and that by countering the "fictions of rumor and the exaggerations of ignorance" it would be possible to generate interest on "behalf of that portion of Miranda's associates, now suffering imprisonment or slavery in that country, where they dreamed they should enjoy and communicate liberty" (ix–x). While John H. Sherman's *A General Account of Miranda's Expedition* (New York: McFarlane and Long, 1808) aimed at providing "a plain, undecorated statement of facts to the public," Congress's *Report of the Committee to Whom was Referred the Petition of Sundry Citizens of the United States Confined at Carthagena, in South America, June 9, 1809* (Washington, D.C.: A. and G. Way, 1809) concluded "that it appears from the statement of petitioners, they were, by various misrepresentations and deceptions, incautiously drawn into the service of general Miranda, in an expedition, *hostile in its intention,* against some of the Spanish settlements, in South America" [3]. Whatever Jefferson knew of or sanctioned beforehand, he did not attempt to liberate the petitioners. See Karen Racine, *Francisco de Miranda: A Transatlantic Life in the Age of Revolution* (Wilmington, Del.: Scholarly Resources, 2003), 168–69.

66. Brown, "Annals of Europe and America," 2:89, 90, 92.

67. Ibid., 92, 93; Thomas Jefferson, "Burr's Conspiracy. Communicated to Congress, Jan. 22, 1807," American State Papers 037, misc. vol. 1, 9th Cong., 2d sess., No. 217 (Washington, D.C., NewsBank, 2005).

68. Brown, "Annals of Europe and America," 2:93.

69. Ibid., 97, 96.

70. Dolores Egger Labbe, *The Louisiana Purchase and Its Aftermath, 1800–1830,* (Lafayette, La.: Center for Louisiana Studies, Univ. of Southwestern Louisiana, 1998), 1.

71. Dooley, *Early Republic,* 137, 167.

72. Brown, "Annals of Europe and America," 2:98.

73. Ibid., 103.

74. Ibid., 103–4.

75. Brown's interest in Miranda and history does not end in his "Annals of Europe and America." Near the end of volume 5 of the *American Register,* under "Miscellaneous articles," Brown includes a British piece entitled "An Historical Sketch of the Projects Lately Adopted for Detaching South America from Spain, and Especially of the Expedition of Miranda: With a View of the Changes Which the Spanish Revolution May Probably Produce in the Colonies." In what are arguably Brown's last editorial comments in the *American Register,* he remarks that the sketch contains useful "facts" but that the "dignity and wisdom annexed to Miranda and his projects, by this writer, appears to the editor quite absurd." In notes appended to the text, he corrects claims in the sketch and writes, for instance, that Miranda often drew "parallels between himself and Washington, and fancied that he was opening in South the same scene that had take place in North America." "The absurdity," he continues, "of such fancies will be best conceived by imagining the English colonies, when all was tranquility, to have the cause of their liberty kindly undertaken by one of their wandering citizens, in France, who was to break the yoke of the mother country, by returning with an army formed of the *French* West Indian garrisons, and ten thousand *Brave Mulattoes,*" Charles Brockden Brown, *American Register; or General Repository of History, Politics & Science* (Philadelphia: C. & A. Conrad, 1809), 5:380, 383.

76. A rich source of documentation on this point is Russel Blaine Nye, *The Cultural Life of the New Nation, 1776–1830* (New York: Harper & Row, 1960). He writes that post-Revolutionary historians studied the colonial period as an "era of genesis and prophecy" and saw the United States on an "upward path" that was "divinely ordained to be permanent" (42–43). The United States, he remarks, viewed itself as "superior to England and Europe" because it was "*not* like them." Its "larger mission" was, according to many, to "exemplify to the world the ability of men to govern themselves, to create and spread new concepts of society and culture, to lead the way to a brighter and better future for mankind" (45–47).

77. Kaplan, "Left Alone with America," 12.

78. Said, *Culture and Imperialism,* 9. On Miranda, whom he appears to have mistrusted, Paine writes, "Miranda was in Paris when Mr. Monroe arrived there as minister, and as Miranda wanted to get acquainted with him I cautioned Mr. Monroe against it, and told him of the affair of Nootka Sound and the twelve hundred pounds. You are at liberty to make what use you please of this letter, and with my name to it." Paine, "To Anonymous," dated March 20, 1806, in *Complete Writings of Thomas Paine,* 2:1481–82.

79. In *Imagined Empires,* Eric Werthheimer defines imperialism in America as "national thinking that envisions an expansionist and portable national presence" and observes, in

a manner that confirms Brown's own intuitions, that American exceptionalism is "partly a product of Anglo participation in the idealized South and Central American Others and their histories" (9, 15).

80. As noted, Duane edited a liberal newspaper in Calcutta, India, before being deported. After moving to Philadelphia, he assisted Benjamin Franklin Bache in running the *Aurora* before taking over himself in 1798. An opponent of the Alien and Sedition Act of 1798, he incurred Federalist wrath, including a physical beating by about thirty anti-Jefferson thugs, which left him unconscious, in his efforts to expose Federalist plots for political power and reform judicial procedures.

81. Michael Durey, *Transatlantic Radicals and the Early American Republic* (Lawrence: Univ. Press of Kansas, 1997), 293.

82. William Duane, *The Mississippi question fairly stated, and the views and arguments of those who clamor for war, examined, in seven letters: originally written for publication in the Aurora, at Philadelphia/by Camillus* (Philadelphia: William Duane, 1803), 37; William Duane, *Politics for American Farmers*, 25.

83. Watts, *Writing and Postcolonialism*, 6

84. Garraty and McCaughey, *American Nation*, 207.

85. Local Philadelphia newspapers like the *United States Gazette, Aurora General Advertiser,* and *Poulson's American Daily Advertiser* carried regular reports on the incident, with Poulson's paper publishing a "List of the Killed and Wounded on Board the Chesapeake" on June 30, 1807, and the *Aurora General Advertiser* on July 2, 1807, resolutions from a "Meeting of the Citizens of the First Congressional District of Pennsylvania," where concerned citizens gathered in the state house yard and resolved "that the conduct of Great Britain, towards the United States, has been too often marked by hostility, injustice, and oppression; and that the outrage committed by the Leopard, one of her ships of war, under the express orders of one of her admirals, upon the Chesapeake, a frigate belonging to the United States, is an act of such consummate violence and wrong, and of so barbarous and murderous a character, that it would debase and degrade any nation, and much more so a nation of freemen, to submit to it." In addition to sharing their sentiments with the president, they also resolved to "make any sacrifices and to encounter any hazards" in the pursuit of the "most rigid retribution" and "full measure of justice" (2).

86. Henry Adams, *History of the United States of America during the Second Administration of Thomas Jefferson*, vol. 4. (1893; repr., New York: Antiquarian Press, 1962), 1, 27.

87. For a more recent assessment of events surrounding the *Chesapeake-Leopard* affair and how American anger over the incident reveals "political and social responses to mariners" and insights into American and British relations at the time, see Robert E. Cray Jr., "Remembering the USS *Chesapeake:* The Politics of Maritime Death and Impressment," *Journal of the Early Republic* 25 (Fall 2005): 447.

88. Brown, "Annals of Europe and America," 3:4–5, 6.

89. Ibid., 7, 8.

90. Ibid., 10, 11.

91. Ibid., 12, 13, 15.

92. Ibid., 17, 18.

93. Ibid., 19, 20, 21.

94. Ibid., 21, 22.

95. Ibid., 23, 25, 29.

96. Ibid., 30, 31, 32.

97. Ibid., 39, 36, 38.

98. Ibid., 44, 39, 40.

99. Ibid., 40, 47.

100. Ibid., 48, 50, 47, 48–49.

101. Watts, *Writing and Postcolonialism*, 99, 121.

102. He identifies, for instance, the 10th Congress's first session, beginning October, 27, 1807, as the most significant in a long time because of unfolding events, the public's heightened interest in congressional proceedings, and the "probability" that its decision would be "a warlike one." Saying that political party differences had largely resumed, he recounts how Jeffersonian Republicans and Federalists each regarded Great Britain and France in light of the situation and how a committee was formed to investigate the circumstances of the attack on the *Chesapeake*. As "an impartial observer," it became readily apparent to Brown how even the process of developing steps of inquiry was fraught with extraordinary emotion and political tension. Brown, "Annals of Europe and America," 3:55, 61.

103. Ibid., 79, 81, 84.

104. Ibid., 88–89, 91.

105. Clark, *Charles Brockden Brown*, 270–71.

106. Jefferson's proclamation was issued in a July 2, 1807, broadside. There were numerous newspaper and periodical publications concerning the embargo's effectiveness and repeal.

Those in favor of the embargo were Samuel Harrison Smith, "The Embargo," *Washington National Intelligencer*, Dec. 28, 1807, Jacob Frank, "Our Situation," *New York Public Advertiser*, Jan. 8, 1808, and William Gray, "Mr. Cushing," *Salem (Mass.) Gazette*, Aug. 25, 1808. In "Embargo," first published in the *National Intelligencer* and then reprinted in *Poulson's American Daily Advertiser*, Dec. 31, 1807, the author asserts that the embargo "destroys the temptation to war" and that an "advantage most to be prized is the death blow which a perseverance in the measure, till the occasion for it be over, will give to the insulting opinion in Europe that submission to wrongs of every sort will at all times be preferred here to a protracted suspension of commerce."

For instances of those against the embargo, see William Coleman, "In 1793 England Issued an Order," *New-York Evening Post*, Feb. 12, 1808; Alexander Contee Hanson, "Embargo," *Baltimore Federal Republican and Commercial Gazette*, July 11, 1808; "Embargo," written by "A Farmer," *Poulson's American Daily Advertiser*," July 28, 1808; and "Mr. Jefferson Disgraced," *Boston Mercury and New-England Palladium*, Oct. 14, 1808. Also, in addition to James Hillhouse, "Speech on the Resolution to Repeal the Embargo" on November 29, 1808 [Boston?: N.p., 1808], Daniel Webster asserted in *Considerations on the Embargo Laws* [Boston: N.p., 1808] that the embargo had moved the country closer to war and that domestically it had "annihilated our trade," reduced fertile lands "to sterility," and "dried up our revenue" (15). James Sloan's December 27, 1808, speech addressed the fifth embargo bill, saying that while he voted for the bill earlier because he considered it a "temporary restriction," he now opposed and condemned a continuance of it, because he believed it would "plunge his country in irremediable ruin." See the preface to "Speech Delivered by Mr. Sloan, of New-Jersey; in the House of Representatives of the United States, December 27, 1808, on the Fifth Embargo Bill," (Newburyport [, Mass]: Thomas and Whipple [1809]), [2].

107. Brown, "Annals of Europe and America," 3:61, 63, 64.

108. The 10th Congress met in Washington, D.C., from March 4, 1807, to March 3, 1809. Members who Brown mentions in his annals are, with the exception of Pennsylvania Federalist William Milnor (1769–1848), Democrat-Republicans from the House of Representatives: Burwell Bassett (1764–1841), Virginia; Joseph Clay, Pennsylvania (1769–1811); Jacob Crowninshield (1770–1808), Massachusetts; Roger Nelson (1759–1815), Maryland; John Randolph (1773–1833), Virginia; John Reah (1753–1832), Tennessee; John Rowan (1773–1843), Kentucky; and John Smilie (1741–1812), Pennsylvania.

109. Brown, "Annals of Europe and America," 3:64, 65, 67, 68. In a footnote, Brown writes, "When we analyze the debates of a public assembly, we are astonished to find how

much of idle repetition, verbose redundance and obscurity, and efforts to explain which make the previous confusion worse confounded, with personal altercation and abuse, compose the motley tissue of the controversy" (64).

110. Ibid., 69, 70, 72.

111. Ibid., 72, 73.

112. Ibid., 74, 72.

113. Ibid., 75.

114. Ibid., 77.

115. For a contemporary analysis of the embargo as it applied to state and local economies like that of Pennsylvania, see Agricola's *An Address to the Farmers of Pennsylvania* (Philadelphia: N.p., 1808), a campaign pamphlet that argues for electing James Ross (Federalist candidate) the governor of Pennsylvania, which may or may not have influenced Brown's own writing. Its arguments, however, against the embargo resonate closely with Brown's own and illuminate rural and class concerns in Brown's pamphlet on the embargo. Agricola's pamphlet provides a larger context for understanding Brown's negotiation of conflicting class and economic interests, especially his principle of "mutual dependence."

116. Brown, "Annals of Europe and America," 5:3–4.

117. Thomas Paine to Thomas Jefferson, July 8, 1808, in *Complete Writings of Thomas Paine*, 2:1497. The Embargo Act of 1807 was a response to repeated British and French seizure of American ships. Jefferson responded to the June 22, 1807, *Chesapeake* affair by prohibiting American exports. Although he hoped to avoid further injury to American merchant ships and put economic pressure on England and France by cutting off American exports of goods, the policy had "catastrophic effects" on the American economy, causing exports to fall from $108 million in 1807 to $22 million in 1808. Seamen, merchants, and eventually farmers were affected greatly by the blockade. See Garraty and McCaughey, *American Nation*, 207–9.

118. Brown, *Address to the Congress*, [iii], vi, 37.

119. Alan Axelrod, *Charles Brockden Brown: An American Tale* (Austin: Univ. of Texas Press, 1983), 175.

120. Tuveson, *Redeemer Nation*, viii.

121. Robert W. Tucker and David C. Hendrickson, *Empire of Liberty: The Statecraft of Thomas Jefferson* (New York: Oxford Univ. Press, 1990), 177. Additional evidence that Brown increasingly critiqued the imperialist dimensions of American exceptionalism can be found in his "Sketch of the Life of General Horatio Gates" (1809–10). Addressing the conflict between England and the United States at the beginning of the American Revolution, Brown says of the geographical-political situation with respect to Canada: "From projects of conquests in Canada, the American government had been compelled to give their whole attention to schemes of defense" (385). Whether or not the United States did in fact initiate plans to conquer Canada, the fact that Brown now identifies imperialist activities or "projects" with the "American government," *not* just "deliverers" like Burr, argues for the continued movement before his death toward a postcolonial sensibility, toward a recognition of the mutually reinforcing relationship between American exceptionalism and imperialism.

122. Tucker and Hendrickson, *Empire of Liberty*, 7, 204, 205.

123. Ibid., 165.

7. Constitutional Limits—and "Liberalism"

1. Kennedy, "Charles Brockden Brown," folder 48, 1970.

2. Willard G. Bleyer, in *Main Currents in the History of American Journalism* (New York: Da Capo, 1973), writes that the flames of political partisanship in American journal-

ism were kept at "white heat" during the War of 1812 but that as early as 1807 Jefferson said of the excesses of partisan papers: "It is a melancholy truth, that a suppression of the press could not more completely deprive the nation of its benefits, than is done by its abandoned prostitution to falsehood. Nothing can now be believed which is seen in a newspaper. Truth itself becomes suspicious by being put into that polluted vehicle. The real extent of this state of misinformation is known only to those who are in situations to confront facts within their knowledge with the lies of the day" (138).

3. Kennedy, "Charles Brockden Brown," folder 48, 1971–72, 1973. The review was published serially in the April 15, 22, and 29, 1809, issues of the *Boston Ordeal* (1:226–29, 241–46, 257–62). As Kennedy points out, it comments on Brown's "lapses of correctness and deviations from authority," particularly in regard to the initial cause of the attack on the *Chesapeake* and the amount of time it took for its commander to surrender to the British (228–29), Brown's willingness to be impartial and see reparation and the right of "immunity" from searches as connected issues, and his reluctance to adamantly defend the position of the United States in regard to Jefferson's embargo (246, 258). On this last point in particular, Brown's reviewer comments that he "does not presume to hazard any political reflections on the various topics . . . but seems contented to offer an abstract of arguments used by others, and *leaves his readers to form their own conclusions*" (257, my emphasis). The reviewer suggests that Brown "sinks into a chronicleer" when he does not allow "his own opinion to be discovered, excepting by some oversight in expression" (257–58). Brown, of course, wrote a separate political pamphlet at this time titled *An Address to the Congress of the United States, on the Utility and Justice of Restrictions upon Foreign Commerce. With Reflections on Foreign Trade in General, and the Future Prospects of America*. At the same time, the reviewer rates Brown's work "very highly" and observes that just as Brown "attaches fault both to the Americans and English" in regard to the *Chesapeake* affair, so with the "controversy between Mr. Rose and Mr. Madison" he "gives a faithful abstract of the arguments advanced on both sides" (226, 227, 260).

4. Clemit, *Godwinian Novel*, 122. By documentary or historical editing, I mean the practice, dating back to Ebenezer Hazard's *Historical Collections Consisting of State Papers, and Other Authentic Documents, Intended as Materials for a History of the United States of America* (Philadelphia: T. Dobson, 1792), of collecting and preserving historical materials with minimal interpretive apparatus. For an explanation of the history of this profession, see Mary-Jo Kline's *A Guide to Documentary Editing* (Baltimore: Johns Hopkins Univ. Press, 1987). She notes, for example, that while documents were being collected and published before the Revolution, the "major phase of American documentary editing did not begin . . . until the second quarter of the nineteenth century, when Jared Sparks of Harvard initiated his work" (2–3). Also see Gordon S. Wood, "Historians and Documentary Editing," *Journal of American History* 67 (Mar. 1981): 871–77.

The conventional belief of historians and editors has been that documentary editors must remain objective and avoid subjective interpretation. Along with Julian Boyd, Lester Cappon was among the first to qualify such a view, with his comment that "if the editor's responsibility requires him to clarify and explain, his mastery of documents in their historical context qualifies him to offer an interpretation as worthy of respect as that of the historian within the framework of his particular subject" ("A Rationale for Historical Editing: Past and Present," *William and Mary Quarterly*, 3d. ser., 23, no. 1 [Jan. 1966]: 73). Fredrika Teute concurs that "ultimately the choice lies with the editor, and concealed within the editor is the historian" ("Views in Review: A Historiographical Perspective on Historical Editing," *American Archivist* 43, no. 1 [Winter 1980]: 47).

5. Barnard, Kamrath, and Shapiro, introduction to *Revising Charles Brockden Brown*, xix.

6. Joyce Appleby, *Liberalism and Republicanism in the Historical Imagination* (Cambridge, Mass.: Harvard Univ. Press, 1992), 1.

7. Dillon, *Gender of Freedom,* 2, 32–33.

8. Cathy N. Davidson, *Revolution and the Word: The Rise of the American Novel* (New York: Oxford Univ. Press, 1986), 255, 253.

9. Bakhtin, *Dialogic Imagination,* 15, 262–63, 17, 39. For a more updated appraisal of Bakhtin's theories of language, ideology, and authority as they pertain to democratic institutions, dialogue, and historical truth, see Amy Mandelker, *Bakhtin in Contexts: Across the Disciplines* (Evanston, Ill.: Northwestern Univ. Press, 1995); Ken Hirschkop, *Mikhail Bakhtin: An Aesthetic for Democracy* (Oxford: Oxford Univ. Press, 1999); and Arnetha F. Ball and Sarah Warshauer Freedman, *Bakhtinian Perspectives on Language, Literacy, and Learning* (Cambridge: Cambridge Univ. Press, 2004).

10. Bakhtin, *Dialogic Imagination,* 324.

11. Brown, "Annals of Europe and America," 1:iv.

12. Ibid., 2:iv, 3:[iii].

13. Ibid., 3:iv.

14. Ibid., 4:[iii], iv.

15. Ibid., [iii], iv.

16. Louis A. Montrose, "New Historicisms," in *Redrawing the Boundaries: The Transformation of English and American Studies,* ed. by Stephen Greenblatt and Giles Gunn (New York: MLA, 1992), 415.

17. For a useful, although somewhat dated, discussion of the relationship between literary reception and historical meaning, see Martyn P. Thompson, "Reception Theory and the Interpretation of Historical Meaning," *History and Theory* 32 (1993): 248–72.

18. Brown, "Annals of America," 5:[iii]–iv. Unlike other volumes of the magazine, Brown's preface to volume 5 follows an advertisement—the announcement that the "original papers and journals" of Captains Lewis and Clark and a "detailed and authentic history of the expedition" would be published and offered to the public ([ii]). The advertisement may or may not have been written by Brown, but it nonetheless reminds us his efforts to market his publication, including his own historical annals, in the increasingly competitive literary and cultural economy in which he was immersed. As Daniel Edwards Kennedy correctly notes, Brown does not actually include an abstract of domestic laws in this volume of the annals. Kennedy, "Charles Brockden Brown," folder 48, 1969.

19. Mark Bevir argues persuasively, in "Objectivity in History," *History and Theory* 33 (1994), that "even though we cannot grasp historical facts as immediately present truths, we can have objective knowledge of the past that is neither relativistic nor irrational" (329). "Objectivity," he says, "arises from comparing and criticizing rival webs of interpretations in terms of facts" and intellectual honesty (334).

However, Brown does make an important distinction between the craft of the historian and the "industrious collector" when he remarks that Proud's narrative is that of "an old man, uninstructed in the arts of selection, arrangement and expression, who always prefers the task of reciting the deeds and papers which he has gleaned from public offices and private libraries, to the more arduous province of stating their contents in his own words. . . . The merit of this author, and the utility of his collection, are enhanced by it being the first publication of this kind. Without his assistance, therefore, future labourers in this field would have been condemned to the drudgery of ransacking libraries, and poring over rolls, a task difficult in proportion to the remoteness of the period to the records of which our searches relate" ("Annals of America," 5:25–26). While such commentary seems to undermine Brown's later rationale for using public documents as part of his narrative, it more accurately points to his early conception of what distinguishes the "industrious compiler" from the "genuine historian" and the degree to which his theory of historiography refashioned itself in philosophically and politically radical ways.

20. Bakhtin, *Dialogic Imagination*, 15.

21. I am indebted here to Janie Hinds for complicating my thinking in the early 1990s about the "linear narrative" element of nineteenth-century histories and for asking how Brown's historiography differs from or resembles elements of the new historicism.

22. Davidson, *Revolution and the Word*, 255; Bakhtin, *Dialogic Imagination*, 300.

23. Bakhtin, *Dialogic Imagination*, 273.

24. This view is confirmed in Brown's last installment of "Sketch of the Life of General Horatio Gates" in Dennie's *Port Folio*. Appearing in late February 1810, the piece includes a footnote in which Brown comments extensively on the current state of less public historical materials, and their value in representing the past:

I have often been surprised to observe that in an age where the facilities of writing and publishing are so great, there should be so few books of the most valuable kind. The memoirs of great men, written by themselves. In times of revolution the number of such men multiply, and in other cases they write and publish by thousands; but in our revolution where can such a performance be found? Excepting slight and contemptible specimens of *self-written* memoirs, I recollect none. The letters of Washington are precious relics indeed, and the letters of all official characters would be valuable beyond estimation. These, indeed, will become of popular value in time; and immense collections of letters will be rescued from the bottoms of mouldy trunks, and make their journey to public libraries. Even manuscript memoirs of that period must start into life in the course of centuries; but in the meantime what havoc will be made among them by the policy, carelessness, or ignorance of families! Thirty years have not been sufficient to give this value to the records of the revolution, and the hand of Time is brushing fast into oblivion the only documents connected with the revolution which are of most value. T [ ] only genuine testimonies to the truth of events. (107)

Port Folio 2, no. 5 (Nov. 1809): 383–90; vol. 2, no. 6 (Dec. 1809): 481–84; vol. 3, no. 2 (Feb. 1810): 102–8.

25. Cathy Matson and Peter Onuf, "Toward a Republican Empire: Interest and Ideology in Revolutionary America," *American Quarterly* 37 (1985): 496.

26. Daniel T. Rodgers, "Republicanism: The Career of a Concept," *Journal of American History* 79 (1992): 37–38.

27. Drew McCoy, *The Elusive Republic: Political Economy in Jeffersonian America* (New York: Norton, 1980), 75.

28. Although dated now, Robert E. Shallope's examination of the role and function of "republicanism" is still useful. No longer, he argues, is it plausible to say that republicanism was merely a "secular faith," anchored in John Locke and natural rights theory, or that it simply meant "maintaining public and private virtue, internal unity, social solidarity, and vigilance against the corruptions of power." "Republicanism and Early American Historiography," *The William and Mary Quarterly* 39 (Apr. 1982): 335.

29. Steven Watts, *The Republic Reborn: War and the Making of Liberal America, 1790–1820* (Baltimore: Johns Hopkins Univ. Press, 1987), xvi–xvii, 221, 238. More recently, Ed White and Andy Doolen have brought perspective to the ways historians have understood "republicanism" and the extent to which a "republican ideology" itself was an established set of values that contributed to the formation of the "early Republic." In *The Backcountry and the City: Conflict and Colonization in Early America* (Minneapolis: Univ. of Minnesota Press, 2005), White reassesses the historical and literary republican "megasynthesis" that has occurred since the late 1980s and argues that historiographical constructions like

the "republican period" artificially isolate the ideals and rhetoric of political elites such as Adams and Jefferson from agrarian, frontier, and other classes and preclude a more complicated understanding of the shaping influences (11).

Doolen (in "Early American Civics: Rehistoricizing the Power of Republicanism," *American Literary History* 19, no. 1 [2007]: 120–40) concurs, adding that scholarship's "self-referential republicanism" continues to ignore "the impact of cultural resistance on the production of republican rhetoric and ideology" and how, say, the reality and "sadism of slavery" factor into the ideological fabric of the Constitution and "inform white republican ideology, laws, and political practices" (130, 133). Within such a theoretical rubric, "the republican synthesis appears like a narrowly construed national genealogy" and historians and literary critics alike might want to "imagine an early American society organized less by enlightenment principles of continuity and coherence, and more by the tenets of resistance and incoherence" (138).

30. Saul Cornell, *The Other Founders: Anti-Federalism and the Dissenting Tradition in America, 1788–1828* (Chapel Hill: Univ. of North Carolina Press, 1999), 31, 246.

31. Garraty and McCaughey, *American Nation*, 192, 203, 208.

32. Hillhouse was elected to the Second Congress in 1790 after having served several years as a representative in the General Assembly of Connecticut. He was also a member of the Third and Fourth Congresses, and in 1796 was elected to an empty seat in the United States Senate; he was reelected three times, and in 1801 was selected as the pro tempore of the Senate. He resigned from office in 1810. See Richard J. Purcell's *Connecticut in Transition, 1775–1818* (Middletown, Conn.: Wesleyan Univ. Press, 1963) and James M. Banner Jr.'s *To the Hartford Convention: The Federalists and the Origins of Party Politics in Massachusetts, 1789–1815* (New York: Knopf, 1970) for a history of Hillhouse's role in politics.

33. Brown, "Annals of America," 5:7.

34. Ibid., 7.

35. Ibid., 7, 8.

36. Ibid., 8.

37. Ibid., 8.

38. Bakhtin, *Dialogic Imagination*, 314, 321, 324.

39. James Hillhouse, *Propositions for Amending the Constitution of the United States; Submitted by Mr. Hillhouse to the Senate on the Twelfth Day of April, 1808, with His Explanatory Remarks* (New Haven, Conn.: Oliver Steele, 1808), [3].

40. Brown, "Annals of America," 5:9.

41. Tucker and Hendrickson, *Empire of Liberty*, 16.

42. Brown, "Annals of America," 5:8–9.

43. Hillhouse, *Propositions for Amending*, 4.

44. Brown, "Annals of America," 5:10.

45. Hillhouse, *Propositions for Amending*, 6.

46. Brown, "Annals of America," 5:10, 12.

47. Ibid., 13, 14.

48. Hillhouse, *Propositions for Amending*, 9.

49. Brown, "Annals of America," 5:9.

50. Ibid., 9, 15.

51. Ibid., 15, 17, 22.

52. Hillhouse, *Propositions for Amending*, 15–16.

53. Ibid., 16-17.

54. Brown, "Annals of America," 5:22, 23, 24–25; Hillhouse, *Propositions for Amending*, 22, 24–25.

55. In reproducing Hillhouse's April 12, 1808, speech on amending the Constitution,

Brown, or the printer, prints Hillhouse's original statement—"All proceedings or nominations shall be with closed doors and without debate; but information of the character and
qualifications of the person nominated shall be received"—as: "All proceedings or nominations shall be with closed doors and without debate? but information of the character and
qualifications of the person nominated shall be received." While insertion of a question
mark after "debate" is possibly accidental, its insertion at that point in the document is
consistent, ironically, with the tenor of Hillhouse's speech and Brown's own concern with
threats to democratic processes. Brown, "Annals of America," 5:32.

56. Ibid., 34.

57. Ibid., 2:159.

58. Ibid., 160.

59. Ibid., 5:35, 71.

60. Ibid., 64–65, 78.

61. Michael Warner, *The Letters of the Republic: Publication and the Public Sphere in
Eighteenth-century America* (Cambridge, Mass.: Harvard Univ. Press, 1990), 166; Bakhtin,
Dialogic Imagination, 400.

62. Winifred E. A. Bernhard, *Political Parties in American History,* 3 vols., gen. ed. Morton Borden (New York: G. P. Putnam, 1973), 298.

63. *Memoirs of John Quincy Adams, Comprising Portions of His Diary from 1795 to 1848,*
ed. by Charles Francis Adams, 12 vols. (Philadelphia: J. B. Lippincott, 1874–77), 1:504–7.

64. Edwin Gray to Stephen R. Bradley, Jan. 21, 1808, Edwin Gray Papers, Special Collections Library, Duke Univ. On April 26, 1808, Mathew Lyon, a member of the Tenth
Congress (1807–09) wrote a circular for his constituents in Kentucky, in which he remarks
on caucus crisis, "I should mention to you the subject which of all others has most occupied the attention of the members of Congress during the last five months, I mean the
approaching election for President and Vice-President. . . . Caucuses, conventions, and
meetings have been set on foot for the nomination of a President in way totally inconsistent with the principles and the letter of the constitution," 589–99. *Circular Letters of
Congressmen to Their Constituents 1789–1829,* vol. 2, *Tenth Congress—Fourteenth Congress,
1807–1817,* ed. by Noble E. Cunningham. Jr. (Chapel Hill: Published for the Institute of
Early American History and Culture, Williamsburg, Va., by the Univ. of North Carolina
Press, 1978).

65. See Noble E. Cunningham Jr., *The Making of the American Party System, 1789 to
1809* (Englewood Cliffs, N.J.: Prentice Hall, 1965) for a selection of representative responses
to the caucus.

66. Everett Carll Ladd Jr., *American Political Parties: Social Change and Political Response* (New York: Norton, 1970), 83. Also see Morton Borden, *Parties and Politics in the
Early Republic, 1789–1815* (Arlington Heights, Ill.: AHM Publishing, 1967) for his account
of Randolph's personal animosity toward Jefferson and reason for division within the Republican party.

67. Brown, "Annals of America," 5:80.

68. Cunningham, *Making of the American Party System,* 126.

69. Brown, "Annals of America," 5:80–81.

70. David Haven Blake Jr. "'Posterity Must Judge': Private and Public Discourse in the
Adams-Jefferson Letters," *Arizona Quarterly* 50 (Winter 1994): 2.

71. Brown, "Annals of America," 5:81–82.

72. The Randolph letter's concern with proceeding "without discussion or debate" also
recalls the April 12, 1808, Hillhouse speech on amending the Constitution and, as noted already, the insertion—accidentally or not—of a question mark in the original text. Given his
efforts to be impartial, it is unlikely that Brown made a conscious editorial or syntactical

intervention here; however, there is no denying that both the Hillhouse speech and the Randolph congressional letter are, like Brown, attuned to democratic processes.

73. Brown, "Annals of America," 5:20–21.

74. Ibid., 82–84.

75. Durey, *Transatlantic Radicals*, 271, 273–74. As Mary Atwell Moore, in "James Cheetham," *Dictionary of American Biography*, ed. by Allen Johnson (New York: Charles Scribner's Sons, 1930), further notes of Cheetham's radical past before coming to New York, he

> was born probably in or near Manchester, England. At the end of the eighteenth century Manchester was restless under the first stirring of the Industrial Revolution and the disquieting news from France. Men of liberal and revolutionary mind were organizing societies for criticism of the government. Of these the most important perhaps was the Constitutional Society, of which Thomas Cooper and Thomas Walker were the leading spirits, and James Cheetham, then a young hatter of Manchester, one of the humbler members. On July 23, 1793, he was arrested with other members of the society charged with conspiracy to overthrow the government. He was freed the following April because of the failure of evidence against him (Proceedings on the Trial . . . against James Cheetham . . . for a Conspiracy . . . 1794). He continued to live in Manchester until the riots of 1798 forced him to remove to America at a time when the United States was passing through the changes incidental to the political revolution of 1800. (4:47)

While after Jefferson's election Cheetham worked diligently on behalf of Republican policies, he eventually opposed—like Brown—Jefferson's embargo, and had a falling out with Thomas Paine.

76. Beyond Machor, *Reader in History* (Baltimore: Johns Hopkins Univ. Press, 1993), background on reader-response interpretive strategies or ways of filing textual "gaps" and making meaning may be found in Wolfgang Iser, *The Act of Reading: A Theory of Aesthetic Response* (Baltimore: Johns Hopkins Univ. Press, 1978), Susan Suleiman and Inge Crosman, *The Reader in the Text: Essays on Audience and Interpretation* (Princeton, N.J.: Princeton Univ. Press, 1980), and Stanley Fish, *Is There a Text in This Class? The Authority of Interpretive Communities* (Cambridge, Mass.: Harvard Univ. Press, 1980).

77. Warner, *Letters of the Republic*, 172.

78. Bakhtin, *Dialogic Imagination*, 314.

79. Indeed, just as Brown's prefaces and idiosyncratic use of documents suggest his progress toward a "novelistic" rather than an "epic" or traditional understanding of history writing, so his later historicism becomes a "disclosure of knowledge," a public act of private resistance in the narrative mode or spirit Foucault identifies with Nietzsche (Michel Foucault "Nietzsche, Genealogy, History," *Language, Counter-Memory, Practice* [Ithaca, N.Y.: Cornell Univ. Press, 1977], 154). Brown's stated preference for "Public documents" appears, of course, to contradict or suppress any "centrifugal" voices that might emerge from unofficial documents, or even from Brown himself as a critic of the status quo (Bakhtin, *Dialogic Imagination*, 273). But similar to Nietzsche, Brown's handling of such documents deviates from a "suprahistorical" representation of history when he juxtaposes conflicting official or "centripetal" (and, arguably, "centrifugal") voices of public officials, thereby promoting in the reader or "the people" an awareness of the potential conflict between constitutional principles and congressional or party practices—the kind of "Nachdenken und Erkennen" (reflection and insight) he encourages in his essays and elsewhere. See Wolfgang Schäfer, *Charles Brockden Brown als Literaturkritiker*, 137.

80. Foucault, "Nietzsche, Genealogy, History," 154.

81. Greene, *Intellectual Construction of America*, 5.

82. Appleby, Hunt, and Jacob, *Telling the Truth about History*, 102.

83. Bernard Bailyn, "The Central Themes of the American Revolution," *Essays on the American Revolution*, ed. by Stephen G. Kurtz and James H. Hudson (Chapel Hill: Published for the Institute of Early American History and Culture, Williamsburg, Va., by the Univ. of North Carolina Press, 1973), 26–27. Also see Bailyn's *The Ideological Origins of the American Revolution* (Cambridge, Mass.: Harvard Univ. Press, 1967), 160–62.

84. In establishing how Brown's liberalism is distinct from "libertarian" thought as it is understood in the twenty-first century, it is necessary to point out that modern "libertarians" are highly protective of individual rights, not affiliated with a particular political party, and generally critical of big government, bureaucracy, and any form of socialism. Although they aggressively embrace free trade and market solutions as opposed to government ones, they also tend toward affiliations with conservative, right-wing political beliefs moreso than social democratic ones. In recent decades, "libertarian" thought has emerged as a center-right or right form of free-market liberalism that embraces, sometimes naively and simplistically, atomistic individualism and property rights.

Like a number of historians, I use the term "libertarian" in significantly more limited ways to describe late eighteenth-century ideas about natural rights; a limited, representative form of government; and the emergence of a free-market economy. To the extent that Brown was critical of the ways England and even the United States pursued political and economic self-interest at the expense of individuals, he may be said to be part of an eighteenth-century tradition of "liberalism" or democracy and dissent. And to the degree he resisted institutional oppression and was sympathetic to the cause of human equality, he may be seen as mingling Quaker beliefs with Godwinian values, late Enlightenment French thinking, and libertarian thought as it existed at the turn of the century. See Henry J. Silverman, ed., *American Radical Thought: The Libertarian Tradition* (Lexington, Mass.: D. C. Heath, 1970).

85. See Leonard W. Levy, *Legacy of Suppression: Freedom of Speech and Press in Early American History* (Cambridge, Mass.: Belknap Press of Harvard Univ. Press, 1960) and his edited collection *Freedom of the Press from Zenger to Jefferson: Early American Libertarian Theories* (Indianapolis: Bobbs-Merrill, 1966), for a standard interpretation of how libertarian thought evolved in early America, especially in relation to the Federalist Sedition Act of 1798, the ability of the public to criticize government, and freedom of the press. Peter S. Onuf, *Jefferson's Empire: The Language of American Nationhood* (Charlottesville: Univ. of Virginia Press, 2000), concurs with Levy, saying that the constitutional crisis produced "a rich discourse on civil liberties and civil society" and that "Jefferson's libertarianism" was intimately connected with his understanding of "the 'people'" (84–85).

86. David Boaz, *Libertarianism: A Primer* (New York, Free Press, 1997), 40–45.

87. Berkhofer, *Beyond the Great Story*, 3, 25, 197. For a more recent discussion of the ways historians are responding to literary and cultural theories, see Elizabeth A. Clark, *History, Theory, Text: Historians and the Linguistic Turn* (Cambridge, Mass.: Harvard Univ. Press, 2004).

88. Berkhofer, *Beyond the Great Story*, 199, 216, 223, 218, 281.

89. For a full discussion of the ways Bayle, Brown, and Berkhofer share similar views about the constructed nature of history and complicate claims of postmodernism, see my essay "Charles Brockden Brown and the 'Art of the Historian,'" 231–60.

90. Bakhtin, *Dialogic Imagination*, 332.

91. James L. Machor, introduction to *Readers in History: Nineteenth-Century American Literature and the Contexts of Response*, ed. by James L. Machor (Baltimore: Johns Hopkins Univ. Press, 1993), viii–xi; Hirschkop, *Mikhail Bakhtin*, 33, 45.

92. Jose Bermejo-Barrera, "Explicating the Past: In Praise of History," *History and Theory* 32 (1993): 17; Foucault, "Nietzsche, Genealogy, History," 154.

Epilogue

1. For additional analyses of the Bush presidency, its interpretation of the Constitution, and legislative history as it pertains to American foreign policy, see John Yoo, *The Powers of War and Peace: The Constitution and Foreign Affairs after 9/11* (Chicago: Univ. of Chicago Press, 2005).

2. Bob Woodward, *State of Denial* (New York: Simon & Schuster, 2007), 490–91.

3. Clyde Prestowitz, *Rogue Nation: American Unilateralism and the Failure of Good Intentions* (New York: Basic, 2003), 277.

4. H. Aram Veeser, introduction to *The New Historicism*, xv.

5. Berkhofer, *Beyond the Great Story*, 16.

6. Alun Munslow, in *Deconstructing History*, writes:

Until relatively recently few history texts were so epistemologically self-referential as to draw deliberate attention to their rhetorical form, preferring instead to foreground the presumed reality behind it. Consequently, texts like Emmanuel LeRoy Ladurie's *Montaillou*, Carlo Ginzburg's *The Cheese and the Worms*, Natalie Zemon Davis's *The Return of Martin Guerre*, Simon Schama's *Dead Certainties* and his *Landscape and Memory* are regarded as exemplars of a new historicist genre because they draw attention to themselves either through their content as studies of the trivial, the anecdotal, the apparently historically marginal, or in respect of their form, as illustrations of where history transgresses the border into fiction through the particular ways in which they organize the content of the past.

While Davis sees her book as questioning "the point at which history ceases to be reconstruction and becomes invention," for Munslow the "deconstuctionist historian is always uncertain about history"—and this resonates with Brown's own philosophy of history.

7. As a historical footnote, if Brown were to analyze and reflect on recent events concerning, say, the Iraqi War and the presidency of George Bush, he would, one might argue, credit Bush's resolve to protect the American people and to pursue the perpetrators of the September 11, 2001, World Trade Center attacks and acknowledge the United Nation's failure to enforce sanctions against Saddam Hussein and stop decades of genocide against the Iraqi people. However, Brown would also, arguably, be candid or impartial concerning American foreign policy as it pertains to Israel, Saudi Arabia, and other parts of the Middle East and the ways, historically, the American government, in the interest of securing oil supplies for its economy, has supported repressive regimes or, until recently, precluded the Palestinian people from their own sovereignty. He would closely analyze President Bush's rationale or reasons for going to war in Iraq and its implications for the integrity of the Constitution, its principles and processes, and a democratic republic.

In that light, and in light of his late Enlightenment ethos, Brown, I think, would conclude that if the war in Iraq has revealed any self-evident truths to the American people, it is this: that when one believes he's been "elected" or chosen by God, and not the people, to lead the nation and relies heavily, if not exclusively, on faith instead of reason in doing so, there is little room for intellectual inquiry, consultation, open debate, critical self-reflection, the admission of mistakes, or ideological change—elements Jefferson himself may not have always practiced but understood, like Brown, are essential to the integrity of democratic processes in a republic. These qualities are, as Brown's historicism suggest, part of a long-standing American tradition of independent thought, political dissent, and "radicalism."

8. Doolen, *Fugitive Empire*, xxvii

9. Doolen, "Early American Civics," 120.

10. In *Fugitive Empire*, looking back to Foucault's 1976 lectures, published as *Society Must Be Defended: Lectures at the Collège de France, 1975–1976* (New York: Picador, 2003) and the idea that the "phenomenon of war" (47) has historically shaped the apparatus and policies of modern nation states, Doolen remarks: "The foreign and domestic 'war on terror' compels American studies to keep adding to this alternative historical memory. It remains one of the few critical spaces to present a politics of anti-imperialism. We can continue to challenge the historical tensions between America's progressive ideals and its imperial practices, and to deepen our understanding of how American writing both sanctions and assists U.S. imperialism" (198, 201).

11. Emory Elliott, *Revolutionary Writers: Literature and Authority in the New Republic 1725–1810* (New York: Oxford Univ. Press), 269–70.

12. David Shields, observation on the relationship between Brown criticism and the Vietnam War (letter, July 2009). For an updated bibliography of Brown's works, see *Comprehensive Bibliography of the Writings of Charles Brockden Brown, 1783–1822*, Philip Barnard, et al. (online).

Index

Aaron Burr Conspiracy, xvii–xviii, 176, 181, 196–207, 209–10, 235–36, 240, 242, 244, 254, 267n11, 307n56, 307n57, 308n58, 308n65, 312n121

abolitionism, 129; arrests of Samuel Swartwout and Peter Ogden, 205

"An Act for Establishing Religious Freedom," 114, 289n10

Adams, Abigail, 66

Adams, Hannah, xvii, 70, 72, 81–84, 261, 283n35, 284n46

Adams, Henry, xiv, 26, 194, 210, 223, 267n11, 305–6n40

Adams, John, 17–18, 66, 110, 115, 186, 234–35; letters to, 131, 299n84

Adams, John Quincy, 131, 246

Adams, Thomas Boylston, 131

An Address to the Farmers of Pennsylvania (Agricola), 312n115

"Address to the Friends of Religion on Civil Government," 114

adventurer, 152, 155, 201, 308n65

Afghanistan, 264

Agricola, 312n115

Ahmed, Siraj, 296n38

Alien and Sedition Acts, 235, 276n21, 310n80

Allen, Paul, 121, 306n48

American Annals; or, A Chronological History of America (Holmes), 25, 92

American exceptionalism, xiii, xiv, 20, 26, 135, 159, 176, 180–82, 208–9, 217, 222–24, 226, 257, 263, 302n6, 310n79, 312n121. *See also* Greene, Jack P.; manifest destiny

American foreign policy, 200, 209, 211, 222–23, 264, 320n1, 320n7

American Indians: Brown's representation of, 34, 45–48, 57, 157, 184, 186, 188–91, 230–32, 277n50, 277n55, 299n79, 300–301n3, 305n31; defrauded, 191; English colonial relations with, 10–11, 20, 47; historical displacement of, 30, 47; small pox, 191; use of gin, 190–91; Volney on, 190, 300–301n3, 304n24, 305n31. *See also* Delaware Indians

American Revolution, history of, 4, 8–9, 15, 107, 134, 201, 238, 283n35; export of revolutionary ethos and ideals, 201, 205–6, 312n121; and God, 15–17, 113; liberalism of, xix, 13, 179–80, 255, 264

American secularism, 113, 115

American shipping, 204, 210–11, 213, 221, 312n117

Anglo-Jacobinism, 44, 274n10. *See also* Woldwinite (Anglo-Jacobin) authors

annalist, 18, 265n7; Brown as, xi, xii, 90

Annual Register (Burke), 7, 15, 294n7

Annual Register (Dodsley), 135

anti-Federalist concerns, 226, 235–36, 245, 247

"An Apology for Apostolic Order and Its Advocates" (Hobart), 116

Appleby, Joyce, 21, 106, 107, 227, 228, 255, 288n106

Arner, Robert, 274n11, 279n67

Atlantic culture, xviii, 65, 113, 115, 223, 227, 279n66, 287n9, 307n50. *See also* transatlantic relations

Axelrod, Alan, 223

Bailyn, Bernard, 255

Bakhtin, Mikhail: Brown's "novel" historicism and, 205, 217, 226, 228, 231, 318n79; dialogical meaning and, 169, 170; discourse theory of the novel and democracy, 228, 233, 257; double-voiced discourse, 157. *See also* heteroglossia